D1478868

CENTRAL PRISON

CENTRAL PRISON

A HISTORY OF NORTH CAROLINA'S
STATE PENITENTIARY

GREGORY S. TAYLOR

LOUISIANA STATE UNIVERSITY PRESS
Baton Rouge

Published by Louisiana State University Press
www.lsupress.org

Manufactured in the United States of America
First printing

DESIGNER: Mandy McDonald Scallan
TYPEFACE: Whitman
PRINTER AND BINDER: Sheridan Books, Inc.

Jacket image: Photograph courtesy the North Carolina Museum of History.

Library of Congress Cataloging-in-Publication Data

Names: Taylor, Gregory S., author.
Title: Central Prison : a history of North Carolina's State Penitentiary /
    Gregory S. Taylor.
Description: Baton Rouge : Louisiana State University Press, [2021] |
    Includes bibliographical references and index.
Identifiers: LCCN 2020028532 (print) | LCCN 2020028533 (ebook) | ISBN
    978-0-8071-7433-3 (cloth) | ISBN 978-0-8071-7487-6 (pdf) | ISBN
    978-0-8071-7488-3
    (epub)
Subjects: LCSH: Central Prison (Raleigh, N.C.)—History. | Prisons—North
    Carolina—History.
Classification: LCC HV8353 .T38 2020 (print) | LCC HV8353 (ebook) | DDC
    365/.975655—dc23
LC record available at https://lccn.loc.gov/2020028532
LC ebook record available at https://lccn.loc.gov/2020028533

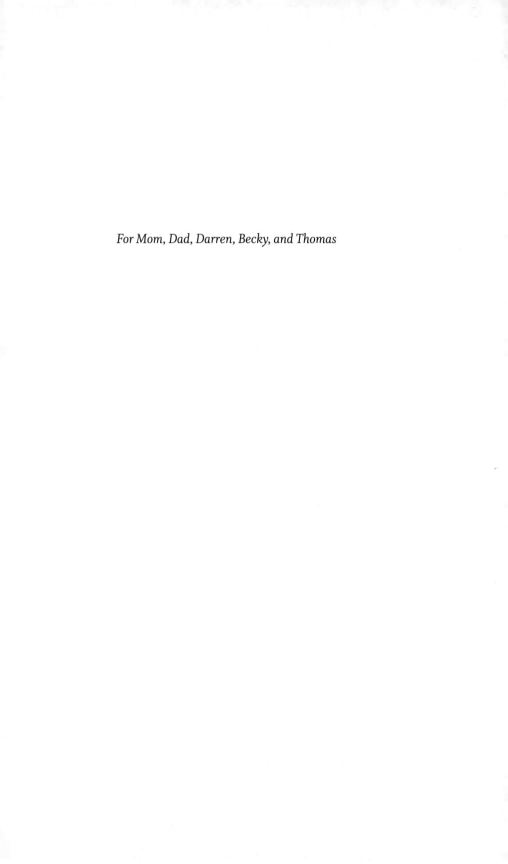

For Mom, Dad, Darren, Becky, and Thomas

CONTENTS

ACKNOWLEDGMENTS

I owe William Hinkle my utmost thanks for introducing me to this topic, for working with me on a previous publication, and for providing some of the foundational sourcing and material. Without his early assistance, this work would not have been possible. Thanks, Bill.

As they have throughout my entire career, my family supported me during this project. They put up with my obsessions and wanderings, humored me as I worked through various drafts, and offered support when needed. I cannot imagine having achieved any level of accomplishment had it not been for them.

The faculty, staff, and administration at Chowan University have been similarly supportive. My colleagues Edward Snyder and David Ballew took on any number of administrative and extracurricular duties that freed me up to research and write. Provost Danny Moore has done even more to ensure I had the time and resources to take on my many projects, and I cannot overstate my thanks to him for all his assistance over the last fifteen years. President Kirk Peterson and Chancellor M. Christopher White have presided over the university during my tenure, and I am thankful for their vision and leadership. And to all those many colleagues who have passed through the Chowan community, whose names are too many to mention, I offer my thanks for your friendship and support.

The North Carolina Collection of the Wilson Library Special Collections unit at the University of North Carolina at Chapel Hill is a wonderful resource. I spent more than a few weeks in the friendly confines, and I appreciate the assistance provided by the archival staff, led by Curator Robert Anthony. Their knowledge, friendliness, interest, and support made the long days of research successful and fulfilling. I always enjoy my trips to Chapel Hill, and look forward to continuing my relationship with the archival staff.

Rand Dotson and the entire staff at the Louisiana State University Press have been a pleasure to work with. I cannot thank them enough for their hard work, patience, guidance, support, and advice along the way. The same is true for Derik Shelor, whose meticulous editing dramatically improved this work. I thank you all.

CENTRAL PRISON

INTRODUCTION

On July 20, 1910, British home secretary Winston Churchill stood before the House of Commons and said, "The mood and temper of the public in regard to the treatment of crime and criminals is one of the most unfailing tests of the civilization of any country." Two generations earlier, having experienced Russian "civilization" during four years in Siberian exile, author Fyodor Dostoevsky allegedly offered a similar sentiment with this oft quoted though unsourced aphorism: "the degree of civilization in a society can be judged by entering its prisons." The present study of the North Carolina State Penitentiary, also known as Central Prison, seeks to demonstrate how apt those thoughts are.[1]

This is not the first study to investigate the social/penological relationship. Writing in the 1920s, historian Harry Barnes saw a correlation between the two when he discussed the reform movements of the nineteenth century. He discovered that the rise of prohibition, abolition, juvenile justice, and mental health advocacy coincided with an effort toward prison reform. Barnes thus contended that the desire to improve society included the desire to help even those whose actions placed them outside traditional social norms. A decade later, penologist Blake McKelvey found the origins of penal reform even earlier when he asserted that Quaker "religious idealism" led Pennsylvania to adopt rehabilitative efforts designed to better both the criminal and society. McKelvey thus affirmed that a societal force, in this case religion, directly affected prison life.[2]

While others made similar claims, the appreciation of a causal relationship between society and prison remained marginal for much of the twentieth century. According to penal scholar Peter Smith, the "critical philosophical and sociological literature on prisons and their relation to society has appeared especially since the 1970s." He links this appearance to the 1975 publication of Michele Foucault's *Discipline and Punish*, which explored the "diffusion of

1

disciplinary mechanisms throughout the social body." Smith acknowledges that Foucault did not view prison "as a reflection of society and modernity," but admits to studying that reflection nonetheless. Unintentionally, Foucault's work sparked a renewed interested in the social/penological relationship and revived the inquiries made by Barnes and McKelvey.[3]

That revival has quickened in recent decades thanks to the work of any number of scholars. Penologist Donald Clemmer asserts that "the prison is a microcosm of society," finds "the existence of numerous parallels between the prison and the free world," and concludes that "the culture of the prison reflect[s] the American culture." Legal scholar Lawrence Friedman concurs, arguing that the "methods of punishment are always related to what is happening in the larger world," with the result that prisons are "a microcosm of the outside world." Countless other scholars agree, and appreciate that developments in the free world are manifest within the prison walls because prisons are a part of the social order populated by members of that order.[4]

That embodiment, however, is not analogous. A decade after declaring prison a "microcosm of the outside world," Friedman revised his assessment and declared prison a warped version of society: a "funhouse mirror," as it were. The relationship between prison and society, he contends, is direct but exaggerated. Others joined Friedman in this interpretation. Criminologists Larry Siegel and Clem Bartollas assert that "poverty, racial and gender discrimination, violent crime, and mental illness are found in exaggerated forms within the prison," while the New York State Special Commission on Attica determined that "prison magnifies and intensifies" social forces. Both assessments portray prison as engendering a distorted version of reality. Such a conclusion seems apposite, as contemporary studies find prison populations younger, blacker, poorer, and less mentally stable than society at large.[5]

The correlation between free society and prison has led scholars to move beyond the foregoing general assessments to explore specific manifestations of the relationship. One of the most common avenues of discourse is race. Lawyer, scholar, and civil rights activist Michelle Alexander sees the nation's willingness to imprison African American males under the cover of "the war on drugs," "stop and frisk" initiatives, and "broken windows" measures as a demonstration of the nation's "stunningly comprehensive and well-disguised system of racialized social control that functions in a manner strikingly similar to Jim Crow."[6]

Historian Robert Perkinson supports Alexander's premise by noting that 1 in 39 white men have been to prison as compared to 1 in 6 African American men. Those numbers, he contends, are the designed goal of a criminal justice system established "to preserve privilege, bolster political fortunes, and, most of all, to discipline those on the social margins, especially African Americans." As evidence, Perkinson notes that while 90 percent of those serving time for drug charges are African American, nearly every study finds that whites use and sell drugs at a higher rate. For Perkinson, that inequity demonstrates American "white supremacy."[7]

Other scholars focus not on race but on the manner in which prisons personify corporate greed. Journalists Joel Dyer and Adam Gopnik studied private prisons and found evidence of capitalism run amok. Dyer notes that private prisons have a statutory obligation to maximize profits, and to do so they require a 90 percent occupancy rate. Gopnik thus notes that "the interest of private prisons lies not in the obvious social good of having the minimum necessary number of inmates but in having as many as possible, housed as cheaply as possible." Consequently, private prison administrators oppose rehabilitation and other potentially beneficial social reforms in order to ensure a literally captive populace. Proof of this disconnect is evident in the 2005 annual report from the Corrections Corporation of America, which warned investors, "The demand for our facilities and services could be adversely affected by the relaxation of enforcement efforts, leniency in conviction and sentencing practices or through the decriminalization of certain activities that are currently proscribed by our criminal laws." Opposition to such reforms has paid off to the tune of $150 billion in corporate profits, while inmates suffer the consequences.[8]

Beyond race and economics, political machinations also become manifest in prison. According to the FBI, from 1995 to 2014 the U.S. crime rate fell from 684.5 offenses per 100,000 inhabitants to 365.5 per 100,000, yet the number of inmates in state or federal custody remained stable at approximately 1.5 million. Scholars contend that one reason incarceration rates remain high is that politicians benefit from both statistics. Lower crime rates allow them to trumpet their success in making society safer, and that success encourages them to push for more prisons and harsher punishments, which they claim facilitated that decline.[9]

Other scholars, however, believe the rates highlight a failure in public policy. Studies show that 65 percent of inmates did not complete high school, 33 percent were unemployed at the time of their crime, 32 percent were employed but living below the poverty line at the time of their crime, 60 percent were under the influence of drugs or alcohol at the time of their crime, and between 16 percent and 24 percent suffer from "extreme mental problems." The figures are staggering, and yet politicians seem little interested in funding or address-ing those underlying causes of criminality. Rather than spend money on better schools, job opportunities, drug and alcohol rehabilitation programs, or mental health services, the nation builds more prisons and passes harsher laws. Worse still, to afford those facilities governments often end up cutting funding for the very programs that might well prevent crime. The irony is that the diversion of funds is uneconomic: it costs approximately $13,000 per year to educate a student in public school and between $17,000 and $20,000 to house a person in a mental health facility, yet it costs approximately $27,000 to house an inmate in a community-based correction center and nearly $30,000 to house them in a federal facility. The mentally ill inmate costs even more, with the figure nearing $50,000. Rather than spend money to benefit the individual and soci-ety, current policies funnel money in a direction that seems to ensure failure, increase expenditures, and crowd the nation's prisons.[10]

Not every scholar, however, is pessimistic about the social/penal relationship. Professor of constitutional law James Jacobs notes that during the civil rights struggle inmates demanded "the rights of citizenship." Like other oppressed groups, inmates fought for recognition as citizens deserving the protections all Americans enjoy. When denied those rights, they protested, rioted, and sued. Jacobs goes further and notes that the rising level of American prosperity after World War II led inmates to demand greater amenities. Calls for radios, televi-sions, movies, and snacks, as well as the right to form unions, to receive pay for their labor, and to enjoy health care and psychological counseling all exploded in the postwar era. Inmates joined the public in the age of consumerism and demanded modern conveniences despite their incarceration.[11]

We could go on, but the impact that civilian ideas, beliefs, and actions have on the prison system is manifest. What is becoming equally apparent, as Foucault related four decades ago, is that this impact often is reversed so that prison culture influences free society. Adam Gopnik notes that "though we avoid looking directly at prisons, they seep obliquely into our fashions and manners. Wealthy white teen-agers in baggy jeans and laceless shoes and multiple tattoos show, unconsciously, the reality of incarceration that acts as a hidden foundation for the country."[12]

It is more than a willingness to dress the part that demonstrates the reversed flow of this relationship. Prison and prison life are common components of popular culture. The success of prison documentaries is but one example. Spike TV's *Jail* takes viewers into local jails, while MSNBC's *Lockup* takes them into the nation's toughest penitentiaries. A&E's reality show *60 Days In*, meanwhile, follows "average citizens" as they spend time in a county jail. Fictional accounts also abound. HBO's *OZ* offers a grim look at the gangs, racism, and administrative struggles behind bars, while Netflix's *Orange Is the New Black* offers a similarly explicit depiction in a women's prison. Movies about prison life are even more common. *I Am a Fugitive from a Chain Gang* (1932) and *Cool Hand Luke* (1967) offer classic accounts of life on the chain gang, while *The Green Mile* and *The Shawshank Redemption*, both from the 1990s, depict life in penitentiaries. Prison movies are popular enough to have inspired their own spoofs, notably Woody Allen's 1969 *Take the Money and Run*, and their own black comedies, including the 1974 Burt Reynolds vehicle *The Longest Yard*. From the manner of dress to television and the movies, prison culture has made its way into popular culture.[13]

The issues herein discussed barely scratch the surface of the multitudinous relationships between society and prison. Although cursory, the point is to demonstrate the existence and nature of those relationships. More importantly, it should make evident the impossibility of studying prisons without appreciating the larger social order or of studying that social order without appreciating prisons. The history of the North Carolina State Penitentiary makes that connection and the utility of this type of study additionally evident, as the institution's origins, development, and legacy serve as a reflection of and a window on any number of the state's political, philosophical, social, and economic circumstances.

From the prison's inception in the late nineteenth century, North Carolina's politicians played a role in locating, planning, building, and administering the facility. Once built, and continuing to the present day, politicians established the prison's budget, chose its leaders, and set policy. While such intervention is an acceptable part of political oversight, what seems less righteous is the manner in which state leaders used those powers as political weapons. The facility served as a means of demonstrating one's "tough on crime" bona fides, as a tool for attacking those who "coddle criminals," and as an easy target of "wasteful spending." It also provided opportunities for political cronyism, corruption, and payback. As a result, politicians alternately splurged on the prison and then needlessly chocked off its funds; they offered principled support for those running the facility and then undermined administrators for political purposes; and they demanded harder time for inmates and then criticized staff for their lack of humane treatment. Politicians of every stripe and from every party have intervened in the prison's affairs, implemented their own policies, and engaged in their own political machinations. In so doing, they made the prison a prime forum for understanding the state's political evolution.

That understanding advances when we consider a second issue: North Carolina's political paradox. Aptly described by journalist Rob Christensen, North Carolinians have a long history of electing both archconservatives and strong liberals. As manifested in the penal realm, that paradox occurred whenever one party replaced the other or when both parties shared power. When the parties cycled from office, the result was a policy reversal as the new regime appointed its own leaders, implemented programs more in keeping with its political persuasion, and funded the prison as it saw fit. This created dramatic swings of penal philosophy, hindered the creation of a stable cadre of experienced administrators, and undermined the prison's financial planning. When North Carolinians elected a divided government, gridlock arose. Few today would be shocked to find politicians refusing to work across party lines, but the occurrence of such intransigence in North Carolina was especially frequent and the prison often served as a tool for political obstruction. Although vigorous penitentiary leaders were able to protect the institution and its inmates despite such political interference, under lesser leaders the results were brutalized inmates, corruption, and fraud. The governance of the prison and the treatment of inmates thus embodied the state's paradoxical politics.[14]

A third issue that demonstrates the prison as a political microcosm relates to North Carolina's progressive reputation. At least compared to many of its southern neighbors, North Carolina tended toward greater industrial development, more moderate race relations, and a more contentious political realm. As Valdimir Orlando Key wrote in his magisterial 1949 work *Southern Politics in State and Nation,* "Many see in North Carolina a closer approximation to national norms, or national expectations of performance, than they find elsewhere in the South. In any competition for national judgment they deem the state far more 'presentable' than its southern neighbors. It enjoys a reputation for progressive outlook and action in many phases of life." North Carolinians are proud of that reputation, and they work hard to protect and advance it. They have done so through their prison by offering work release programs, vocational training, modern capital punishment techniques, and model mental health and juvenile treatment facilities.[15]

Reputations, however, are not always representations of reality, and just as often state leaders resorted to policies that mitigated progressive reform. Indeed, Key couched his praise by dubbing the state "a progressive plutocracy" dominated by "a financial and business elite" who controlled the state's "political and economic life." The result was another paradox, in that the state's progressivism remained narrowly bound. As evidenced by the state's early and enthusiastic use of convict leasing, North Carolina's progressivism, while expressed as a means of serving the masses, actually served the elite.[16]

The state's finances offer one final example of political influence. North Carolina's politicians have a long history of financial conservatism, and that parsimony has had a direct impact on the penitentiary. Prison administrators frequently pressed politicians for funds, while politicians responded with claims of poverty and pushed administrators to seek self-sufficiency. That push forced the first inmates to construct the prison, later led to convict leasing, and eventually resulted in the use of parole, probation, and work release programs. Although the responses reached the desired ends, the financial squeeze has had negative consequences. It cost prison administrators their freedom when the Highway Department assumed control of the system in the 1930s, it led to overcrowding in the 1980s, and it resulted in fatal shortcomings in inmate healthcare in the 2000s. While tight finances inspired prison officials to create cost-effective methods of confinement, they also cost bureaucrats their independence and inmates their lives.[17]

That politics played a role in Central Prison's development should come as little surprise. More surprising is the myriad additional points where we can see the social/penal relationship. Sectionalism is a prime example. From the state's inception, North Carolinians have had to overcome the existence of three distinct regions: the coastal plain, the central piedmont, and the western mountains. The regions' geographical, cultural, political, racial, and economic peculiarities led to bruising debates over where to place the state capital, where to run the earliest railroads, and where to place state universities. They also affected the penitentiary, with arguments over its location, funding, and expansion all influenced by regional differences.[18]

The regional divide also helps explain the state's lackluster early history. When compared to Virginia and South Carolina, North Carolina lagged in terms of economic development, social consciousness, and political organization. North Carolina thus earned the "Rip Van Winkle" sobriquet as it fell asleep, bypassed by the world. Although it overcame that lethargy, for much of the state's early history it failed to keep up with its neighbors. That failure is apparent by the simple fact that North Carolina was one of the last to construct a state prison. It also emerges when we appreciate that even after it built a prison, North Carolina failed to implement the most modern penal philosophies. The state's struggles with modernity are thus evident in its penal system.

The most visible demonstration of the prison as a social microcosm may be

the one North Carolinians are least likely to acknowledge: race. While segregation and racial violence were less egregious in North Carolina than in the Deep
South, African Americans still faced Jim Crow, intimidation, and violence. The
penitentiary was part of the state's racial struggle if for no other reason than the
disproportionate number of African American inmates. While the state's African American population hovered around 22 percent, their numbers among
the prison population frequently exceeded 70 percent. At the same time, the
percentage of white guards and administrators often exceeded 90 percent. The
prison thus embodied the state's racial disequilibrium, as whites dominated and
African Americans suffered.[19]

But it is more than numbers that tell the story. The widespread use of convict
labor meant inmates often worked in some form of unpaid toil. They helped
build the very walls and cells of their incarceration, and then moved to in-house
industries in an effort to offset the costs of their confinement. When such
labor proved financially insufficient, administrators leased inmates to private
firms. Although the labor was difficult, dangerous, and often resulted in injury
or death, the fact that most of those impacted were African American made it
easier for the public to accept that exploitation.

Such treatment was not simply evident from inmate labor. Prison administrators obeyed the state's Jim Crow dictates and mirrored its response to desegregation. For the better part of a century, African Americans and whites had
separate cellblocks, dined at different times, and used segregated facilities.
When desegregation finally arrived, officials again followed the state's lead,
engaged in massive resistance, and kept the facility segregated until lawsuits and
the threat of a federal takeover forced their hand in 1965. Even then, however,
Jim Crow's vestiges remained, and it was not until the 1980s that segregation
finally ended. As historian Dan Berger notes, "the South's political geography
seemed to mirror that of the prison."[20]

Lastly, it is worth noting that the prison had its own place in the state's civil
rights history. Not only did inmates adopt civil rights techniques to demand
equitable treatment, but the impact also flowed back on the movement. According to Berger, "The Black Power and New Left movements gathered energy from
news of prison unrest." The result was "a series of political linkages, connecting
the inside to the outside." As with popular culture, civil rights also demonstrate
the two-way flow of the social/penological relationship.[21]

All of these issues should make clear the utility of studying the North Carolina State Penitentiary. Not only can we appreciate the institution, its gover-

nance, and its inmates, we can gain a new perspective on the state's history. What makes this facility an even more valuable tool is that the lessons are not restricted to North Carolina. Central Prison also serves as a means of appreciating the history and evolution of American penology.

When construction on the penitentiary began in 1870, the Auburn system was preeminent. Devised in the 1830s, the system housed inmates individually and in complete silence, requiring daily work from all. Authorities believed isolation and labor gave inmates time for reflection and growth, preparing them to re-enter society as upstanding citizens. The theory failed in practice due to cost, crowding, and mental health issues, and by the 1870s the reformatory model arose. This system, centered on the Elmira Reformatory in upstate New York, focused on the inmate's moral regeneration through education, hard work, and enforced good conduct. As with the Auburn model, the reformatory sought to prepare the inmate for his return to the free world. Unlike the Auburn model, the reformatory actively engaged inmates in that preparation. While more successful than the Auburn system, by the turn of the century it too fell into disuse.

The cause of the reformatory's collapse was the realization that inmates were a profitable labor source. Convict leasing subsequently emerged, as profit replaced reform. Despite the dangers inherent to the system, for much of the twentieth century the exploitation of inmate labor was a central feature of the nation's prison systems. That was true despite the development of the rehabilitative model in the 1920s. Based on the idea that inmates could benefit from educational or vocational training, as well as individualized treatment for mental health, drug, and alcohol issues, the object was to address the factors that drove criminal behavior. Although a step forward, until the 1950s the drive for profit overshadowed rehabilitation.

In the 1980s, after three decades of rehabilitation, the pendulum moved in the other direction. With rising crime rates, crack cocaine, and gang violence, public sympathy for inmates waned and a new "law and order" mentality emerged that demanded harsher sentences, fewer rehabilitation programs, and a focus on punishment. Prison officials dropped the rehabilitative model, and inmates suffered accordingly from a lack of health care, counseling, education, space, and simple activities to pass the time.

Central Prison has embodied all of those eras and methodologies. When conceived, politicians and administrators intended to employ the Auburn system. By the time construction was complete, however, the reformatory approach had won favor and the prison's earliest wardens appreciated the benefits of preparing inmates for their freedom. Quickly, however, politicians succumbed to the financial opportunities of convict leasing and employed nearly every able-bodied inmate in some form of productive labor. That employment lasted even as administrators implemented elements of the rehabilitative model in the 1920s. Only after inmates rioted and took the prison to court in the 1970s did political leaders fully appreciate rehabilitation's benefits. That appreciation proved short lived, and by the 1990s the public pushed back against inmates who seemed to have it "too good." A return to "hard time" ensued.

Although today's inmates contend that those "hard times" remain, presently Central Prison offers an amalgamation of each model. A large segment of the population is isolated in some form of restricted confinement for rules violations, as punishment, or for their own protection. Those inmates do not achieve self-actualization, but rather suffer for their behavior. They certainly are doing "hard time."

Most inmates do not suffer so, and instead have opportunities to engage in reformative and rehabilitative activities. The prison provides educational and vocational training programs, job opportunities, drug and alcohol counseling, mental healthcare, and juvenile detention facilities as well as numerous parole, probation, and work release programs. All of those components offer inmates some level of hope and the opportunity to prepare for their post-prison futures. And yet, few would argue inmates have it "easy." Discipline at Central Prison is strict, freedoms are few, the ever-present threat of violence hovers over the facility, and questions remain about the treatment of mentally ill inmates and the excessive use of solitary confinement. In the end, prison officials try to balance punishment with rehabilitation based on the understanding that most inmates eventually will return to polite society. While they must pay for their crimes, they are not beyond hope.

The story of that effort to find a balance is a tale in and of itself, and when combined with the state's ever changing social, political, and economic history it becomes that much more intriguing. Central Prison has served North Carolina for more than 140 years, and during that time those varied elements have shaped and been shaped by the state penitentiary. The penitentiary truly is a social microcosm that reflects larger forces at work in the state. Appreciating that reflection is fundamental to understanding both the state and its prison, and it is to that historical relationship we now turn.

1

THE PENITENTIARY ARGUMENT

The origins of both Central Prison and its reciprocal relationship with the state emerge in the early nineteenth century, amid a revolution in penal theory. Key to that revolution was the penitentiary. Designed to punish the criminal through the loss of freedom and the requirement of hard labor, to protect the public by removing offenders from society, and to offer both groups hope for a better future via individual reformation, the penitentiary seemed the answer to society's search for law and order. North Carolinians, however, largely ignored the revolution and clung to traditional forms of punishment longer than people in nearly every other state. The reasons for that refusal were many: a stubborn traditionalism, worries about cost, politics, and the regional divide. Whatever the causes, even at this early stage penal policy reflected public sentiment.

The origins of the penitentiary system date to the 1790s, when Americans came to believe the penal system was broken. Local jails often were unsanitary, ill-suited for long-term confinement, and insecure, while the use of public sham- ing and corporal punishment (which included the pillory or stockade, physical mutilation such as branding or the loss of an ear, and public whipping) left the criminal depraved, separated him from society, and increased recidivism. Physi- cian, social reformer, and signer of the Declaration of Independence Benjamin Rush was a leading advocate of this perspective, and as early as 1787 he asserted that corporal punishment neither reformed the criminal nor affected deter- rence. He therefore called for the creation of a "house of repentance" to punish and rehabilitate criminals.[1]

Other supporters argued that incarceration was a more civilized and flexible form of punishment, while those who blamed society for causing crime asserted that imprisonment removed criminals from corrupting social influences and offered time for contemplation. Those who blamed the individual for his crimes also came to support incarceration, and argued there could be no greater penalty than preventing someone from enjoying America's "openness" and its "boundless frontier." For a variety of reasons, and from nearly every competing perspective, Americans seemed to be turning toward incarceration, with the result that by 1800 eleven states had replaced traditional punishments with jail time.[2]

In the 1820s, Pennsylvania and New York took incarceration a step further and created the penitentiary. The Pennsylvania model tried to "separate offenders from all forms of earthly corruption, contamination, or infection," but to do so without leaving them "insane or physically broken and debilitated beyond repair." It did so by shaving the inmates' heads, referring to them by their prison issued identification numbers, and preventing any contact with the outside world. The inmates received no mail, newspapers, or visits, and lived in individual cells in a state of total and constant silence. Those who behaved earned small jobs, while those who misbehaved remained idle to bide their time. The system's creators argued that "shut out from a tumultuous world, and separated from those equally guilty with himself, [the inmate] can indulge his remorse unseen, and find ample opportunity for reflection and reformation." The concept proved popular, but it had a notable problem: cost. Since inmates worked only as a reward for good behavior, the state covered virtually all expenses.[3]

To solve that concern, the Auburn system arose. Used first in New York, this system employed the same model as Pennsylvania except that all prisoners worked. Each day, guards led inmates from their individual cells to a communal work area. The products of their labor were used within the prison walls to save administrators from having to purchase supplies, or were sold on the open market to earn revenue. In either case, the inmates offset some portion of their confinement costs. Those who devised this system asserted the isolation and silence reformed the inmate by convincing him "that he is no longer his own master," while the hard work taught him "some useful trade, whereby, when he is let out of prison to obtain an honest living." Historian Edward Ayers further notes that the system's economics satisfied "budget-conscious legislators," while its isolation convinced the public the penitentiary was not a breeding ground or training site for crime and criminal behavior. Auburn's economics made it more popular, and most states that adopted the penitentiary model followed New York's lead.[4]

North Carolina attempted to join in the penitentiary movement, but the going was slow. In 1791, legislators first proposed building a state prison. The *Raleigh Star, Raleigh Register, Greensboro Patriot,* and the *Hillsborough Recorder* supported the proposition, but most North Carolinians rejected the idea.

One reason for that opposition was the regional divide. The aforementioned newspapers represented the state's central piedmont, where law enforcement remained problematic. The population of the coastal plain, where no such problem existed, saw little need and opposed the institution. Even as the population shifted westward, the coast continued to dominate politically, and, according to historian William Powell, that domination was "the predominant cause of the state's failure to move forward."[5]

A decade later, in 1801, Absalom Tate, the County Representative from Hillsborough, introduced to the House of Commons the first formal prison bill. It called for the creation of a facility large enough to house seventy-five prisoners in cells so constructed as to isolate each inmate and to prevent communication with others. The bill set first-degree murder as the only crime punishable by death, but implemented imprisonment for second-degree murder, rape, and arson. Those convicted of crimes not listed faced traditional punishments, such as the pillory, whipping post, and stockade. Opponents of the bill argued it was too expensive, that only physical punishment truly deterred, and that such an institution would increase crime by creating a school where young criminals could hone their techniques and experienced criminals could plot new assaults. Such counterarguments prevailed, and Tate's bill failed 73–44.[6]

Dr. Calvin Jones, a representative from Johnston County, was one of the opponents, and on November 20, 1802, he delivered a speech opposing yet another bill to bring forth a state prison. Calling it "a project to save from the gallows, a set of wretches, who so far from being entitled to the bounties of community, have by the atrocity of their crimes, justly forfeited a right to existence," he then joined the ranks of those who feared a prison would become a crime school: "Murderers, robbers and horse thieves are not suitable persons to teach good morals. By such company bad men are made worse. There they lay plans for future villainies, and after a few years, they are turned out upon society as abandoned and as vile as the influence of such infamous society can make them." Prison did not reform men, he argued, but rather made them worse individuals and better criminals.[7]

After covering well-trod ground, he then offered a new argument by asserting that traditional punishments were by no means cruel, especially in comparison to those inflicted in places like Russia. He even claimed that by their very comforts American prisons attracted criminal immigrants. Indeed, he argued that states with prisons suffered crime waves because foreigners "think themselves happy if they can be accommodated with a place in it" because they could then "live in affluence." He believed North Carolina would suffer similarly from those determined to live a posh life at the state's expense.[8]

After that rather preposterous argument, Jones claimed Americans too innocently accepted human reclamation, and asserted instead that some men were evil and beyond repair. Even were they not, he continued, criminals responded only to physical suffering. The physical pain and social consequences of corporal punishment and public humiliation were thus more effective means of reform.[9]

In the end, Dr. Jones concluded that if the state wanted to end crime, the way to do so was to focus on positive factors. He therefore proclaimed, "Endow your University, establish schools in every part and corner of your counties, and you may then hope for a time to exercise the virtues of humanity in a manner not inconsistent with the stern demands of justice."[10]

The problem with Dr. Jones's argument was that as the nineteenth century progressed there was a growing sense that the humiliating and violent punishments he supported were too extreme. This caused prosecutors to fear jury nullification, by which jurors refused to convict those they believed were guilty because the potential penalties revolted them. Indeed, by 1837 the North Carolina law code required death for those convicted of being mere accessories to robbery, burglary, arson, or mayhem. As a result, many prosecutors dropped cases whose punishment they feared juries might find excessive or repellant. Even when prosecutors went forth and juries did their job, governors often commuted the sentences. There thus seemed to be a breakdown in the criminal justice system.[11]

Supporters of a state prison used jury nullification and a rising crime rate to further their agenda. In 1810, legislators reintroduced Absalom Tate's bill. While it passed the House, it died in the Senate. In 1812, with the state enjoying a rare financial surplus, the House of Commons passed yet another bill to construct a prison and set aside $60,000 for the purpose. The Senate vote, however, ended in a tie, with Speaker of the Senate Joseph Riddick of Gates County holding the deciding vote. Believing a state prison remained too revolutionary, Riddick voted no. The legislature redirected the money to other internal improvements, and the state continued forth without a central prison.[12]

Undaunted, proponents pressed on. In 1815, Priestly Mangum gave a speech to his graduating class at the University of North Carolina at Chapel Hill entitled "Whether North Carolina Ought to Establish a Penitentiary." He began by asserting that the "disproportionate severity of our laws does not prevent, but encourages the violation of them." As had others, he contended the very harshness of the state's laws led to jury nullification, which bred criminal behavior. Mangum argued that deterrence came from the certainty of punishment, not the severity. The way to get that certainty was to create a system by which juries felt comfortable punishing criminals, and he believed a state prison was that mechanism.[13]

Mangum went on to argue that there were further benefits to a prison. First, he noted that it punished the inmate. He believed too many county jail inmates lived in idleness, while a prison required them to labor. Labor for the criminal, he argued, would first be "irksome and compelled." But prisons could be reformative, and he believed over time the inmate would find labor "more tolerable than idleness," and would emerge a reformed and productive citizen. In a similar vein, he argued that many crimes were the result of dissolution, but incarceration forced sobriety upon inmates and taught them a temperate lifestyle.[14]

In the end, Mangum concluded, "If you wish to wipe away the stain of blood from your penal code—to make a body of useful mechanics and manufacturers of those who are now emptied out of the prison into the grave—to cure the idle, to reclaim the intemperate, to turn despair into hope and beggary into comfort—to preserve your wives from portionless widow-hood, your children from orphanage, and some of (the most) valuable of your countrymen from suicide, erect a penitentiary."[15]

Whether his speech had any impact or not is hard to tell, but in 1816 the House of Commons passed a bill (61–56) to construct a central prison in Raleigh. While the Senate supported the concept, sectionalism derailed the bill when a majority of senators wanted the prison located in Fayetteville. Unwilling to compromise, the Senate refused to vote on the House bill and the measure died. When similar legislation failed in 1817 and 1818 due to renewed financial concerns, one citizen asked, "Is North Carolina too poor to be just?"[16]

In 1828, legislative supporters tried again and organized a joint select committee to investigate and report on the two penitentiary models then dominating the nation's penal systems. The committee studied both methodologies and presented its findings to the legislature, but refused to make a recommendation on whether or not the state should build a penitentiary or which model to adopt. The result was that North Carolina remained among the small minority of states doing without.[17]

Penitentiary supporters hoped to use the state's lethargy to their benefit and in 1844 convinced the legislature to organize yet another committee to study the issue. It produced a *Report of the Committee on the Penitentiary,* which went well beyond the 1828 study. Delivered on December 28, 1844, it argued that the experiences of other states proved a penitentiary "conclusively" and "materially . . . diminished the commission of crime." It found the Auburn model most successful, and echoed the model's creators in arguing that confinement reformed inmates by cutting them off from the people and temptations that led them astray, while the labor requirement gave them "a habit of sober industry" and provided the opportunity to "find a profitable trade." The system, in other words, enabled inmates to achieve moral reformation and provided them the tools needed to avoid a return to criminality.[18]

The report not only pointed to the benefits of the Auburn model, it stressed the shortcomings of the state's present model. It called the state's use of corporal punishment "uncongenial to the spirit of the age, and revolting to humanity," and it argued that public humiliations marked the victim with "the brand of Cain," which created an "impassable barrier" in his return to polite society. The result was that no matter how badly the criminal wanted to reform, there were "no obvious waters in public sentiment that can wash out the scars of his lacerated flesh." The Auburn model punished, reformed, and enabled the criminal to return to civil society; the state's existent system certainly punished, but it failed to reform and actually prevented social reintegration.[19]

The report concluded by turning to the issue that had so often before torpedoed the proposition: cost. The committee found that inmate labor enabled most states to cover all the costs of upkeep; several emerged with a profit. While some states failed to cover costs, the shortfall was never more than $20,000. The Auburn model, the committee therefore asserted, not only punished, reformed, and enabled inmate reintegration, it was so cost effective it left the state with only a minimal outlay. To demonstrate its true financial value, the committee noted that North Carolina spent $15,000 annually to house in county jails inmates who otherwise would have been in the penitentiary. That meant, at worst, the state could expect the penitentiary to cost $5,000 more than the present system, but with better results for all involved.[20]

Knowing the next concern would be construction costs, the report finished by estimating expenses at $100,000, based on real estate, supply prices, and a construction cost of $500 per cell. The way to meet that expense was simple: an added tax of 3 cents on land and 8 cents on the poll tax. The taxes would raise $25,000 per annum and would last four years. The committee acknowledged that raising taxes would not be popular, so it suggested a public referendum.[21]

Moved by the committee's report, legislators decided to follow its recommendations. In 1846, therefore, the General Assembly offered North Carolinians a statewide referendum on penitentiary construction funded by modest, temporary tax increases. With the votes tallied, legislators were shocked when only 28 percent supported construction. Studies found that "in exactly half of the reporting counties, fewer than one-fifth of the county voters approved the innovation. Indeed, the vote was so overwhelmingly negative that no clear patterns of support emerge from the numbers." Cities, towns, and rural areas all voted in nearly the same numbers, as did members of the competing Whig and Democratic parties. North Carolinians simply were not ready to enter the modern age of penology.[22]

While "no clear patterns of support emerged," the history of the state's multiple failures indicate that financial considerations engendered the most opposition. Additionally, the theft of funds set aside for infrastructure development in the 1820s and 1830s might well have convinced the public that politicians could not be trusted with the amount of money needed to build a penitentiary. Finally, the fact that the state paid to house state inmates in county jails might have raised additional financial concerns at the county level.[23]

Finances and the fear of graft were not the only factors that influenced public sentiment; so too did race. Although a slave state, in 1830 North Carolina had a "free black" population that numbered nearly 20,000. In 1831, the General Assembly created a convict lease system for "free Negroes" facing a fine they could not pay. In this system, the county sheriff oversaw a bidding process during which anyone willing to pay the fine, or the highest bidder if no one would pay the full fine, purchased the right to employ the individual as he saw fit. The employer had to guarantee the inmate's safety and security, and was required to release the individual after a period determined during the bidding process. When combined with the fact that slaves remained under their owner's control, this lease system meant imprisonment was unlikely for a sizeable number of African Americans. With the number of potential inmates limited due to slavery and leasing, the question for many was why build a penitentiary that might well lose money?[24]

Despite that question, during the two decades prior to the Civil War public sentiment began to change. The question no longer was why build a penitentiary, but why not? The cause of this change, in part, was the rising power of the central piedmont. The people there had long supported a penitentiary, and with its increasing population and power in the state legislature, the region's inhabitants enjoyed more political heft. A second factor was the rise of the Whig Party and the inauguration of "a generation of honest, progressive, and enlightened government," which gave citizens confidence the government would spend tax revenue as intended.[25]

Determined to press their apparent advantage, those who advocated for a penitentiary took to the press. On April 7, 1846, a letter writer to the *Raleigh Register* complained about "the most humiliating scene that has ever been exhibited before us." The letter described how local authorities stripped two white criminals, fastened them to a post, and flogged them thirty-nine times "until their skin was rough with whelks and red with blood." The writer asserted, "We have never beheld a scene more degrading to the noble sentiments that should be nurtured and cultivated in the heart of every freeman." Sickened by the use of corporal punishment on white men, the letter writer called for the legislature to ban such barbaric practices. He then concluded: "Had North Carolina a State Prison for her convicts, she might, from it, derive a revenue to the state, bring the erring to reflection, and probably to reformation, and teach them that which they will not learn of their own accord, trades and arts, by which they may obtain an honest and honorable livelihood." While the racial implications of the letter are clear, so too are the changing sensibilities.[26]

Others supported a penitentiary because it could better adjust the punishment to fit the crime. One advocate wrote to his local paper and asserted, "The penitentiary graduates not only the quantity, but the quality or degree of intensity, which depends on the grade of the crime, age of the criminal, his conduct after conviction, [and] his degree of depravity which is indicated by his obedience or disobedience, his livelihood or penance." This same person further argued that corporal punishment scarred the criminal forever and offered little chance for reform. Isolated in a prison cell, however, an inmate could "commune with the silent monitor of his heart," reflect on and feel remorse for his crimes, and look forward with "hopes of the future."[27]

A letter writer to the *North Carolina Standard* came at the issue from a different perspective:

> I have an unprincipled, mischievous, thievish neighbor who trades with my negroes, lets down my fences, and turns his stock into my fields, steals my lamb and pigs etc. What shall I gain by having him convicted in our courts? Conscience will not allow me to have his life taken on account of a little pelf; and if I have him whipped, what do I or the community

gain by it? But if North Carolina built a penitentiary, where he could be kept at work and out of the way of doing mischief, for five or ten years, then there would be a strong motive for me to have him caught in his villainy and convicted.

This citizen saw no benefit to himself from the current penal system, but saw great benefits from a penitentiary.[28]

Other supporters perceived the penitentiary as a moneymaking operation, as a job-creating institution, or as an opportunity for political patronage. Finally, those embarrassed by North Carolina's Rip Van Winkle image considered the penitentiary a means of joining modernity. Editors for the *Raleigh Star* gave expression to such sentiment when they wrote, "We believe in the expediency of establishing a Penitentiary in North Carolina, and of doing it now. We have been dilly-dallying about it long enough." Whatever the reasoning, by the 1850s there existed a wave of support for penitentiary construction.[29]

But not everyone was caught up in the wave, and many continued to oppose construction. Rockingham legislator Theophilus Lacey asserted, "I cannot believe this penitentiary is calculated for humane purposes, since it proposes that an unfortunate criminal shall drag out, in some cases ten or twenty years, and in others the whole of his life, in prison; whereas if the offender was punished with death at once, he would be forgotten, and not be a living monument of misery and distress." Another opponent questioned the power of the penitentiary to reform: "how can a person repent and reform in a state of constant punishment, the mind strained to a state of endurance and the person in distress?"[30]

Others saw the penitentiary as a threat to American values and the nation's founding ideals: "In the time of the Revolution it was admitted that taking away any part of our labor, without our consent, amounted to slavery, and that any such slavery was worse than death; but under the penitentiary system the free-born citizen is made to labor directly under the lash as a slave, and is not this worse than death? What legal or moral right has a State to inflict upon them this horrid tyranny, which would disgrace the most barbarous and savage times?" Another citizen worried penitentiary walls hid potentially evil acts, and argued it was better to keep punishment in the daylight to ensure it did not become a tool of state coercion. Finally, some simply believed individuals could settle disputes on their own.[31]

Whatever the argument, and despite growing support, North Carolina remained without a penitentiary and relied on the county jails, pillory, whipping post, and branding iron well into the nineteenth century. The reasons for that are evident: The regional divide initially pitted inhabitants of the coastal plain against those of the interior over the very existence of a penitentiary. Once they agreed on its need, they split on its location. Cost concerns also influenced public sentiment, as did worries about the government's ability to administer penitentiary funds. Race too played a role, as slavery and convict leasing meant most African Americans would never see the inside of a prison cell. Location, finances, and race thus conspired against a penitentiary, leaving North Carolina's penal system, like the state at large, lagging behind its neighbors.

Events were about to transpire, however, that changed virtually every one of the aforementioned factors. Federal intervention amid the Civil War and Reconstruction subsumed sectionalism, finances, race, and politics, and pushed the state forward. While North Carolinians were unable or unwilling to build a penitentiary, the federal government proved much more capable. Through the processes of defeat, reconciliation, and renewal, North Carolina was about to enter the penitentiary age.

2

THE CIVIL WAR ERA AND THE PENITENTIARY

The Civil War cost the South 260,000 dead, and of that number nearly 20,000 were North Carolinians. The war also devastated the state financially, as abolition cost slaveholders millions in property losses, the repudiation of Confederate bonds cost investors millions more, and the destruction of cities, towns, railroads, and farms by Union troops caused additional untold sums of damage. Reconstruction further challenged North Carolina, as southern hostility and northern vengeance made the effort to rehabilitate the Union more difficult than anticipated. Worse still was the subsequent era of Redemption, when white Democrats sought to reclaim the state from Republicans, African Americans, and the federal government. Together, the sixteen years of war, Reconstruction, and Redemption altered many elements of life in North Carolina, including the penitentiary. In that case, however, the impact was riven: on one hand, there emerged a constitutional requirement for penitentiary construction, something politicians and supporters had been unable to achieve on their own. On the other hand, the era's violence, financial difficulties, racial unrest, corruption, and wild swings in political leadership undermined fulfillment of that requirement. Once again larger social forces reflected on penal policy, and the state, forced by external circumstances to move forward yet constrained from so doing by domestic developments, carried on without a penitentiary.

While North Carolinians had long experience in debating the need for and feasibility of a penitentiary, upon the outbreak of war in 1861 politicians had no experience with mass or extended incarceration. That shortcoming proved notable, as the state housed one of the largest and most infamous Civil War prisons. Opened in December 1861, the Confederate prison in Salisbury served as a holding place for Confederate soldiers under court-martial and for Union prisoners of war. According to historian Milton Ready, "from August 1861 until

November 1864 conditions at Salisbury seemed tolerable for a nineteenth-century prison." Then the population spiked from seven hundred to more than two thousand. There were not enough tents to house the inmates and many had to sleep under the stars. Meat, flour, and water were in short supply and death stalked the prison, yet new inmates kept arriving. Between October 1864 and February 1865, 3,419 inmates died; 500 more escaped.[1]

Fortunately, as the war wound down the influx ebbed and prisoners moved to Greensboro or Wilmington. On April 12, 1865, three days after Lee's surrender at Appomattox, Union General George Stoneman liberated the prison and burned it to the ground. According to historians, some five thousand people died during the prison's operation. Although overshadowed by the atrocities inflicted at the Andersonville prison in Georgia, where nearly thirteen thousand died, the horrors of Salisbury were immense and demonstrated that North Carolina had little competence in administering a large penal institution. Despite that incompetence, the momentum for a state penitentiary, which had been building prior to the war, returned in its aftermath. That revival, however, was not the consequence of internal forces. Instead, it came from without.[2]

Radical Reconstruction divided the former Confederate states into five military districts. A military authority governed each district and oversaw the writing of new state constitutions, the granting of universal male suffrage, and ratification of the Fourteenth Amendment. Only after completing those tasks could states seek readmission. North Carolina was part of Military District 2 along with South Carolina, and General Daniel Sickles governed the region. One of Sickles's first tasks was to address the region's postwar crime wave. He did so by creating a committee to oversee construction of a temporary penitentiary. Consisting of M. L. Wiggins, chairman of the Senate Finance Committee; R. Y. McAden, speaker of the House of Commons; J. C. Harper, chairman of the House Finance Committee; Kemp Battle, the public treasurer; and Governor Jonathan Worth, the committee's initial meeting took place on August 15, 1867. Amid the meeting, the committee learned that Sickles also wanted them "to take into consideration the probable erection later on of a permanent penitentiary and the employment of the prisoners therein in mining or other work in metals, quarrying stone, brick making or manufacturing, whereby the penitentiary may be made self-supporting and the convicts taught some useful work." Members decided they did not have enough information to address those considerations, so they called on local sheriffs to gather data about the number of felons in their care and on state geologist W. C. Kerr to help determine where to find the resources Sickles hoped to exploit.[3]

As the committee gathered information, North Carolina politics changed dramatically. First, on August 26, 1867, President Andrew Johnson removed Sickles as commander of District 2 and replaced him with General Edward Canby. Then on January 14, 1868, the prescribed constitutional convention met in Raleigh to write a new governing document. African Americans voted in the statewide election for constitutional representatives, and the Republican Party benefitted from their presence at the polls. Of the 120 representatives, 107 were Republican, including fifteen African Americans, and the constitution they drafted was "one of the most forward-looking and progressive documents in the state's history." Known as the "Canby Constitution," one factor that made it so progressive was its clear "assumption that government . . . had a collective responsibility for the overall welfare of the citizens of North Carolina." Proof abounds throughout the document, which abolished property qualifications for voting and office holding, expanded the number of elective offices, ordained a free public education system, and mandated the establishment of a permanent state penitentiary.[4]

During the convention, a Committee on Punishments, Penal Institutions, and Public Charities examined that final issue. It subsequently authored a report recommending substantive changes to the state's criminal statutes, all focused on the goals of "satisfying justice" and "reforming the offender." Among the recommendations were calls to abolish corporal punishment and to reduce the number of capital crimes to four: murder, arson, burglary, and rape. Members understood that reducing the number of capital crimes and abolishing corporal punishment meant more criminals would face prison time, so they supported General Sickles's policy of building a penitentiary. The committee recommended locating the new building "at some central and accessible point within the state" and determined it should be "as nearly self-supporting as is consistent with the purposes of [its] creation." Finally, members called for the maintenance and expansion of county jails, where criminals with sentences of fewer than two years would serve their time. As historian Susan Thomas explains it, the committee envisioned "a dual penal system" with long-term sentences served in the state penitentiary and short-term sentences served in county jails.[5]

The constitutional representatives in Raleigh adopted the committee's recommendations completely, and they became Article XI of the new state constitution. Sent to the public in April 1868, voters ratified the constitution by a vote of 93,086 to 74,016.[6]

They not only voted in favor of the new constitution in April 1868, they also voted for a new governor. Jonathan Worth chose not to run for reelection out of his disdain for the new constitution, but Democrat Thomas Samuel Ashe and Republican William Woods Holden, who had supported the Union during the Civil War and governed the state for five months in its immediate aftermath, both vied for the office. Thanks in part to the African American electorate, Holden won with 56 percent of the vote.

By the time Holden took office, Sickles's 1867 committee, created to study the location of a temporary penitentiary, had received all the requested documentation, digested the information, and offered a suggestion. It determined Lockville, southwest of Raleigh on the Deep River in Chatham County, was the perfect place to locate what would now be a permanent penitentiary. Centrally located, the site offered access to a variety of natural resources and provided numerous opportunities for inmate labor.

Holden failed to act on the recommendation due to larger political concerns. Specifically, he faced impeachment. Democrats charged Holden with arresting political opponents under the guise of a crusade to quell Ku Klux Klan violence, and they campaigned furiously on the charge during the 1870 election cycle. The campaign succeeded and the party reclaimed the legislature. Invigorated, Democrats went after Holden directly, and on December 14, 1870, the House of Representatives voted to impeach him on eight counts. The trial dragged into the new year, but on March 22, 1871, in a near straight party-line vote, 36–13, the Senate convicted Holden on six counts. He became the first governor in American history to be impeached, convicted, and removed from office.[7]

Facing such political turmoil, it should come as little surprise that constructing a penitentiary was not Holden's focus. Not everyone was so distracted, however, and legislators continually reminded the governor of his constitutional mandate. They also pointed out the presence of "many prisoners now supported in idleness in County jails, at great expense." Determined to address both issues, regardless of the other political issues then swirling, on August 24, 1868, the General Assembly ratified "An Act for the Employment of Convicts and the Erection of a Penitentiary." The act ordered a seven-member purchasing committee, consisting of three members of the Senate, three members of the House, and the superintendent of public works, to purchase a site and gather inmates to grade and prepare the grounds for construction of a permanent penitentiary. Additionally, the act created a separate board of directors, consisting of the governor, the Council of State, and the seven-member purchasing committee, to select the best architectural design and to oversee construction. The board also would employ inmate labor in the construction process and would sell $200,000 worth of bonds to pay for the project.[8]

The various bodies abided by the act's dictates and selected representatives to the purchasing committee. Colonel Cebern L. Harris, by virtue of serving as the superintendent of public works, was the first member, and R. W. Lassiter, Hugh Dowing, J. H. Renfrow, J. H. Harris, and William Robbins, all of whom were white, soon joined him. Also a member of the committee, and evidence that Reconstruction was beginning to have an impact on North Carolina, was John Hyman of Warren County, one of three African Americans elected to the state Senate. On September 14, 1868, the interracial committee met in Raleigh and elected Colonel Harris chairman. It then examined a series of property propositions.[9]

Members heard thirteen offers, all located in the piedmont: six were in Wake County, one was in Orange County, one was in Johnston County, two were in Guilford County, and three were in Chatham County. The committee deemed Chatham County the preferred location. It was centrally located and had railroad access that facilitated the journey from the state capital in about one hour. Of the three possible sites in the county, the committee eventually concurred with the 1867 assessment and supported the site in Lockville. The land included a twenty-five-acre site for the penitentiary and eight thousand neighboring acres of timberland. Beyond its central location and access to Raleigh, the committee supported the location because access to the Deep River offered transportation opportunities and the potential for waterpower to run the penitentiary's industries. The land beneath the eight thousand acres, meanwhile, supposedly contained deposits of granite, iron, and coal. The committee also found the cost amenable: members believed they could get the twenty-five-acre site for $20,000 and the eight thousand-acre plot for $100,000.[10]

The committee's decision, however, was not unanimous. William Robbins dissented, and in a scathing memorandum he laid out a multitude of concerns. First, he deemed the purchase of the eight thousand acres unwise because it lay ten miles from the penitentiary site, making the employment of inmates problematic and increasing the transportation costs for any products mined. Robbins next raised concerns about the twenty-five-acre site. He argued it was rough and uneven land that needed extensive grading before construction could begin. Finally, he asserted that waterpower was a thing of the past and that the time had come to employ steam. Access to the river, therefore, was irrelevant. In the end, he argued cheaper sites closer to Raleigh were better options.[11]

The majority ignored Robbins's objections and voted to go forth. On December 2, 1868, the state paid David J. Pruyn $44,000 in bonds for the twenty-five-acre site, and a day later it paid John Heck $56,000 in bonds for the eight thousand-acre site. While the committee paid more than double what it expected for the main site, it paid half what it planned for the larger site, and in the end members believed the $100,000 total price tag was money well spent.[12]

Almost immediately, however, accusations of fraud and incompetence arose. The *Roanoke News* made the first charge, and state Senator W.H.S. Sweet, from Craven County, soon thereafter introduced a bill alleging corruption. The committee defended itself against the charges in a letter to the General Assembly. Members asserted, "it is central in position, has marvelous resources of coal, of iron and other mineral and metallic ores, unlimited water power, fertility of soil, and healthiness of location." They went on to argue that the site offered "valuable water power on the Deep River and means of access by navigation works to the coal deposits above, and the iron deposits, granite quarries and timbered lands below." They also assured critics that the "quality of this ore and granite have been tested" and "their quantity is believed to be inexhaustible." After defending themselves and their decision, committee members attacked the allegations as "unfounded and false representations" made by those who hoped to benefit financially from the selection of another location, and challenged their critics to prove their charges.[13]

Amid the political battles of the era, Democrats were not about to let such an opportunity pass and took up the challenge. On December 18, 1868, the Senate created a committee to investigate the charges. Consisting of George Welker of Guilford County, Silas Burns of Chatham County, and W. Levi Love of Macon County, the committee spent three weeks investigating the land and the deal. The three physically traversed the property, visiting first the twenty-five-acre site. They found it included but 150 yards of river frontage, with the main acreage 100 yards from the river up a steep slope. They recognized that this meant employing waterpower would require the construction of an aqueduct and holding tank, the cost of which would be "enormously expensive." They also found the site uneven, and acknowledged that grading it would be expensive.[14]

The three men next visited the eight thousand-acre site. They found some signs of natural resources, but the quantity and accessibility were unclear.

Equally problematic was the distance to the penitentiary site. While the river seemed to offer an easy route to cover the ten-mile span, the members discovered the locks were in disrepair, making travel impossible in the short term. Finally, they learned that 6,550 of the 8,000 acres of timberland consisted of "pine barrens of no marketable value." Members left the site unimpressed and determined that the land, for which the state paid $12.50 an acre, was worth not more than 10 cents an acre.[15]

Worse was to come. After leaving the sites, the members did some additional investigative work and discovered that a previous owner of the eight thousand-acre site had found the land of so little value that he had considered dividing it up and parceling it out "as a gift to freedmen" in order to save on taxes. Ultimately, he sold the land for 65 cents an acre. Two subsequent investors purchased the land for $1.50 an acre and $7 an acre respectively. The investigative committee also learned that the hoped-for natural resources on the site were nonexistent. While there was some iron on the property, its extent was unknown. There was no granite or coal, however, and the land proved "valueless for farming purposes."[16]

More damning, the investigators discovered that of the purchasing committee members, only Colonel Harris had visited the land, and he examined only a small portion of it. He knew it so poorly, in fact, that he claimed the eight thousand acres were one single tract, when the investigators knew it was two separate parcels. Most damning of all, the investigators proved unable to determine with whom the purchasing committee had negotiated and what that person's connection was to the land. Indeed, the purchasing committee members admitted, "it is hard to say of whom we purchased."[17]

Despite such appalling findings, the investigative committee was rather gentle with its final assessment. Their report concluded, "We will permit the Senate to draw its own conclusions. That the state is deeply wronged we are satisfied; that the penitentiary commission was imposed on by persons who cared only to make a good thing out of the state is equally true." The committee did not accuse the purchasing committee of wrongdoing or unethical behavior, although its assertion that members never visited the site came close. Instead, it determined that unscrupulous actors had duped the committee, and suggested the state find some way to unload the land as best it could.[18]

Later assessments were more severe. Journalist Jonathan Daniels contends that a conspiracy to defraud the state government emerged centered on a group called "The Ring." Leading members included industrialist George Swepson, "notorious carpetbagger" Milton Littlefield (with whom Swepson later defrauded the state of $4 million in a railroad deal), and Daniel J. Pruyn, another "notoriously corrupt carpetbagger." Using bribery and their connections to powerful politicians, they hoped to reap a fortune by purchasing cheap land and then selling it to the state for an inflated price. Daniels found Swepson acted as the "moneyman," Littlefield served as the "lobby lawyer," and Pruyn was the go between who handled the negotiations and sale. Their scheme nearly succeeded, Daniels contends, because the purchasing committee acted as willing allies. They were not duped as the final report suggested, but instead directly served the conspirators.[19]

Hilda Zimmerman offers less detailed analysis but similar findings, concluding, "the building of the penitentiary in North Carolina . . . became entangled in the general corruption of the reconstruction years." Others suggest it was simple party politics, and that while battling with the governor Democrats sought a second political front with the penitentiary as the ostensible cause. Finally, the possibility remains that as Democrats reclaimed the state they were determined to roll back every Republican achievement, including the penitentiary, and used the investigation as a political cudgel. Whatever the motivations, the committee's findings forced the General Assembly to accept the unacceptability of the Lockville site. Legislators wrote off the financial losses and determined to start again.[20]

Such was North Carolina's make-up during this era that legislators proved unable to complete the simple purchase of land for a penitentiary. Six decades after the first penitentiaries arose, a combination of corruption, incompetence, and political infighting made this first effort at penitentiary building an abject failure. That failure not only left the state without a place to house its prisoners, it left North Carolina even further behind its neighbors in terms of social organization and penal philosophy. At the same time, however, the Reconstruction-era dictates forced North Carolinians to grapple more formally than ever with penitentiary construction. For good and ill, social forces found expression in the state's penal policy. The only question that remained was when those forces would bring about an actual prison.

3

CONSTRUCTION BEGINS

Embarrassed by the failed purchase of penitentiary land and the resultant investigative findings, politicians briefly foreswore the previous shenanigans and
by 1870 had authorized an appropriate site and begun to erect a penitentiary.
Construction initially went well and seemed to suggest the state would match
its neighbors in penal policy. As so often before, however, problems arose that
undermined the early success. The trouble came in two forms. The first was the
General Assembly's traditional penny-pinching, which slowed construction. The
second was a series of reform demands by penitentiary officials. Even before the
first cells arose, administrators worried about the future and demanded the full
employment of inmates, training programs to prepare inmates for their post-
prison lives, the proper treatment of mentally ill inmates, and the segregation
of youthful offenders from older, hardened prisoners. Those proposals were in
keeping with the penitentiary model, but were too much for the state's legislators, who simply wanted to build the prison as cheaply as possible and move on.
Prison officials and politicians thus found themselves on opposite sides of yet
another penitentiary debate, as politics, economics, and penal policy clashed.

That debate and the related political battles began in February 1869 when the
state legislature repealed the "Act for the Employment of Convicts and the Erection of a Penitentiary" and passed a new law that called for the creation of a five
hundred-cell penitentiary located "at or near Raleigh." On April 12, 1869, it then
created a new committee to fulfill that endeavor. Consisting of white members
Colonel Cebern Harris, who had chaired the previous, unsuccessful committee,
General Alfred Dockery, Samuel Patterson, and George Welker, and African American member Alfred Howe, the committee set out to purchase land, visit other
prisons to learn from their administrations, hire staff, and begin construction.[1]

On May 4, 1869, the new committee held its first meeting in Raleigh and elected Alfred Dockery president and George Welker secretary. It also welcomed in two new white members, as Augustus Lougee and John Harrison replaced Harris and Patterson, who declined the appointments. The committee then solicited bids for twelve- to twenty-five-acre tracts of land. It settled on a twenty-two-acre site located one mile south of the present capital district in Raleigh and mere blocks from North Carolina State University. Purchased from Miss Kate Boylan for $4,468.75, the deal also included the right to lease a neighboring quarry. The committee then selected Ohio-based architect Levi T. Schofield to draw up the blueprints and named William J. Hicks superintendent and assistant architect. Finally, it budgeted $14,000 for construction of a wooden stockade and temporary holding cells for the prisoners, who would assist in the construction of the permanent structure upon completion and approval of the architectural plans. After decades of debate and years of false starts, North Carolina finally was on the path to constructing a penitentiary.[2]

There was, however, much more to do. Having purchased land, hired architects, and set a budget with surprising speed and bipartisan support, the committee set about investigating the administration of the permanent facilities. Secretary Welker visited several northern penitentiaries to determine the most appropriate layout and discipline methods. Dr. G. W. Blacknall, although not a committee member, also visited a number of prisons and reported back on his findings. What both men discovered was that northern prisons were more advanced than the southern institutions with which they were familiar. One element that especially impressed them was the focus on reform, and Blacknall reported that northern states "wished [inmates] to reform and become not only useful to themselves and families, but to society and their fellow-man." He called for the new penitentiary to follow the northern model by offering inmates religious services and educational opportunities. He also demanded the segregation of young and first-time offenders. In the end, Blacknall envisioned a penitentiary where "justice [was] ever tempered with humanity."[3]

Committee members agreed, and decided to employ the aforementioned Auburn system since it focused on reform and proved more cost effective than the Pennsylvania model. With that determination made, the committee laid out the penitentiary's administration in a document entitled *The Rules and By-Laws for the Government and Discipline of the North Carolina Penitentiary*. The rules created a Penitentiary Commission to oversee the construction and operation of the prison site until the facilities were complete. The commission would appoint penitentiary officials, authorize expenditures, provide annual reports on the progress and cost of construction, ensure prisoners were treated humanely, and offer suggestions for any needed legislation. To facilitate the day-to-day operations, the *Rules and By-Laws* created the temporary position of superintendent of the prison building, and the committee appointed William J. Hicks to that role.[4]

The *Rules and By-Laws* continued by declaring that the commission and the position of superintendent would dissolve with the completion of construction, to be replaced by a board of directors and a warden. A deputy warden, a clerk, a physician, a steward, and various guards would assist the board and warden in governing the completed facility. The deputy warden had the daily task of running the prison, and was to oversee the opening and closing of cells, food preparation, inmate employment, the enforcement of punishments, and the maintenance of prison records. The commission selected W. H. Thompson as the first deputy warden. The clerk kept track of inmate admissions and releases, chronicled visitors, inventoried the prison's supplies, and chaperoned visiting dignitaries. The physician was to visit the prison every day and attend to any inmate requesting aid. He provided a full medical examination to incoming inmates to determine whether or not they were fit for labor, made alterations in the labor or housing of inmates whose health suffered from their confinement, dispensed medicine, and recorded the cause of any deaths. The steward, meanwhile, purchased the prison's supplies, fed and clothed the inmates, and employed prisoners in the kitchen, laundry, and bakery.[5]

At a level below those administrators came the men who interacted more directly with the inmates, and the *Rules and By-Laws* organized several different positions to oversee the prisoners. The "guards" ensured inmates did not escape, the "overseers" guarded inmates during work hours, the "gate-keepers" controlled access into and out of the penitentiary, and the "yard overseer" kept the grounds neat and secure. Since those individuals had the most intimate contact with the inmates, they faced a litany of regulations. They had to "be at the prison day and night, unless specially excused," were to remain in the guard house at the completion of their shift, and were required "always [to] be ready for any emergency." They were not allowed to speak with prisoners, were to enforce silence among the prisoners at all times, and were forbidden from cursing, abusing, ridiculing, threatening, or striking an inmate. The "Sergeant of the Guard" was in charge of these men and was to ensure they performed their assigned duties. George Faribault, who had served as a colonel in the 47th Regiment, North Carolina Infantry during the Civil War, was the first "Sergeant of the Guard."[6]

Committee members next devised the regulations by which the inmates would abide. Not surprisingly, the *Rules and By-Laws* included extensive guidelines regarding their control and behavior. Upon receipt at the prison, guards stripped the men of their clothing, directed them to the showers, and issued a prison uniform consisting of a jacket and pants, underclothes, shoes, a cloth cap, and two handkerchiefs. After the men were properly attired, the deputy warden and as many guards and penitentiary officials as could be spared examined the inmate. The examination served two purposes. First, it was an opportunity to record all the requisite information about the inmate, including his name, height, age, crime, and sentence. More importantly, it offered officials an opportunity to interact with the inmate and to learn his proclivities. New inmates spent the next two days confined to their cells. During that period a prison official visited each man to "assure them of interest in their welfare; explain the object of the incarceration; urge upon them motives to reform; explain their duties as prisoners; read to them the prison regulations and perform such other acts as will serve to win the confidence of the convict and inspire them with hope for the future." Among the rules the inmates had to learn were bans on alcohol and cigarettes, that they were not allowed to receive food from visitors, and that they would be allowed visitors and mail privileges only if they behaved "to the satisfaction of the officers."[7]

Not only did the inmates face strict rules, they also faced a strict daily regimen. Reveille occurred at 5 A.M. in the summer and 6 A.M. in the winter, when they were to wash, dress, and make their beds. Guards then did a count, opened the cell doors, and led inmates to breakfast. After the meal, inmates headed to their job assignments, at which they toiled until noon, when they received an hour break for lunch in the summer and forty-five minutes in the winter. They returned to work until 7 P.M. in the summer or sundown in the winter. After the evening meal they returned to their cells, and at 9 P.M. a bell sounded requiring them to go to bed. As per the Auburn system, all of this was done in silence to provide the opportunity for moral reflection and personal growth.[8]

As the committee created the foundations along which the institution would function, the Penitentiary Commission assumed control of construction and budgeted $600,000 for completion of the permanent structure, based on the use of inmate labor. Quickly, however, commission members found themselves hamstrung when the General Assembly announced it would only authorize $50,000 per year for construction costs. Prison officials pointed out that this would extend construction time and could affect the payment of contractors. Legislators refused to budge, and there was little the commissioners could do but set to work.[9]

They did so by dividing the construction bids into eight categories and advertising nationally. The Coleman Brothers Company from Cincinnati, Ohio, won the bids for the stonework and brickwork, taking on the two largest tasks. Along with the other six categories (plastering, wrought ironwork, galvanized ironwork, carpentry, painting, and plumbing), the bid total was $609,595.18. Although this price slightly exceeded the commission's budget, contractors agreed to employ inmates at an average wage of 65 cents per day. The inmates would not see that money; instead, each company deducted that amount from its bid, reducing the costs below the $600,000 threshold. Indeed, during the first two years of construction inmate labor saved the state $53,716.39.[10]

On January 6, 1870, Charles Lewis, Eliza Lewis, and Nancy Richardson, three African Americans convicted of robbery in Johnston County, became the penitentiary's first inmates when they arrived at the barren construction site. Others soon followed, and by November 389 inmates crowded the location. Of that number, 286 were African American men, sixteen were African American women, eighty-six were white men, one was a white woman, and one was a Native American man. Whatever their race or gender, they built the temporary structures, and by the end of the year had erected a 2,965-foot wooden pole stockade, complete with twelve sentry boxes and four gates, along with twenty cell houses, two hospital rooms, a guardroom, a kitchen and bakery, carpentry and blacksmith shops, bathing rooms, and an 870-foot stockade around the quarry. The cost for the temporary structures was $37,298.06.[11]

While inmates labored on the temporary fixtures, Coleman Brothers began work on the permanent structures. To facilitate that work and the future delivery of material and supplies, the commissioners contracted with the North Carolina Railroad to build a "turn-out" from a nearby line directly into the prison. By December 1870, the 850-foot track was complete and supplies flowed into the site. Those supplies enabled the Coleman Brothers' team to lay the foundations for several buildings. Expecting to continue at the same pace, the company planned to complete construction on the exterior brickwork by August 1871, at which point the other firms could begin their tasks. The first year of construction thus went well, and it seemed the state was on its way to entering the modern age of criminal justice.[12]

That initial success led commissioners to look forward on several fronts. In December 1870, they raised the issue of post-construction inmate labor. Although several inmates acted as tailors, cooks, and bakers, while others did the laundry or made shoes, the vast majority of inmates worked in construction. The commissioners believed labor was an integral part of the penitentia-ry's purpose, and asserted that it was "not proper that a penitentiary should be a mere receptacle where convicts are kept in idleness, and time given them to plan new crimes and to become adept in their commission." Similarly, they made the questionable claim that inmates benefitted from the labor, going so far as to argue that "a convict can realize a profit from his labor for the state" by learning a trade or the temperament and discipline needed to abide by tradi-tional social dictates. Indeed, the commissioners specifically required that during their period of incarceration inmates "be taught some knowledge at least of a trade that will afford them the means of an honest living, and also to give to their lives such habits as will serve to make them good citizens."[13]

The commissioners not only were concerned with the inmates, they also worried about finances. They were determined to make the inmates cover the cost of their upkeep, and they understood the continual and long-term need to find inmates useful forms of labor. Finally, the commissioners understood that hard labor was part of the penal process and accepted the idea that "enforced labor is felt to be punishment for [the] crime." In order to avoid idleness, to fund the prison, and to reform and punish the inmate, the commissioners asked state legislators if they could contract with external companies or if the prison could create on-site industries. While the commissioners did not support one form of labor over the other, even at this early date they were prodding legislators to think about the future.[14]

As the commissioners awaited a response to their inquiry about labor, they also proposed implementing newly emergent penal philosophies. The first was a call to end determinate sentences, by which inmates merely served their term. The commissioners asserted that such punishment offered "no gratification to the State and work no advantage to the criminal," who emerged from prison unreformed, unrepentant, "more hardened and a greater adept at crime." In its place they proposed the use of indeterminate sentences, by which inmates received a minimum and a maximum term limit. Once the inmate reached the minimum term, he was eligible for release if he proved ready to re-enter society as a productive citizen. The commissioners saw the penitentiary as a place of reformation, arguing at one point that one of the goals of imprisonment was to "allow at least the opportunity to accomplish some good for the criminal," and they believed indeterminate sentences, by encouraging proper behavior, were the best way to facilitate that good.[15]

Not satisfied with helping the inmate solely during his incarceration, the commissioners also urged the state to take direct action in helping him upon release. They feared many inmates would return to their criminal ways unless they received help finding work. It was not enough to train inmates in a skill and disposition, the state also needed to help them find a job. Although an element of new penal thinking, this proposal was not as selfless as it may seem. The commissioners worried inmates might remain in Raleigh upon release, and left to their own devices they might well "assort with the vilest of the population and soon return to their former habits." For the good of the inmate and for the good of the city, therefore, the commissioners wanted to help inmates find employment.[16]

As prison officials waited for politicians to digest the various proposals, the commissioners urged legislators to create two additional institutions. First, they called for an "asylum for the insane." Worried that mentally unstable inmates stirred up others, they asked for a separate facility to house the criminally insane. Second, they called for a facility for youthful criminals. Believing association with older inmates would corrupt and harden the young, the commissioners called for their removal and placement in a separate institution.[17]

Legislators failed to address any of those proposals, however, as a new issue dominated their focus. The issue began in April 1871 when the prison's board of directors, which was to assume control of the penitentiary upon completion, held its first meeting. The all-white board elected Moses A. Bledsoe president and C. H. Coffield clerk, and then announced its intention to supersede the commission and oversee construction. It did so as a result of reports that construction on the permanent structures had fallen behind schedule and that costs had ballooned to $143,000, even with the savings resultant from inmate labor. That cost put the project well over its $50,000 per annum budget, and the governor refused to provide additional funds. As a consequence, the state owed Coleman Brothers money. Unwilling to carry on with the outstanding bills unpaid, Coleman Brothers slowed its construction schedule. The expectation had been that as the prison arose inmates would reside in the completed quarters and new inmates would fill the vacated temporary cells. New inmates continued to arrive, but since the permanent buildings were not yet complete there was no place to house them. The housing shortage forced the erection of additional temporary quarters and resulted in added costs. The penitentiary commissioners begged for additional funds, noting that otherwise they were wasting money on quarters that were "likely to prove in the end almost an entire loss." When politicians refused to act, the board of directors, believing they would have more pull, stepped in.[18]

Almost immediately the board demonstrated that pull when, in late 1871, it ordered Coleman Brothers to cease construction. During depositions in January 1872, board president Moses Bledsoe asserted that he ordered the halt because "the work was not being done according to the contract and specifications." He claimed eleven particulars, and noted that according to the contract those violations gave the state the right to break the agreement. Coleman Brothers, by contrast, believed Bledsoe was playing hardball and was trying to force it to speed up construction, thereby completing the buildings needed to house the influx of inmates without costing the state additional revenue.[19]

Wary of breaking a duly signed contract, even if there was cause, the General Assembly ordered the board of directors to appoint a "practical skilled architect" to examine Coleman Brothers' work. The board did as ordered, contracting with an architect who found that large portions of the company's work failed to meet code. The General Assembly demanded a second opinion, and that architect also condemned the work. Despite evidence of shoddy construction, the legislature still did not want to break the contract, so it reached an accord with Coleman Brothers, which agreed to rebuild the condemned work at its own expense.[20]

Bledsoe and the board of directors were frustrated with the agreement because they no longer had the right to abrogate the contract. Part of that unhappiness was the poor work, but part of it also came from the realization that the demolition and reconstruction processes further slowed the construction schedule. There was one other factor as well. Board members believed the experiences inmates had gained gave them the skills needed to construct the penitentiary on their own. As proof, the board noted that convicts, working with the help of two stonemasons, two blacksmiths, and one quarryman, had raised large portions of the exterior wall at one-third the expected cost. In other words, the board's actions may have had nothing to do with the quality of work, but rather were the result of simple economics: they did not need Coleman Brothers to complete construction.[21]

Although forced by legislators to continue employing Coleman Brothers, board members did not give up on ridding themselves of the company's services, and they soon urged the General Assembly to buy out the contract. After presenting evidence that inmates could do the work cheaper and just as effectively, in 1873 legislators followed the board's suggestion and paid Coleman Brothers $35,000 to relinquish the remainder of its contract. Thereafter, inmates assumed the majority of the construction tasks.

While the penitentiary's first year went well, the next several proved more difficult. During the early 1870s, legislative penny-pinching, shoddy construction, and battles between penitentiary officials and state leaders slowed construction. Those factors demonstrate well the complicated relationship between prison staff and politicians. That relationship was even more evident in the direct and thorough manner in which legislators set rules and regulations. Even before the first prisoner arrived, politicians took a hands-on approach in determining nearly every aspect of the penitentiary's governance. That did not mean prison officials had no say in the matter, as they demonstrated their adherence to the penitentiary model, showed a prescient preference for providing inmates with reformative and rehabilitative opportunities, and proved more than willing to push legislators to enact such policies. The problem was that politicians all too often believed they knew best, and proved less motivated to implement the new penal models. Administrative philosophies and political realities thus clashed early in the process. Other clashes, however, had even more significant impacts on the construction process, and as the penitentiary slowly rose the impact of those clashes proved not just fraught, but destructive.

4

POLITICIZING THE PENITENTIARY

Cost overruns, a lagging schedule, battles with contractors, and prescient worries about the future slowed the penitentiary's rise during the early 1870s. While the problems were not beyond the pale for a construction project of such complexity, they demonstrated some deep-seated issues with which politicians and prison administrators had to deal. More notably, the issues began to affect the inmates. That impact became especially apparent in the mid-1870s as a political battle erupted that made the immediate postbellum clashes seem mild. Republicans clung desperately to the political gains they made during Reconstruction, while Democrats fought even more desperately to reclaim control of the state. In such a battle nothing seemed out of bounds, and both sides employed dirty tricks and questionable tactics. Those incidents had a direct and significant impact on inmates and prison officials, who became tools in the political struggle. The result further undermined construction, harmed those inmates housed in the still incomplete facility, and make evident the clear, continued, and problematic link between the state's history and that of the prison.

The political turmoil originated in 1871 when several members of the board of directors resigned and the General Assembly selected their replacements. Tod Caldwell, a Republican who became governor in March 1871 after the impeachment of William Woods Holden, questioned the legality of the selection process, believing he had the right to appoint the replacements. When advisors pointed out that the General Assembly had appointed the entire board, he demanded the right to remove all the members and to replace them with his own. While some of that determination was Caldwell's honest desire to maintain the governor's authority and engender his own oversight, much of it had to do with the continuing struggle between the two political parties.

Democrats dominated the state legislature and were determined to undermine Republican influence as much as possible. That determination resulted not only in Holden's impeachment, but in a decades-long effort to crush the African American vote, reinstate white supremacy, and turn North Carolina into a one-party state. Caldwell was the Democrats' next target, but he proved willing to fight back. He did so by appointing his own board of directors. The sitting penitentiary board charged Caldwell with playing politics, and they refused to step aside. Caldwell retaliated by refusing to authorize payment of the board's debts, in part causing the aforementioned conflict with Coleman Brothers.[1]

The governor then went further. He first accused the board of insubordination by claiming it purposefully kept him ignorant of the penitentiary's progress. He then accused it of malfeasance by presenting allegations that "the treatment of some of the convicts has been inhuman, and that punishments have been inflicted which were both cruel and unusual." Finally, he dared the Democrats to call his bluff by asserting, "if the legislature shall deem it proper and expedient to institute an enquiry as to the truth or falsity of these rumors . . . it will afford me great pleasure to give such information as I have upon the subject."[2]

In January 1872, the General Assembly obliged the governor and organized hearings into allegations of misconduct by the board of directors and penitentiary staff. Board president Moses Bledsoe and D. C. Murray, the penitentiary steward, faced the first round of questioning. The investigative committee first asked if they properly fed, clothed, and cared for the inmates. Both assured their questioners that the inmates were well attended and denied allegations that guards served rotten food or failed to provide adequate clothing. The committee then challenged the men about alleged pay raises. Both admitted to altering the remuneration of various officials, but asserted that those modifications were the result of changed circumstances, not political favoritism. They noted specifically that Murray received a raise because "his duties are much more onerous" than originally thought, while guards and overseers saw their salaries reduced due to "the appreciation of currency and decreased costs of provision." Finally, they fended off suggestions that they had associations with companies with which the penitentiary did business, and denied allegations of bribery and kickbacks.[3]

Prison physician Dr. William G. Hill testified next, defending himself and the treatment of prisoners. He did so by reminding investigators that the inmates were criminals and were expert in lying and subterfuge. As such, when challenged with claims that inmates did not get enough food, he charged them with eating portions of their meals and passing off the remainder as the entire meal. He also asserted that inmates, either intentionally or through disregard, destroyed their own clothing and were responsible for any shortcomings in dress. When asked about diseases, he admitted some inmates suffered from scurvy and typhoid, but assured investigators they entered the penitentiary with those ailments and that he had cured the men of their suffering. As proof, he claimed in 1870 there were no major epidemic outbreaks.[4]

What Dr. Hill failed to admit was the wide array of diseases he himself had documented. In November 1871, just months before his testimony, he noted that an "epidemic" of measles, eighty-one confirmed cases, had ravaged the prison. He also failed to note that in June he acknowledged a dysentery "epidemic," in which "many cases were violent, not yielding readily to treatment," as well as an outbreak of hemorrhagic fever that killed seven. While he admitted inmates suffered from scurvy, in a formal written report he noted it had affected sixty-three inmates—a quarter of the entire population. Worse still, he also wrote, "persons in confinement require good, solid, substantial food, both of meat and vegetable. . . . I consider such a diet a sanitary matter of the first importance." The implication was that the prison lacked such fare. Despite those inconsistencies, the investigators left Hill's testimony, and that of all the prison officials, relatively unchallenged.[5]

After deposing administrators, the legislators called on inmates. Twenty-three-year-old inmate Columbus Summey, who was serving time for larceny, testified first. He reported that inmates received between four and eight ounces of meat per day, but said they subsisted mostly on a diet of bread and the occasional serving of rice, potatoes, or greens. He also complained about a lack of underclothes and the presence of vermin in the clothes they did receive. While damning testimony, his next story proved even more so. He told of an occasion when he and several inmates killed, butchered, fried, and ate a cat. When asked if he normally ate cats, he said no. When asked why he did this time his reply was simple: "because they did not give us enough to eat." For good measure, he reported eating rats for the same reason.[6]

Inmate John Edmondson, a twenty-four-year-old serving ten years for assault with a deadly weapon and horse theft, also testified. Edmondson reported that he was the one who skinned the cat before the men ate it. Like Summey, he testified to doing so "for lack of something to eat." When asked about a normal meal, he reported that his most recent one consisted of "about an ounce of meat, about four spoonful of peas and a corn dogger." Other inmates followed and offered similar testimony, alleging they received diseased meat, lacked adequate clothing and protection from the weather, and faced cruel treatment from the guards.[7]

After hearing from inmates, the committee called several guards. Miles Goodwin, an overseer, testified that during his two years on the prison staff he had "reported to [the] Steward, [the] Superintendent and one of the Directors (Mr. Boylan) that the food given to the convicts was insufficient in quality and quantity." He noted that inmates had to perform hard labor but did not have enough food to do so. He admitted that after one complaint the food improved, but claimed it quickly returned to the poor quality about which the inmates had protested.[8]

Charles Irwin, a guard, testified next. He reported that he was the one who found the head and skin of the cat the inmates allegedly ate. He said he could not know for a fact that they ate it, but he admitted some inmates went hungry. Irwin concluded by asserting that often the men did not receive a change of clothes for more than a week.[9]

Other guards testified to alleged bribery and corruption. Several asserted that various jobs in the prison were sold or promised for political considerations, while others claimed officials took kickbacks or made deals with companies supplying the prison. None could offer more than vague proclamations to support their accusations, and officials examined under oath denied making any such deals.[10]

After dozens of additional inmates, guards, and others associated with the penitentiary told similar stories, B. E. Coleman of the Coleman Brothers Company took the stand. Coleman testified that on several occasions he saw inmates who were not working. When he asked them why, they told him it was because they were weak from a lack of food. Coleman thought they were malingering, but investigated their claims nonetheless. He explained that he examined the meals and found them inadequate. Coleman testified that he still did not believe what he saw, so he spoke with several guards. Each one, he asserted, assured him that what little food he saw was the entire meal, and told the committee he was appalled anyone could think two ounces of meat and three inches of hard bread was an adequate diet. He further alleged that many of the inmates were unable to work in the winter due to a lack of clothing. While Coleman's testimony seemed damning, he surely had an axe to grind as a result of the board's efforts to remove his company from the work site.[11]

That potential for bias, of course, was widespread. The inmates had reasons to complain, while the very essence of Caldwell's charge was politically motivated and focused on the Democrat-controlled legislature. The legislators were astute enough to see the investigation for what it was, so there was little doubt about what they would find. The investigative committee declared there was no evidence of "unauthorized, unusual or inhuman punishments," and deemed all punishments in line with what was necessary to maintain order. It found the food "generally sufficient in quantity and good in quality," and noted that while on occasion the quality was poor and the quantity small, those instances occurred when the governor refused to appropriate money to the prison amid his battles with the board. The committee further determined that inmates received adequate clothing, and concluded, "the convicts are as fully provided for as the incomplete condition of the Penitentiary will admit." The report exonerated the board from Caldwell's charges, laid blame for any shortcomings at the governor's feet, and determined no action was needed. Any real inmate suffering or official transgressions were ignored, as the investigation served simply as a tool in this political battle.[12]

Although seemingly the end of the case, the petty jealousies between the board, the legislature, and the governor smoldered, and the prison continued to serve as a political weapon. In his annual report for 1872, Moses Bledsoe took shots at those who accused the board of malfeasance. He complained of the "many absurd, groundless and slanderous reports . . . about the Board of Directors and their management of the Penitentiary," and claimed any contrary testimony were acts of revenge from inmates, fired employees, or people who failed to win jobs. Governor Caldwell read Bledsoe's allegations as a political attack, so on November 14, 1872, he returned the board's report and complained that it "was not properly addressed; that it was not accompanied with a note transmitting it to him, and that he objected to the subject matter of the report and did not consider it respectful to him." Bledsoe attached a note of address and transmission to the report, but made no amendments to its content. Caldwell again refused to accept it, and complained to the General Assembly about the board's insolence. The General Assembly responded by creating another joint committee to investigate the governor's charge.[13]

Caldwell clearly was interested in more than the letter's content. He saw these hearings as another opportunity to attack Democrats and the board members he sought to displace. He consequently collected and offered the committee a series of inmate affidavits that claimed mistreatment at the hands of prison officials. The documents included charges that guards gagged and tied inmates to posts, physically struck and beat inmates, had sex with female inmates, reported to work drunk, bound inmates and bathed them in cold water outdoors during the winter, and left bound inmates chained to poles outside in the summer heat.[14]

The stories seemed damning, but the committee heard exculpatory testimony as well. Guard H. M. Ivey turned allegations of bribery back on the governor, claiming the governor's office had attempted to bribe several guards to offer negative testimony. Columbus Fowler, whom the prosecution invoked as having admitted to accepting bribes, testified that his statements were part of a misunderstood joke. In regard to inmate treatment, several guards explained that while they gagged inmates for various infractions, the gagging never lasted more than thirty minutes. Former prison employee Miles Goodwin acknowledged dousing them in water and putting the wet inmates in cold, dark cells for rules violations, but he asserted the punishments were short lived and deserved. He further argued that anyone who became ill as a result of punishment received medical assistance and that no one who was ill faced punishment. Guard H. B. Whitaker, meanwhile, challenged many of the claims made in the affidavits by explaining that the accusers could not have seen the things they reported. He noted the stations of various guards and demonstrated that the accusations, at best, were hearsay. When asked about testimony in the previous hearing that inmates ate a cat, Whitaker said he personally asked Edmondson why he did so, and that Edmondson replied he simply was curious. To prove the point, he said Edmondson told him it tasted like squirrel.[15]

Dr. Hill returned to the witness stand for this second hearing. He acknowledged the punishments but noted they were the result of rules violations, including escape attempts and inciting to riot. He thus argued that the punishments were deserved and necessary to keep inmates in line, and asserted that no inmate died as a result of his punishment. Investigators challenged him with the story of Granville Ferrell, who died after being placed in balls and chains. Hill explained that the punishment was for an escape attempt and asserted that while Ferrell did die, it was from dysentery eight days after the punishment. Such was proof, Hill argued, that the punishment did not cause his demise.[16]

The issue of food also returned during this round of hearings. Inmate Thomas Scott told the committee there was a brief period when rations declined, but explained he "had no apprehension of starving." A former guard testified that guards ate the same meals as inmates and that he never received rotten food. Turning allegations of inadequate food back on the governor, guard Basil Sanders reported that in March 1872 Bledsoe sent him to tell the governor he had three options: give the prison money, free the inmates, or let them starve.

Sanders reported that the governor refused to authorize additional funds and warned that if any inmates died "he would indict the last one of [the guards] for murder." Sanders reported that when he informed his fellow guards of the governor's pronouncement, many feared indictment and quit.[17]

When inmates caught wind of the pronouncement, they rioted. According to inmate Eaton Mills, however, "when we attempted the revolt we were getting full rations, and did not attempt it because we were hungry." Inmate Perry Williams affirmed that statement, explaining that the cause of the uproar was not hunger, but hope. The inmates believed the guards were wary of using their weapons due to the governor's threat to indict them for murder. They concluded they had the upper hand and saw a chance to escape. Indeed, guard Martin T. Whitlock testified: "I was present at the revolt and was also present at the examination of the revolters . . . who swore that they engaged in the revolt by reason of having heard that Governor Caldwell had said that he would have the guard punished for murder if they fired on the convicts while attempting to escape."[18]

According to Eaton Mills, the inmates planned the riot for days. They decided to look for a guard unawares, steal his gun, put him in a cell, and then fire the gun to draw a crowd. In the ensuing chaos, they planned to seize more weapons, free additional inmates, and escape en masse. While the inmates succeeded in seizing weapons, the tumult they hoped to create failed to emerge. Guards descended quickly on the scene, opened fire, reclaimed the stolen weapons, and brought the brief episode to an end. The story supported claims that inmates were not being mistreated and demonstrated that Governor Caldwell, the prison board, and the guards were all partially to blame for any disorder and unrest.[19]

By the end of the hearing, everyone appreciated its futility. The committee determined Bledsoe unintentionally omitted the traditional letter to the governor on his report, and that he did so without malice. The committee also noted the governor previously accepted reports that omitted the letter, implying his recent actions were the consequence of political calculation, explained that other governors received reports without the requisite note, and asserted that Caldwell's response was one "not heretofore observed on the part of the Governor." After criticizing Caldwell's actions and disposing of the report issues, the committee returned to the penitentiary. It once again rejected claims that prison officials mistreated inmates, and it determined that the sitting board, not the governor's, was legitimate.[20]

Despite all of that, the true end of the battle still had not been reached. Caldwell could not have been surprised that the Democrat-dominated legislature failed to find in his favor, so he undoubtedly was pleased when the North Carolina Supreme Court did. In 1872, Governor Caldwell's board of directors sued the sitting board for refusing to disband. In January 1873, the court issued its verdict in the *Welker v. Bledsoe* case. The court ruled that the General Assembly had the power to make regulations and create necessary offices, but "filling these offices by competent men is a different matter—that is an executive function." The court not only ruled in favor of the governor's board, but asserted that the governor, not the General Assembly, had the right to appoint all subsequent board members and replacements. The court thus handed Caldwell a clear victory—one he must surely have enjoyed, having otherwise been bested by the Democrats. He responded by replacing the sitting board with members of the original penitentiary committee: Alfred Dockery, George Walker, Alfred Howe, Augustus Lougee, and John Harrison. The appointment of Howe was especially galling to the Democratic legislature. As an African American, he represented everything to which they were opposed, and his placement in such a high-ranking position undoubtedly rankled.[21]

Although entertaining and instructive from a historical perspective, the political mudslinging did little to speed up penitentiary construction. Work on the structures continued, but the lack of guidance and oversight, and the focus on politics rather than penology, slowed progress and raised costs. More notably, the shenanigans demonstrate well the relationship between the prison and state politics. The penitentiary took center stage in this contest between Democrats and Republicans, and prison administrators, employees, inmates, and even contractors found themselves pawns in the larger struggle—a struggle that embodied the state's political divide. While political intervention into prison affairs previously had a mixed impact on the penitentiary's development, little good came from this intrusion as nearly everyone associated suffered.

Fortunately, as the 1870s progressed the political machinations abated. Unfortunately, a new and even more powerful force soon arose: convict leasing. Desperate for revenue to fund the ever-costlier penitentiary, in the mid-1870s politicians found themselves dazzled by the prospect of making money from inmate labor and turned out inmates to construct railroads, buildings, and dams. While they reaped a financial windfall, they also reaped the whirlwind, as leasing brutalized inmates, facilitated hundreds of escapes, and further slowed construction.

5

CONVICT LEASING

The political skirmishes of the early 1870s slowed penitentiary construction and caused undue inmate suffering. As the battles ebbed and the politics of destruction faded, nearly everyone hoped state leaders would refocus their efforts on erecting the prison. That hope proved misplaced, as businessmen pleaded for cost-friendly laborers while politicians grew increasingly desperate for new forms of revenue. The solution to both desires emerged in the form of convict leasing, and by the mid-1870s North Carolina adopted the system with verve and a determination to extract every last cent of labor from the penitentiary's inmates. While the revenue raised was substantial, so too were the consequences: brutalized inmates, an empty penitentiary, and a near halt in construction. Greed, endemic racism, and the obvious and utter contempt for the lives of those in the state's care emerged as fundamental characteristics of the era, characteristics that shaped not only the state but the penitentiary as well.

It all began on December 10, 1874, when the board of directors sent a letter to Governor Curtis Brogden, a Republican who ascended to the position after Tod Caldwell died from cholera on July 11, 1874, pointing out that the number of inmates had risen to 455. The number was only going to increase as counties abided by the constitutionally mandated dual penal system and emptied their jails of long-term prisoners, and the board warned that the incomplete facility was ill-equipped to handle the influx. It was overcrowded, dangerous, and unhealthy, and many inmates lacked work. Although most helped build the prison or worked in on-site industries, many were underemployed or were incapable of performing physical labor. The board worried that inmates with time on their hands would use it to "create conspiracies and revolt," and noted that the site was not yet secure and the escape risk remained real. As a potential solution, the directors suggested leasing inmates to outside firms. An added benefit was that leases would produce revenue. Indeed, historian George Washington Cable contends that convict leasing sprang "primarily from the idea that the possession of a convict's person is an opportunity for the State to make money."[1]

But there was more to it than the state's need for income. Railroad construction, which began before the war, exploded in the postwar years. As historian Milton Ready argues, after 1870 "North Carolinians began an almost paniclike building of new railroads." The problem was that low pay, dangerous working conditions, and unsanitary housing and dining facilities made raising adequate construction crews difficult. Realizing inmates could serve as a cost-effective, exploitable, and management-friendly labor supply, railroad officials pushed for convict leasing.[2]

Urged on by business leaders and prison administrators, in 1872 the General Assembly authorized the penitentiary to lease convicts to "railroad companies and other public corporations." Few took advantage of the opportunity, however, as elements of the law remained unclear. Over the next two years, as the prison's crowding issues grew, the board pressured legislators to tighten up the law. On December 12, 1874, Governor Brogden joined that effort. He noted that inmates at the penitentiary site lacked labor, passed along the board's concern that inmates were growing restive as a result, reminded legislators about industry's desire for an exploitable labor force, and urged them to pass new legislation clarifying the lease system.[3]

Acceding to the governor's request, the General Assembly passed two new laws. The first, 1875's *Act to Authorize the Hire of Convict Labor in or Outside the State's Prison, and to Regulate the Same*, required prison administrators to advertise inmate labor by noting the number of men available, the length of time they were available, and a bid schedule. Each bidder had to explain what they planned to do with the prisoners and offer an annual price per inmate they were willing to pay. The law further required companies to cover the costs of inmate feeding, clothing, guarding, and health care. Finally, it banned inmates convicted of murder, manslaughter, rape, attempted rape, and arson from outside labor, but made eligible all other physically able inmates.[4]

In 1876, the legislature passed an additional law that required inmates to remain "under the supervision and control of the penitentiary board or of some other officer of the State penitentiary" while laboring outside the penitentiary walls. Rather than require the civilian firms to maintain oversight, penitentiary guards would secure the inmates. Author Hilda Zimmerman notes that it was this "limitation on the convict leasing system which gave the system in North Carolina its peculiar characteristics. It was unlike the system in any other state. In fact, the term 'lease system' applied to North Carolina has been questioned since the state leased only the labor of the convicts and not the convicts themselves. Individuals or corporations who contracted for the labor did not gain any control over the convicts, who remained under the absolute control of the board of directors of the penitentiary." Despite that lack of control, companies had to pay the annual fee for any inmate who escaped, ensuring that the penitentiary received full payment even if the guards failed to do their job.[5]

The legislation proved an immediate sensation, and railroad companies statewide leased hundreds of inmates, making North Carolina the first state to employ prisoners in such a fashion. In 1876, 332 inmates worked on the Western North Carolina Railroad, two hundred worked on the Spartanburg and Asheville Railroad, and fifty worked on the North Carolina and Georgia Railroad. Such labor proved amazingly cost effective, as the Western North Carolina Railroad reported that it had saved between $35,000 and $50,000 in 1876 alone by employing inmates rather than free laborers. With such a financial boon available, it should be no surprise that by 1878 additional railroad companies joined the convict labor frenzy: the Chester and Lenoir Railroad and the Mount Airy and Central Railroad soon employed their own cadre of inmate workers.[6]

Railroads were not the only companies to partake, so too did construction firms. Companies building the Hospital for the Insane in Raleigh employed fifty inmates, while the firms building the Western Hospital in Morganton hired fifty more. Even the companies constructing the new governor's mansion hired inmates. Prisoners ultimately laid one-third of the state's railroad mileage, helped construct dozens of buildings and state facilities, and saved the contracting companies hundreds of thousands of dollars in labor costs. The companies also avoided union problems, enjoyed more control over the labor force, and benefitted from an all but endless supply of workers. Prison labor thus proved a godsend to the state's industrial base.[7]

Industry clearly gained from inmate labor, but so too did the state. With hundreds of inmates laboring away from the prison, overcrowding concerns and fears of inmate unrest faded. Even more notable was the flood of cash. While the fees varied, they were substantial. In 1878 the state earned $96,514.05 from inmate labor, while 1883 and 1884 combined saw income balloon to $363,998.73. By 1885, administrators were leasing inmates from a low of $8.00 per inmate per annum to a high of $125.00 per inmate per annum. And those figures only account for income; the state also saved money as the outside firms housed, fed, and cared for the inmates. North Carolina was not alone in this endeavor; by the 1880s, 80 percent of states leased inmates to private firms, earning $29 million dollars.[8]

As those figures demonstrate, crime and punishment had become linked with economics. Indeed, in his study of convict leasing in Alabama, Florida, and Georgia, journalist Douglas Blackmon found that "arrests surged and fell, not as acts of crime increased or receded, but in tandem to the varying needs of the buyers of labor." Lacking detailed crime reports makes proving such an assertion difficult, but legislation suggests such a connection. In 1879, the North Carolina General Assembly passed a law making it illegal for African Americans to change jobs without permission. Violators were employed by the state for internal improvements or leased to private businesses. Later the legislature added a new element to its vagrancy policy when it made subject to arrest those unable to demonstrate gainful employment. According to historian Jennifer Roback, both laws enabled the state to gather a labor force whenever it saw fit. Historian William Cohen even found the *Atlanta Constitution* newspaper baldly making this point when it urged the police, "Cotton is ripening. See that the 'vags' get busy."[9]

Not only did the drive for cheap labor affect policing, it also hit at the very heart of the penitentiary system. Previous rhetoric about rehabilitation disappeared, replaced by a system in which inmates suffered mightily. Historian Herbert McKay makes this point well when he notes, "the lessee was motivated by the spirit of enterprise and the temptation to exploit cheap labor; state officials were influenced by eagerness to put money in the treasury." He goes on to assert that "the thinking of penitentiary officials, governors, legislators . . . was almost wholly directed along the lines of self-support and cheap labor for internal improvements. . . . Very little thought was given to the reclamation, reformation, and rehabilitation of the convicts; and few efforts were made to improve the penal organization."[10]

That greed directly affected the prisoners, as was made apparent in 1882 on the construction site of the Western North Carolina Railroad. Since 1875, more than five hundred inmates a day had been laboring on the road. Focused on profit and speed, the railroad's owners drove the inmates at a frantic pace. That pace, combined with an "inadequate diet" and substandard living conditions, meant inmates perished by the dozens. While many died during construction, the single most horrific episode occurred on December 30, 1882. After laboring on the Cowee Tunnel near Sylva, about fifty miles west of Asheville, inmates proceeded back to camp, chained together. The campsite lay across the Tuckaseegee River and was accessible only by ferry. As a result of heavy winter rains, the river was swollen and treacherous that December evening. As the twenty convicts and one guard crossed, the ferry capsized, dumping them all into the icy water.[11]

What happened next is unclear. One version claims nineteen convicts who were chained together drowned. African American inmate Anderson Drake, a trustee, was not chained to the others, and he not only survived but saved guard William Foster, who was unable to swim. After the rescue, however, Foster accused Drake of stealing his wallet. Fellow guards searched Drake and found it. As punishment, Drake lost his trustee status and the day after the tragedy was back in chains working on the tunnel. A similar version has Drake facing a whipping for the theft, but receiving a reward for saving the guard. Yet another has him receiving an additional thirty-year sentence. A different account of the tragedy contends that two inmates escaped their chains and swam safely to shore; the other eighteen succumbed. One final account has African American prisoner Sam Pickett escaping his chains and risking his life to drag several men to safety. In this tale, the state recognized Pickett's heroism with $100 and a pardon.[12]

While the truth remains unclear, what is clear is that the leasing system was dangerous and that such tragedies were common. Prison records indicate that in 1878 ninety-four inmates died on various lease assignments. Hilda Zimmerman confirms that this was not an isolated problem. She notes that "convicts who were sent to work on railroads died and were killed at a shocking rate," and calls the 1880s "the darkest in North Carolina's prison history." It was not simply a North Carolina problem either, as studies demonstrate that "leased Southern convicts died at up to eight times the rate of convicts in other parts of the country." Businessmen and prison administrators, however, gave little thought to those statistics. Historian Matthew Mancini contends that the "lessee in many cases actually had an economic incentive to abuse their prisoners." Employers needed to get as much out of the inmates as possible, and thus drove them mercilessly. Inmates were expendable and interchangeable, mere commodities to exploit. As one lessee observed, "One dies, get another." Prison administrators, by contrast, simply were blinded by corporate lucre.[13]

What caused such callousness was not simply greed, but racism. According to Homer Carson, between 1874 and 1892, 85 percent of North Carolina's inmate population was African American. African American life was cheap in the American South in the late nineteenth century, and the deaths of a few more during railroad construction was not something that worried most citizens. Indeed, a report on the Tuckaseegee deaths found the guards and overseers guilty of a complete disregard for the prisoners' lives and safety. Penitentiary administrators denied the charges, and since the dead were African American there was little public outcry. North Carolinians quickly forgot the tragedy and accusations, and moved on with their lives. Such indifference made it easy to continue the exploitation.[14]

But there was more than popular indifference at work. Many scholars contend the white public actively approved of the leasing system and its brutality as a useful mode of social control. Historians Jesse Steiner and Roy Brown assert that the "prison system in the South cannot be understood without reference to the fact that within two decades following the Civil War the problem of the Southern prison . . . became preeminently the problem of dealing with the Negro." Dan Berger concurs, and writes, "southern states used their jail cells to aggregate racial injustice" in the hopes of "enforce[ing] docility." Lawrence Friedman goes a step further and writes, "During the long night of segregation and white supremacy, criminal justice systems in the southern states served as foot soldiers in the army of the dominant race. The black population was a kind of caste of untouchables. Keeping them in their place was a primary function of courts, laws, and police."[15]

Several historians assert that the penitentiary and leasing systems went even further than seeking to control and punish, contending that the systems actively endeavored to re-enslave African Americans. Historians James Cobb and Alex Lichtenstein argue that southern states passed laws to increase the number of convicts in order to fill the labor void that emancipation created. Matthew Mancini asserts that "control of black labor was a leading motivation behind every significant effort to establish and maintain convict leasing." Douglas Blackmon goes even further, arguing that since there was no penalty if an inmate died in custody, and since another black laborer always could be had, "there was no compelling reason not to tax these convicts to their absolute physiological limits." By contrast, "slaves of the earlier era were at least minimally insulated from physical harm by their intrinsic financial value. Their owners could borrow money with slaves as collateral, pay debts with them, sell them at a profit, or extend the investment through production of more slave children."

African American inmates, he implies, were more degraded than slaves.[16]

Statistics from the Western North Carolina Railroad seem to support all of those assertions. Of the 3,644 inmates who worked on the railroad, 461 (12.6 percent) died. When addressing that excessive rate, the board of directors determined that the cause was the large number of African Americans working on the project. The board suggested that since most were from the piedmont or coastal plain, their constitutions were not hardy enough to withstand the western winters. Although the board believed it had identified the cause of the excessive death rate, it continued to send African Americans to the mountains, where they died in great numbers.[17]

This racist, dangerous, and exploitative relationship was the worst element of the convict leasing system, but it was far from the only problem. As money flowed into the state's coffers, politicians believed they had found the solution to all their fiscal concerns and willingly leased inmates by the hundreds without regard to the penitentiary's needs. In other words, administrators lost control of their own labor force. In 1876, the state leased 456 of its 794 inmates, and in 1878 it leased 737 of 1,102. Of those remaining, most were physically unable to perform the hard labor required on the work sites. That shortcoming, of course, also meant they were unable to help build the penitentiary. The prison thus went from an oversupply of labor to a dramatic undersupply that hampered and slowed construction efforts.[18]

In 1879 it got even worse, as politicians not only ignored the penitentiary's needs but reality. That year they authorized the leasing of 2,325 inmates, a figure nearly 1,000 inmates greater than the number actually assigned to the penitentiary. As Zimmerman explains, "Not all of these assignments could be carried out since the number of state convicts was never as large as the number allotted to the railroad building; and yet each session of the legislature passed laws making such assignments because the legislators were working for the support of their constituents who were demanding convict workers for railroad building. If a reasonable penal policy were considered at all it received secondary consideration."[19]

Another problem was the prevalence of inmate escape. In 1875, twenty-six inmates escaped from their work sites; in 1876, sixty-eight escaped, including twenty-two from the Spartanburg and Asheville Railroad and fourteen from the Western North Carolina Railroad; and in 1877, fifty-seven escaped. Even a decade later the issue plagued the lease system, as 1889 and 1890 saw another 167 inmates escape from the railroads or other work sites. Although inmates escaped from the penitentiary as well, the vast majority of incidents happened on the work sites, where inmates took advantage of the relative isolation and lack of security. As the fundamental purpose of any penal system is to hold secure those convicted of crimes, the escapes demonstrate the relative failure of convict leasing as a penal policy.[20]

One final problem with the convict leasing system was the appreciation that the railroad building boom would not last forever. In July 1878, the board of directors removed two hundred inmates from the Spartanburg and Asheville Railroad after the company failed to pay for their labor. The board transferred the inmates to the Western North Carolina Railroad and continued to employ them in a useful and financially beneficial manner, but the failure of the Spartanburg and Asheville demonstrated the underlying financial weakness of much of the railroad system. Similarly, board members appreciated that eventually railroads would cover the state and that the need to add more track would end. The question of where else to employ inmates thus pulled at penitentiary administrators even as they enjoyed the system's immediate economic benefits.

Despite the obvious problems that the leasing system presented, "the revenue which poured into the state treasury seemed to dazzle the highest officials and to blind them to the abuses of the system." Penitentiary administrators forgot the original reason for seeking outside labor, virtually abandoned inmate labor on penitentiary construction, ignored facts, and succumbed to railroad gold. All of this had negative consequences for the prisoners and the prison, yet it remained policy for decades.[21]

With railroad jobs beginning to dry up, convict leasing eased in the 1880s and prisoners slowly returned to the prison to help complete construction. They eventually fulfilled that task, but during the era of convict labor it was far from a prime focus. Avarice and racism infected both politicians and prison administrators, and led each to abandon thoughts of inmate rehabilitation and to acquiesce in their exploitation. The willingness of politicians to intervene in prison affairs, the focus on income over reform, and the obvious refusal to treat African Americans as human beings exemplify well the continued reflection of public life in the penitentiary. That reflection would linger as the inmates returned. Fortunately for them, it soon offered some hope.

6

COMPLETING THE PENITENTIARY

As inmates flooded work sites throughout the 1870s, the penitentiary rose but slowly. Lacking inmates, confronting often oppositional legislators, and worrying about future economic opportunities, prison administrators had to make their way amid an obstacle course. In the 1880s, however, the political battles briefly waned, the economy stabilized, convict leasing eased, and prison administrators breathed a sigh of relief. The result was the completion of the prison facility and a returned focus on inmate rehabilitation. While the changed circumstances and completed penitentiary made life somewhat easier for the inmates, those same factors led administrators to adopt the era's racism and formally segregate them by race. The newly completed prison, for good and ill, thus continued to imbibe the state's social, political, and economic ethos as the nineteenth century neared its end.

That embodiment initially exposed some of the state's worst attributes. In 1872, penitentiary physician Dr. Hill raised alarms about the impact the lack of permanent structures was having on the inmates' health. He noted that the insufficient heating, restricted living space, and inadequate ventilation in the temporary quarters led to an inmate mortality rate of 4.5 percent. While that was half the rate at which inmates died on the lease system, Hill found it unacceptable. Two years later the situation was even worse. Hill reported that "disease was terribly rife" and listed numerous cases of dysentery, cholera, and typhoid fever. He tried to absolve himself of any blame by resorting to racial stereotypes and exclaiming that "the large excess of colored prisoners [384 of 455], accounts in a great degree for the sickness, mortality, medical expense and labor." This was so, he asserted, due to "their characteristic improvidence, recklessness and disregard of sanitary regulations." Despite blaming African Americans for their suffering, he reiterated his previous assessment, acknowledged the lack of sanitation, ventilation, and space, and demanded the state complete the permanent structures in the interest of inmate health. As he told the legislators, "when completed, [the permanent structures] can be thoroughly ventilated and adequately warmed, and will doubtless furnish all sanitary appliances and arrangements essential to the physical well-being of the convicts."[1]

Hill was not the only one to push for a more focused effort on completion; so too did the board of directors. In 1874, the board reminded the General Assembly that the state had purposefully adopted the Auburn system as its penological model based on the belief that isolation gave inmates time to reflect on their crimes. In the current setting, however, inmates were neither isolated nor reflective. Instead, they crowded together and spent their time "plotting mischief and escapes." Worse still, the board worried that the lack of isolation made it nearly impossible to separate the younger and more impressionable inmates from "the vilest of the offenders." Rather than uplifting inmates, the prison, as then organized, degraded them.[2]

Whether or not Hill's concerns or the board's fears had any impact is unclear, but the General Assembly briefly refocused on the prison facility and opened its pocketbook. In 1872, the legislature provided money to purchase land on Walnut Creek, not far from the prison site. The land contained large amounts of clay, which inmates gathered and molded into bricks. Although an important step forward, legislators failed to provide adequate funds to fire the kilns, and the prison had to warehouse 870,657 unfired bricks. Eventually the General Assembly appreciated the absurdity of the situation and provided the requisite funds. With the kilns ablaze, inmates fired 1.8 million bricks in 1875 and 1876, and ultimately produced 12 million bricks. Leased inmates employed many of that number in the construction of state buildings, but a substantial portion went toward completing the prison.[3]

In 1873, the board again acted to speed up construction when it bought the nearby stone quarry it had been leasing for three years. Purchased from William Boylan for $6,000, the deal made economic sense: the rock was of high quality and could be used for the main prison wall, the administration buildings, and the cellblocks (which were to include 640 cells, up from the original plan of 500). Additionally, administrators foresaw the opportunity to sell stone on the open market and viewed the quarry as a place for continued inmate labor after construction was complete.[4]

Legislators next authorized the use of inmates in the manufacturing of cell doors and cell frames. The board of directors was wary of working inmates at the tasks since it had signed contracts for the manufacture of both products with outside firms. Unsure whether to push forward with the legislative mandate and risk a lawsuit or to abide by the contracts, the board asked for guidance. During the 1873–1874 legislative session, the General Assembly authorized administrators to go ahead with the ironwork regardless of the contracts. Prison officials opened an on-site metal shop, and inmates set to work fashioning their cells.[5]

Other developments also seemed to point to progress. By 1874, state funding allowed for the creation of an on-site shoe shop, which produced shoes for inmates, guards, and the general public. By 1876, a tailor shop produced all the prisoners' clothing, and inmates in a mattress-making shop made all the mattresses used by prisoners and guards. The legislature also authorized construction of a tin shop to produce needed tin-ware and a soap factory to make the detergent employed in the laundry and the soap used in the baths. Inmates who were not leased out labored in those facilities, and also did the cooking, washing, and cleaning. They even raised much of their own food by farming several acres of leased land and raising hogs for slaughter.[6]

Happy with the progress, delighted that legislative intervention had turned to the benefit of the prisoners, and hoping the speedy completion of the permanent structures was now just a matter of course, the board was even more thrilled when the General Assembly acceded to previous requests and passed a new commutation law. The law allowed inmates to earn time off for good behavior, shortening their terms of incarceration. Previously only the governor could commute a sentence, but now inmates had a means of improving their station. Although it was vague and continued to give the governor the final say in setting a prisoner free, the board found the law "has proved quite an inducement to good conduct . . . so that quite a number of [inmates] have been singularly obedient and industrious." Board members believed this good behavior would carry on after the inmates left the prison as they came to appreciate the benefits of hard work and clean living. In other words, the board continued to support the prison's reformative elements. Indeed, as early as their 1874 report the board of directors explicitly wrote, "it is better to reform a man—qualify him to live—make of him a productive citizen, and restore him to the State and society by the reforming and educating discipline of the Penitentiary than to degrade him by brutal punishments—imbrute him by idle and corrupting confinement and then turn him loose to depredate on the public and become a confirmed burden to society." After the brutal treatment inmates faced on the lease assignments, this return to reformation was a notable development and suggests that legislative action could benefit the prisoners, not just harm them.[7]

As inmates escaped the temporary quarters, found adequate labor, and benefitted from the new commutation law, construction continued apace, and by the end of 1875 inmates occupied the first sixty-four permanent cells. The result was a measurable improvement in their health, and Dr. Hill reported a significant decrease in inmate illness. He credited the new structures for that decrease and continued to urge completion of the entire facility in order to bring those health benefits to all.[8]

Beyond the new cells and better health, there were other signs of improvement. Ministers from various Raleigh churches volunteered their time to provide regular chapel services, and a small library arose with books purchased from a 10-cent fee charged to all visitors. By 1881, the number of library books had reached four hundred, thanks to several book donations, while the YMCA provided additional reading opportunities through a literacy program. Finally, prison administrators acknowledged the legitimacy of the inmates' previous complaints about the quality and quantity of the food, and worked to improve their diet. In 1878, the steward reported spending just 9 cents per day to feed each inmate, but by 1882 expenditures had increased modestly to 11 cents. Inmate complaints about the food continued nonetheless, but prison administrators alleged inmate treatment was improving across the board.[9]

The good news continued when, in 1878, the exterior stone wall reached fifteen feet. Although it was yet to reach its completion height, and it did not yet fully encircle the penitentiary grounds, Warden Hicks lauded the progress in his biennial address to the General Assembly. He noted that when complete the wall would rise another five feet, and explained that the incomplete portion was the section that would connect with the main administration building. Although this was good news, Hicks worried that the closing in of the wall, combined with the weakness of the incomplete section, tempted the inmates. While escapes were rather common, it was clear that with the wall's completion future escapes would be more difficult. Inmates were thus likely to take their chances while the opportunity remained.[10]

And there was a notable escape attempt on July 9, 1878. While most inmates were in the dining hall for dinner, six African American and two white inmates attempted to flee. Guards thwarted the attempt by opening fire, killing one inmate, wounding another, and scaring the other six back to their cells. Warden Hicks worried the failure would not prevent future attempts. As such, he ordered guards to increase their vigilance. He also used the threat to request additional funds from the General Assembly.[11]

Thanks to the legislature's continued support, by June 1880 construction crews had completed the entire exterior wall. It rose twenty feet above the ground, with a base buried sixteen feet below the surface; it was seventeen feet thick at its base but tapered as it rose to four feet, eight inches at its peak. A fence and a walkway for the guards topped the structure, which also included guard towers at regular intervals and at each corner. Warden Hicks was so pleased that he boasted, "I believe it may be truthfully said, that North Carolina has as good, if not the best, prison wall in the United States."[12]

While the wall's completion marked a milestone, the lack of permanent cells remained a problem, and by the 1880s the prison once again faced crowding issues. The crowding was a result of several policy changes. First, prison officials determined that certain types of inmates should not be leased. There was thus a growing number of inmates who were required to remain in the penitentiary. The list of those statutorily banned from release included those considered too dangerous or too prone to escape, women, and those whose physical infirmities prevented them from performing hard labor. The board referred to those later inmates as "decrepids," and lamented that they did not suffer the pains of hard labor as the prison charter required, did little to subsidize their existence, and proved difficult to remove from the penitentiary grounds.[13]

An additional cause was the expense of sending out small groups to various work sites. The inmates needed to be guarded and fed along the way, and the constant transport of small groups proved costly. As a result, prison administrators determined to transport only larger groups. Although cost effective, the consequence was that physically capable inmates often remained in the prison for months until their numbers were large enough to make moving them economically sound.

The response to this population growth was yet another call on the state legislature. This time, Warden Hicks urged the state to purchase some nearby farmland. He noted that by 1881 there were more than two hundred inmates who were performing little or no labor, but who were capable of handling farm work. He argued that not only would such labor ease the crowding, but the fresh air and exercise could prove healthful. The state already leased six acres bordering the penitentiary, and with legislative support Hicks leased additional acreage just outside of Raleigh in 1882. Nearly two hundred inmates, mostly "decrepids" and female prisoners, set to work on the land. According to an official report, "the health of many has much improved by the outdoor work, and women and old men and unsound men have by this means been made to yield to the State an income greater proportionally than that derived from any other sources." Additionally, the report noted that farm work did not upset free labor, as had some of the prison's other enterprises, because farming was "too broad to admit of competition in the sense in which it is generally used."[14]

The cost savings that accrued from inmate work on the farms offered one final benefit: it enabled the board to hire additional craftsmen to assist the inmates who remained behind working on the permanent penitentiary structures. As a result, completion of the buildings neared. By 1882, workers had completed the east cell house. The kitchen, dining hall, hospital, and laundry were nearly complete, and the whole complex was far enough along that E. R. Stamps, president of the board of trustees, described the prison as "one of the most substantially constructed and conveniently appointed prison buildings in the country."[15]

Enjoying two more years of relative stability, and free from prisoner turmoil, financial distress, or political meddling, the final buildings continued to rise. On December 1, 1884, the board of directors formally declared the penitentiary complete and celebrated a job well done. Critics since have argued that it actually took another fifteen years to complete the work, pointing to the main administration building as evidence. It was incomplete in 1884 and remained skeletal and unused until 1899. While correct, the assertion is mere quibbling, as the cell houses, guardrooms, and general facilities were operational by the end of 1884.

Whenever it was complete, the buildings, wall, and the entire complex were impressive. Adorned with cupolas, spires, and assorted gothic architectural affectations, the exterior was striking. Future superintendent George Pou called the prison "an imposing castle-like structure which in all probability was the most modern prison in the United States. At the time, from an exterior view, it was certainly one of the most magnificent looking of the various state buildings." Another observer described it as "a dark, feudal fortress, ancient and dreary, a place certain to have damp dungeons and loathsome torture chambers."[16]

The interior was equally commanding. The three-story central administrative building extended north beyond the prison walls. It included business offices, the employee dining hall on the ground floor, and bedrooms for the guards above. A lengthy corridor extended south from the administrative building through the exterior prison wall and into the main facility. Continuing straight back, the corridor led into the bakery, kitchen, and inmate dining hall, beneath which resided the prison's power plant. Just south of this section, although separate from the main facility, was the four-story, sixty-four-cell "female building." Able to meet all the needs of the female inmates, it included a laundry, kitchen, bakery, dining facilities, hospital, and workroom. It served the state until 1935, when women moved to their own separate site.[17]

Spanning east to west from the main facility's central corridor were the prison's two wings, each five stories tall and divided into two separate cellblocks. The cellblocks contained thirty-two eight-foot by six-foot cells per floor. With each cell housing a single prisoner as per the Auburn system's call for isolation, this allowed the prison to hold 640 inmates. The cells had seven-foot ceilings, lacked plumbing, and included but the simplest of strap-iron beds. Although a walkway around each floor provided guards the ability to monitor inmates, the layout of the cells, with doors located on the far right, proved problematic because inmates were able to hide or otherwise escape surveillance behind the solid wall that enclosed half the cell front. Not until 1934 was that design flaw corrected. The lowest floor of each block housed the inmates' baths as well as the segregation and isolation units used to punish rule breakers. Extending out beyond the west cellblock was the inmate reception area, where new arrivals were processed, while extending beyond the east wing was the "chapel and hospital building." The chapel was segregated, with African American inmates and white inmates assigned to different pews, while the hospital placed ailing inmates on separate floors. The entire facility similarly was segregated by race, with the original blueprints defining the east wing as the "white prisoners' cellblock" and the west wing as the "colored prisoners' cellblock." Although it took fourteen years and cost $1.25 million dollars, more than double the original estimate, by December 1884 North Carolina finally had its state penitentiary.[18]

The journey to complete the penitentiary had been long and winding, and throughout the process the state's essence was apparent in how politicians and the public treated and viewed the institution. Demonstrating that the state may have turned a corner, the final years of construction saw a returned focus on inmate rehabilitation and a renewed legislative interest in the prison that included increased funding, the opportunity for early inmate release, and new job opportunities for those inmates who remained incarcerated. Although this era also witnessed the formalization of racial segregation within the facility, completion of the penitentiary seemed a net positive for the inmates, who now inhabited a more secure, sanitary, and stable institution. Almost immediately, however, prison officials faced questions about the administrative model, threats to their employment policies, and continuing calls for reform. As the societal peace that had facilitated completion came to an end, a new era of change and unrest forced prison administrators to confront a new set of worries.

7

THE FIRST TWO DECADES

With construction on the North Carolina State Penitentiary fundamentally complete by December 1884, officials turned their attention to a new array of issues. Although many were of long-standing concern, with construction no longer a focus the matters finally took center stage. The issues included questions about the prison's underlying penal philosophy, its employment of inmate workers, its placement of youthful offenders, and its finances. Throughout the 1880s and 1890s, penitentiary administrators navigated those issues by aping politicians and society at large: they remained stubbornly wedded to the past in a manner that recalled the state's Rip Van Winkle reputation, they affected changes that appeared progressive but altered little, they battled with organized labor, and they relied on the traditional employ of farming. Although officials escaped the impact of political intervention during the penitentiary's inaugural years, their efforts continued to emulate North Carolina's larger traditions, beliefs, and practices.

Among the first issues administrators addressed was the prison's purpose. A penitentiary is more than a complex of buildings; it also must have a penal philosophy. As noted previously, penitentiary officials originally found their philosophy in the Auburn system, which they discovered during examinations of other penal systems in 1868 and 1869. At the time, it was the most widely accepted and cost-effective criminal justice system in the United States. As a result of crumbling prisons, rising costs, charges of guard brutality, and the revolutionary social changes wrought by the Civil War and the postbellum immigration boom, however, by the 1870s many were rethinking the Auburn model.

That rethinking began with a growing belief that crime was a "learned behavior" resulting from "inadequate socialization." Criminals, in other words, did not choose the wrong path, but rather social forces beyond their control led them astray. As such, inmates could not reform themselves through Auburn's combination of isolation, reflection, and hard work. Instead, they were "sick" and needed to be "'cured' of their criminality in a setting that approximated a normal society." Isolation, of course, was far from normal.[1]

The desire to cure inmates led the New York Prison Association to commission Congregational minister Enoch Wines and Columbia University Law School professor Theodore Dwight to conduct a nationwide prison survey. The result was their *Report on the Prisons and Reformatories of the United States and Canada*, which argued that nowhere in the nation were jailors actively engaged in reforming inmates. Even should they have tried to do so, the report asserted, inadequate facilities, poorly trained staffs, and the lack of oversight would have doomed the effort. To fix what they viewed as a broken system, the authors called for a new model with larger cells, better trained guards, state boards of inspection, and systems designed to allow inmates to "demonstrate and earn their advance toward freedom by moving through progressively liberal stages of discipline."[2]

Based on those ideas, New York State opened the Elmira Reformatory in 1876. All inmates were required to enroll in school, with classes offering everything from basic reading, writing, history, and math to advanced courses in philosophy, literature, and the sciences. The reformatory also offered vocational training and required inmates to work in one of the several on-site industries. To determine the amount of moral regeneration the inmate underwent, the reformatory implemented a classification system. Inmates entered at the "Second Grade," and for six months administrators judged them on their conduct in the classroom and the work site, as well as on their demeanor. Good conduct afforded the inmate the opportunity to earn promotion to "First Grade," which entailed greater freedoms and benefits, as well as the potential for a reduced sentence; poor conduct led to a demotion to "Third Grade," with the requisite loss of freedom and benefits. Elmira superintendent Zebulon Brockway claimed great success in reforming inmates and reducing recidivism, and the system "was hailed the world around as the greatest forward step in penology since the substitution of imprisonment for medieval maiming and execution." As a result, the Elmira model supplanted the Auburn model by the turn of the century, and was the dominant penal methodology for much of the twentieth century.[3]

Despite the rise of that new model, officials in North Carolina remained wedded to the Auburn system. In 1882, with construction still ongoing but nearing its end, the board of directors made clear its philosophy when president E. R.

Stamps wrote, "The correct theory of a penitentiary . . . is *locus penitentie*, a place for repentance." Envisioning the state as "the mother of its citizens," he stated that the purpose of sending people to the penitentiary, beyond punishing lawbreakers and protecting the public, was "to reclaim [the inmates] from habits of vice and crime to the paths of virtue and sober industry." Continuing, he asserted that prison should "take them from evil and debasing associations and build them up into useful if not respectable characters." It was for those purposes that the state was proud to include a chapel, basic schooling, and the commutation system in its version of the Auburn model.[4]

While this may sound similar to the Elmira system, in practice the North Carolina State Penitentiary operated along quite different lines. Guards brutally enforced the rules and referred to inmates by their numbers, while administrators ignored inmate suffering on lease assignments and acquiesced to the near reintroduction of slavery. Even elements of the Elmira system that officials did employ were mitigated by the limited nature of the educational and vocational training opportunities. Such practices and limitations were anathema to the very essence of the Elmira model, and they demonstrate how far North Carolina was from fully implementing the new system. In other words, although the buildings were new, the methodology was old. The state once again found itself lagging behind its neighbors. As one scholar put it: "Central Prison was outmoded before its permanent buildings were even begun."[5]

That outdated theory resulted in some problems for officials as they turned their attention from building to administering a fully functioning and self-sustaining institution. While they may have been relieved to be done with the headaches of construction, they found running a penitentiary made the problems of the past seem like child's play.

Among the earliest problems administrators of the mid-1880s had to address was the ongoing concern about future inmate employment. Historian Susan Thomas notes that the penitentiary's very organization forced the board to run it like a business. Finding labor for its "employees," therefore, remained central. The Western North Carolina Railroad annually employed approximately five hundred inmates, but it was nearly complete and those inmates soon would return to the prison. Other railroads were nearing completion as well, and the general railroad building boom was beginning to wane. While the penitentiary always had leased inmates to other types of industries, the figures were insignificant in comparison to the number employed and the revenue generated from the railroads. Officials scrambled to find new avenues of employment.

One idea was to expand on-site industries. The penitentiary already employed those who were unfit for the hardships of railroad labor in the prison laundry, kitchen, and shoe shop, while the rented farmlands offered further employment. Once again, however, the numbers were minimal. If the penitentiary was to make up for the loss of railroad labor, it needed to expand dramatically the size and number of those industries.

Increasing the number of on-site industries, however, raised two related problems. First, when convicts were employed off-site the prison received a direct payment and was freed from the costs of inmate housing, feeding, and care. If inmates worked in the prison, the state lost the fees and had to pay for their upkeep. Thus, even should the penitentiary create on-site industries, the cost of inmate care diminished the economic return. Second, when inmates worked off-site the firms covered the mechanical expenses. To expand existent industries or to move new industries to the penitentiary required the state to cover the costs. Prison administrators thus faced the unenviable task of asking the legislature for additional funds to purchase industrial machinery after having spent $1.25 million to build the penitentiary. Undaunted, Warden Hicks attempted to procure such funds by scaring legislators, whom he warned of an imminent "calamity, both to the prison and to the prisoners," should something not be done. Legislators remained more afraid of costs than unruly inmates, and Hicks's effort made little legislative headway.[6]

What made the administrators' efforts to find new labor for the inmates even more difficult was the growing opposition to the use of inmate labor in competition with free labor. In the 1880s, organized labor and business leaders began to object to what they viewed as unfair competition. It was one thing for inmates to produce for their own consumption, although companies would have preferred access to that market as well, but what infuriated the business and labor communities was the use of inmate labor in the free market. Present scholarship asserts that convict labor's impact on wages was virtually nil and that it flourished only in places or industries where free labor failed due to conditions or costs. Contemporaries, however, believed it artificially lowered wages and overhead, and harmed both employees and competing employers. Free workers also claimed inmate labor "demeaned and devalued the 'honest'" labor they performed and "fostered an association . . . between the otherwise honorable trade of the workingman, and the dishonored and 'depreciated' convict." Others claimed it was "undemocratic" or that it "presaged an [era of] 'industrial slavery.'" In the end, workers and business owners opposed the system.[7]

The penitentiary's board of directors acknowledged "the opposition manifested by a large portion of the people of the United States to the use of convicts upon mechanical enterprises upon the 'contract system,'" and closed the shoe shop in 1886 as a result. But it was more than the shoe shop that was affected. That same year several companies with contracts to employ inmates, as well as several that were considering signing contracts, cancelled their deals or broke off negotiations. When Warden Hicks inquired as to the cause, nearly every firm informed him that it was public "opposition to the contract system of convict labor" that drove their decision. The penitentiary thus not only faced the loss of inmate labor on the railroads, it faced losing previously agreed to labor contracts as well as potential future contracts as companies grew skittish of facing public outrage over their association with convict labor. As we shall see, that opposition waned and the on-site industries and contracts with private firms eventually returned. In the late nineteenth century, however, opposition to inmate labor created a grave employment shortage and concerned prison administrators.[8]

Administrators had other reasons to fret as well. From its earliest incarnation the prison employed "certain docile and short-term convicts" as trustees. Those inmates had proved their honesty and dependability, and as a result were largely free from oversight and assisted the guards in administering other prisoners. An 1885 state Senate report, however, noted that some trustees were serving life sentences or had committed violent crimes. Smelling a powerful campaign topic, senators expressed their outrage and moved to ban the practice. During subsequent hearings, penitentiary officers assured legislators that they took every precaution to ensure trustees did not abuse their positions or take advantage of their freedoms to escape. Warden Hicks even argued that a ban on trustees would be a "fruitful cause of escapes." Despite such testimony, the Senate determined there was no legal authority for the program and shut it down. Combined with the issues caused by the return of inmates due to the decline in railroad construction and the lack of on-site industry, Hicks worried that the end of the trustee system would not only lead to escapes, but to unrest and riot.[9]

A third concern administrators faced during the penitentiary's early decades was the growing population of youthful and first-time offenders. Prison officials long believed the penitentiary was the wrong place to send impressionable individuals. Board members complained that judges sentenced boys as young as eight to the penitentiary, and noted that in 1886 the prison housed forty-six inmates between the ages of eight and fifteen and another 352 between fifteen and twenty. Placing such youngsters in prison, they contended, resulted in "manufacturing hardened criminals out of boys and girls that might be reclaimed and made valuable members of society." Warden Hicks seconded this concern and noted specifically that those numbers meant one-third of the prison population was under twenty. Placing them alongside hardened felons turned the youngsters into career criminals, and he encouraged state legislators to create separate facilities for youthful offenders.[10]

There was precedent for such a move, as New York City opened the first such facility in 1825 with the New York House of Refuge for Juvenile Delinquents. Boston and Philadelphia followed suit, and by 1850 there were more than twenty-five additional institutions. North Carolina's legislators, however, ignored the trend and the advice of their prison officials.[11]

Administrators eventually changed tactics and suggested legislators pass a law to prevent judges from sentencing anyone under the age of fifteen to the penitentiary. While this would have incarcerated young offenders in local and county jails, officials believed inmates housed in those facilities were less corrupt and the impact would be less deleterious. Legislators, however, rejected even that suggestion as too radical, and throughout the nineteenth century young inmates continued to find their way into Central Prison.[12]

Although the first four years of the fully functioning prison proved problem-filled, administrators handled the issues, found creative ways of addressing their concerns, and made do as best they could when confronted with a recalcitrant General Assembly. By 1888, the prison employed inmates on various state work projects, with prisoners laboring on the North Carolina Supreme Court building and on the capitol grounds. Inmates also produced 750,000 bricks used in the construction of the North Carolina Agricultural and Mechanical College (now North Carolina State University), and by 1890 inmates had renovated elements of the penitentiary's western cell house to make it available for prison industries.[13]

As a result of such labor, in 1890 the board reported that the prison was financially self-sustaining with a $113,069.98 surplus. Warden Hicks warned, however, that the prison still needed the state's support, both financially and legally, to remain solvent. Only the money provided from on-site industries would allow the prison to remain liquid, he explained, as railroad construction was nearing its end. Indeed, by 1892 the prison confronted the return of five hundred inmates who had been employed off-site working on the railroads. While there was room to house the men, due to the lack of industry or jobs they were idle and unruly. Administrators put some of the men to work digging canals for the state or diking and ditching the penitentiary's farms, but they remained worried about the financial and behavioral consequences of the lack of long-term labor. Despite that concern, in 1892 the prison once again proved self-sufficient, ending the year with a $92,202.51 surplus. Determined to maintain that financial success, and without any obvious industrial focus or substantive help from the state, penitentiary officials decided to make the leap into large-scale farming.[14]

According to historian Hilda Zimmerman, the reasons officials turned to farming were numerous: most inmates knew how to farm, unlike industrial labor there was little opposition, it offered opportunities for inmates who could not perform heavier labor, and it offered inmates the opportunity to escape the prison's confines and enjoy fresh air and sunshine. Inmates were already working small farms around Raleigh, so the move to large-scale farming would have seemed obvious. And yet, "North Carolina was the first southern state to use convict labor for extensive farming activities."[15]

It did so beginning in 1882 when legislators approved a ten-year lease on a large tract of farmland along the Roanoke River in Northampton County. Two hundred inmates farmed the land, and by 1891 they were producing nearly $30,000 worth of cotton, corn, oats, peas, potatoes, turnips, and wheat. They also raised hogs and cows. By 1892 the state had added another eight thousand acres, and 80 percent of all inmates sentenced to Central Prison (935 of 1,122) were engaged in farm labor. By 1893 the prison had more than thirteen thousand acres statewide, and in 1895 the farms recorded a profit of $44,699. The growth continued, and by 1898 prisoners farmed more than fifteen thousand acres scattered across three farms on the Roanoke River (in Northampton and Halifax Counties), one in New Hanover County, one in Wadesboro, and one on the Cape Fear River. The state possessed 11¾ acres of land for every inmate, and farming "monopolize[d] convict labor." It was "the chief source of employment for the state's prisoners" for the next several years.[16]

The use of farm labor not only ameliorated the financial concerns that came with the end of railroad labor, it also eased crowding issues. One report found that by the late 1890s fewer than two hundred of the fourteen hundred inmates assigned to the penitentiary actually resided in the prison; the vast majority served their time on the farms. Inmates lived on the farms and, for all intents and purposes, served their terms in these rural settings. This marked the beginning of the statewide prison system that soon would include more than eighty separate institutions. Although that required additional expenditures on buildings, fences, and guards, at least in the case of the farms the income, the appreciation that the need for farm labor never would abate, and the realization that it did not upset organized labor or big business convinced prison officials to go forth. Farming seemed like the perfect solution to several of the penitentiary's problems. The danger, as penitentiary officials soon learned, is that farming is a precarious endeavor.

In 1893, legislators abolished the position of architect and warden, and replaced it with two new positions to deal with that risk. Former deputy warden John Fleming assumed the rank of warden and ran Central Prison. Former architect and warden William Hicks assumed the rank of superintendent and managed the entire prison system, including the farms. The governor selected the superintendent, pending Senate approval, and he served a four-year, renewable term. Hicks had overseen the construction process, managed the conversion from the temporary to the permanent facilities, and run the prison from its opening in 1884. He had twenty-three years of experience and understood well how to govern the prison and handle politicians. The appointment was thus no real promotion, and in 1894 Hicks retired. The Senate subsequently confirmed Augustus Leazar to complete Hicks's term, and it was he who learned the dangers of an overreliance on farm revenue.

In his first report to the General Assembly, Leazar, who had long served as the penitentiary's general manager, addressed the changeable fortunes of farming. He noted that despite spending $20,000 on dike construction, in 1893 eight separate floods ruined one-third of the corn crop. Although he reported that the farming efforts, despite the failures, still resulted in the prison ending the year with a profit, he warned about relying too heavily on farming. Those warnings proved prescient in 1894 when low yields and low prices brought on in part by the Panic of 1893 forced the prison to request $30,000 to cover operating expenses. Another flood in July 1895 breached levies, flooded three different farms, and destroyed 100,000 bushels of corn (85 percent of the crop) and 425 bales of cotton (16 percent of the crop). Similar problems in 1896 again left the prison in financial straits and forced Leazar to request state aid. Unfortunately for Leazar, that funding request became entangled in the lingering financial crisis of the late nineteenth century and, more importantly, in yet another period of political turmoil.[17]

The relative financial success that prison administrators enjoyed in their first years under normal operating conditions was contingent, in part, on the hands-off approach adopted by the state legislature. While that approach caused some problems, most notably the refusal to fund on-site industries or to deal with youthful offenders, it benefitted the prison by allowing administrators to govern the institution as they saw fit. And yet, that governance still mirrored many elements of North Carolina's larger social, political, and economic makeup. It remained behind the times, as evidenced by its slow adoption of the reformatory model, it confronted the growing power of organized labor and big business, and it relied on farming for financial support, a job in which most North Carolinians engaged. Unfortunately, as many Carolina farmers knew all too well, farming was a changeable endeavor, and the state's inmate farmers found themselves at Mother Nature's mercy. Such was the case for other elements of the prison as well, as the institution, its administrators, and the prisoners remained subject to external forces. The power of those forces became even more apparent as the century waned thanks to a grassroots political movement that swept the nation and upended politics as normal. While the Populist movement sought to help the common man, it impacted and reshaped nearly every element of North Carolina's public life. Among the elements affected was the penitentiary.

8

THE EXPLOSIVE POWERS OF FUSION

North Carolina's fraught political history continued into the 1890s, and penitentiary administrators again found themselves to be tools in a political battle. This time the battle pitted Democrats against the emergent Populist movement, and the vitriol had negative consequences for nearly every segment of society, including inmates and prison staff. Once the battle was fought, however, and with the Democrats again dominant, politicians came to appreciate the need to serve those they represented and offered prison officials some assistance. Although the political pendulum swung wildly, as the century waned North Carolinians, inmates, and prison administrators alike eventually enjoyed slight improvements in their circumstances.

The origins of the era's tumult began in 1877 when the people of North Carolina elected Democrat Zebulon Vance as governor. Vance had served the state as governor before, during the Civil War, and his reelection was a sign of the political times. Democrats had dominated the state legislature since 1870, when they used their power to impeach Republican William Woods Holden. Despite that control, and thanks to the public's "paradoxical" voting, Republicans maintained the governorship until Vance's election. Now with the entire government under their control, Democrats set about implementing their program with little to stand in their way. Convinced of their invincibility, however, they moved slowly and did little to benefit the poor whites who made up the majority of their electoral base. That sluggish response and lackluster performance created a political void into which the newly emergent Populist movement neatly fit. In 1894, Populists and Republicans "fused" their votes and won 116 of 170 seats in the state legislature. In 1896 the "fusion" vote won 136 seats and sent Republican Daniel Russell to the governor's mansion.[1]

That electoral success had a real impact on the penitentiary. In 1895, the "fusion" legislature abolished the office of superintendent, fired Augustus Leazar, and created a new, albeit remarkably similar position to which it appointed its own choice. Leazar refused to give up his position, and sued. He won the case and remained in office, but relations with the General Assembly proved implacable. The legislature slashed penitentiary spending and refused to fund flood control or internal improvements on the farms. Leazar eventually realized his presence was hurting the penitentiary and stepped down on April 1, 1897. John Smith succeeded Leazar and served out the remainder of his term.

In 1898, Governor Russell selected James Mewboorne to serve the next full term as superintendent. Not surprisingly he was a Populist, and he worked to repair the damage between the penitentiary and the General Assembly. His political affiliation made this reconciliation possible, but so too did his communication skills. Whereas Leazar asked for more money, Mewboorne worked to cut costs and streamline the penitentiary's farming operations so as to reduce state funding. In a letter to the General Assembly, he specifically suggested running fewer farms and purchasing the land rather than leasing.[2]

Legislators appreciated Mewboorne's ideas and ended the state's leases on the Cape Fear and Northampton farms after finding them "unprofitable and a burden." They then purchased a seven thousand-acre Caledonia farm in Halifax County for $61,000 in 1899. The state had been leasing it since 1892 at the cost of $3,350 per year, so the purchase made economic sense. It also purchased a farm in Anson, which Mewboorne converted into "a reformatory for young criminals," physically segregating them from older criminals. He also gave them regular uniforms rather than prison stripes and implemented a training program. His thinking was that

> if the object of the law is as much to *reform as it is to punish,* then there ought to be some means provided by which they can be separated from the hardened criminals, and given such *moral and religious training* as is calculated to make them better, so, when they shall have been discharged and enter again among good citizens, the latter would feel and know that their country was better, perhaps, by receiving back among themselves those who had been taught and trained rather than those who had been continuously in company with the hardened convicts of the State Prison.

Elements of the state's progressive tradition, as well as the fulfillment of Warden Hicks's long-standing request, thus became manifest in this new youth center.[3]

Mewboorne clearly was more successful working with legislators than was his predecessor. He also proved more creative in his financial dealings, overseeing a period of strong financial growth. In 1900 the prison ran a $101,668 surplus, produced sufficient food for the prisoners and hay for the animals, and employed inmates in a shirt factory and a brick making shop that earned the prison $4,000 per month. Mewboorne used that revenue to improve the penitentiary's water supply system, which allowed more frequent inmate baths, and to wire the prison for electricity, which provided lighting for each cell and powered machinery in the various industries. Mewboorne thus took advantage of the era, mirrored the "fusion" legislature's focus on helping the masses, improved the penitentiary's relationship with the state government, stabilized its finances, and modernized elements of the superstructure.[4]

The new superintendent did not stop there. Mewboorne next moved to improve the entire prison system's administration. He did so by firing a number of individuals, including the Halifax farm's supervisor and the penitentiary's steward, physician, and overseer. He publicly, although kindly, charged all of them with incompetence. Reports soon emerged that one of those discharged had a "fondness for the women . . . the negro female convicts" and that one female inmate "had a room in his own house fitted up for her." Others allegedly allowed inmates to venture outside the walls to hunt, to have access to alcohol, and to pass counterfeit currency. In general, the dismissed officials violated prison policy or failed to enforce discipline, and Mewboorne swept them out of office.[5]

All those developments seem like steps forward for the still young institution, and the last years of the nineteenth century appeared productive. Sadly, the political infighting that Mewboorne's appointment solved reemerged with a vengeance.

The problems began in 1898 when Democrats inaugurated a plan to regain power. Framing it as an effort to reclaim the state from outsiders, incompetents, and African Americans, party leaders authored *The Democratic Handbook, 1898*, a two hundred-page document that laid out the campaign. Much of it was avowedly racist and focused on reestablishing white supremacy, but the penitentiary fell within its purview as well. Democrats attacked across the board, claiming "fusionists" turned the penitentiary into a cesspool of corruption, incompetence, and financial misdealings. They asserted that during Smith's brief term as superintendent "there were rumors of peculations and thefts and scandalous proceedings." While admitting they had no proof, they turned that lack of evidence back on the "fusionists" by asserting they were stonewalling and hiding financial improprieties. Indeed, the handbook concluded, "enough appears to justify the public in believing that there has been not mere malad-ministration, but a decided absence of honesty. To what extent the Penitentiary has been pillaged we cannot know until the details are laid bare; and until we can get a look at the books, we can only feel that another miserable disgrace has befallen the State." It was a consequence of those issues, Democrats claimed, that Mewboorne replaced Smith as superintendent in 1898.[6]

The problem, they went on, was that under Mewboorne nothing changed. They charged him with withholding information about the penitentiary and pronounced their astonishment at such a brazen willingness to put party ahead of state: "no State officer had ever before concealed from the public the reports and records of his office, because they might militate against the party to which he belonged." Democrats went on to claim that it was not just Mewboorne but the entire board of directors who were involved in a cover-up because they "could not afford to let the people know the real facts concerning the manage-ment of the Penitentiary by the present administration."[7]

Stirred by such language, state Democratic Party chair Furnifold Simmons wrote several letters to Mewboorne demanding the penitentiary's financial and administrative records. Mewboorne refused, seeing it for the political stunt that it was, and instead authored a vitriolic attack on Simmons in the press. Published on July 27, 1898, in the *Raleigh Post*, Mewboorne declared Simmons insincere, dishonorable, and a liar. He accused the party chair of actively deny-ing African Americans the right to vote, called him the "commander-in-chief of the perjurors [sic] of the precincts and the robbers of the returning boards," and asked "how many votes did your party steal in the election of 1892?" A man with such a past and associations, Mewboorne asserted, had no right to demand information from a duly appointed government official. He then went further, asserting that Simmons and the Democrats had used the penitentiary to enrich themselves and their friends, and laughed at the thought of Democrats decrying corruption.[8]

Simmons returned fire:

I denounce the statements made in your letter, personal to myself, as emanations of a vile heart, devoid of any restraint of conscience, and as the impotent vaporings of a miserable liar. There has grown up in North Carolina during the last few years a horde of which you are one, who seek, by detraction and defamation of their betters, to deceive and mislead the people, and gain for themselves positions which they are notoriously unfit to hold. The time has come when these miserable slanderers and hypocrites will not only be exposed, but fittingly denounced and pilloried before an outraged public.

Such rhetoric played well among poor whites and business leaders, and in 1898 Democrats not only regained control of the General Assembly, they had a near seventy-seat majority. Two years later, in 1900, Democrat Charles Aycock won the governor's office by sixty thousand votes over his Republican rival, Samuel Adams. The margin was a record to that point in the state's history, and it left Democrats in firm control of the state.[9]

The resurrection of the Democratic Party boded ill for Superintendent Mewboorne. He appreciated that fact, and on January 1, 1899, he resigned. In an effort to prevent Republican governor Daniel Russell, who was not up for reelection until 1900, from filling the vacancy, on February 15, 1899, the legislature passed the "Prison Administration Bill," which abolished the office of superintendent and created a twenty-one-person board appointed by the General Assembly. Governor Russell ignored the law and selected W. H. Day as superintendent. Russell did not send Day's nomination to the Senate for confirmation, and simply installed him in office. Not about to allow those acts to go unchallenged, the legislature sued, claiming Day's assignment was invalid because the Senate had not confirmed him and because the office no longer existed. Day's camp contended that the new board was simply a ruse "to deprive the defendant of his office on the part of the general assembly . . . contrary to the provisions" of the state and federal constitutions. In April 1899, the state Supreme Court issued its *State v. Day* decision, in which it ruled that while the General Assembly did have the right to abolish an office it created, it could not "oust an incumbent of an office, and continue the office afterwards." The court thus agreed with Day's contention that the board was a ruse. It also ruled that Day did not need Senate confirmation since the governor had the constitutional right to fill a vacancy.[10]

Although stymied by the courts, the legislature sought to drive Day out by other means and launched an investigation "to inquire into and investigate any and all charges of fraud, negligence, immorality, incompetency and mismanagement on the part of any officers or employees of said Penitentiary." After extensive hearings, the committee expressed shock at the "recklessness which characterized the management of almost every department of the State Prison," found it $120,000 in debt, and determined that under recent management the "depreciation in the value of the State's property amounted to at least $75,000." The committee allegedly found "everybody from the bell-boy to the Superintendent making purchases," asserted that "the system of bookkeeping was poor," argued that "practically, no business rules or principles were applied to any of the departments," and reported waste on the farms, drunkenness and incompetence in the administration, and cruelty by the guards.[11]

Despite that litany, the committee determined the penitentiary had the fundamental resources necessary to return to profitability since the problems were recent and the direct consequence of mismanagement under Superintendents Mewboorne, Smith, and Leazar. Indeed, it specifically asserted that "up to the year 1897 . . . the management was competent, business like, economical and honest, and a great many permanent improvements were made on the property under control of the State during that time, which should have been of great assistance to the future management in helping to put the prison on a self-sustaining basis. . . . But since that time . . . we find incompetency and extravagance on almost every hand."[12]

Superintendent Day played a role in the hearings, and he went out of his way to support the committee's findings. Whether or not he did this to protect his precarious position is unclear, but his comments about Smith and Mewboorne were brutal. He declared Smith "absolutely incompetent," found Mewboorne "incompetent" and "weak," and labeled numerous other prison officials as inept, corrupt, violent, and drunk. The committee also heard from guards, overseers, supervisors, and inmates, who provided additional testimony to support Day's allegations. Based on that testimony, the committee concluded the system could be saved only with a dramatic overhaul, but it implied that the overhaul required a new administration—undoubtedly one appointed by a Democrat.[13]

Despite the findings, Day survived the hearings, remained superintendent for the duration of his term, and implemented some needed reforms. He authorized "general leases," which allowed firms to hire inmates for unspecified labor. Unlike previous leases, which worked on annual contracts, the general leases required a daily payment. In 1902, for instance, the Southwestern Railroad Company paid the state 75 cents per day per inmate. The different renumeration and the unspecified nature of the labor diminished the obvious competition with free labor, and firms proved more willing to partake, with the percentage of inmates employed in this manner hitting 60 percent by 1902.[14]

Day also oversaw efforts to improve the inmates' health. In 1900 he replaced all the old wooden bunks with new iron beds made in the penitentiary machine shop. Prisoner mattresses, made in the penitentiary mattress shop, similarly were improved with a change from stuffed straw to shuck and eventually to cotton. Both the new beds and mattresses proved more comfortable, safer, and healthier for the inmates. To further address the inmates' health concerns, the prison also added a physician to each off-site work farm. Not only was he there to address inmate health needs, he had supervisory responsibilities to ensure they were not overworked or treated cruelly, and to attest to the quality and quantity of their meals.[15]

Two even more important reforms followed. The first was the creation of a separate cellblock for tubercular inmates. Initially those inmates resided in their own unit but worked and exercised with the other inmates. Realizing this did not go far enough to protect the healthy prisoners, in 1903 penitentiary officials fully segregated the tubercular inmates from the rest of the penitentiary. They resided and worked in their own unit, ate in their own dining hall, and exercised alone. In keeping with the racial sensibilities of the era, the unit itself was further segregated by race. Although this separation proved beneficial for the healthy inmates, it was not so useful for the ill. The tubercular ward was on the penitentiary's fourth floor, and the difficulty ailing inmates had in ascending and descending the stairs meant many never left the ward to enjoy and benefit from the warm air and sunlight. Although a step forward, administrators clearly had more to do to assist these ailing inmates.[16]

The same year that segregation of the tubercular inmates began, so too did the separation of the "dangerous insane" inmates. In 1901, legislators ordered the creation of the State Hospital for the Dangerous Insane, placing it under the administration of the prison's board of directors. The General Assembly required the board to build the facility on prison grounds and to administer it under the direction of a trained medical doctor. The state supplied $5,000 a year plus $3,000 for construction costs. To fulfill the requirement with the funds available, Day decided against constructing a new edifice. Instead, he simply closed off a portion of the penitentiary's western cell house that traditionally held the dangerous insane. As with the tubercular unit, the dangerous insane unit was further segregated by race: the first floor was for African American inmates and housed the kitchen and dining room, the second floor was for administrative offices, the third floor was for white inmates, and the fourth floor was for female inmates with the races divided by a small partition.[17]

Unfortunately, almost immediately the unit proved inadequate. In 1905, physician James Rogers complained that while it was built to house fifty inmates, it already held fifty-four. Although Rogers applauded the fact that the block had been upgraded with new plumbing and heating, he worried about the impact overcrowding might have on the mentally ill. In 1909, he again raised concerns when he reported that the number of inmates had risen to sixty-one. He also asserted that the inmates really were not criminals, in that they were not aware enough to understand their actions. As a result, Rogers argued the facility either should be a standalone institution or it should be connected with other institutions for the insane throughout the state. Although not yet ready to create a statewide mental health facility, by 1911 legislators provided sufficient funding so the prison could expand the dangerous insane unit by fourteen rooms. As a result, the inmates were "much more comfortable."[18]

Despite the animosity he faced, Superintendent Day modernized the facility and slowly pushed it toward a more complete implementation of the reformatory model. Unfortunately, economics and Mother Nature conspired to undercut much of that progress. In 1901, Day closed the shirt factory due to a lack of demand. While it initially made prison uniforms and then expanded to make shirts for various clothiers, opposition from the state's powerful textile firms limited sales opportunities and eventually made the shop uneconomical. At virtually the same time the penitentiary faced a dramatic decline in the demand for bricks. After having provided bricks for any number of state buildings, construction projects dried up. With them went the demand. The result was the loss of two major sources of revenue and labor.[19]

Worse was to come. In May 1901, a flood destroyed the dike protecting the Caledonia prison farm in Halifax County and buried two hundred acres under three feet of sand. The flood also destroyed the corn, cotton, and peanut crops, costing the penitentiary most of its expected income from its largest farm. Inmates rebuilt the dike and added to its height, but in January 1902 another flood destroyed much of the new barrier. Although that second flood did not destroy any crops, the costs entailed in rebuilding the dike for a second time in eight months were substantial.[20]

There were other difficulties as well. In January 1901 a fire destroyed the cotton gin at the Caledonia prison farm. The fire resulted from a random metal wire that was swept into the gin with a bale of cotton. The wire sparked when it hit one of the gin blades, igniting the cotton. Inmates saw the fire and put it out, but at some point that night a lingering ember hidden in a dust heap reignited and destroyed the building, machinery, and cotton. Authorities deemed it an accident, and insurance money enabled prison officials to purchase a new gin and rebuild. Although spared the expense of having to pay for construction, the penitentiary lost the cotton destroyed in the fire as well as months of production during the rebuilding process. General leasing remained a cash cow, but the floods, fire, and other the financial mishaps ate into the prison's budget and stymied the penitentiary's economic growth.[21]

Administrators and inmates in Central Prison, along with the public, endured an era of great turmoil during the "Populist Moment." As "fusionists" and Democrats fought for control of the state, they employed slander, political patronage, racism, and violence, and the penitentiary found itself to be an unwitting weapon in that battle. While the consequences of that involvement initially were negative, in the form of an undermined administration and legislative investigations that sidetracked administrators from the real work of governing the prison, in the long run inmates benefitted thanks to a renewed focus on reform, which gave them a healthier environment and better treatment for the ailing and insane. The same results could be found in society at large, which endured political unrest but subsequently enjoyed a newfound political willingness to serve the masses. Even that service, however, had its downside, as North Carolina became a one-party state and institutionalized racism became the law of the land. In more ways than one, therefore, the prison continued to mirror developments in the outside world. In the years to come that mirror continued to reflect tumult, as the first decade of the twentieth century was only slightly less chaotic than the final decade of the nineteenth. While reforms continued apace, so too did the turmoil.[22]

9

THE ERA OF HIGH HOPES

Upon entering a new century, both legislators and Central Prison administrators hoped to build on the reformism of the Democratic return to power subsequent to the Populist-led political challenge. That hope was furthered by the then developing Progressive movement, which sought to create a state-sponsored social safety net. The results of those hopes and developments were mixed, but they demonstrate well the prison as a social microcosm. Indeed, historian Rebecca McLennan asserts that at the turn of the century, "despite the high walls of the prison and the persistence of laws mandating the separation of convicts from society, prisoners, guards, and administrators by no means confronted one another in a social or political vacuum. Just as in the past, when legal punishment had become embroiled in controversy in times of massive structural changes and deep social conflict . . . the prison was a critical referent, and even a lightning rod, in the much larger debates taking place around America over the meaning of a just economy and society, and the proper means and ends of government." Simply put, "the prison . . . became an intensely contested institution in the early Progressive Era." Evidence of that contest is clear thanks to questions about the chain gang, the development of new youth facilities, and the organization of a new death penalty model. As North Carolina made its first, tentative steps toward progressive reform, prison officials and inmates alike had high hopes.[1]

The era of high hopes began on April 3, 1901, with the expiration of Superintendent W. H. Day's term. Although Day oversaw some notable improvements, the General Assembly's Democratic majority found his political affiliation unacceptable, and they replaced him with J. S. Mann. Mann was a Democrat, but he looked at his job, not his party, as his first concern and he worked hard to improve the penitentiary. He did so by taking advantage of the emerging progressive sensibility to implement a series of reforms.

One of his first efforts centered on the state's chain gang system. In 1867, the North Carolina legislature had passed a law giving county judges the power to assign nonviolent offenders to chain gangs. The entire basis of the chain gang was economic: county jailers wanted to make inmates contribute to their own upkeep. They dug ditches, graded roads, and performed other menial forms of labor to benefit the county. Although historians Jesse Steiner and Roy Brown, who studied chain gangs in North Carolina, contend that the system actually cost counties money, local politicians believed the opposite, and gangs were a common sight throughout the late nineteenth and early twentieth centuries. Economics thus trumped rehabilitation, and the result was prisoner misery and abuse.[2]

Some of the abuse was a result of the system itself. To prevent escape, jailers chained inmates together with "thirteen-inch chains connecting steel bands locked around their ankles. The best a shackled prisoner could manage was a shuffling gait." Not only did chain gang crews have to manage the chains, they also worked hard. S. T. McGinnis was a white inmate who served time on a chain gang in Andrews. He worked in a quarry, swinging a fourteen-pound sledgehammer from 8 A.M. until 5 P.M., and he did so on a diet of pinto beans, corn bread, and, "if lucky, a cup of strong, black coffee." He served another stretch on a chain gang in Cary, during which "his crew, herded like chained cattle along the roadways, spent endless days, rain or shine, cutting rights-of-way, digging roadside ditches, unloading and spreading gravel from trucks, and sometimes they were taken into the gravel pits to load trucks under a blistering sun."[3]

Only the strong could survive such labor, and judges sentenced healthy inmates to the gangs and shipped off to the penitentiary those too old, ill, or infirm to work. The penitentiary thus filled with the physically unfit and those too violent or uncontrollable to work beyond the confines of its forbidding walls. This infuriated penitentiary officials, who found themselves swamped with inmates who offered nothing toward their upkeep, while the county jails seemed to be enjoying a financial boon.

As early as 1896, when the penitentiary was looking for some way to employ those inmates no longer working for the railroads, Superintendent Leazar had complained about the practice and accused county officials of conspiring to let the state bear the burden of those inmates who could not labor. Conspiracy or not, the system caused real problems for the state. Although counties completed local projects, large-scale state projects that might have benefitted from inmate labor remained incomplete. Although "occasionally the legislature directed the counties to make their prisoners available for large-scale construction projects," in most cases the state suffered while the counties gained.[4]

The problem only grew worse at the turn of the century with the birth of the "good roads movement." Launched in North Carolina in 1899 with the formation of the Buncombe County Good Roads Association, other counties followed suit and by 1902 the desire for good roads led to the formation of the North Carolina Good Roads Association. Although setting out to build more roads and improve those already in existence, the movement also sought to minimize costs. Realizing the labor involved was relatively menial and that inmates offered the opportunity for cost-effective labor, counties throughout the state tasked chain gangs to their road building programs. As a result, the flood of inmates to the chain gangs and away from the penitentiary continued. The consequence, Hilda Zimmerman notes, was that in the early days of the twentieth century Central Prison "emptied of its occupants, [and] declined in importance as a part of the state's penal system. More and more the central prison in Raleigh became a mere asylum for the 'prison paupers'—the decrepit and diseased criminal offenders."[5]

It was for this reason that Superintendent Mann made the chain gang among his top priorities upon taking control. In 1907, he first critiqued the system's shortcoming as a means of housing inmates. He argued that judges often sent criminals with long sentences to the county work crews. Those criminals were desperate, and thanks to the counties' inferior facilities they often managed to escape. Although he offered compliments to county guards, he noted the sites could not match the penitentiary in terms of security, and he chided state officials for putting financial considerations ahead of security.[6]

When that argument failed to resonate, Mann turned to the impact the chain gang had on inmates. Noting the average life span on a gang was five years, he contended that inmates with longer sentences faced the equivalent of a death sentence. Not only was that unfair, he argued it was unconstitutional as counties were usurping the judicial power to set punishments. In a related argument, he noted that each county had its own rules and standards. This was unfair as inmates incarcerated for the same crimes with the same sentences faced remarkably different circumstances. This too, he worried, was unconstitutional. To avoid lawsuits, he urged the state to place all inmates under penitentiary control to ensure constitutional and equitable treatment.[7]

In 1909, Superintendent Mann expanded on that argument by focusing on the dangerous or unhealthy circumstances in which inmates worked and lived. Those circumstances, he argued, threatened both the inmates' physical and psychological health. He claimed the conditions warped prisoners and caused good men who had erred to become pathological. Worse still was that minor criminals often ended up serving harsher sentences than violent felons: "The law evidently intends the punishment to fit the crime, and that persons convicted of felony and given long terms shall be sent to the State's Prison, while those convicted of less serious offenses, especially misdemeanors, shall be given shorter terms and lighter work upon the roads. And yet, under existing conditions, it is strangely true that harsher and more vigorous punishment is inflicted upon the petty offender than upon him who commits the more serious crime."[8]

Evidence of all of those concerns was plentiful, and inmates who served time on the chain gangs were more than happy to join Mann in his condemnation. Frank Watson, a white chain gang inmate, explained that one cause of the horrendous conditions was that jailers kept inmates shackled constantly—even at night, in bed. That made it difficult to change clothes, especially pants. If an inmate proved unable to remove his pants while enchained, he was stuck wearing them until "the pants rot off." He noted further that the sheer filth of the gangs, with little opportunity to clean up, made life unhygienic. Indeed, a 1923 study of North Carolina's chain gangs described how "food was regularly passed out an open unscreened window of the kitchen over a barrel of slop around which the flies were literally swarming." The same study noted that tubercular inmates lived alongside healthy inmates, that one inmate had "running syphilitic sores on his legs," that "the meat was lying on this block of wood exposed to flies and dust," and that the bedding, which consisted of "a bundle of filthy rags," had not been changed in a month.[9]

Civil rights icon Bayard Rustin did time on a chain gang in Roxboro in the 1940s, and even at that late date he found appalling conditions. He explained that there was little privacy because the "double-decker beds stood so close together that to pass between them one had to turn sideways." The lack of space was made worse by the fact that inmates remained locked in the dorm from 6:30 P.M. to 5:30 A.M. Worst of all, however, were the unsanitary conditions. Rustin complained that "roaches were everywhere," and he explained that inmates ate meals "without so much as a chance to wash their hands and face." George Smith, a white inmate who served time on a chain gang in Goldsboro, found similarly unsanitary conditions: "Everybody had to wash in the same bucket and same water, about seventy-five of us, on the road, white and black."[10]

What added to the misery was that many gangs were mobile, meaning their housing was temporary. The lucky ones enjoyed rickety wooden structures, but others had to make do with tents. The least fortunate lived in "cages on wheels." These contraptions looked like railroad cars and housed twelve to eighteen men. They contained beds stacked one above the other, often with as little as thirteen inches of separation, a stove for heat, and a simple slop bucket to collect waste. Made of steel, they offered little escape from the weather. Frank Watson noted that one winter he spent time in a mobile cart that got so cold "one boy's foot froze, so they had to amputate." Inmates additionally hated the cars because they often found themselves locked up on Sundays, holidays, and in bad weather. In the other settings, at least, inmates had some mobility and freedom when not employed. Administrators, however, preferred the mobile units because they were easy to move and offered more security.[11]

When the General Assembly proved intransigent and refused to address Mann's concerns despite all of the charges, allegations, and horror stories, he authored a series of suggestions calling for a radical overhaul of the entire penal system. He wrote, "Every person in North Carolina under conviction and serving a term of imprisonment . . . should be under the direct, immediate and exclusive care, management and control of the State." That meant the board of directors would take charge of everyone convicted of a crime. The directors then could move inmates and assign them as they saw fit, but with two provisions: First, Central Prison would house every felon, and felons and misdemeanants would never mix. Second, Mann suggested that if a county wanted inmate labor it should purchase that labor at the cost of $1.00 per day per inmate. The county had to provide the living quarters, transportation costs, drinking water, and firewood, but the state would cover all additional costs and would maintain control of the inmates during their employment.[12]

Those reforms, he contended, addressed all the problems he saw with the system: they ensured the state labor, or at least income from inmate labor; they allowed counties access to inmate workers; they ensured uniform inmate treatment; they protected the inmates' health; and they ensured the proper execution of court-determined punishments. Although the main issue clearly was money, and the reforms did nothing to address concerns about sanitation, Mann did his best to bury those oversights.

Legislators fended off Mann's demands for years, and it was only in 1917 that the General Assembly required the state to send all convicts with terms of five or more years to the state penitentiary. That pacified officials somewhat, since it ensured for them "at least a share of able-bodied convicts theretofore retained by county courts to work county roads." Although Mann was not around to witness this concession, his years-long effort against county-based chain gangs was a notable campaign that served notice that he was serious about advancing progressive reform through a more rational, humane, and cost-effective penal system. Equally notable, however, is that North Carolina's politicians did not enact the ideas Mann suggested.[13]

While the chain gang attracted much of Mann's focus, he also spent time thinking about the penological theory underlying the prison's basic administration. Those thoughts, though, were mixed. He embraced the general concept of reformation:

There are some reformatory features in prison life. Many of those who are sentenced here are the thriftless and idle whom want has led into crime. During the term of their imprisonment they are required to perform regular and effective work of some kind and are taught to do skillfully whatever work is required of them. They must also retire at night at a particular hour and arise in the morning with equal regularity, and take their meals punctually at the appointed time. These requirements must stimulate habits of industry and regularity of life and be very beneficial to that class of people who, as a rule, find their way into prison life.

At the same time, however, he questioned its effective practice: "[I] am doubtful if a term of imprisonment here can have any permanent reformatory effect upon the ordinary inmate. The association is vicious."[14]

Mann especially worried about the penitentiary's failure to reform youthful inmates. He thus took up the long-held argument that the state needed a separate facility for the young. While he supported the youth farm at Anson and concurred with former Superintendent Mewboorne's call to reform young inmates along moral and religious lines, he believed the state needed to do more. So too did others. Several women's organizations, including the King's Daughters and the North Carolina Federation of Women's Clubs, saw the placement of children in the state penitentiary as inhumane and a travesty of justice, and they made their own efforts to convince legislators to create reformatories for youthful offenders.

The groups understood well their state and did more than simply pressure politicians. They raised money to help defray the costs and announced that they wanted to name a reformatory after Confederate general Stonewall Jackson.

With the promise of outside financial help and the prospect of remembering Jackson, the push for a youth reformatory succeeded. On March 2, 1907, the legislature authorized construction of the Stonewall Jackson Youth Development Center.

The General Assembly only provided $10,000, but thanks to money raised by groups like the King's Daughters there were sufficient funds to purchase 288 acres just north of Charlotte. Construction on two dormitory buildings took slightly less than two years, and the center opened on January 12, 1909. It housed white, youthful offenders accused of minor crimes. They were required to take academic classes, work, learn a trade, and generally prepare to reenter the world as productive members of society. To further that goal, each dorm had a house father and mother who oversaw the boys' moral, spiritual, and academic development. A farm, gymnasium, pool, bakery, and print shop filled out the campus. Many of the first attendees emerged reformed, and word of the center's success spread. Politicians realized the center's benefits and provided additional funds to expand it, while local and private donations rolled in. The two dormitories soon grew to seventeen, with approximately thirty boys per building, and at its peak the school housed five hundred individuals.[15]

Although reformers and supporters saw the center as a success, those who served time there disagreed. The aforementioned S. T. McGinnis, who at the age of twelve spent thirteen months at the facility for breaking, entering, and theft, explained, "the school was not a picnic. It was tough. But it reformed no one." Indeed, he later asserted that administrators "didn't really try to train us or teach us anything; their only thought was to beat the meanness out of us—and they were experts." McGinnis endured that meanness on at least one occasion: "The house father entered with a stout grapevine stick, flexible enough to work exactly as he wanted it to. He made S. T. lie on his stomach on his bed and grasp the bedstead with his hands. The house father pulled the long sleeping gown up to S. T.'s shoulders, exposing his naked body. Viciously, he lashed S. T.'s body with the stick from his ankles to his shoulders until his body was red." McGinnis's time in Jackson ultimately did little to uplift: "his vocabulary did not increase a great deal and neither did his knowledge of necessary educational subjects." What his time there did do was teach him the crafts of a criminal: "he learned how to pick locks, how to play cards, how to gamble in a dozen different ways. He learned how to lie in ways that would never have occurred to him; and he learned useful shortcuts to thievery." This was far from what the school's creators had intended.[16]

Despite that divergence, the facility's apparent success led to the construction of additional facilities. In 1917, the General Assembly authorized a reform school for white girls. Called the State Home and Industrial School, but better known as Samarcand Manor, the school opened in 1918 in Eagle Springs. It initially accepted females between the ages of five and thirty, but eventually it restricted residents to those between ten and sixteen. The home originally had room for 150 girls, but by the 1930s it housed nearly two hundred. The girls spent much of the day doing outdoor activities as a way of getting healthy, while teachers did their best to educate the young women and to "restore ladyhood to poor white girls."[17]

In 1925 the state afforded the same reformative opportunities to African American youths when it opened the Morrison Training School in Hoffman. The school operated along the same lines as the Jackson youth center, and offered classes in English, history, math, and science as well as vocational training. The school housed over two hundred African American boys under the age of sixteen, and served the state until the legislature closed it in 1977 and repurposed the facility as a prison. The Eastern Carolina Industrial Training School for Boys, which housed white youths under the age of twenty in Rocky Mount, and the North Carolina Industrial Home for Colored Girls, which housed African American girls in Efland, also opened in 1925.[18]

The era's reformism carried on in two additional developments. The first had its origins when Joseph John Laughinghouse took over as superintendent on April 7, 1909. In January 1910 he issued new regulations for the guards. The penitentiary had purchased new Remington semi-automatic rifles and shotguns, and Laughinghouse required each guard to do target practice with the weapons. With the guards now better armed and trained, Laughinghouse announced that he would fire any guard who allowed a prisoner to escape "without being able to stop him with a fair chance to shoot." The result was that in 1910 only twelve inmates escaped (the lowest number to that point in the prison's history). Guards shot and killed seven others during escape attempts.[19]

An even bigger reform came when the state took from the counties control of capital punishment. There were two reasons for this change. First, in 1868 legislators had banned public executions. Most county sheriffs ignored the law, however, bending instead to the will of local businessmen who hated the thought of passing up a day of public spectacle and the money that went with it. The second was the desire for a more humane form of execution than hanging, which often failed to break the victim's neck and left the individual to strangle. Indeed, historian Seth Kotch contends that the state's politicians viewed hanging as "fundamentally antimodern," and sought out a "painless method of execution" that would "burnish the reputation of the state." With the advent of the electric chair in 1888, that new method seemed apparent. The cost, however, was prohibitive at the county level. Thus determined to end the spectacle of public executions, to offer some level of humanity to those facing death, to accomplish both feats in an economically viable manner, and to demonstrate the state's progressivism, in 1909 the General Assembly passed legislation that made Central Prison the site of all future executions and authorized the installation of an electric chair within its confines.[20]

Legislators contracted with Edwin F. Davis for the construction and installation of the chair. Davis agreed to a fee of $1,500, while the state agreed to prepare the death chamber and other necessary facilities. Davis faced numerous technical failures and delays, and he missed the contracted September 1909 delivery date. The chair finally arrived in December, but the transformer needed to supply electricity remained incomplete. When the transformer arrived, it broke down during testing and Davis spent another two months correcting the problems and finishing the installation process.[21]

The delays were notable as they forced Governor William Kitchin to stay the execution of Walter Morrison, a thirty-seven-year-old African American laborer who was to be the chair's first victim. A judge had sentenced Morrison to death for rape and the attempted murder of police officers, and his original execution date was September 10, 1909. The installation delays forced several stays, but on March 18, 1910, authorities strapped Morrison into the electric chair. Jailers placed one electrode on his head and then affixed another to his leg to complete the circuit. Warden Thomas P. Sale then flipped a switch and eighteen hundred volts of electricity roared through Morrison's body. When doctors examined Morrison after the first jolt, they found him still alive; it required three additional shocks, and fully seven minutes, before they pronounced him dead. Despite those facts, legislators and prison officials deemed the execution a success, and North Carolina became just the sixth state to employ this new technology.[22]

During the first decade of the twentieth century, the chain gang, juvenile justice centers, and death penalty reforms emerged as major penal innovations. Those innovations altered fundamental elements of the prison system and affected inmates throughout. More notably, the reforms demonstrate the questionable nature of North Carolina's progressivism, as the chain gang engendered exploitation and brutality and the electric chair raised fundamental debates about humane punishments. Even the seemingly altruistic move to incorporate new juvenile justice facilities further cemented the state's racial segregation policies, mitigating somewhat its progressive nature. As the progressive ethos spread throughout the public and political realms, prison administrators and inmates alike enjoyed the benefits and bore the burdens. Those varied consequences continued in the ensuing decade as progressivism carried forth and began to affect inmates on a broader and more intimate level.

10

"AN ALMOST PERFECT LAW"

During the second decade of the twentieth century, North Carolina's prison system continued to undergo substantive reforms while suffering from various crises and concerns. Under the guidance of Joseph Laughinghouse and J. R. Collie, penitentiary administrators pleaded with the state legislature for additional funding, infrastructure improvements, and a more modern penal methodology. Confronted by racial violence, a scathing critique of the prison system, and the reform momentum built up over the previous years, the General Assembly came through and created a piece of legislation that seemed to give penitentiary administrators and, more notably, inmates virtually everything they wanted. Thanks to the Democratic Party's continued appreciation that it needed to serve its constituents, the desire on the part of politicians and the public to maintain at least the facade of progressivism, and a period of relative economic prosperity brought about by the continued success of the state's industrial base, prisoners and prison administrators enjoyed several more years of progressive reform.

Superintendent Laughinghouse implemented a number of improvements during the century's first decade, and he was determined to continue modernizing the prison system into the second. In 1910, he oversaw significant renovations to Central Prison's infrastructure. He closed one vehicle entrance through the exterior wall, painted the main administration building, cellblocks, hospital, laundry, and women's ward, opened new dining facilities, and installed new beds and washtubs throughout the institution. He also purchased a new organ and electric lighting for the chapel, and had the room reorganized with sections segregated by race and gender; the later change allowed for fewer services while ensuring everyone who wanted to attend could do so. Laughinghouse next replaced the wooden cell doors in the women's ward with iron ones, purchased new porcelain dishes to replace the tin-ware in the dining hall, and improved the library by increasing the book selection and implementing a segregated schedule by which white and African American inmates used it on alternating weeknights and Sundays. The library further benefitted from a 1911 decision to sell prison postcards, the proceeds of which went to purchase books. While an impressive list, even bigger reforms were yet to come.[1]

In 1913, Superintendent Laughinghouse proposed several changes in the treatment and handling of inmates. First, he called for North Carolina to join the growing number of states employing a parole system. Developed in Australia by Captain Alexander Maconochie in the 1840s, expanded on in Ireland by Sir Walter Crofton in the 1850s, and introduced to the United States in the 1870s by Zebulon Brockway, the basic concept was to induce inmates to obey the rules by rewarding good behavior with an early release. Not only did the system create inmates who were more compliant, it theoretically reformed them by teaching the benefits of obedience and it saved the state money, as the cost of parole supervision was significantly lower than the cost of incarceration. By 1901, twenty states had adopted the parole model, and Laughinghouse wanted North Carolina to join that number. Warden Thomas P. Sale concurred, arguing that prison officials should help inmates learn to do "right because it is right," not because they were afraid of punishment. The parole system, he further noted, required the inmate to earn early release by good behavior, but also required him to maintain that behavior once free. The system thus offered inmates benefits and lessons while ensuring the public some level of protection.[2]

Laughinghouse and Sale also called for a revision of the indeterminate sentencing procedure by which "the prisoner himself fixes the maximum [term] according to the progress he is able to make in morals and industry." Specifically, the two administrators wanted inmates to earn a set number of days off their term for good behavior. In this way, inmates had tangible proof of the benefits of proper conduct. Prison officials had been calling for such a system for decades, yet into the 1910s the governor alone had the right to commute a prisoner's sentence. The problem with gubernatorial commutations was that there was no standard and no way for an inmate to see himself progress toward possible freedom. Indeed, one inmate later describe his shock at being set free:

"Come on," the guard grinned. "You've been paroled, man." "Wait a minute," S. T. said. "Somebody's got something messed up here. My

mama don't have no money. She can't hire a lawyer. There's nobody working to get me out. You'd better check and make sure you've got the right
man." The guard read off the number. "Is that your number?" "Yes, that's
mine." "That's the number on this piece of paper." There in the middle of
a dusty road, the guard handled S. T. his parole. It was signed by . . . the
governor of North Carolina. Despite that, the inmate remained incredulous: "I don't understand this," S. T. said, "I've served less than three
years [of a five-year sentence], and I don't know of anyone who has been
working to get me out. I hope it isn't all a bad mistake."

It was not a mistake, but such uncertainty undermined commutation's positive
possibilities.[3]

As a final reform, Laughinghouse and Sale wanted to move away from dress-
ing inmates in striped outfits, and instead to dress them in "a more agreeable
uniform." They suggested stripes could remain as a form of punishment, but
argued that allowing inmates to wear less suggestive attire would help them
maintain their humanity and better prepare them for a return to society.[4]

The administrators appreciated the benefits these "carrots" afforded, but
understood the need for "sticks." They thus called for a new law to extend the
time an inmate served if he attempted to escape. As the system currently stood,
inmates lost any benefit toward commutation if they escaped or attempted to
do so. Laughinghouse and Sale suggested adding one to five years to an inmate's
sentence. Doing so, they contended, would reduce the incentive to flee.[5]

While the legislature contemplated those many suggestions, a 1916 investigation of conditions at the penitentiary and associated farms and work sites
unearthed some disturbing findings. The report found that the dormitories at the
Caledonia prison farm lacked proper sanitation, with men having to share beds
and sheets, and recorded the resultant frequency of communicable diseases.
Central Prison was little better. Inmates received cold food, often had to eat
without washing their hands, and did not always receive their required two baths
per week. As a result, disease was rampant. The report further noted that guards
at Central Prison raped some of the female prisoners, that there was little recreation, entertainment, or reading material, that whipping was the main means
of discipline, and that administrators provided few opportunities for inmates to
improve their moral or mental capacities. In other words, despite the high praise
Laughinghouse, Sale, and prison authorities heaped on themselves, this investigation found disturbing allegations of misconduct and lackluster oversight.[6]

Rather than simply lament the poor state of the penal system, legislators responded to the report vigorously. In keeping with the era's progressive sensibilities, in 1917 the General Assembly passed a law designed to modernize the penitentiary. Called *An Act to Regulate the Treatment, Handling, and Work of Prisoners*, the wide-ranging legislation capped nearly a decade's worth of reform and brought to fruition many of the most urgent proposals the superintendents and wardens had long been making.

In an effort to reduce escapes from county jails and work crews, the act required every convict sentenced to a term of five years or more to serve their time in Central Prison. Those inmates sent to the penitentiary had to work ten hours a day except for Sundays and holidays. That work was limited, however, as the law prohibited the state from leasing inmates to private industries and forbid the production of goods for sale on the open market, with the exception of farm goods. Instead, the act authorized the use of inmates on roadwork, where the state could employ inmates on grading, maintenance, and construction. It also authorized the use of inmate labor on county roads as long as the county paid the state $1.00 per day per inmate. In other words, this act finally addressed the long-standing concerns about varied inmate treatment, the counties' abuse of their inmates, and the lack of viable laborers among those housed in the penitentiary. Now the state controlled all long-term convicts, leased them out, and enjoyed the chain gang's alleged financial benefits. Former Superintendent J. S. Mann, who had proposed all those reforms a decade earlier, would have been pleased.[7]

While notable, especially for the potential financial benefits, the act also addressed more substantive reforms. Again following Mann's suggestion, the act required the penitentiary to place every inmate into one of three grades, and implemented probationary concepts in conjunction with those grades. "A Grade," or honor inmates, included prisoners who "observe the rules and regulations and work diligently, and are likely to maintain themselves by honest industry after their discharge." Those inmates lived in their own camps or cellblocks, where they received "not very conspicuous uniforms" and were neither guarded nor chained while at work. They received eight days off their maximum sentence for every month of good behavior and earned 10 cents per day for their labor.[8]

"B Grade" inmates included "those prisoners who have not as yet given evidence that they can be trusted, but are competent to work and are reasonably obedient to the rules and regulations of the institution." Those inmates wore "conspicuous uniforms" and worked under guard but not in chains. The superintendent had the discretion to decide whether or not inmates working on farms or work sites were chained in bed at night. The inmates received six days off their maximum sentence for every month of good behavior and earned 5 cents per day.[9]

"C Grade" inmates included "prisoners who have demonstrated that they are incorrigible, have no respect for the rules and regulations, and seriously interfere with the discipline and the effectiveness of the labor of the other prisoners." Those inmates wore conspicuously striped uniforms, worked under guard, were chained while at work and in bed at night, and were not allowed to mix with inmates of other grades. The act also suggested, but did not require, that they work only in stockaded areas. The inmates received no time off their sentence for good behavior and earned only 2 cents per day.[10]

The act continued by instituting additional punishments for rule breakers. Any inmate guilty of a first offense of "misconduct or infringement of the rules and regulations" lost 10 percent of the time off he had accumulated and 10 percent of the money earned. Subsequent violations cost him all of his time and money, and made him subject to a lower grade. If an inmate subsequently regained his former grade, the board of directors could return any portion of his time and money it saw fit. The act further stated that an A or B Grade prisoner who escaped or attempted to escape earned C Grade status and lost permanently all his time and money. Whipping remained a permitted form of punishment for C Grade inmates only, but the punishment had to occur at least twenty-four hours after the event that brought it about, and it had to take place in the presence of a doctor or a priest.[11]

The new act was not only about punishing and controlling inmates, however, as it also set new rules for their benefit. The act required the prison to provide inmates with games, lectures, and "other forms of amusement." Additionally, administrators were to provide educational opportunities and allow educated inmates to teach other prisoners. Inmates also gained the right to write letters, although their grade dictated the frequency. Most notably, the act granted inmates the long-sought parole for first-time offenders. The act authorized judges to sentence inmates to a minimum and a maximum term, and it created a parole board to advise the governor, who maintained sole power to grant parole. An inmate became eligible for parole once he had achieved the minimum term, and if he failed to make parole the board would reconsider him every six months.[12]

Superintendent J. R. Collie, who took over from Laughinghouse in December 1917, called the legislation "an almost perfect law," and the reforms put the state in line with its contemporaries, who had adopted the Elmira model of prisoner management. Even the inmates agreed, as they reported the new policies "helped to improve the morale of the men."[13]

While the reforms improved the administrator's ability to govern the penitentiary and made the inmates' lives a bit easier, they were expensive to implement. This expense was important as the law banned convict leasing and cut off a major source of income. Appreciating the General Assembly's legacy of financial parsimony, Superintendent Collie set about looking for new revenue. In 1919, he decided to sell the Caledonia prison farm. The plan was to subdivide the land into fifty-three plots with the goal of raising $500,000. Well aware of the land's propensity to flood, few investors expressed much interest. As the land lay fallow, Collie had second thoughts about giving it up. Although the penitentiary needed money to cover costs and make up for lost revenue, many inmates still resided on the farms. Penitentiary records indicate that of the 900 inmates assigned to Central Prison in 1916, only 138 actually lived there; the others served their time on the farms. The numbers were similar in subsequent years, with only 130 of 760 inmates serving time in Central Prison in 1918 and 136 of 753 in 1920. Collie realized that losing the Caledonia prison farm would swell Central Prison's population, moving inmates to a facility that gave them few opportunities to labor.[14]

As Collie began to rethink the sale, he also realized that selling the land offered a one-time-only cash infusion. While it might alleviate the immediate financial concerns, it did nothing to address longer-term worries, nor did it do anything to address the loss of labor resultant from the 1917 act. Holding on to the land and continuing its cultivation, regardless of the flood danger, offered both long-term economic returns as well as continued inmate labor. Fortunate not to have sold much of the land, Collie called off the sale, the prison retained the five thousand unsold acres, and in subsequent years it repurchased the majority of the plots that had been sold.[15]

In completing this turnabout, the board of directors next spent $282,000 purchasing a 2,860-acre plot that formerly was part of Camp Polk, one of three World War I military training centers set up in North Carolina. The prison populated the new facility, called the Cary prison farm, on March 1, 1920, and inmates worked to turn the land and buildings into profitable and livable entities. Collie warned legislators that it might take some time to make the farm cost-effective, but he assured them it would become so. He also noted that much of the Caledonia prison farm had become overgrown during its time on the market, so that land too would need time for reclamation. With neither farm earning money, the question for administrators was where to put the inmates to profitable work.[16]

Fortunately for penitentiary officials, in 1919 the General Assembly amended the 1917 act and reauthorized inmate leasing. This was a major gain, and inmates returned to several projects they had abandoned in 1917. For instance, in 1916 the Hardaway Company employed 220 inmates on the construction of a dam across the Yadkin River. The company paid an average of $1.62 per day per inmate, but at one point it was so desperate for workers that it offered $2.00 per day. Despite an average convict maintenance cost of 50 cents per day, the offer was so good that the state withdrew inmates from other projects and employed them on the dam. The loss of such income due to the 1917 act helps explain the decision to sell the Caledonia prison farm. With the ban on leasing rescinded, inmates returned to the Yadkin River project, with the Hardaway Company paying the state $2.08 per prisoner per day.[17]

Unfortunately for the penitentiary, as the General Assembly giveth, so it can taketh away. When the state began its good roads project at the turn of the century, the focus was on making the roads passable for horses and carriages. The birth of the automobile, however, made the need for better roads even more imperative. By 1921, North Carolina had more than 150,000 registered vehicles, and the demand for good roads led the state to claim an ever-increasing number of inmate laborers. The problem was that inmates working on state roads labored without earning the penitentiary any compensation, as the state, unlike the counties, did not reimburse the prison. With inmates on other sites averaging a return of $1.75 per day, and those employed by the counties earning $1.00 per day, Collie calculated that the penitentiary lost $95,288.15 per year in potential earnings.[18]

The lost revenue certainly worried the superintendent, but he was even more concerned when he realized that his predecessors had included as real income the money state-employed inmates would have made had outside firms employed them. The result was an impressive but false financial balance sheet. Unwilling to partake in such fiscal manipulations, yet worried about appearing to have overseen a dramatic decline in the penitentiary's financial standing, Collie requested official recognition of the labor inmates provided the state. Legislators ignored his concerns, leaving the superintendent unclear of his position.[19]

Collie was further distressed when, on March 15, 1920, the main penitentiary administration building caught fire. Although only partially destroyed,
the building was uninsured and Collie had to cover the $17,000 cost to rebuild
it out of the prison's general operating budget. To add to his misery, not long
after the fire the penitentiary's physician demanded a new operating room.
He complained that the penitentiary lacked an "antiseptic" environment, and
carped that under such conditions "the risk of operations . . . would be so grave
that no conscientious surgeon could justly be expected to assume it." After issuing what was basically an ultimatum, he softened his tone a bit by noting that
several physically incapacitated inmates could be made productive with the
help of surgery. Aware of to whom he was writing, the doctor made clear that
despite the cost, which he pegged at $2,000, the investment would save money
by creating a larger pool of inmates who were physically able to work and earn
the penitentiary money.[20]

Nothing came of the doctor's request, and Collie, probably happily, stepped
aside as superintendent on May 10, 1921. While fiscal concerns marked the
end of Collie's term, the preceding decade witnessed some impressive financial
and organizational reforms that modernized the prison and improved the lives
of inmates and guards. The era's progressive sensibility, the determination of
politicians to uphold that sensibility, and their continued willingness to intervene directly in prison affairs created a circumstance by which requests made
by prison administrators resulted in real reform. As North Carolina entered
the roaring 1920s, the reflection of the state in the prison was thus as clear as
ever. The question, however, was whether or not the benefits of that reflection
could be sustained. The man confronted with that question was George Pou,
and during his lengthy tenure he did everything in his power to ensure that the
answer was affirmative.

11

GEORGE POU

During the 1920s, North Carolina's prison system benefitted from the dynamic leadership of George Pou, who became superintendent on May 10, 1921. The son of Edward Pou, a longtime congressman from Smithfield, he took office at the tender age of twenty-six. Although young, Pou brought a personality of insistence and determination to the office, as well as an awareness of his predecessors' reformism. Building on their progressive efforts, Pou prodded politicians to implement far-reaching changes to the manner in which the prison system functioned and the policies by which officials treated inmates. Taking advantage of societal changes that created an inmate population boom, political circumstances that encouraged intervention in prison affairs, and the ongoing desire of state leaders to appear progressive, Pou enacted reforms that continued to make life easier for administrators and better for inmates.

The system Pou inherited was in the midst of a dramatic expansion. In the years following World War I the number of inmates serving time in the penitentiary or at one of the eleven road camps or two farms soared: from 753 in 1920 to 2,317 in 1930. Pou thus faced a population that more than tripled in a decade. While the penological consequences of that influx might have overwhelmed lesser administrators, Pou saw an opportunity for reform.[1]

Numbers, however, were only part of the reason for Pou's efforts. He also wanted to minimize the system's infamous brutality. Among those who had exposed this brutality was African American inmate J. J. Lindsay, who penned a short book entitled *Inside the Prison, or, In Chains and Stripes*. In it he described his time at Central Prison as a "living death," and complained of a monotonous diet, a lack of underclothes, and the complete absence of religious services. He described working in freezing cold conditions that left his feet so frostbitten he lost his toenails, of being whipped when a supervisor thought he was not working hard enough, and of being bunked in dorms so overcrowded that inmates "could hardly turn over for lack of room." He further asserted that guards "paid more attention to the condition of the mules" than to the inmates, and concluded that though "the prison is in North Carolina . . . it makes one think he is in some cruel Russian prison."[2]

A subsequent study of the same era affirms Lindsay's assessment. Author Alfred Cooke argued that "rehabilitation did not appear to be the function of the State's Prison," and if practiced it was done so "through the application of a perforated leather strap applied to the naked back." He concluded, "Among the prisoners the law of the jungle evidently prevailed. A prisoner had to be tough to survive." Whatever progress the system had made during the previous two decades seemed to have done little to change the brutal reality of life in Central Prison.[3]

Pou refused to condone such jungle law, but initiated his reformism rather modestly by joining the long list of administrators who called for the establishment of on-site industries. He suggested inmates could produce goods for sale to other state agencies in a manner that would save the state money, earn the prison income, and provide inmates a sense of purpose. He even got specific and suggested that prisoners could make desks and chairs for the state's schools.

Although politicians met that modest suggestion with reluctance, Pou continued to propose new policies. Arguing that most inmates serving time in the dangerous insane unit were unaware they had committed crimes and did not deserve to be in prison, he wanted to close the unit and transfer the inmates to traditional hospitals for the insane. He argued similarly to end the tubercular ward and instead to house inmates in sanatoriums. Penitentiary physician Dr. J. H. Norman joined Pou in this call. He reiterated earlier complaints that segregating tubercular patients on the fourth floor meant few got outside to enjoy the fresh air, and he warned of the incomplete segregation of infected inmates. The latter issue occurred despite the guards' best efforts, and it resulted in an ever-growing number of infected prisoners. Only removing them to a hospital of their own would solve the problems.[4]

Much to Pou's delight, in 1923 the General Assembly passed laws addressing both concerns. Legislators first agreed to establish an inmate division at the North Carolina State Sanatorium. Located in present-day McCain, the sanatorium opened in 1908 and in 1925 added an inmate division to house all the state's ailing prisoners. To ensure no new tubercular cases entered the prison, the General Assembly further required the testing of all incoming inmates, with those found ill sent to the new institution.

The legislature also established a white criminal insane ward at the State Insane Hospital at Raleigh and an African American criminal insane ward at the State Insane Hospital at Goldsboro. Additionally, legislators opened the checkbook and authorized $40,000 to build new quarters at the Cary prison farm, $50,000 for new quarters at Caledonia prison farm, an additional $58,000 to rehabilitate the farmland at Caledonia, and $25,000 for infrastructure improvements at Central Prison. Thanks to the money for Central Prison, Pou improved the sidewalks, driveways, and drainage, installed new water mains that connected the prison to the city's water and sewage system, placed fire hoses throughout the prison, and updated the heating and lighting systems. The inmates at both farms, meanwhile, benefitted from new concrete dormitories, while Caledonia prison farm officials used the funds to clear over a thousand acres and to repair nearly one hundred bridges, more than fifty miles of roads, and several dikes.[5]

The money for those projects came from a dramatic increase in taxes and government spending under Governor Cameron Morrison. In 1921, he convinced the General Assembly to fund a six-year, $20 million program designed to expand, improve, and more fully fund the state's "asylums, reformatories, sanatoriums, and schools for the deaf and blind." Although the expenditures still left North Carolina third from the bottom in terms of government spending, this newfound largess benefitted a wide swath of state agencies, including the penitentiary. Pou took Morrison's willingness to spend as a sign he should offer more advice and suggestions—and he had plenty.[6]

In 1920, Governor Thomas Bickett had asked Superintendent Collie to determine whether or not to ban corporal punishment. Collie did not respond to the governor's query, but Pou did. He determined no alternative form of punishment existed and supported whipping as a punishment for "C Grade" inmates who violated rules. Indeed, when a bill to ban whipping arose in the General Assembly, Pou opposed it. The bill failed, but Pou then had a change of heart. In 1922, he banned corporal punishment at the Cary prison farm and instead had disruptive inmates punished with solitary confinement on a diet of bread and water. The experiment worked, as inmate behavior improved. Pou then banned flogging at most other camps, and allowed it at the remainder only in extreme situations. In 1926 Pou informed legislators that no inmate had been flogged in four years, yet discipline remained good.[7]

Although still not ready to call for a formal legislative ban on corporal punishment, Pou did call for another major change. In 1917 the General Assembly authorized judges to assign indeterminate sentences, but those already in prison suffered under determinate sentences. Pou urged making all determinate sentences indeterminate. As had others before, he contended that so doing provided "the prisoner hope for reward for good behavior," taught "the prisoner self-restraint," and created "in the prisoner a desire to do right." On June 29, 1923, Governor Morrison acceded to Pou's request and placed all inmates then on a determinate sentence on an indeterminate sentence. The only exceptions were those serving life terms.[8]

Pleased that politicians twice had listened to his suggestions, in 1924 Pou continued his offensive with a revision of the 1917 classification system that divided inmates into A, B, and C grades. He proposed a detailed list of rights for each inmate grade as well as a designated list of punishments, believing that a clear enunciation of both the requisite "carrots" and "sticks" would induce good behavior. The incentives included time on the yard, the right to attend entertainment events, mail privileges, visitation rights, access to newspapers, and expanded personal possessions. As inmates moved up the grades, they enjoyed access to more of those opportunities. The punishments, meanwhile, included reprimand, loss of privileges, reduction in grade, double shackles, solitary confinement, and a restricted diet, and increased as inmates descended the grades.[9]

Undaunted when the General Assembly balked, Pou offered several additional recommendations. Among them was a call to create a state bureau of identification housed in Central Prison. He wanted the bureau to maintain the records of all inmates passing through any element of the state's penal system, with a special focus on fingerprinting. At the time the state employed the Bertillon record, which "consisted of a series of eleven standardized measurements of the convict's body, a photographic record of the prisoner's distinguishing characteristics, and standardized notes written on a simple card." Pou noted that fingerprinting was a simpler, less expensive, and more useful practice that "would within a few years prove of untold benefit to the various solicitors in the State." This time Pou's persistence paid off. In 1925, the General Assembly created the State Bureau of Identification and tasked the agency with recording and collecting all inmate data.[10]

Later that year, Governor Angus McLean, known as the "businessman's governor" for his efforts to make the state government function more efficiently, further rewarded Pou's persistence when he offered a "Special Message" to the General Assembly. Much of that message focused on the penitentiary. He began by noting that from November 30, 1921, through December 31, 1924, the various prison enterprises earned $1.164 million dollars. Despite that revenue, and in large part thanks to the presence of three hundred inmates who were unable to labor, the prison ended up losing $186,000. Added to that were $112,000 in unexpected expenditures, leaving the prison with a three-year deficit of $298,000. What made the financial concerns even worse was the diminishing use of inmates on road crews, as employers demonstrated a growing preference for free laborers, whom they found performed better work with fewer disciplinary issues. McLean thus concluded, "unless new policies are adopted and new methods employed the Prison will become more and more of a serious burden to the taxpayers of the State."[11]

Among the policies McLean proposed to prevent that development was making the prison system "a regular department of the State government" rather than a "separate corporation." This would allow the General Assembly to fund the prison in the same manner as all other state agencies. He also proposed a "state-use" policy by which prison laborers produced goods required by state agencies. To facilitate the production of those goods, he further proposed $245,000 in improvements to Central Prison as well as additional funds to purchase machinery. Finally, he called to transfer the prison's $298,000 debt to the state treasury's general fund, absolving the prison of the obligation. All four reforms fit nicely with the governor's drive for efficiency; they also fit well with Pou's previous demands.[12]

McLean's proposals paid quick dividends, as later that year the General Assembly fulfilled one of his requests by making the penitentiary a regular division of the state government. Legislators created the State Prison Department and put funding for the new department into the state budget. While this meant all the money the prison earned went to the state, it also meant all the money the prison needed came from the state; the prison no longer needed to fund its existence.[13]

Pleased to be free from concerns about the prison's financial status, and determined to continue its forward momentum, in 1926 Pou implemented new admittance policies. According to physician Dr. J. H. Norman, new arrivals received a bath, a haircut, and a shave, and donned their prison garb. Guards then took photographs, fingerprinted the inmates, noted their physical characteristics, gathered their personal histories, and lectured them on the rules.

Physicians then examined them for mental and physical ailments, vaccinated them for smallpox and typhoid, and did a blood test for syphilis. Those testing positive or suffering from any medical malady received treatment before entering the main unit. According to Deputy Warden H. H. Honeycutt, the policies benefitted both the inmates and the administration. The vaccinations and blood test made the prison a healthier place for inmates and guards, while the inmates' physical and mental health records made it easier for guards to handle them. Finally, the fingerprints and photographs facilitated recapture should an inmate escape. Indeed, between 1926 and 1929 the state recaptured four hundred inmates; in nearly every case fingerprints played a role in the re-apprehension.[14]

The same year he implemented the new admittance policies, Pou also set about beautifying the prison grounds. He did this by removing the last vestiges of the temporary buildings and stockade. Many of the old structures served as storage buildings and barns for animals, but many more were decomposing, creating an unappealing atmosphere. Pou had inmates tear down the buildings, grade the land, and build a baseball diamond. The ballfield not only spruced up the grounds and gave prisoners a new recreation area, it gave them the opportunity to excel, as the prison baseball team became the first in the nation to play civilian teams beyond the penitentiary walls when it joined the Raleigh City Baseball League. Appreciating the benefits of such recreation, Pou expanded other entertainment opportunities. He authorized weekly boxing matches between inmates, showed films once a week, and sanctioned frequent concerts. The renovations and recreational opportunities also offered an added incentive for inmates to earn A Grade status so they could participate fully and enjoy the new amenities.[15]

The good news continued in 1926 when the General Assembly passed legislation allowing penitentiary officials to open additional on-site industrial plants. Pou took advantage of the law and opened six new industries. He started a culvert-making shop, which produced concrete culverts for local, county, and state services that needed drainage and piping. A new chair-making shop opened and proved especially useful in employing inmates who were otherwise unfit for labor, as they could do their jobs seated and with only minimal physical exertion. Pou also opened a print shop, which produced a wide array of printed material for the state; a hot house, which produced an abundance of flowers for local florists; a dairy to produce milk, butter, and cheese for inmate consumption; and, in 1930, a license plate manufacturing plant. He also reopened several previously shuttered industries. The tailoring shop and the mattress factory recommenced operation and produced goods for use in the penitentiary, on the farms, and at the work camps. The soap-making unit also reemerged and made all the cleaning products the prison system needed.[16]

The state benefitted financially from the new industries and the inmates appreciated the opportunities to labor at a variety of tasks; they did not, however, benefit monetarily. In 1925, North Carolina ended the policy of paying inmates for their labor and replaced payment with a plan by which the state might "pay such sums to prisoners at the expiration of their sentences as may in their judgment adequately aid such prisoners in securing employment and defraying their expenses to the place of such employment." The always fiscally conscious legislature thus allayed somewhat the costs of these reforms by taking money out of the inmates' hands.[17]

While the inmates lost financially, other elements of the prison system continued to gain. By 1926, the resurrection of the Caledonia prison farm was complete, with new concrete and steel buildings to house the inmates and guards. It also had a new flour mill and grain elevator, a sawmill, and a cotton gin, and it benefitted from modern lighting, electricity, and sanitation. Inmates completed all of those improvements, saving the state $100,000.[18]

While the renovations at Caledonia proved useful, the construction of new concrete and steel buildings was especially important as the type of inmate sent to the farm began to change. Although previously required to reside in the penitentiary, a state investigation found many murderers, rapists, and arsonists serving their time on the farm. The new buildings thus were necessary to better secure those inmates.[19]

Despite the renovations, and likely due to the type of inmates then residing, Caledonia faced some problems. In May 1927 and April 1928 the inmates rioted. They complained about poor food, abuse, long workdays, and the lack of educational and recreational opportunities. After the May riot, Governor McLean visited and assured inmates that if they had real concerns he would address them. He warned, however, that riot was not the proper method to bring about change. Even some prisoners were unhappy with the unrest. After the April riot, The Prison News, an inmate-run newspaper, criticized the outburst as the work of "the youth of today . . . [who] have little respect for the law and [are] senseless enough to rebel against reasonable punishment from the society which they have offended."[20]

Among the inmates who lived through the riots and called the renovated

Caledonia farm home was one of North Carolina's most famous prisoners: David Marshall "Carbine" Williams. Sentenced to thirty years for killing a police officer in 1921, Williams did a brief stint in Central Prison but spent most of his confinement on the Caledonia prison farm. During a stint in solitary confinement for rules violations, he had a vision:

> I could see the firing pin strike the cap of the cartridge, the explosion of the powder, the movement of the bullet through the barrel, and I began to examine the vast amount of energy that was being wasted, especially in automatic weapons as the bolt was blown back. I began to get the idea of the floating chamber, looking at it somewhat like putting your foot on a croquet ball and then driving another ball by hitting the one you had your foot on with the mallet. Also, I saw the gases burning and realized, some damned how, that this energy should be captured and used.

In other words, he saw a way to improve the semi-automatic gun.[21]

Williams explained his ideas about the floating chamber to Captain H. T. Poole, who allowed him to work on his ideas in the prison's blacksmith shop. Outraged when he learned that Poole allowed an inmate to work on weaponry, Pou demanded it stop. Poole was so impressed by Williams's ideas, however, that he promised, "If Marshall Williams tries to escape with the weapon that he's building, I will serve the balance of his time. I will assume full responsibility. I trust this man." Pou acceded to his request, and Williams returned that trust. By 1929 he had made six guns with the new mechanism, and gun manufacturers were anxious to get their hands on his invention. As a result, Pou, in consultation with the deceased officer's wife, urged Governor McLean to commute Williams's sentence. On September 29, 1929, McLean freed Williams, and he returned to his home in Godwin, North Carolina. He eventually earned fifty-two patents, worked for the War Department and several gun manufacturers, and saw his life depicted on the silver screen in the movie *Carbine Williams*, with Jimmy Stewart playing his part. Williams remained in Godwin for the rest of his life and died on January 8, 1975.[22]

While Williams became famous as a result of his technological skills, Pou deserves the real approbation. He was a man of vision who took chances, pressured his superiors, and changed long-accepted practices. He also bragged about his achievements. In 1928, he informed the General Assembly he had studied forty-one state prisons, and only seven, including North Carolina, operated in a self-sufficient manner. He noted even more proudly that North Carolina's fourteen prison camps, two farms, and main penitentiary were the second most financially successful institutions in the nation. Pou further lauded the success of minimizing corporal punishment by noting that fewer than 10 percent of inmates were in the C Grade (down from 50 percent in 1921) while 30 percent were in the A Grade. His decision to abandon formally the silent system, which never really worked in practice, also may help explain the improved numbers.

Pou continued to boast about his achievements when he noted the ongoing effort to prepare inmates for productive labor upon their release. In this case, he used Williams as an example of what a little trust and faith could accomplish. Certainly not every inmate had Williams's technical skills, but Pou explained that prison administrators provided inmates the opportunity to learn the vocational skills needed to earn an honest living. He further claimed that prison officials placed them in jobs for which they were best suited and trained them in skills for which they showed the most aptitude. As an additional part of the effort to find inmates the right type of labor, Pou added to his classification system a physical assessment: A inmates could perform any manual labor; B inmates could perform general farm labor and road work; C inmates could perform light duty; D inmates could perform practically no labor, and E inmates were "totally disabled."[23]

As Pou expressed it, "Every effort is made 'to fit a round peg in a round hole and a square peg in a square hole.'" He further asserted that the efforts showed real success:

Many prisoners who have come to the Prison without any trade whatso-ever have been released and immediately employed at good wages at the trade they have learned while in Prison. This work is deemed construc-tive and important, as the discharged prisoner with a trade stands a better chance to earn an honest living, thereby causing him to lay aside his life of crime, and in such instances such prisoners become an asset to the State rather than a continuing liability in the destruction of life and property, which would place the State to untold and continued expense in Court trials and in maintaining such prisoner in Prison.

Pou was proud of such achievements, and he wanted the world to know of his success.[24]

While he undoubtedly overstated both the opportunities inmates had and the successes they achieved, his claims struck a chord. Prison officials from other states lauded his efforts, and one wrote, "Pou is a live wire as a Superintendent of Prison. He is thought a great deal of by prison officials over the country and his policies are given much consideration even when they have not yet been put into effect." The state of Texas even sent a delegation to examine the prison as a model.[25]

Journalists also praised his agenda, with the *Asheville Times* asserting that Pou had created "Probably the most perfect criminal system in the United States, which means the world in this respect." The *Raleigh Times*, the *Rocky Mount Telegram*, and the *Newton News Enterprise* all praised Pou's effort to segregate young inmates, while other papers commended his financial management and his medical, organizational, and industrial reforms. Determined to announce the state's progressive achievements to the world, the press fawned over his leadership.[26]

Pou clearly achieved a great deal during his first decade as superintendent. Determined to implement actual progressive reforms rather than relying on the mere appearance of such, he pushed the General Assembly to enact any number of new policies. Prodded by an exploding inmate population and aided by activist governors, state legislators proved amenable. They funded the prison like never before, acceded to a series of new policies, and largely put aside their own egos to acknowledge Pou's expertise. The worry for Pou was whether those factors would continue. As the decade turned and the nation faced the onrushing Depression, he soon got his answer.

12

O. MAX GARDNER

As the 1930s wore on and the horrors of the Depression became evident, Superintendent George Pou found an ally in Governor O. Max Gardner. In many ways, in fact, Gardner overshadowed Pou's efforts to improve the prison. While running for office in 1928, he promised to reshape and modernize the state, and he publicly stated that "the State Prison system constituted a key battleground" in that effort. Arguing that "the object of our penal system is, in part, to bring about reformation," he set out to "reform prisoners by vocation and education rather than by punishment." To fulfill that goal, he commissioned a study by the North Carolina State Board of Charities and Public Welfare. The 1929 report recognized "several starts toward real prison reform" and acknowledged that "something had been accomplished" in that endeavor during Pou's tenure. Despite those accomplishments, the report concluded that "fundamentally the prison system remained unchanged." Pou was shocked by the report, as it called into question not only his achievements but the very myth he and others had created. In reality, however, Pou had nothing to worry about as the report provided Gardner the justification to intervene aggressively in prison affairs. That intervention was wide-ranging, addressed foundational issues of penal practice and theory, and ultimately benefitted both prison administrators and the inmates.[1]

Part of the governor's effort to modernize the state through penal reform focused on one of North Carolina's most infamous criminals: Otto Wood. Convicted of murder and sentenced to thirty years, he arrived in Central Prison in 1924. By 1928 he had escaped three times, leading Warden S. J. Busbee to place him in isolation, where he remained for two years.[2]

Despite Wood's obvious contempt for the law and his genius at escape, Governor Gardner saw something in him and during a visit to Central Prison in

1930 demanded a meeting. According to historian Trevor McKenzie, the Wood who emerged was "a gaunt, frail figure shriveled by two years of extreme isolation. . . . Wood's health declined steadily and left him with a hacking cough that made the politician fear it might soon kill the notorious prisoner." Affected by Wood's appearance and his own progressive sensibility, Gardner decided to use him as an "experiment in humanity." Specifically, Gardner envisioned Wood as a "figurehead" for his penal philosophy: if treating someone as incorrigible as Wood with humanity could turn him around, then anyone could be reformed. But the experiment was about more than just the penal system. As McKenzie writes, "the infamous convict encapsulated everything the governor wished to restructure within his state" and served as a perfect means of "cast[ing] a light on issues of education, poverty, and crime."[3]

Wood initially lived up to Gardner's hopes and seemed to confirm the possibilities of social reform. After regaining his health, he worked in various prison industries, taught other inmates, and eventually earned honor status. On July 10, 1930, however, Wood escaped Central Prison yet again and went on a five-month crime spree. On December 31, 1930, authorities caught up with him in Salisbury. A gun battle erupted when police attempted to pull over the stolen car he was driving, and Wood died in a hail of bullets. The escape, Wood's crime spree, and the violence that ended his life not only embarrassed Governor Gardner but potentially undermined his drive for reform.[4]

Fortunately for Pou and other reform-minded advocates, the governor proved undaunted. He remained committed to improving the penal system, and soon embarked on a plan to address the needs of female prisoners. By 1930, the women's ward in Central Prison housed seventy-seven inmates. A year later the number had exploded to 111, about two-thirds of whom were African American. The problem was that the separate building constructed for female prisoners was designed to hold only sixty-four. That meant prison officials had to double bunk the inmates, which created unhealthy conditions, escalated the potential for violence, and wreaked havoc on the guards' efforts to run the facility smoothly.[5]

Sadly, double bunking was but one of the problems with the women's ward. The building itself was one of the oldest on the prison grounds. According to historian Karin Zipf, the ward was a fire hazard that offered a "deplorable" and "dangerous" setting, with cells "crowded and in disrepair," little opportunity for rehabilitation, and "a marginal medical system." Female inmates suffered from "neglect, isolation, and endangerment," and while authorities tended to "excuse women from rules and assigned them to less physically demanding labor," the result was that they "had fewer opportunities for fresh air, had less surveillance and less protection, suffered from loneliness more often, and felt more stigmatized than men." To make matters even more degrading, guards in the ward were men, giving women "little privacy from the opposite sex" and creating the potential for "threats of forced prostitution and rape."[6]

Female inmates faced another sexual threat as well: sterilization. Zipf explains that prison physician Dr. J. H. Norman and prison surgeon Dr. Kemp Neal handled the health concerns of the female inmates. This included all manner of reproductive and gynecological issues, from births and abortions to sexually transmitted diseases. They also performed what seem to be unrequested sterilizations. Zipf notes at least four cases between 1930 and 1932 when the doctors, while operating on female inmates for various ailments, performed a "nonconsensual sterilization." Amid the era's eugenics craze, authorities feared women who committed crimes were likely to have children who did the same, and thus took as their right the power to prevent the creation of more criminals. Here, at the most intimate level, state officials intervened in the affairs of inmates and, in the process, reflected the state's values on the prison and the prisoners.[7]

While Pou did nothing to address the sterilization issue, by 1931 he demanded that Governor Gardner do something to improve the women's ward. He specifically urged the governor to construct a separate facility for women, located off-site from Central Prison. Nationally, the first separate facilities for women emerged in the late nineteenth century, and by the time Pou made his case sixteen separate female facilities were in operation. Pou hoped to join that list, and prodded Gardner to action.[8]

Gardner needed little urging, as an infamous group of inmates provided him all the impetus for reform he needed. The group consisted of twelve teenage white girls housed in Samarcand Manor who, in March 1931, set fires to protest the conditions of their confinement. Hoping the fires would improve conditions or get them expelled, and unaware that arson was a felony, the young women believed they were taking control of their lives. In fact, they lost control. The fires did more than $100,000 in damage, and the judge hearing their case sentenced the twelve to five years in Central Prison.[9]

Fearful the girls would resort to arson yet again, Pou housed them in the only section of the prison that was fireproofed: the isolation cells just above death row. What that meant, however, was that the "teenagers lived in proximity to the very worst adult male offenders." Not only that, they endured some of the harshest conditions in the prison. Their cells "had concrete floors, were inadequately ventilated, and were practically dark. Only a few slats in the solid wood doors allowed any light or air into the cell. The girls likely spent almost every moment in these cells without exercise or socialization." Appreciating that such treatment was inhumane, Pou eventually moved them to the women's ward. The problem was that the ward was not fireproof, and when the insurance company learned of the girls' presence it threatened to revoke the prison's policy. Fearful of losing coverage, and appreciating the inhumanity of keeping the young women in such brutal conditions, authorities released them in the summer of 1932 after they had served but one year.[10]

In part due to this incident, Gardner authorized construction of two new, separate female facilities. The most notable was the North Carolina Correctional Institution for Women (commonly called the Women's Prison), which opened in 1933 on the former site of a men's road camp just a few blocks east of Central Prison. The new prison was racially divided, with Dorm A for African Americans and Dorm B for whites. The dining room was "divided down the middle with one side for whites and the other for blacks," while the various jobs at which the inmates worked (sewing, cleaning, canning, gardening, and cooking) were segregated as well. Some women remained in Central Prison until the new facility was complete in 1935, and Central Prison administrators oversaw the institution until 1938, when it formally separated and acquired its own administrative organization. With that, North Carolina joined a minority of states with enough vision to house female inmates in their own facilities, a minority that included only two other southern states: Arkansas and Virginia.[11]

The stand-alone Women's Prison was not the only effort Gardner made in that realm. He also oversaw construction of a farm colony for women. The impetus for this reform came, in large part, from the efforts of Marie Long Land and Kate Burr Johnson, both of whom had served as president of the North Carolina Federation of Women's Clubs. In 1927 they began to demand the General Assembly do something to guide back to the proper path those women who had strayed. As Land expressed it, "Throughout the state there are girls who might be reclaimed, now held in idleness in jails, with no chance for physical, moral and spiritual rebirth that would make them changed citizens." Their suggestion for achieving that rebirth was a farm colony. Advocates envisioned "a campus of small, cottage-style buildings, which would allow a homelike atmosphere. . . .

The facility was to be built more like a school than a prison, with most of the inmates having their own rooms." It would house white misdemeanants, and "officials hoped to change women's lives before they had fallen so far as to be convicted of a felony."[12]

The General Assembly appropriated $60,000 for the farm, and construction began at a site five miles from Kinston. To isolate the farm and prevent men from trying to infiltrate the facility and further the women's fall, it was set apart by leaving the roads adjacent purposely rough. Completed under Gardner's watch, the colony, although scheduled to house upward of three hundred women, held but thirty-five in 1931. Attended by a staff of four, inmates were young and poor, most were illiterate, many had children, and 80 percent suffered from venereal disease. Residents served three-year terms—six months in the colony and two a half years on parole.[13]

During their six months at the facility, staff sought "to cure venereal diseases, teach basic literacy skills, provide industrial training, and work a personal reformation that would . . . keep the individual woman on a respectable path for the rest of her life." As a part of that reformation, the staff "worked to make inmates dutiful daughters, faithful wives and self-sacrificing mothers," with the goal of getting them to "internalize the controls on female behavior." That is, they were taught to "act like ladies." Beyond individual redemption, the staff also believed their efforts could elevate "whole families out of squalor and immorality and into the joys of a healthy, productive and respected life." Colony leaders claimed 80 percent of the inmates achieved those goals and "became productive members of society. . . . Even critics of the colony conceded that a surprisingly high percentage of farm colony inmates appear to have turned around their lives." Although successful, the population never reached much above one hundred and tended to hover around thirty. Worse, it cost twice as much to house inmates at the colony than at other facilities. Unwilling to continue such a small and expensive program, the state closed it in 1947.[14]

Although the results of Gardner's first efforts toward reform were mixed, he carried forth and in March 1930 appointed a committee to determine how to modernize the entire penitentiary system. Rather than address elements of the system, Gardner wanted a fundamental overhaul. The committee tasked with that effort consisted of former Governor Angus MacLean, the chairman of the prison's board of directors, J. W. Bunn, board members T. L. Bland and E. B. Jeffress, and Superintendent Pou. It met first on March 11, 1930, and created a subcommittee to investigate the penal systems in other states, specifically

Alabama, which had "one of the most modern [prison plants] in the country." The committee also sought advice from experts.[15]

The expert from whom they were most interested to hear was Dr. Howard Odum, a University of North Carolina at Chapel Hill sociology professor, creator of the Institute for Research in Social Science, and a man hailed by historian Milton Ready as "the state's greatest social scientist and visionary of the early twentieth century." Odum studied the state's prison system and the prisoners it held, and proffered three major conclusions. First, he determined most inmates came from broken families, unhappy homes, or grew up in poverty. Second, he found those who turned to crime were poorly educated and had "wanderlust" (18 percent never attended school, 50 percent attended only grammar school, and 68 percent left home before they were twenty-one). Third, he discovered that while 83 percent were employed at the time of their arrest, in general arrests rose and fell with the changing economic conditions. For Odum, crime was a socio-economic phenomenon and needed to be dealt with as such.[16]

The committee accepted Odum's findings and, in conjunction with what the subcommittee found at other state penitentiaries, began its final report with a statement of purpose: "The object of prison administration is not only to punish the guilty but to reform the prisoner as much as possible. It is not primarily to make money out of the prisoner, but we believe that the more intelligent handling of prisoners and the proper co-ordination of farming and industry will go a long way toward reclaiming the prisoners for useful lives and thus reducing the burden upon the taxpayers." Acknowledging that inmates were not bad people but rather victims of circumstance and environment, the committee sought to rescue them through reformative labor.[17]

With its penal philosophy set, the committee made seven recommendations. First, it called for a new parole law with adequate funding. The committee called parole "the keystone in the arch of the . . . prison system of North Carolina" and argued it enabled a more useful and economical management of the inmates. The members also asserted that parole improved inmate morale by making clear that "faithful service" would speed their release, and ensured that inmates were not "cast out upon society at the end of the term . . . without friends or money," thus offering them a better chance for success.[18]

To achieve that success, the committee argued the parole agency needed to be fully staffed and to have oversight of all inmates released on parole, be they from the state penitentiary or county jails. It encouraged the state to place the parole board under the direction of the Commissioner of Public Welfare, who could better integrate the parolees into society and help them find jobs. The committee also noted that Public Welfare often had knowledge of the prisoner's family by having to assist them while their family member was in prison, so it had a head start on providing assistance. Finally, the committee asserted that "a proper system of parole" would save the state $100,000 a year. The committee concluded, "It is, therefore, a mandatory economic step for the State to take."[19]

Second, the committee called for the expansion of inmate work projects and suggested that "as many as possible should be placed upon the highways, and also used for the production of road materials." It further called for "intelligent farm operations" through the establishment of "cold storage plants, granaries and canneries," and the production of more cash crops that could be sold to the general public and not simply used to feed inmates. As a part of that, members urged the expansion and more extensive cultivation of the existing farms. Finally, they suggested introducing new industries, such as an automobile repair shop in which inmates could repair state vehicles. That would save the state money and provide inmates vocational training and practice.[20]

Third, the committee demanded the modernization of Central Prison and the various camps and farms. The report asserted that Central Prison "is unsafe from the stand-point of fire protection; it is costly to heat; it is expensive to operate; it is devoid of proper sanitary facilities; it lacks adequate hospital facilities; and, in general while possessing an imposing appearance, its condition as a central plant is thoroughly uneconomic, and it possesses the danger of a fire trap." Such conditions demoralized inmates and staff, so renovation would benefit the entire penitentiary community. To fund the renovations, the committee called for a $400,000 bond issue.[21]

Despite this call to modernize Central Prison, in its fourth suggestion the committee proposed moving Central Prison to the site of the Cary prison farm. The committee argued that the farm was more centrally located and offered more land to expand the prison and prison-related industries. It also noted that the penitentiary was showing its age and would require significant expense to modernize, while a new prison could be built inexpensively and would employ the latest architectural and penological designs. The old site, meanwhile, could be converted into "a central State warehouse to be utilized as a part of the State central purchasing agency."[22]

Fifth, the committee called for employing expert opinion and advice in administering the prison facilities, arguing specifically that prison officials and inmates would benefit from the insights of the faculty at the North Carolina State College of Agriculture and Engineering (later North Carolina State University) and employees of the State Department of Agriculture. The hope was that such individuals could help prison administrators find new ways to work the inmates and new methods to exploit the prison's resources.[23]

Sixth, the committee argued that the prison would benefit from the employment of people trained in criminal justice administration, and it encouraged the University of North Carolina and the North Carolina State College to create such programs. This was especially important, the committee suggested, if the state followed its recommendations and built a new penitentiary. Members argued that the new facility would involve a different means of handling inmates, that "many of the old type prison guards will be found unsuited, and . . . it will be necessary to bring in other men of a different type." Creating training programs at the state's universities would ensure a supply of qualified labor once that new penitentiary was up and running. Indeed, the American Prison Association did a study of prisons employing the rehabilitative model and discovered that most "old-time wardens" did not understand the concept. While they abandoned "brutality and strict discipline," they did not introduce any real treatment programs and undercut the system's reformative elements. The committee sought to avoid that shortcoming by hiring a cadre of well-trained guards and administrators.[24]

Finally, the committee urged the state to take control of county convicts. Members argued that most county jails and nearly all county work sites failed to meet modern standards of security and sanitation. From a simple health and safety perspective, therefore, the state needed to end county control and create a single statewide criminal justice system.[25]

The committee concluded its report by arguing that if the state followed the suggestions "it will result in better discipline and morale; . . . it will give the prisoner a more hopeful outlook on life with the State assisting him in the problem of re-adjustment in after prison life; and . . . it will be economically beneficial to North Carolina."[26]

This was an epochal document that called for systematic changes and demanded a complete rethinking of the manner in which the North Carolina prison system operated. Indeed, its calls to expand parole, modernize the prison, and rely more heavily on expert administrators and college-trained staff seemed to demonstrate a truly progressive agenda. More importantly, the committee's arguments were hard to rebut. While Pou may have been embarrassed to have his previous achievements called into question by the 1929 report, he must surely have been satisfied with this committee's findings, as they supported nearly every one of his demands. Gardner too surely was pleased. Despite the qualified success of his efforts with Otto Wood and the female inmates, here was encouragement to carry on.

The fact that two legislative committees and the state's leading sociologist joined with the governor and the prison superintendent to support continued reforms speaks volumes about the public's sensibilities. By the 1930s, North Carolinians appeared on the cusp of accepting the benefits of progressive penal reform. Showing faith in the most degraded of inmates, moving to improve the lives of female inmates, and supporting a wide-ranging and exhaustive overhaul of the state's prison system suggest a state ready to move forward.

The deepening Depression, term limits that prevented Gardner from serving a second term, and changing social mores, however, altered the order of things. That alteration, for the first time, calls into question the concept of the prison as a social microcosm and makes clear that the reflection between the prison and the state, while ever present, was not always complete. The later years of the Depression, in other words, challenged both the emergent and beneficial relationship between prison administrators and politicians and the reformism of the previous decades. It was left to Pou, once again, to lead the prison through that trying time.

13

THE DEPRESSION YEARS

As the Depression deepened and John Ehringhaus succeeded O. Max Gardner as governor, the reformism of the previous decades threatened to wane. Increased crime rates led to packed prisons, overwhelmed staffs, and charges of brutality, while financial exigencies led to the absorption of the prison system into a larger state agency. Despite those problems, George Pou, who remained superintendent for much of the era, was able to convince legislators to direct some level of financing to the prison, and North Carolina's prisoners enjoyed some surprising gains. The result was a dichotomous era during which developments within the penitentiary both replicated and diverged from the changes taking place in the outside world. Regardless and through it all, the prison continued to reflect substantial aspects of the state's social, political, and economic development.

Much of that reflection, at least initially, was negative. As a consequence of the economic collapse, the state dropped any thought of moving the penitentiary to the Cary prison farm. Legislators simply refused to spend money on a new prison when the one it had, regardless of its shortcomings, still stood. A second consequence was a substantial increase in population. From 1928 to 1932, the number of inmates in Central Prison doubled. Two related factors made this population boom especially problematic.

Overwhelmed with inmates, prison administrators had trouble finding room for all their prisoners, let alone trying to segregate them. As Pou lamented, "there were no provisions at the prison for the proper segregation of prisoners by race or by sex, nor for the segregation of youthful offenders from the old and hardened offenders, nor for the isolation of prisoners with contagious diseases." Instead, they all crowded together in a circumstance that undermined health and security and threatened the well-being of everyone inside the prison's walls.[1]

The second factor was that inmates often found themselves idle. The Depression forced prison-made goods "off the open market," as businesses fought for every last customer. While the penitentiary continued "production-for-state-use," that market was much smaller than the open market and offered fewer financial rewards. At the same time, the economic decline reduced tax revenue and gave the state less money to spend on any type of commodity, so the limited state market contracted even further. Indeed, between 1928 and 1932 the prisoners' annual per capita production fell from $212.20 to $65.76. Beyond income, the decline meant fewer jobs and left little to help prisoners pass their time. As administrators were well aware, a bored inmate was a dangerous inmate.[2]

Pou, however, was not one easily stymied, and he saw a glimmer of hope with the emergence of a new penal philosophy that came to dominate the nation's prison systems in the 1930s. Called rehabilitation, it maintained many of the reformatory ideas, including indeterminate sentencing, parole, classification, segregation, education, and job training, but it ended the silent system and the use of stripes, used solitary confinement only for punishment, and, more importantly, it focused on diagnosing and treating any physical, mental, or emotional problems from which the inmates suffered.[3]

Inspired by his earlier successes, fortified by the continued calls for reform developed by the governor's 1929 committee, but stung by the inability to implement those reforms, the newly emergent model enthralled Pou. Determined to use it to benefit the prison, in 1932 he shrugged off the Depression and set out to convince politicians to implement rehabilitation regardless of the economic crisis.

He did this first by demonstrating how prisoner treatment had improved over the previous decade. In 1921, he asserted, an inmate

was given a prison uniform and assigned to some form of hard manual labor—usually the first job that revealed itself. From then on, the individuality of the prisoner was forgotten. Usually he was just one of a large group of prisoners who moved from one type of manual labor to another. Without the benefits of sane occupational placement, without adequate medical attention, without sanitary quarters and a balanced diet, and without the other provisions characteristic of a constructive prison program, the inmates of our North Carolina state prisons led a miserable existence which could hardly be expected to awaken and develop their finer qualities.

Prisoners thus enjoyed neither reform nor rehabilitation.[4]

Under his watch, he claimed, things had improved dramatically. First, he had instructed officers to treat "each prisoner . . . as an individual" so as to preserve their humanity, win their trust, and prepare them for the real purpose of prison: education. Asserting that a prison sentence should be "educative rather than punitive," Pou then explained that his men worked to "help the prisoner learn how to respond to life situations" in appropriate manners. As a part of that, prisoners acquired healthy living techniques, learned "faithful citizenship," mastered "the tools, techniques, and spirit of learning," were encouraged to make "wise use of leisure," and generally studied "the habit of correct living." The purpose of it all, he concluded, was "to reduce the number of prisoners convicted of second offenses," to keep to a minimum those "who are classed as habitual offenders," and to provide the fullest protection "to the free citizenship of North Carolina."[5]

After applauding the achievements thus made, and ignoring the criticisms of the 1929 investigation, Pou warned that all their success was at risk. He reported that "present conditions at the Central Prison are indeed deplorable," called the facility a "fire trap," and proceeded to give a full accounting of the overcrowding and lack of proper segregation. Resurrecting one of the main suggestions put forth by the 1929 committee, Pou argued the only thing that could save the system was "the erection of a new and modern Central Prison" organized around the rehabilitative model. He asserted that the new prison could be built for $300,000–$400,000, and suggested that politicians could not object to righting the aforementioned wrongs for such a reasonable price regardless of the state's other financial considerations.[6]

The General Assembly surely knew Pou was right and appreciated the efforts he made during the previous decade, but it was not about to spend the sums he suggested amid the Depression. Aware, however, that something needed to be done, legislators eventually pushed forward with a massive reconfiguration of the penitentiary administration. This reconfiguration was nothing along the lines Pou envisioned, and instead was part of the larger effort to cut costs, reduce waste, and limit bureaucratic overlap by consolidating state agencies.

The result was that in 1933 Governor John Ehringhaus ordered the state's entire prison system absorbed into the State Highway and Public Works Commission. The motivation was simple economics: since so many inmates worked on the roads, the prison system and the highway commission were administering the same duties. It only made sense, Ehringhaus concluded, "to make the two departments one." Future prison superintendent Vernon Leland

Bounds concurred, and later he explained that the 1933 merger was "motivated frankly by financial considerations. The Prison System had to secure support from a source apart from the General Fund; the Highway System needed a pool of cheap labor. The Prison System had idle prisoners; the Highway System had the Highway Fund. The union of the two agencies was a marriage of convenience." Historian Charles Craven agrees, and writes, "the reasons the two systems combined in 1933 were never seriously related to penal considerations directly. It was purely an economically dictated maneuver."[7]

Whatever motivated the move, prison administrators found themselves playing second fiddle in the newly consolidated agency. As Bounds noted, "the fact that the controlling body of the new agency was called the State Highway and Public Works Commission, rather than the State Highway and Prison Commission, is perhaps indicative of the subordinate status of the State Prison System in the new organization." While the penitentiary lost its independence and Pou saw a dramatic decrease in his power, the merger did offer some benefits. Most notably, it allowed the penitentiary to access gasoline tax revenue and additional sources of otherwise inaccessible highway funds. There was, therefore, some hope that consolidation would lead to the implementation of Pou's reforms.[8]

That hope, at least initially, was not to be. The act creating the new organization required that "as many qualified prisoners must be assigned to [road] work as the Commission can economically use." Once the state employed all the inmates it needed on the roads, the law allowed the commission to put inmates to work for the state on agricultural or forestry work, to lease inmates to private employers, or to put them to work producing for "state use." To create a market for "state use" goods, the law required the Department of Motor Vehicles to purchase all of the state's license plates from the prison, and encouraged, but did not require, other state agencies to purchase inmate-produced goods. As one final element, the law allowed the prison to sell agricultural goods, stone, and coal on the open market.[9]

Those new policies increased the Highway Commission's revenue, but emptied the state's prisons and jails of laborers. Work on the roads and on agricultural and forestry projects engaged nearly every able-bodied inmate, once again leaving behind only those too weak to labor elsewhere. The prison industries thus lacked workers and proved unable to produce for "state use," let alone for the open market. As a result, the penitentiary's income fell markedly and it began operating at a deficit in excess of $200,000 per year. While the deficit was irrelevant since the Highway Commission funded the prison, Pou was a proud man who felt emasculated by the consolidation process and the prison system's ensuing loss of economic independence.[10]

While Pou licked his wounds and prison administrators adjusted to their second-class status, prisoners encountered a new system that proved a double-edged sword. According to historian John Hackney, "living conditions were improved for many prisoners" as they were no longer subject to the whims and wills of each county. The food, the environment, and the discipline were more uniform and generally better than most prisoners had previously experienced. At the same time, however, Hackney found "the exploitation of [inmate] labor was apparently intensified under the new system." With more inmates available, the Highway Commission went into overdrive employing them at a frantic pace throughout the state.[11]

Although disquieting for nearly everyone involved, consolidation's impact ultimately proved limited. In 1935, New Deal legislation required states to employ Civilian Conservation Corps workers for roadwork. This sent the vast majority of inmates back to the county jails or the penitentiary. Ironically, this return proved beneficial to the prison system as inmates once again worked at on-site industries. The license plate-making shop, the mattress-making shop, and the soap-making shop produced goods for "state-use-only," while a newly created tobacco processing plant arose where inmates made two commodities that were virtually Depression-proof: cigarettes and chewing tobacco.[12]

Even more beneficial was a sudden and surprising willingness on the part of legislators to spend money on penitentiary improvements. Funded in part by a 3-cent sales tax, in 1933 the legislature authorized $125,000 to modernize Central Prison. By 1935, officials had spent $75,000 on a new dining hall, print shop, and bakery. By 1938, renovations had provided hot and cold running water, electric lights, and ventilation systems to each cell, while 1940 saw completion of an industrial building to house the print shop, paint plant, and license plate-making shop. That same year the prison constructed a canteen for inmates where they could purchase tobacco, cold drinks, candy, canned goods, and various toiletries. Warden H. H. Honeycutt noted that revenue from the canteen went to support the prison recreation fund that purchased balls, bats, gloves, boxing paraphernalia, and other recreational necessities. While the inmates subsidized their own recreation, it is important to note that the other sources of funding came from tax revenues. Whereas the legislature sought all manner of consolidations and cost-cutting measures to save money, here were legislators proving surprisingly generous. As the public at large suffered from a stingy government, prisoners benefitted from at least a limited level of government largess.[13]

Among the recreational opportunities that largess subsidized was an inmate-run newspaper titled *The Prison News*. For nearly a decade amid the Depression, inmates published this monthly paper that provided news from both inside and outside the prison and allowed prisoners to spread their thoughts on any number of issues. Each edition, for instance, included the results of athletic events held within the prison walls. The paper covered the outcomes of boxing matches and baseball games, and analyzed each as if it was a heavyweight championship bout or the World Series.[14]

More remarkable may be the insights the inmate-journalists provided into their beliefs and values. In the inaugural issue, inmates noted that while they had it rough, others had it worse:

When we think of the men, women, and children in the world who are destitute, who have no place to call home, or of the little children in our orphan asylums who have no one to call Father or Mother and must depend on strangers to help them thru the early years of their lives, we then know that we have a lot to be thankful for even tho we are in the penitentiary. There is in this old world of ours plenty of people who would gladly exchange places with us and whose daily life is far worse than ours.

Some inmates, at least, saw the world in perspective.[15]

Other writers used the paper to lecture fellow inmates on proper behavior. One issue included a letter from "Joe Burnett" in which he described the hardships resultant from his escape: "I had no freedom, no enjoyment, no pleasure, absolutely nothing but a load of suspense. There were restless nights from fear of officers swooping down on me, perhaps killing me." In a later edition, journalists employed a different tactic and argued that escapes hurt those who remained behind by causing administrators to crack down: "we may expect prison rules and regulations to become more rigid, and not one of us will have the right to blame the officials, the supervisors or the guards for the part we unsuccessfully play in the game of 'doing time.'"[16]

In a similar vein, writers criticized riotous inmates. The authors of one article noted that the state spent vast sums making life better for individuals who had violated the state's laws. They worried that riots would turn the public against further expenditures and could result in making life worse for all inmates in the system. To prevent that possibility, they called for an end to prison riots and for "good" inmates to step in and prevent disturbances when "bad" inmates tried to cause trouble. The paper even included a "dishonor role," which served as a form of peer pressure by listing all those sent to solitary confinement for rules violations.[17]

In the end, the paper lasted as long as it did in large part because it served the needs of the administration. From distracting inmates with sports, news, and information to preaching the benefits of good behavior, the paper helped administrators maintain discipline. Indeed, the paper's tagline was: "strengthening the morale and improving the efficiency of the prisoners by keeping them in touch with prison affairs." Penitentiary officials could have wanted little more from its inmates, and they funded the paper throughout the Depression.[18]

Sadly, the prisoners may have wanted more from the officials. Despite all the reforms and high-minded philosophies, a series of abuse scandals rocked the prison system and again called into question claims of rehabilitation. The scandals began when *Success* magazine published former Central Prison inmate John Kennard's essay "Confessions of a Boy From Hell's Forty Acres." A white inmate who served sixteen years in Central Prison for armed robbery, he described his time there as a horror that left him "infinitely more hardened when I got out." He exclaimed that prison "taught me how cruel men can be. Everything they did to reform me, only made me worse—more vindictive—more revengeful."[19]

That process began as soon as he entered Central's walls:

First of all they stripped me naked. They put a black cap over my head, a cap such as they put over the head of a man that is to be hanged. With the aid of a rope and pulley they lifted me in the air until my toes just touched the ground. Then they beat me with a big strap which was four and a half feet long and eighteen inches wide by one fourth of an inch thick and filled with rivets. After every blow they drew the strap through sand, hot sand. The sand created more pain, intensified the agony; festered the sores. They gave me forty-five licks. Then I was thrown into a dungeon for twenty-four hours after which they took me out and beat me again. They kept this up for ten days, at the end of which I was raw from my hips down to my knees. I had to lie on my stomach for four weeks. They were trying to break me—trying to reform me—but they didn't break or reform me, they simply brutalized me and made me worse than ever.

Kennard survived that initiation, found God, and, with no thanks to the prison guards, reformed himself. That reform did not lessen his outrage at the jailers, but he hoped his descriptions would bring about change.[20]

They did not, as proved by events that transpired in 1935 when news broke that African American inmates Woodrow Wilson Shropshire, aged nineteen, and Robert Burns, aged twenty, had their feet amputated after being "chained in an upright position in solitary confinement as punishment" for cursing at guards and refusing to work while serving their time at the Mecklenburg County Prison Camp. Further investigations discovered that another African American inmate, L. Bogan, had died in shackles, hanging from the wall of a solitary confinement cell at the same Mecklenburg camp. At the time, officials claimed he died five days after the punishment, but inmates disputed that assertion. Public outrage was swift, and the state legislature held hearings, during which even more disturbing testimony emerged.[21]

The hearings began with investigators asking Director of the State Penal Division J. B. Roach if guards at the Mecklenburg camp violated prison policy in their handling of Bogan. Roach said they had not, and testified that chaining an inmate to his cell in a standing position for eight to twelve hours was an approved punishment. L. G. Whitley, assistant superintendent of the State Penal Division, supported Roach and testified that he had approved the practice. While shocked by the admissions, as politicians probed deeper they were absolutely horrified.[22]

During testimony about the use of confinement cells, inmates testified that "prisoners confined in 'solitary' were given no way to relieve themselves of normal bodily wastes except in their clothes and were given no change of clothes when in dark cells." They further described the cells as "infernos in summer and refrigerators in winter." Most damning was testimony that revealed "North Carolina prison camp officials had made a practice of secret burials for friendless victims of their disciplinary measures. The committee was told that when beatings, chained suspensions and other forms of punishment proved fatal to the prisoners, the victims' bodies were carted off to lonely spots in the mountains and buried."[23]

Author John Mebane, who documented the abuses in an essay entitled "The Torture Chamber in North Carolina," lamented that North Carolina had "devised a new mode of torture: the dark cell where men are chained until the bitter cold stiffens their bodies and the blackness drives them mad." The aforementioned Frank Watson, writing about his experiences in the 1940s, was even more graphic and explained that not only were inmates chained, but often they were chained in a suspended state: "Hanging there with your feet just off the floor, your face mashed against the wall, your wrists and ankles breaking, does something horrible to your mind as well as your body." And he spoke from experience, having once suffered such confinement for seventy-four straight hours. It was such a brutal experience that he later wrote, "even being in the hole without food and sometimes water is more humane than hanging on a ring on the wall, no matter how long."[24]

Despite the chilling nature of Mebane's prose and Watson's firsthand account, with so much other suffering going on amid the Depression public outrage quickly dissipated and the investigation had little effect. Pou suspended three guards, two camp superintendents, and one doctor, but the practices continued and the abominations persisted.[25]

In an effort to move beyond the testimony and outrage, in 1936 legislators singled out the prison system for a financial windfall when they authorized another $470,000 to renovate Central Prison. The upgrade included "fire-proofed cells equipped with lavatories, toilets, cotton mattresses, and a new locking device similar to ones installed at Alcatraz Prison." It also provided a lighter color scheme designed to make the interior less depressing. Further reforms included showing more movies, implementing more formal racial segregation, improving food service, reducing the workday from twelve to ten hours, installing radios for inmate entertainment, and expanding the number of authorized sporting activities. The reforms even altered punishments, with whipping formally abolished in all instances. In its place, authorities suspended inmate privileges or placed them on a limited diet. Notably, however, the reforms did not include a ban on chaining inmates to their cells.[26]

Pleased with the funding and resulting reforms, but wary that state money could disappear at any time, in the late 1930s Pou focused on cost-effective alternatives to incarceration, most notably the creation of new parole and probation systems. His updated parole plan required the inmate to complete half his sentence before he became eligible. Once eligible, he had to obtain a "First Friend" who would help the prisoner find work and would make monthly reports regarding "the prisoner's work, habits, associates, behavior, etc." The inmate then had to collect letters supporting parole from the trial judge, the lawyer who prosecuted his case, and the sheriff of the county where the crime occurred. Pou believed those requirements would increase the number of inmates who successfully completed their parole.[27]

Pou also suggested the creation of a probation system. First introduced in the United States by John Augustus, whose pioneering efforts began in Massachusetts in the 1840s, by 1920 twenty-two states had adopted probation laws. Pou argued that probation prevented the creation of career criminals by diverting individuals from the prison system, where they could become habituated to a life of crime. Again remembering to whom he was appealing, he further suggested it would be cost effective since the savings resultant from not having to imprison people would offset probation officers' salaries.[28]

In 1937 state legislators acquiesced and implemented new parole and probation systems, although not exactly along the lines Pou suggested. According to the new parole law, inmates became eligible after serving one-quarter of their minimum sentence or ten years of a life sentence. A parole board judged each eligible inmate based on the "reasonable probability that the prisoner will live in free society without violating the law," that his release "is not incompatible with the welfare of society," that he has shown "obedience to prison rules and regulations, proper respect for prison officials, and due regard and consideration for fellow prisoners," and that he "harbors no resentment against society, the judge, prosecuting attorneys or convicting jury." The parole board also considered the crime, the inmate's previous criminal record, and his psychiatric and medical reports. Those deemed worthy of early release received a suit of clothes, $25, and travel funds. They also were assigned a welfare officer, whose task was to help the inmate reenter society, and a parole supervisor, whose job was to ensure the inmate abided by the rules of his release. Any inmate who violated his conditions or broke the law while on parole had to serve the remainder of his time.[29]

While parole was designed "to facilitate the proper adjustment of a parolee to free society," the new probation law "aimed at arresting the growth of a criminal character and rehabilitating an offender without resort to incarceration." When a potential probation case arose, a probation officer gathered a report on the offense, the person's criminal record, their social history, and their present condition. A judge then used the report to determine the utility of sentencing the individual to probation rather than prison. Any person convicted by a jury or pleading guilty or *nolo contendere*, except those subject to death or life in prison, was eligible, and the judge could impose any conditions on probation he saw fit, except that the term could not exceed five years.[30]

As it turned out, both probation and parole served North Carolina and the convicts well. The state saved substantial sums of money by redirecting individuals away from expensive incarceration, while the convicts avoided the stigma and trauma of prison time.

Pou, who had championed both plans, was not around to enjoy their implementation, having left the prison in 1937. During his sixteen years of service, however, he had convinced the state to fund numerous construction projects, implemented several fundamental reforms, improved the quality of life for most inmates, successfully guided the prison system through the Depression, and even managed to overcome the system's loss of freedom and the damning allegations of prisoner abuse. While legislators did not enact the full scope of his agenda, administrators remained a long way from fully implementing the rehabilitative model, and some prisoners continued to suffer brutalization, Pou did more to improve the prison system than any previous superintendent. He certainly benefitted from the active support offered by Governors Gardner and Ehringhaus, but Pou deserves the lion's share of the credit.

Whomever we credit, the mid- to late 1930s were a difficult time for the people of North Carolina as the Depression deepened and the population suffered. That suffering, however, was not fully reflected in the prison, and for one of the rare moments in the state's history the social/penological relationship was incomplete. Administrators found themselves awash with money at a time when governmental spending was at its nadir and virtually every other state agency saw its financing slashed. Inmates, meanwhile, gained ever more recreational opportunities at a time when many North Carolinians lacked the financial wherewithal for any form of entertainment. The reflection did not disappear completely, however, as the consolidation of the prison system within the Highway Department and the creation of new probation and parole programs mirrored similar external cost-cutting developments. The Depression was thus an era of contrast and change, at once demonstrating the continued link between the prison and society while also indicating the imperfect nature of that relationship. As the nation plunged from the crisis of the Depression to the crisis of World War II, however, the reflection cleared and the prison once again closely resembled free society.

14

DEATH PENALTY REFORMS

The first evidence of the re-emergent public/penal relationship was in the realm of capital punishment. Amid the lingering horrors of the Depression and with war looming on the horizon, administrators decided to bring some compassion to the prison system by replacing the electric chair with the gas chamber, an allegedly more humane form of capital punishment. Sadly, the effort toward humanity not only failed, it led to some of the most horrific events in the state's penal history. It also demonstrated the state's ongoing struggle with race, made clear the continued determination of politicians to intervene in the prison system, and once again called into question North Carolina's progressive reputation. While the mirror returned, the problems of old remained.

Since 1910, all executions in North Carolina had occurred in Central Prison's electric chair under the administration of state authorities. Although executions no longer were the public spectacles of the eighteenth and nineteenth centuries, historian Trina Seitz explains that the "vivid, colorful accounts and descriptions of executions . . . shed light on the reality of state-sanctioned violence." People no longer witnessed executions, but the press provided lurid accounts that proved nearly as provocative as the real thing. While the verbal spectacle that journalists produced titillated many, it outraged others. Descriptions of burning flesh, bulging eyes, and contorted faces wrought by seemingly endless jolts of electricity led humanitarians and activists alike to question the system and call for reform.[1]

The questions and calls became louder thanks to a 1929 study by the North Carolina State Board of Charities and Public Welfare entitled *Capital Punishment in North Carolina*. The study found that most of those sentenced to die were African American, male, illiterate, and had "no memory of a home, a church, a school or a community whose influence might have led the wandering feet of childhood along a path that had a happier end." Doomed by the ill luck of fate to grow up amid a cruel environment with few positive influences, those inmates, the report argued, were "for the most part the children of ignorance and neglect" for whom the public should seek sympathy, not vengeance.[2]

That sympathy did not mean those sentenced to death should escape their fate. Instead, the 1929 study found that North Carolinians supported the death penalty but wanted a more humane technique. In 1935, state Senator Charles Peterson, a practicing physician from Relief, proposed just such a technique when he introduced a bill to replace the electric chair with the gas chamber. Peterson did not make this proposal reflexively; prior to his election he had contacted governors in states that used the gas chamber, and from those conversations became convinced it was a more just form of execution. In March 1935, the Joint Committee on Penal Institutions held hearings on Peterson's bill and took testimony from an array of physicians. The legislators were especially interested in those familiar with anesthetics, and from them they heard assurances that death by lethal gas was less painful than jolts from an electric chair.

While those supporters viewed the gas chamber as a progressive advancement in capital punishment, other supporters simply wanted to speed up the process. State Senator J. T. Burrus of Guilford complained that "each of the triple executions last year took nearly an hour," and he suggested a gas chamber would speed things along: "Another feature of the gas chamber is that double and triple executions take no longer than a single execution, as two or three chairs may be installed in the chamber instead of one, and the same lethal does administered to each of the condemned prisoners."[3]

There was one final reason people supported the change—racism. According to historian Seth Kotch, officials hoped that a less violent form of execution would prevent the emergence of white sympathy for African American victims. Fearful that such sympathy might lead to challenges against the state's segregation laws, he contends, politicians and prison administrators sought to avoid the spectacle and instead worked to push "the death penalty out of the public square and onto the fringes of social and cultural life." To protect white privilege, state leaders thus sought to make executions too clinical to excite an emotional response. As Kotch writes, "the death penalty in Jim Crow North Carolina expressed the state's firm commitment to a criminal justice system created to control the bodies and lives of African Americans, but only as subjects, never as actors."[4]

Convinced by this odd mixture of racism, vengeance, and humanity, the joint committee supported the bill. The House passed it in April, the Senate followed suit in May with a unanimous vote, and Governor Ehringhaus subsequently signed the bill into law. That signature made North Carolina just the fourth state in the nation, and the first east of the Mississippi River, to employ the gas chamber. Legislators and capital punishment reformers could now take pride that North Carolina was on the cutting edge of penal policy.

By December 1935, workers had constructed a gas chamber at Central Prison and administrators were preparing it for implementation. That first use took place in January 1936, when Jimmie Lee "Allen" Foster entered the chamber. Foster was nineteen years old and mentally feeble. An African American originally from Alabama, he had a long history of run-ins with the law, and in 1935 he was serving time in Birmingham for his latest arrest. At Foster's request, Alabama transferred him to a North Carolina Civilian Conservation Corps camp in hopes that a new setting away from bad influences would help set his life straight. It did not. On September 28, 1935, he escaped from the Hoke County work camp to which he was assigned and assaulted, robbed, and raped a white woman. Authorities captured Foster and a jury convicted him of rape. Sentenced to death, on January 24, 1936, guards led Foster to the gas chamber.

Although the underlying premise of the gas chamber was that it was more humane than the electric chair, this execution proved revolting in its brutality. Guards strapped Foster into a chair beneath which sat a vat of sulfuric acid. Suspended above the vat by a quick-release mechanism controlled by the warden was a hydrogen cyanide capsule. After strapping in Foster, the guards exited the chamber and sealed the airtight doors. The warden then released the mechanism dropping the capsule into the acid. The resulting poison gas was supposed to kill rapidly, but the prison staff was unaware that cold temperatures greatly reduce the gas's potency. The chamber that January day was near freezing, and the result was a weak gaseous cloud that led to a prolonged and gruesome death. It took three minutes before the gas rendered Foster unconscious, and it then took another eight minutes for him to die. According to the *Raleigh News and Observer*, Foster's "small, but powerfully built torso began to retch and jerk, throwing his head forward on his chest, where witnesses could see his eyes slowly glaze. . . . The torturous, convulsive retching continued spasmodically for a full four minutes." It took eleven minutes from the time the cyanide pellet dropped until doctors finally pronounced Foster dead.[5]

Witnesses were horrified, with Warden H. H. Honeycutt complaining that a hanging would have been more humane. Even Wake County coroner Lawrence

Waring, who had witnessed five hangings and seventy-two electrocutions, was outraged, stating: "This was one of the most terrible and horrible things I ever looked at." Further proof of the revulsion many observers felt is that some sympathized with Foster and even "forgot that the Negro in the chair was paying the penalty for raping a white woman." Such sympathy was nearly unheard of in the American South in the 1930s, and serves as an all too clear sign of the execution's horror.[6]

When news of the spectacle hit the public, they too were outraged. Calls soon arose to abolish executions completely or to return the state's mode of death to the electric chair. Unwilling to admit they were wrong, legislators made inquiries and learned they needed to keep the chamber warm to facilitate the gas; they also adopted a different formulation of the hydrogen cyanide compound to produce a more effective poison. With those changes in place, on January 31, 1936, guards strapped into the chamber its second victim, Edward Jenkins, a white man convicted of murder. The alterations to the temperature and formula worked, and witnesses reported a speedy and allegedly painless death. Satisfied, and believing they had taken a major step forward, legislators maintained the gas chamber, which served the state for the next fifty years.

Whether or not the gas chamber was a more humane form of punishment is open to debate. What is not debatable is that those who died in it remained largely the same: African American men. In keeping with much of the state's unfortunate history, of the eighty-four executions performed in the 1930s, sixty-eight were of African Americans. This was nothing new. Between 1910 and 1929, North Carolina sentenced two hundred people to death: 149 were African American and only fifty-one were white (including one white woman). One hundred of those so sentenced, however, had their sentences commuted to life in prison, but once again the racial discrepancy is apparent. Of those spared death, sixty-six were African American men, thirty-three were white men, and 1 was the lone white woman. In other words, while 64.7 percent of the white men had their sentences commuted, only 44.3 percent of the condemned African Americans received similar reprieves. Race clearly affected the sentencing and implementation of capital punishment, and according to a 1930 study, "In North Carolina the man who goes to the electric chair, almost without exception, is poor, uneducated, and feeble minded. Race, also, is an important factor. The Negro here, as elsewhere in the administration of justice, is at a disadvantage even in comparison with the least privileged white group." This point is even more obvious when we remember that Superintendent Pou granted a white man, "Carbine" Williams, the right to work on weaponry while incarcerated. It is hard to imagine an African American inmate earning the same freedom.[7]

The statistics not only demonstrate the over-representation of African Americans, but the underrepresentation of women. Official records list twenty-one women as having been executed in North Carolina between 1720 and 1892. Eighteen of that number were African American, enslaved, and had been convicted of murder. By the dawn of the twentieth century, however, the state dramatically reduced the practice. That change may have had something to do with Caroline Shipp. In 1892, the petite, eighteen-year-old, African American woman faced hanging for the murder of her infant child. It was a grisly execution. The fall did not break her neck, and according to the *Gaston Gazette* the gathered witnesses heard "a horrible sound of suppressed breathing" and saw her chest "heaving and struggling in a terrific effort of nature to supply the lungs with air." Subsequent studies suggest spectators had to pull on Shipp's legs to break her neck, that she may have miscarried during the hanging, and that she may well have been innocent. As a result, North Carolina did not execute another woman for fifty years. The gas chamber's "success," however, changed public sentiment, and in the 1940s two women found their way to the death chamber. The first was Rosanna Lightner Phillips.[8]

Rosanna Lightner was born on December 25, 1917. The daughter of unmarried African American parents, she was raised in poverty by her grandmother until she was seven, when she reunited with her mother. Like her mother, who dropped out of school to give birth, in 1932 Lightner ended her education to raise a child. She earned about $2 a week working as a nurse and domestic servant, but was young and had a wild streak. Arrested multiple times for larceny, public drunkenness, and assaulting police officers, in 1935 a jury sentenced her to two years in the Women's Prison. Upon her release in 1937, she met Daniel Phillips, a twenty-five-year-old farmer who was married to another woman. They began a tumultuous relationship and lived together in Gastonia, High Point, and Durham. Wherever they lived they fought, with Lightner bearing the brunt of the violence. Her body was scarred with knife wounds inflicted on her by Phillips during their many arguments, and one especially heinous scar stretched eight inches across her stomach. Despite the violence, the two remained together.[9]

In April 1942, they settled on the land of Harry F. Watkins and began work as sharecroppers. The two remained on the land until August, when violence once again erupted. The victim this time was Watkins. The story remains unclear, muddied by competing assertions, but it ends with Watkins's death on August 3, 1942. Lightner later claimed she was in Watkins's home doing the dishes and looked out the kitchen window to see Phillips and Watkins loading watermelons into the trunk of a car. As she watched, Phillips hit Watkins in the head with an axe and then struck him again in the neck, nearly severing his head. She testified that Phillips then took Watkins's wallet, wrapped his body in towels, loaded him into the trunk of the car, cleaned up the blood, and went back to work. She claimed she never left the kitchen.[10]

Phillips testified to a different story. He claimed Lightner had argued repeatedly with Watkins over the quality of her work. He testified in court that Lightner had previously tried to poison Watkins and that she had planned his murder in the days leading up to August 3. According to Phillips, Lightner struck Watkins first, hitting him in the back of the head and killing him immediately. She then had Phillips cut Watkins's throat just to make sure he was dead. After killing Watkins, they loaded his body into the car and washed up the bloodstains.[11]

While the two disagreed on how the murder transpired, both confirmed what happened next. They dumped the body in a nearby well and fled the farm a day later, taking Watkins's car to South Carolina, where they married (despite the fact that Daniel remained married to his first wife). The Phillips returned to Watkins's farm that same evening and lived there for several weeks before fleeing to Gastonia at the end of the month. During that time Watkins's family grew concerned by his absence, and eventually reported him missing.[12]

On the evening of September 19, 1942, James Walters was out walking when he discovered human remains at the bottom of a well in Orange County. Harry Watkins owned the land, and local officials determined the remains were his. Three days after they discovered the body, police arrested the Phillips in Gastonia. They were transported back to Durham County and charged with first-degree capital murder. Their trial began on October 13, and the two faced an all-white jury who heard the defendants implicate each other. Not only did they indict each other for the murder, they exchanged charges of witchcraft. Rosanna claimed Daniel cast a spell on her, while Daniel claimed an unknown person cast a spell on him. According to the *Statesville Daily* newspaper, Rosanna said, "That man has me crazy as a bedbug right now, and I swear I ain't had nothing' to do with no killin'. Danny stole a lock of my hair and three pictures and put a spell on me." Daniel, meanwhile, claimed, "Long time ago she went to South Carolina to a root doctor; to have him put a spell on me." In neither case did the two deny the murder, they simply deflected the guilt. Their testimony lasted thirteen hours and ended on the afternoon of October 14; forty-eight minutes later the jury returned with two guilty verdicts.[13]

Consigned to death, both settled in Central Prison's death row to await their January 1, 1943, execution date. In the interim, Rosanna appealed to Governor J. Melville Broughton, asking him to commute her sentence to life in prison. The *Greensboro News* supported a commutation, arguing it was inappropriate to execute women. Broughton rejected that argument and Rosanna's appeal, calling the crime "one of the most brutal murders ever committed in the state." The executions thus went forth. At 10 A.M., guards strapped Daniel Phillips into the gas chamber. Authorities purposefully executed him first in hopes he would claim responsibility for the murder, setting the stage for Rosanna's last-minute reprieve. Daniel made no such claim, so moments after doctors declared him dead and guards removed his body, Rosanna entered the chamber. Strapped into the chair, Rosanna waited to die. That wait proved slightly longer than anticipated as the mechanism to drop the hydrogen cyanide capsule failed and prison guards had to enter the chamber and adjust it. On the second try the execution proceeded, and a cloud of poison gas engulfed Rosanna. According to witnesses, she died in seven minutes and twenty seconds—the fastest death in the chamber's history.[14]

Having broken the taboo of executing women, the state acted again two years later when African American Bessie Mae Williams followed Rosanna Phillips to the gas chamber. Left an orphan at a young age, Williams quit school in the fifth grade and largely raised herself working as a maid. She committed a few minor crimes and spent some time in jail for being drunk and disorderly, but nothing in her past indicated she might play a role in murder.

On the evening of April 28, 1944, Williams and her friends Annie Mae Allison, Ralph Thompson, and Cleve Bryant Johnson wanted to have some fun in Charlotte. Lacking money, they decided to rob a taxi driver. They flagged down a passing cab and asked to be taken to an isolated spot. Once there, Johnson ran away, but the other three proceeded to kill white cab driver, Mack Minyard. Allison hit him with a brick while Thompson stabbed him as he tried to fight back. Williams, meanwhile, grabbed the cash—a grand total of 50 cents.[15]

Police arrested all four, and Johnson agreed to testify against the others for a reduced charge of second-degree murder. Prosecutors were unclear how old Williams or Allison were, although it now seems Williams was eighteen and Allison fourteen. They looked alike, but the court determined Williams was older. That decision was key as a jury convicted all three and sentenced them to death.

Despite the fact that Allison actively hit Minyard with a brick while Williams played little role in the actual murder, Governor Broughton commuted Allison's sentence to life in prison due to her age. Williams received no such reprieve. She died in the gas chamber on December 29, 1944. Thompson preceded her to the grave earlier that day.[16]

While the use of the gas chamber initially appalled many, and the decision to execute women raised some eyebrows, prison officials and state politicians believed the changes were in keeping with their reformist agenda. That assessment is questionable, but the new policy certainly demonstrates the impact social and political forces had on penal policy. Convinced by a legislative study, determined to speed up the execution process, and once again hoping to bolster the state's progressive image by doing something no state east of the Mississippi had yet done, legislators authorized the installation of a gas chamber. Sadly, those developments did little to change the racial sensibilities that continued to skew punishment of all sorts. African Americans, even African American women, found themselves overly represented on death row, and just as in society at large the welfare of minority groups proved of little interest to the white public or politicians. That reality once again makes clear the limits of the state's progressivism.

The war years were thus a time during which the conjoined nature of the state and the prison carried forth. That link continued after the war, as administrators faced a rising crime rate and stark criticism for the manner in which they governed the facility. They also faced new financial concerns, political intervention, and inmate unrest. As with the rest of the state, and the nation as a whole, the postwar years were a time of upheaval. Prison officials employed a deft hand and a willingness to change in navigating this tumultuous era, and in the process continued to demonstrate the close relationship between the prison and society.

15

THE MACCORMICK REPORT

Bessie Mae Williams's execution came eight months prior to the end of World War II. Like most Americans, North Carolinians celebrated the war's end but worried about the future. The Depression remained an all too recent memory, and many feared that the end of wartime production would lead the nation back into economic collapse. That collapse did not occur, but the postwar era proved unsettled nonetheless, as judicial decisions, social unrest, and continued political intervention affected prisoners and prison administrators alike. Public issues thus continued to cross into the penal sphere. While some of those issues improved the prison experience for inmates and provided hope for rehabilitation, the refusal of politicians to relinquish control of the penitentiary and the eruption of several prisoner riots make clear that time in Central Prison remained hard and that politicians remained intent on preserving their influence over the prison system. While elements of the progressive tradition remained and administrators succeeded in more fully implementing the rehabilitative model, they still had to subordinate their agenda to the whims of the political class.

The era's developments began with a 1948 court case that originated in a Richmond County work camp. As punishment for saying "I wish I had a case of that beer" when a beer truck drove by, guards handcuffed a white inmate to his prison bars for fifty-two hours in a "spread eagle" fashion. News of the punishment leaked, and the press, remembering the exposure of similar punishments during the Depression, descended on the camp. Ned Carpenter, the work camp superintendent who ordered the punishment, justified it by claiming the inmate had violated policy by inciting his fellow prisoners. Neither the press nor the public bought that claim. Unlike the response to similar abuses thirteen years earlier in Mecklenburg County, this time the public outrage was loud and sustained. That reaction forced prosecutors to act, and Carpenter faced charges for the cruel and unusual treatment of an inmate.[1]

During his trial, Carpenter again asserted that the inmate violated camp rules, and his lawyers claimed the punishment was constitutionally protected. State Superior Court Judge Susie Sharp, who in 1949 made history when Governor Kerr Scott appointed her as the state's first female Superior Court judge, rejected both arguments and sentenced Carpenter to pay a $200 fine and serve a nine-month suspended sentence. Although overturned on a technicality, the ruling caused prison administrators to realize such treatment opened the possibility of further lawsuits and their own imprisonment, so in 1949 they made some reforms. Most notably, while handcuffing inmates to their cells remained policy, the punishment was limited to twenty-four hours, was to be used only in emergency cases, and was not to be used for minor offenses. Those inmates who remained a problem after twenty-four hours of confinement were removed to a more secure location.[2]

That secure location was Central Prison, where the second reform came with the creation of three versions of solitary confinement. Eleven "dark sol" cells served the most extreme cases. These six-foot by eight-foot rooms were located on the bottom level of the cellblock and remained pitch dark, a "Stygian darkness" as one author describes it. The cells contained a thin cotton mattress, a toilet, and a bucket of water. Originally, inmates "were fed a full meal only after 72 hours of confinement," and for the remainder of their term, which was limited to ten days, they received bread twice a day and a ten-quart bucket of water once a day. Inmate S. T. McGinnis noted that when he first spent time in isolation he devoured the bread, but he soon learned to cherish it and eventually "would pick up the bread, lie back on his mattress, and place the slices over his nose, breathing through them, inhaling the aroma. Then he would nibble a little of the bread and put it back on his nose for his olfactory senses to savor. He chewed each tiny bit a hundred times to make it last as long as possible, and then swallowed it slowly and gently." By the mid-1960s the meal had changed, although to many inmates it had not improved. As one inmate from the era explained, "here's the way they did it: ground-up liver, onions, carrots, turnips, and God knows what else, maybe a rat or two because they had plenty, all mixed together, cooked into the most ungodly mess you can imagine. You could smell it coming and it would make you puke." This inmate claimed the new meal, the "monotonous diet" as it was known, was created "so it would still be punishment but not such downright cruelty," and later asserted, "I'd rather starve" than eat it. And starve many did, to the extent that upon being released most had lost substantial weight, were in no position to perform hard labor, and spent time doing farm work until they regained their strength.[3]

Located just above the "dark sol" cells, the "hard sol" cells were a lesser form of isolation. Although the cells received light, inmates otherwise faced the same conditions as those in "dark sol." "Plain sol" isolation was the least penal form of isolation. It consisted simply of keeping an inmate in his normal cell twenty-four hours a day. He had no access to work or recreation, was required to maintain silence at all times, and received reduced rations. In each instance, a physician examined the inmates daily to check for physical or mental distress.[4]

Penitentiary officials believed the reforms enabled staff to punish deserving inmates in a manner that upheld their constitutional rights and ensured the penitentiary would not find itself back in the courts. While a noble effort, the problem was that moving all the difficult cases to Central Prison, isolated or not, meant a greater likelihood for trouble; and during the early 1950s there was a great deal of trouble. In May 1952, the prison faced four separate incidents in which inmates "went berserk" and destroyed property or attacked guards. One of the incidents was a massive brawl in the recreation yard that officials believed was the result of inmates being "pepped up by a drug prison inmates know as 'yellowjacket.'" In June, yet another assault occurred when African American inmate William Rook, who was serving ten years for breaking, entering, and larceny, stabbed Captain Thomas Jefferies in the shoulder.[5]

Frustrated by the continued assaults and disruption, prison guards complained to Warden Robert Allen. Rumors even began to swirl that they were considering a strike. Allen mollified the guards by assuring them he was working on a plan to reduce the inmates' ability to make or procure weapons. He also instructed guards that they had the right to use "whatever force they found necessary to protect themselves, prison property and their prisoners."[6]

Although Allen's assurances placated the guards, the inmates remained on edge. Privately, prison officials acknowledged that many inmates were unhappy with their treatment and with the actions of specific guards. The violence, in other words, may not have been the result of drug abuse, it may well have been a form of acting out against a system the inmates found intolerable. Indeed, prior to his assault on Captain Jefferies, Rook had filed a petition claiming his treatment was cruel and unusual. As proof, he asserted that he had been transferred to Central Prison in order to receive medical care, but after more than a month he still had not seen a doctor. Despite complaining of abdominal pain, the guards refused to provide him medical service, and when he slashed his own arm in an effort to force their hand, they simply took him to a nursing station where another inmate applied some stitches. Worse still, for the act of self-mutilation guards ordered Rook to solitary confinement. It was on the day they informed him of his punishment that he attacked Jefferies.[7]

Other inmates made similar claims of abuse and neglect, and many pointed to one guard in particular as the worst of the lot: Captain W. G. Meadows. Rook later explained that he "was afraid Meadows would beat him and perhaps kill him." Others alleged Meadows had "beaten and kicked prisoners, knocked a man down a flight of stairs, cut the rations of men on punishment already lower than the already low standard, and generally acted rough." When nothing came of the inmates' protests, they joined Rook in acting out—this time on a much larger scale.[8]

The incident began at 1 P.M. on June 4, 1952, when an interracial group of inmates working in the industrial building took three guards and seven civilian employees hostage. After seizing the hostages, all of whom were white, the inmates barricaded themselves inside the building and issued three demands: better food, the right to air grievances, and the dismissal of Captain Meadows. They also demanded to speak with Warden Allen. The meeting with Allen took place, and at 6:30 P.M. the inmates released the hostages after the warden publicly promised "to check on the cooking, hear occasionally from inmate spokesmen, suspend Captain Meadows, and, finally, to exact no reprisals."[9]

In the aftermath, a state Bureau of Investigation examination into the charges against Meadows led to his dismissal and the firing of five other guards. Furthermore, Allen and State Prisons Director Walter Anderson met to discuss reforms to keep drugs out of the prison, to prevent future hostage takings, and to address other organizational issues that might make handling inmates easier and safer.

Despite those efforts and the incident's peaceful resolution, Warden Allen faced criticism for caving to the inmates' demands. Indeed, in the aftermath the press questioned inmates about the impact their actions might have on Allen. The inmates assured the press that they liked Allen and preferred him to his predecessor, Joseph Crawford. When journalists told inmates that public outrage might cost Allen his job, they went out of their way to explain that the issue had nothing to do with him and that they just wanted to get rid of Meadows. They also assured the press that they were "satisfied" and had "no more demands." To further make the case that no one should blame Allen for the incident or his handling of it, in July inmates issued the second edition of a newspaper called *The Inner World*. In it, they apologized for the hostage taking, offered their "sincere gratitude and honest admiration" to the warden, and pledged to him their "full support and cooperation." Allen ultimately kept his job.[10]

Although authorities quelled this riot, within a month four other uprisings occurred that resulted in the stabbing of three inmates and one guard. Staff determined the cause of the violence was "the concentration at Central Prison of prisoners recognized as dangerous and clever troublemakers." To solve the problem, administrators moved some inmates to indefinite segregation within the prison and moved others to different facilities. The hope was that dispersing the miscreants would end the trouble. In reality, all it did was spread the trouble and undermine rehabilitation efforts in other facilities. Those inmates who remained in segregation at Central Prison, meanwhile, continued to file lawsuits alleging cruel and unusual punishment.[11]

The unrest of the era was not limited to the male prisoners. On August 13, 1954, guards at the Women's Prison placed Eleanor Rush, an eighteen-year-old African American woman who was serving a six-month sentence for forcible trespass, in isolation for threatening a guard with a rock. On the seventh day of isolation, guards failed to deliver her any food for sixteen hours. When she yelled demanding a meal, guards placed her in a restraining belt and gagged her. Twenty-five minutes later, when the guards next checked on her, she was dead. When Rush's fellow inmates learned of her death at 9 A.M. the subsequent morning, they rioted. They destroyed property and hurled debris at the guards. The rebellion lasted four hours and ended only after guards from Central Prison augmented the Women's Prison force. Administrators punished the ringleaders by sending them to isolation, Central Prison, or the Caledonia prison farm.[12]

The rioters, however, were not the only ones facing punishment. Coming barely five years after the Ned Carpenter case, state prosecutors realized they needed to make a formal inquest into Rush's death. A six-person coroner's jury performed the investigation and determined that Eleanor died from a broken neck. It further found evidence that she had been restrained, gagged, and perhaps even beaten. One inmate told the jury she saw Superintendent Ivan Hinton "beat Eleanor to death," while another asserted that "Mr. Hinton rammed a towel down Eleanor's throat, and tied another one over her mouth. Then the guards put steel handcuffs on her, and forced her hands behind her." The same inmate claimed guards tied Eleanor to her bed and beat her; she also reported seeing guards remove a bloody mattress from the cell.[13]

Despite such testimony, the jury blamed Rush's death on "her own violent efforts against necessary restraint." The *Raleigh News and Observer* called the result "a shocking verdict," and the public was similarly perplexed. Seeking to quell the furor and put the matter behind them as quickly as possible, in 1955 Industrial Commission Examiner Hugh Currins ordered the Highway Department to pay Eleanor's mother Genevieve Gould $3,000 in damages. Highway Department officials objected, believing the courts had absolved them of any wrongdoing, and appealed the order. In 1957, the State Supreme Court upheld the fine after it determined, albeit in a split decision, that the state was responsible for Rush's death.[14]

The riots and lawsuits convinced Governor Kerr Scott to intervene. In 1949 he thus created the Prison Advisory Council, whose task was to promote "practices consistent with the best modern concepts and experience, directed toward rehabilitation of prisoners." The council turned to Dr. Austin MacCormick, a professor of criminology at Berkeley College in California, to assist in the task, and requested he perform a complete analysis of the prison system with recommendations for improvement.[15]

When MacCormick proffered his findings in 1954, he was brutal in his assessment. He called the state's penal system "a disgrace" and pointed to "inefficiency, politics, road gangs, and lack of rehabilitation" as its "most glaring ills." He described Central Prison as "a mediocre institution at best," found nearly half of all inmates idle, and asserted that former Warden Joseph Crawford had been "appointed for political purposes" and possessed "neither the training nor the understanding for the position." Surprisingly, he claimed there existed no brutality within the system, but he found "the methods and discipline . . . archaic." He further determined that guards made no effort to rehabilitate inmates, and explained that this led to a high level of recidivism and the "loss of life and property and increased human misery caused by preventable crime."[16]

From this litany of shortcomings, MacCormick moved to a series of recommendations. He first urged the state to separate the prison system from the Highway Department. He wrote, "While it is possible for Highway Officials to build and maintain good roads and also operate good prisons, it is not realistic to expect them to serve with equal devotion both objectives." This recommendation superseded all others, and until addressed none of his other suggestions would be impactful. If the state truly was serious about solving its penal problems, divorcing the prison system from the Highway Department needed to be its first act.[17]

Once divorced, MacCormick suggested the independent prison system devise a new organizational structure. He recommended the establishment of a seven-person board of correction who were free from political influence and were "fully qualified on basis of ability, training, experience, personality, and character." To assist the board, MacCormick suggested hiring additional staff, including an assistant director of administrative affairs, a chief medical officer, a chief chaplain, a psychologist, a supervisor of social services, and a supervisor of educational and vocational training. He was, in other words, demanding that administrators adopt fully the rehabilitative model and make use of experts and trained staff as George Pou had suggested two decades earlier.[18]

Beyond those calls, MacCormick recommended better wages, shorter workdays, better working conditions, and more training for guards. He suggested that the prison do more to employ inmates in on-site industries to produce goods for on-site consumption. He called for better educational opportunities through a more deliberate employment of local teachers and professors, with the goal of raising every inmate to at least a fourth-grade reading level. He suggested a dramatic expansion of the youth centers. He urged the state to "replace Women's Prison with a modern reformatory," or at the very least update its medical facilities, heating unit, and visitor's center. He also called for the construction of a separate medium security facility so that Central Prison could focus on maximum custody inmates, and then suggested the more formal segregation of incorrigibles, honor inmates, and the old and ailing. Finally, he called for more individualized treatment and increased aid to inmates' families.[19]

To ensure the success of the reforms, MacCormick concluded his report by urging the prison to adopt a more modern classification system. The cornerstone to his proposal was a "traveling card system." The card would follow an inmate wherever he went within the system, and would include "a brief digest of the classification summary, and all transfers, promotions, demotions, [and] disciplinary actions." Such information, he asserted, would facilitate inmates' integration into a new facility and would prevent cases of mistaken identity. This new system, combined with all the other suggestions, MacCormick ultimately declared, would solve the problem of prisoner unrest and would further benefit the inmates, the prison administrators, and the state through reduced recidivism and decreased expenditures.[20]

Although a devastating report, not only in its direct condemnations but in the implicit criticisms raised by the litany of suggested reforms, few of the ideas were original and most fell in line with the state's progressive tradition.

A state that proudly proclaimed its position as among the first to adopt the gas chamber surely would find it hard to reject such logical and beneficial penal programs. And indeed, officials in the Highway and Public Works Commission accepted MacCormick's analysis and suggestions, and "instructed the Director of Prisons to apply as many of the recommendations as he found feasible and desirable."[21]

Over the course of the next six years, prison administrators fulfilled that instruction. They increased the salaries of guards and trained fifteen "key officials" by sending them to a five-day seminar at the University of North Carolina Institute of Government. They created new youth and first-time offender camps, and they transformed the Caledonia prison farm into an honor camp for African American inmates. As a part of that transformation, Caledonia gained a vocational training program, library, classrooms, and recreation accessories. Prison officials also introduced several psychological testing programs and expanded the literacy classes and vocational training programs system wide. Among the new vocational programs was a food service school at Central Prison, which not only trained inmates in the culinary arts but saved the state money by employing the trainees as cooks. Additional reforms included a more complete segregation of misdemeanants and felons, and the segregation of physically handicapped inmates to their own facility. Finally, each work camp employed a newly hired physician to ensure the health, safety, and welfare of every inmate. Although still part of the Highway Department, leaving in place the fundamental change for which MacCormick called, these new policies demonstrate a clear willingness on the part of state officials to reform the system.[22]

In 1956, the reforms became even more meaningful when prison officials fully adopted the rehabilitative model by introducing six services: classification, medical, consolidated records, education, religious and moral training, and recreation, all of which sought "to provide a program for inmates that will enable them to return to society rehabilitated to the point that they will become acceptable citizens in normal society." The classification and medical processes began when inmates entered the reception center at Central Prison to be fingerprinted, photographed, interviewed, given an IQ test, "tested for educational achievement," given a physical exam, assigned a physical rating, and asked about their social history. The inmates then spent two weeks in K-dorm, isolated from the main body of inmates, during which time a classification committee reviewed their file and assigned them to one of four "custody requirement" levels: maximum, close, medium, and minimum. The committee made the assignments based on the information gathered during the inmate's reception, as well as the observations guards made during the inmate's two weeks in the reception center.[23]

After the inmate received his classification, administrators assigned him to one of fifty-six units throughout the prison system. Twenty-six served medium custody inmates, nine served youthful offenders, nine housed close custody inmates, six housed minimum custody inmates, five served physically handicapped inmates, and all maximum custody inmates resided in Central Prison. Wherever the inmate served his time, the consolidated records provision ensured the accessibility of his criminal, behavioral, and medical information. Unlike MacCormick's "traveling card system," a central facility maintained the records and distributed the information as needed.[24]

The final three services were more easily addressed. The system achieved the educational element through course work, vocational training, and library opportunities. Religious leaders from the area volunteered their time and provided spiritual and moral training, and recreational opportunities, in the form of boxing, baseball, board games, and television, continued at each facility.[25]

The services proved a rapid success and facilitated five minor reforms in 1958. First, the state increased its rehabilitative efforts by employing additional high school teachers and college professors to further the inmates' education. Second, it opened Alcoholics Anonymous programs with the realization that many inmates got into trouble as a result of alcohol abuse. Third, it added a full-time psychologist to the staff and began to employ group counseling sessions. Fourth, it implemented the "continuous testing and adjustment of classification criteria." The purpose of this reform was to subject inmates to repeated re-evaluations of their "custody requirements" in order to determine when they were ready to move to a lower classification level. The move served as a reward for achievement, bolstered morale, and saved the state money since lower level facilities were cheaper to administer. Cost had always been a concern, so it is surprising that the fifth reform, the hiring of a comptroller, took so long. Tasked with ensuring strict financial accounting, the comptroller and his team of field auditors and accountants implemented "proper procedures for calculating, processing, and reporting of all financial data." To assist the comptroller team in those endeavors, the legislature also authorized the purchase of a punch card computer.[26]

The implemented reforms went a long way toward solving many of the issues confronting the prison. Administrators noted that the improved classification and record keeping systems resulted in more inmates earning honor status, which improved behavior throughout the system. Improved segregation reduced prison violence, and prisoner complaints about brutal guards declined dramatically. Here was proof that when they wanted to be, state legislators and prison administrators could be truly progressive. The results also seemed to prove that the rehabilitative model worked, and that Pou had been correct in his calls to adopt it.

Despite that success, one fundamental problem remained: the prison's continued subordination to the Highway Department. Politicians refused to make the change, and not only violated the foundational issue for which MacCormick called, but mitigated many of the aforementioned achievements. In a formal in-house analysis, prison officials recognized that fact. The analysis began by noting that "North Carolina is the only state whose prisons are administratively under the Highway Department." While acknowledging the consolidation occurred for financial considerations during the Depression, the report argued, "there is now no justification for putting a dollar sign on every prisoner and continuing a system of prison administration which is inconsistent with the national reputation of North Carolina for progressive thought and action."[27]

But more than state pride was at stake, and the analysis warned that under the Highway Department

virtually no effort is being made to rehabilitate prisoners . . . and the result is that prisoners released from the penal institution repeat their crimes over and over again. Repeated crimes, committed by offenders who could have been salvaged, exposes the persons and the property of the public to a menace which could be removed and subjects the tax-payers to heavy costs for the apprehension and conviction of repeaters. Even if one leaves out of consideration the needless loss of life and property and the human misery caused by preventable crime, the financial costs alone would be enough reason for the change advocated. These long-range costs far outweigh the apparent immediate savings that come from financing the prison system by turning it over to the Highway Department.

Prison officials thus agreed with MacCormick's findings.[28]

The analysis continued with a critical survey of the impact that Highway Department control had on inmates working the road camps: "Nothing worthy of note is done to improve them while they are serving sentence, or to prepare them for free life, or to help them when they return to freedom." Worse, the report contended that "it is an inescapable fact that a stay in the camps is much more likely to do harm than good to men committed to them and tends to confirm them in a criminal pattern." This was caused by the fact that those who ran the camps had a very different goal than those who ran the prison: those overseeing the road crews wanted to get the job done, those overseeing the prison sought inmate reform.[29]

Not only did the Highway Department's control of the road camps injure inmates, the analysis discovered it hurt the penitentiary as well. It noted that none of the industries at Central Prison produced at full capacity, nor were they employing a full work staff. It further asserted that the state had needs that prison industries could address, including the production of road signs, metal filing cabinets, and printed paper products. The reason prison industries were not fully exploited and the needs of the state were left unaddressed was that the Highway Department worried only about roads and ignored other opportunities. The report ultimately concluded that "the best interests of the State" required "abandoning this administrative set-up" and replacing it with one in which the prison system had "separate and independent status in a State Department of Correction."[30]

That separation would come, but throughout the early 1950s inmates and prison staff struggled amid an era of change. Those struggles challenged the public's perception of the state as being forward looking, but thanks to the intervention of Dr. Austin MacCormick and the willingness of officials to follow some of his suggestions, the perception rebounded to the state's benefit. The refusal of the state's politicians to remove themselves from prison governance, however, undermined the effective power of those reforms and called into question the political motivation. Such paradoxical behavior continued throughout the decade, as inmates won greater opportunities and more representative treatment, yet faced ever more stringent controls. Administrators, by contrast, won their freedom from the Highway Department yet faced new financial constraints and the difficulties of governing a growing penal system. The issues of finance, progressivism, political intervention, and the state's paradoxical history thus remained relevant as prisoners and administrators dealt with the social, cultural, and political upheavals of the late 1950s.

Arial view of prison, circa 1926.
Courtesy of the North Carolina Museum of History.

Inmates on convict lease assignment.

Inmates picking cotton on a prison farm.
Courtesy of the North Carolina Department of Public Safety.

Inmate band. Courtesy of the State Archives of North Carolina.

Chain gang inmates in mobile cells.

Central Prison's Warden H. H. Honeycutt in the State Bureau of Identification office.
Courtesy of the North Carolina Museum of History.

Cellblock with segregation cells on the bottom level.
Courtesy of the North Carolina Department of Public Safety.

Double bunking, circa 1970. Courtesy of the State Archives of North Carolina.

Yard area. Courtesy of the State Archives of North Carolina.

Arial view of prison with newly constructed industrial building. Courtesy of the
North Carolina Museum of History.

Evidence of overcrowding, 1970s.
Courtesy of the North Carolina Department of Public Safety.

Inside of new Central Prison, 1980s.
Courtesy of the North Carolina
Department of Public Safety.

Exterior of new Central Prison.
Courtesy of the North Carolina Department of Public Safety.

16

FREEDOM

The reforms of the early 1950s were but a prelude to three major changes that emerged at the end of the decade. The construction of several new facilities offered administrators multiple options for segregating and reforming inmates, and demonstrated the legislature's continued willingness to fund the penitentiary system. The second major reform came when politicians freed the prison system from the Highway Department. The final change came when legislators made history by implementing a first-in-the-nation work release program designed to better prepare inmates for their transition to the outside world. The combined result exemplified the state's paradoxical nature: the creation of new programs to more securely house and punish difficult inmates arose alongside ground-breaking new programs to better rehabilitate them. As the 1950s came to a close, punishment and rehabilitation once again clashed.

In 1954, legislators inaugurated the era's reforms when they approved funds for construction of an eighty-bed facility in Caswell County. It took two years to construct, opening for service in 1956. Called Ivy Bluff, but known by inmates as "Little Alcatraz," it housed "prisoners who would make necessary a repressive program and curtail opportunities for effective rehabilitation programs at other units if they were not removed and segregated in a facility specially designed for such prisoners." It was thus "reserved for prisoners who [were] too troublesome to be retained in the regular population of other units, but who [were] found by the prison physician and prison psychiatrist to be fit for its rigorous regime." Simply put, it housed the worst of the worst.[1]

Despite that, there was a rehabilitative side to the new facility. As administrators explained it: "It was hoped that the very existence of an institution where privileges are limited, supervision is strict, routine is exacting, and discipline is firm but fair would act as a deterrent to misconduct by inmates of other units of the prison system, and that the lack of opportunity for serious misbehavior would enable those sent to Ivy Bluff to acquire habits of good behavior." Indeed, officials designed Ivy Bluff's policies "to make assignment there undesirable from the inmate's viewpoint." No inmate went directly to this facility, and guards used the threat of being sent there as a corrective to inmate behavior at other facilities.[2]

According to inmate Frank Watson, who served time in the institution not long after it opened, "Ivy Bluff's main building was T-shaped, with offices and dormitories to the front, the mess hall and kitchen to the rear. The lockup and sickbay were over the kitchen. Each side of the T had two dormitories, each with about twenty beds. The beds were solid steel with legs sunk in the concrete floor so they couldn't be moved or torn apart and used as weapons. The sinks, commodes, and showers were built so they couldn't be torn from the wall and destroyed." To ensure further control and to limit the inmate's ability to cause trouble, initially prisoners could possess only a comb, a toothbrush, and toothpaste. As Watson noted, "no radio, no TV, no books, no reading matter of any kind, not even a newspaper or a Bible." Additionally, guards strip-searched inmates in the morning before they headed to work at a nearby quarry and in the evening upon their return. Intimidation also played a part, with Watson recalling that upon entering the prison the warden warned the men, "You guys been sent here to git killed. Any of you gits out of line, you're dead." In his own way, the warden was making clear that the inmates had reached the end of the line.[3]

For the first twenty-two months of its existence, everything went fine. Apart from two unsuccessful escape attempts, Ivy Bluff proved secure, trouble at Central Prison and the other facilities in the system declined, and several inmates who served time at Ivy Bluff successfully reintegrated into the general population. That success, however, hid a darker perspective. Prison administrators declared those sent to Ivy Bluff were "usually psychopaths suffering from a distorted personality that renders them especially unreliable." As a result, guards allowed inmates little leeway and strictly enforced every regulation. Lacking traditional forms of agency, frustrations among the prisoners quickly reached a boiling point, with the result that a number "resorted to hunger strikes and self-mutilation." In 1958, several inmates went so far as to smash their own legs with sledgehammers in an effort to win transfer or more privileges. Those same inmates often refused medical treatment or reinjured themselves to avoid returning to Ivy Bluff.[4]

In response, politicians and prison administrators implemented three reforms. First, legislators passed a law giving doctors the right to perform medical procedures on inmates suffering from self-inflicted wounds. Second, politicians passed a law making a self-injury that prevented an inmate from working a felony punishable by up to ten years. Third, prison officials created a new three-tier classification system unique to Ivy Bluff. New arrivals entered in classification stage 1. Each new inmate resided in a segregation cell for an orientation period, during which he learned the rules and adjusted to the prison. After the inmate demonstrated his willingness to abide by the rules, he moved to classification stage 2. At this stage, the inmate earned mail and visiting privileges and had access to magazines, religious services, and games. An inmate who behaved in stage 2 could win promotion to classification stage 3, at which point he received a radio, additional reading opportunities, and canteen privileges. An inmate who remained in stage 3 for six months became eligible for return to the general population upon successful completion of an interview with Ivy Bluff staff.[5]

Despite the reforms the prison remained oppressive, and many inmates attempted to escape. In 1959 they succeeded. On December 7, 1959, Charles "Yank" Stewart, a white inmate who previously had escaped from Central Prison by sawing through prison bars, shimmying down a rope made from bed sheets, and scaling the wall with a homemade ladder, made a similarly daring escape from Ivy Bluff. At 1 A.M. Stewart lured a guard into his cell, overpowered him, and seized his keys. He then freed nineteen other inmates. In one of the largest prison breaks in the state's history, the twenty inmates seized a prison truck and escaped. State police eventually recaptured all twenty, but Stewart went on a crime spree during his several months on the lam and served federal prison time in Atlanta and Alcatraz before he returned to North Carolina in 1963.[6]

Despite the escape's infamy, officials believed the new facility was secure and were happy that it eased tensions and unrest at other institutions. Politicians, meanwhile, prided themselves on their willingness to fund the prison and implement a new penal program. And finally, prisoners at the state's other detention centers appreciated the improved atmosphere created by the new prison's threatening existence. Ivy Bluff served the state for four decades, remaining open until 1999.

An even bigger reform came when the prison system finally gained its freedom from the Highway Department. The journey began in 1952 when the state legislature created a separate Prison Department under the umbrella of the Highway Department. Although not fully independent, the hope was that with more autonomy penitentiary administrators could better address the inmates' needs. While the autonomy helped, penitentiary officials argued they needed complete independence from outside oversight.[7]

As a part of that argument, in 1956 officials produced their *Report on the Feasibility of Separating the State Prison System from the State Highway and Public Works Commission*. The document began with an extensive history of the system since World War II. Among its findings was that "for the last 20 years, repeaters have never constituted less than 57 percent of the total number of prisoners committed to the State prison system in the course of a year. Recidivism has registered as high as 67.9 percent." Those numbers were higher than in neighboring states, and administrators argued that the cause was a lack of focus on rehabilitation brought about by the prison's subservience to the Highway Department.[8]

The document then criticized the shortcomings of the state's parole and probation systems. It noted that in 1955, 32.5 percent of those released from the North Carolina prison system were paroled. In a majority of states the figure was above 50 percent, and in fifteen it was above 75 percent. It further argued that when the cost of housing an inmate, the welfare funds that went to families with husbands in jail, and lost income taxes were added together, the state could save $4.34 million per year by more fully employing parole. It offered similar figures for probation, noting that in 1956 it cost $878.92 a year to keep an inmate in prison but only $66 to place him or her on probation. The report also reiterated previous calls for more "pre-release" programs to help inmates prepare for the transition to freedom. Administrators then tied all of this together to assert that the cause of those problems was Highway Department control.[9]

To make the causation evident, the document next explored the administrative consequences of the relationship. The writers noted that due to the political nature of the Highway Department, new commissioners appeared virtually every time the state elected a new governor. Indeed, the report noted that between 1933 and 1953 the director of prisons changed twelve times. As a result, the report found the "development of a professionalized prison service has not been possible. Rapid turnover of personnel . . . precluded effective training programs. There were too few tested leaders ready for the responsibilities of the next higher position." This led to unfilled vacancies, low morale, excessive costs, and high recidivism rates.[10]

Although the legislation granting the prison autonomy was a step in the right direction, the report concluded by criticizing the fact that the Highway Department still managed the prison's funds: "It seems unlikely that anyone advocating separation of the State prison system from the State Highway and

Public Works Commission would want the Commission to retain fiscal control over prisons. Prison administrators without fiscal authority would be puppets dangling from the purse strings controlled by the Commission. On the other hand, it would be unsound to hamper the Highway Commission in its control over funds appropriated for road maintenance. Therefore, it appears that prison separation should be accompanied by a change in the statute requiring payment of prison costs from road maintenance funds." Prison administrators were willing to forego the financial benefits of their association with the Highway Department in return for freedom.[11]

The same year the report appeared, prison officials hired an accountant tasked with creating a budget to demonstrate how an independent prison department would fund itself. The accountant determined that without access to the highway funds the prison would run a $3.8 million deficit in 1957–1958 and a $2.9 million deficit in 1958–1959; money to cover that deficit would have to come from the state's General Fund. However, the accountant did not include in those estimates a $1.3 million "revolving fund" that would "permit savings resulting from bulk purchasing on a buyer's market." When projected forward, and with the "revolving fund" taken into consideration, the accountant determined the prison would run at or near self-sufficiency by 1960. With that, prison authorities justified their call for separation on the grounds of rehabilitation, institutional stability, and economics.[12]

On July 1, 1957, politicians accepted that judgement and granted the prison system its freedom with the creation of the North Carolina Prison Department. For twenty-four years it had been part of the Highway Department, but under the new arrangement a seven-member commission and a director of prisons governed the Prison Department. The governor appointed the commission members, who served four-year terms and, in consultation with the governor, selected the director. W. F. Bailey was the first director, serving through 1960, and he assumed control of a sprawling and racially segregated system that included eight institutions: Central Prison, Women's Prison, the Caledonia prison farm, Polk Prison, Ivy Bluff Prison, Umstead Youth Center, Goldsboro Youth Center, and the Inmate Division of the North Carolina State Sanatorium, as well as eighty-six field units. The system that Director Bailey oversaw was thus massive and diverse. It also mirrored the state, with facilities scattered throughout its three regions, racial segregation being a fundamental component of each facility, and progressive elements being built into an otherwise oppressive structure.[13]

Among Bailey's first tasks as head of the newly independent Prison Department was to require each institution to improve its economic productivity. Appreciating that he had to compete with other state agencies for General Fund money, he wanted to reduce the department's reliance on state resources and increase inmate-generated revenue. To achieve those goals, he enhanced industrial training for inmate workers, improved the quality control of prison-produced goods, and modernized the packaging and marketing of prison-produced goods. The result was a 22 percent increase in prison industry sales in the 1957–1958 fiscal year. Inmates under the supervision of civilian foremen manufactured metal and wood products, soap, paint, signs, and clothing, and sold products to "tax supported agencies of the state and its political subdivisions." None of the products were sold to the general public.[14]

The farms, meanwhile, produced "food in sufficient quantities and varieties" to meet the daily nutritional needs of the inmates. Each site grew its own vegetables, and inmates at the Caledonia prison farm and the Women's Prison canned goods for later use. The Caledonia prison farm also produced a majority of the meat and 75 percent of the eggs that the prison system needed. The food service school at Central Prison taught inmates from throughout the system how to turn those products into meals, and after completing classes the inmate-students returned to their institutions to prepare the thirty-eight thousand meals per day that the prisoners consumed.[15]

Bailey's efforts to reduce expenditures and increase profits succeeded surprisingly well. A study found that "control of its own fiscal affairs has enabled the prison department to make marked improvements in the accounting, budgeting, and business operations of the prison system." Those improvements were across the board, and included a $418,728 budget savings for the 1957–1958 fiscal year and an increase in the system's sanitation scores from 72.6 percent to 91.2 percent.[16]

Those achievements encouraged Bailey to implement additional reforms aimed at benefitting the inmates. He introduced new vocational training programs, expanded literacy training and the libraries, and updated each facility's recreational, medical, educational, and religious facilities. He also changed the dress code by abolishing the use of striped clothing and instead assigning inmates different colors. Minimum security and honor grade inmates of any security level received blue uniforms; medium, close, or maximum security inmates who were not honor grade received brown uniforms; and close or maximum security inmates who had a "C" conduct grade received gray uniforms.[17]

One final reform demonstrated that Bailey understood he was dealing with dangerous men and that for every benefit he provided he needed to ensure they remained under tight control. Thus, in 1958 he added "additional security facilities . . . at close custody field units, including fencing around segregation units, yard activities fencing, a barred section for the guard in the mess hall, barred sections in the cellblock corridor, interior emergency lighting, and exterior wall lighting." A year later, he created "a special security work squad . . . at each close custody unit to provide additional guarding for the fraction of close custody prisoners considered to be the greatest security risks."[18]

Taken together, Bailey's achievements are notable. He guided the Prison Department through its first years of independence, improved its financial balance sheet, granted additional benefits to the inmates, and strengthened prison security. All of those reforms became possible by the freedom the prison system enjoyed after its release from the Highway System, and demonstrate well the move's propriety. Although long overdue, once the Prison Department gained independence it did not take long for it to regain its forward momentum.

That momentum continued with the era's final major reform. In 1957, North Carolina introduced a daytime work release program. Select inmates earned the opportunity to leave the penitentiary unattended each morning to work at off-site jobs, with the expectation that they would return to the penitentiary on their own each evening. Inmates in the program earned a salary, from which the state deducted expenses, with any money left over entered into a trust fund for the inmate to enjoy upon release.[19]

The initial law limited participation to those serving misdemeanor terms who had not served more than six months for any prior crime. The result was that only twenty-four inmates were eligible in 1958, so in 1959 legislators amended the law to make eligible any felon serving fewer than five years. Additional amendments allowed inmates with longer terms the opportunity to participate with the approval of the board of paroles.[20]

Subsequent examinations of North Carolina's work release program seem to demonstrate its success. In 1956, a study by scholars at the University of North Carolina at Chapel Hill predicted the state would have nearly fourteen thousand inmates by the late 1960s. Thanks in part to the work release program, in 1968 the number of inmates was ten thousand. A 1977 study found that on average fourteen hundred inmates participated in the work release program per day, and the author of that study, Ann Witte, a professor of economics at Chapel Hill, asserted that "it has the effect of reducing the propensity of releasees to commit serious crimes. This finding serves as a rebuttal to the claim that 'nothing works' in the field of criminal rehabilitation. Something does work, and, fortuitously, it is a program that is generally compatible with other objectives of the criminal justice system, including incapacitation, deterrence, and reasonable criminal justice system budgets."[21]

Director of Prisons George Randall, who assumed the position in 1960, also approved, and in 1962 he offered an extensive summary of the work release program, which he believed benefitted inmates and the state. He noted that in 1960, seventy-four inmates were part of the program, but by 1962 the number had increased to 571. He went on to assert, "possession of money and productive employment on final release from prison are two positive factors contributing importantly to the low rate of recidivism for inmates granted work release privileges. (16 per cent; general rate, 64.5 percent). Less tangible but probably even more important are the increased self-respect and self-confidence frequently found in those inmates who serve all or the final part of their prison sentences on work release." Another cause of the low recidivism level, he argued, was that in the process of working, inmates were "facilitating development of an acceptable parole plan."[22]

The work release program demonstrated that North Carolina had successfully adopted the rehabilitative model. Indeed, in 1962 Director Randall proudly reported that the prison system's inmate population had declined by over one thousand prisoners between 1960 and 1962, and he argued that "it seems certain that considerable credit for this achievement is ascribable to our various efforts to promote the rehabilitation of offenders while they are serving terms of imprisonment in the State prison system." He praised the educational and vocational training programs, Alcoholics Anonymous, and the work release program, but acknowledged the further benefits that resulted from improved classification, improved medical and psychological services, added group counseling sessions, expanded religious services, and the more frequent and varied recreation opportunities. Rehabilitation worked, and with administrators free to run the prison without political intervention, that fact became ever more obvious.[23]

Although he did not do so, Randall might also have credited the impact of another of his reforms. In 1960, he had increased guard training and enacted more selective criteria for their hiring. Those standards included raised educational requirements and the expectation that all employees would "have a record and reputation that will provide no basis for questioning his or her integrity, sobriety, and moral fitness." Additionally, he implemented "a policy for standardization of custodial officers' uniforms" and began to employ "a consistent set of military titles" in an effort to raise the "personal pride and organizational efficiency" of the guard staff. The result, Randall explained, was that by the mid-1960s Central Prison was "a hybrid institution including characteristics found in a military organization in terms of custody, in a business concern in terms of prison industrial operations, and a school and hospital in terms of rehabilitation programs."[24]

Randall's explanation summarizes well the varied nature of the prison system and the changes it underwent in the 1950s. Politicians accepted a diminished influence in prison affairs by granting the system its freedom from Highway Department oversight. In response to their newfound ability to govern themselves, prison administrators cut costs, created a new system to better prepare inmates for their release, and even devised a better method of training guards. At the same time, however, those guards were militarized, while Ivy Bluff punished those inmates who refused rehabilitation. As with much of the rest of the state's history, developments in the state penitentiary demonstrated an odd combination of forward-looking reform and a determined effort to maintain close control of circumstances. Politics, finances, progressivism, and paradoxical programs thus remained fundamental elements of the era. But times change quickly, and almost before anyone could adapt to those developments a new set of challenges emerged. Like the nation at large, prisoners and prison officials struggled with the turbulent 1960s, as racism, violence, and a general unease descended on the sprawling system and threatened to undo all that administrators had so recently achieved.

17

RIGHTS AND REBELLION

Although the 1950s saw the state's penal system undergo some significant reforms, the ensuing two decades proved problematic. The civil rights movement and the resultant white backlash saw North Carolina "pull back from its midcentury liberalism," first electing conservative Democrats and then turning toward the Republican Party. While the penitentiary had long endured political interference, the impact of this change was especially notable as legislators and the public alike turned on the rehabilitative model and pushed for inmates to do "hard time." That push fostered a level of inmate unrest that was matched by an authoritative and violent administrative response. As the state and nation lived through an era of social and political ferment, so too did the prison.[1]

To be fair, North Carolina's prison system was not the only one to endure unrest in this era. According to scholars Peter Carlson and Judith Garrett, prior to the 1950s prisoner riots were "relatively rare, spontaneous, opportunistic events not intentionally launched to air collective complaints." That began to change in the 1950s. Between 1950 and 1953, fifty major prison uprisings exploded nationwide, and the unrest continued through the 1970s. Not only were those riots more numerous, they were unique due to their interracial nature and the fact that they "began to display political and activist overtones." Prisoners purposefully organized, but rather than seek escape they sought to change the circumstances of their confinement.

Scholars contend that one reason for the explosion in inmate activism was the simple fact that it was an era of activism and fear. James Jacobs writes, "prisoners, a majority of whom [were] black and poor, . . . identified themselves and their struggle with other 'victimized minorities,' and pressed their claims with vigor and not a little moral indignation." Just as civil rights protestors took to the streets to foment change, so too did inmates. Penologist John Martin notes,

"Prisoners are like the rest of us; they lived through the same history as the rest of us. . . . They feel all the pressures the rest of us feel." With American society in an uproar, and protest, demonstration, riot, and violence endemic, that similar events transpired in prison should not be a surprise; inmates simply behaved like the rest of the population.[2]

Judicial decisions also played a role in increasing inmate activism. In the 1961 *Monroe v. Pape* case, the Supreme Court ruled that the Civil Rights Act of 1871 gave inmates the right to sue in federal court for abuses suffered in state prisons. This ruling was key, as state courts often were "inhospitable to claims against state and local agencies. In addition, some states . . . put legal limits on the ability of state courts to grant judgments against state and local agencies." The *Monroe* decision demolished those restrictions and provided inmates a way to overcome laws designed to limit the liability of state agencies.[3]

The *Cooper v. Pate* verdict followed in 1964. In ruling that inmates had the right to access religious literature, Justice Byron White asserted, "there is no Iron Curtain between the Constitution and the prisons of this country." Constitutional law professor James Jacobs expands on White's assessment, explaining that the ruling declared unequivocally that "prisoners have constitutional rights" and that "prison officials were not free to do with prisoners as they pleased." Together, the *Monroe* and *Cooper* rulings marked the end of "the authoritarian regime in American penology" and encouraged inmate activism.[4]

A third factor leading to increased inmate unrest was the rising crime rate. The annual rate rose in nine of the ten years from 1950 to 1959, and according to the FBI's *Uniform Crime Reports,* in 1959 the United States suffered "69 percent more crime than 1950 and 128 percent more over 1940." The period from 1960 to 1975 was even worse, with a 232.6 percent increase in crime. That increase packed prisons, raised tensions in already tense settings, and led many inmates to lash out.[5]

Scholar Lawrence Friedman contends that the rise in crime also created a public backlash in the form of demands for harder time: "in an age of paralyzing fear, the middle class gives off as it were a great shout 'We don't care *who* these people are, and what excuses they give, or what their backgrounds are. We want them caught, convicted, and put away.'" Unhappy that criminals seemed to have it "too good," with access to television, radio, games, and recreation, the public wanted inmates to suffer for their crimes. Politicians responded by imposing new restrictions, and as privileges disappeared and time became harder, inmates rose up in protest.[6]

North Carolina was not immune to those larger social forces, and in the late 1960s and early 1970s inmates staged several significant actions to improve their circumstances. The first occurred in 1968, a mere twelve days after the assassination of Dr. Martin Luther King Jr.

April 16, 1968, began like most days at Central Prison. Inmates awoke, ate breakfast, went to work, and broke for lunch. At 12:30 P.M., with inmates gathered in the recreation yard, the whistle ending the lunch break sounded. Rather than return to their jobs, most of the 529 inmates remained in place. According to Vernon Bounds, who was then the commissioner of Central Prison, officers were aware trouble was brewing and that inmates were plotting to seize hostages in an effort to force the prison to accede to various demands. Officers had investigated the plot, confirmed it through the use of informants, and had devised plans to deal with the threat. They were thus somewhat prepared for trouble. When the prisoners refused to go back to work, Officer T. J. Burns initiated the protocol.[7]

Burns informed Chief Custodial Officer Major Fred Briggs, who met with the administrator of the penitentiary, David Henry, who was operationally in charge that day as Commissioner Bounds was out of town. Henry told Briggs to meet with the inmates and see what they wanted. Briggs attempted to meet with James Castellot, a thirty-eight-year-old white inmate who was serving fifteen to twenty years for kidnapping and assault with a deadly weapon. According to Bounds's later assessment of the incident, Castellot had long wanted to be a leader but other more powerful figures overshadowed him. With those other figures locked up in segregation units as part of an administration effort to assert more control on the cellblocks, he assumed some level of power. As leader, however, Castellot refused to meet with Briggs and instead sent his "spokesman" Jerry Jarrett, a white inmate serving twenty years for armed robbery.

Jarrett demanded to speak with Commissioner Bounds. When informed he was away, Jarrett announced that the prisoners "would not work, eat, nor move" until Bounds met with them in the presence of reporters from two Raleigh newspapers and acceded to seven demands: the return to general population of all inmates sent to segregation, the elimination of shakedowns in the segregation units, the establishment of a five-member inmate grievance committee that would meet with administrators once a month and had the power to remove guards who mistreated inmates, the payment of a legally mandated daily wage of $1.00 for every working inmate, the service of hot meals rather than cold cuts and salads for lunch, the installation of additional television sets, and an increase in visiting hours.[8]

As prison administrators digested the demands, they remembered that inmate informants claimed the rebels planned to take hostages. When they failed to do so and simply refused to go back to work, administrators determined there was incomplete prisoner support for the action. This apparent divide led officials to decide that "countering action could now be more open." In other words, they could do more than passively wait out the protest. They determined that force was a legitimate response.[9]

There were only forty-three guards on duty at the time of the protest, and 463 of the original 529 inmates remained in the yard. With force now an option, and in an effort to even the balance of power, Administrator Henry called in all off-duty prison guards and requested twenty-five additional guards from nearby youth centers. He then locked the striking inmates in the yard to isolate them from the other cellblocks, informed Castellot that the administrators would not negotiate, and ordered the men back to their cells.[10]

During the course of the next several hours 109 of the inmates surrendered. In the meantime, guards locked down the rest of the prison, established a command post, and passed out walkie-talkies. Henry also contacted Commissioner Bounds, who was on his way to Washington, D.C. Bounds ordered Henry to inform Governor Dan Moore of the trouble and of his intention not to yield to the inmates' demands. He further ordered Henry to keep the rebellious inmates in the yard and to handle them peacefully as long as they acted peacefully in their own right.[11]

As Bounds made his way back to North Carolina, additional guards arrived on the scene. Henry dispersed them throughout the prison and issued firearms to those placed on the roof and wall. To those assigned to the grounds and cell houses he supplied mace, tear gas, batons, and baseball bats. The growing official presence made the inmates restive, and Castellot, through Jarrett, warned that he would not be able to control the rebels if the officers remained. Henry refused to pull back, and the inmates responded by breaking benches and other objects, which they fashioned into weapons. One group of armed inmates then feigned an attack on officers, but retreated when guards on the wall gathered their weapons. Another group of inmates set fire to trash cans, while another, just before dark, broke into and looted the barbershop, where they armed themselves with a variety of sharp objects. As night descended, the inmates gathered together the material they had seized and set about creating additional weapons, including "torches, spears, clubs, and crude maces."[12]

Bounds arrived at the prison just after 8 P.M. and conferred with Henry. The two administrators decided they could not negotiate with the inmates, as that would give them a sense of power. Instead, they decided Henry would try one more time to convince them to return to their cells. Bounds also told Henry to remind the inmates that guards had the right to "use any means necessary" to combat an insurrection. As Henry communicated with the rioters, Bounds gathered the assembled guards and police officers. He told them they had the right to use force, but only in self-defense, in the defense of property, to prevent an escape, or to quell a disturbance. He further explained that they could use only enough force to achieve the objective given, they could use firearms only if there was a risk to human life and tear gas would not work, and they were to employ their firearms only to incapacitate, not kill. He then dispersed the men throughout the penitentiary.[13]

Bounds later wrote that as long as the inmates simply refused to leave the yard, containment was enough. Once they began to set fires and fashion weapons, however, he had to consider more forceful measures. Those considerations grew when, at 11:15 P.M., officers reported that the inmates were "getting out of hand" and appeared to be preparing for battle by soaking torches in flammable liquids, forming crude armor, and collecting their weapons. Bounds responded by calling for even more reinforcements, with officers from the Raleigh police force and the state highway patrol attending to the matter. By midnight there were nearly one hundred additional officers on scene. They also brought in security dogs.[14]

With the numbers in their favor, officers designed a plan to retake the yard. An unarmed group, covered by officers on the wall and roof, would enter the yard. Once in place, guards would give the inmates one final chance to surrender. If they did not, the guards would move in, corral them against the wall, and take them into custody. As Bounds later wrote, "It was our hope that they would see the futility of resistance and would submit without compelling us to use force to bring them under control." That hope was dashed.[15]

At approximately 2 A.M. the guards issued an ultimatum. When the inmates refused to surrender, the guards moved in. As they did so, inmate John Stinnett lit a torch and ran in front of the officers, dragging it along the ground and leaving behind "a wall of fire." Additional inmates followed to keep the wall burning, while others taunted the officers or lobbed debris. Major Briggs, who directed the guards on the ground, reported, "We were preparing to move in. I gave the instructions to different officers to move out closer to the rioting inmates. And as the officers and security dogs started out, the inmates began to light towels and bed clothing saturated with some kinds of flammable material. As the officers approached they were met by a wall of fire thrown by 35 to 40 prisoners. Fire got on one security dog and one officer. I saw one officer go down when he was hit by a stick. It appeared that the inmates were going to override the officers." The guards advanced nonetheless, but debris continued to fly. In response, officers on the exterior wall and roof fired tear gas and several warning shots. When the gas and warning shots failed, Commissioner Bounds issued the order to open fire.[16]

The shooting lasted less than one minute, and most inmates quickly laid down and surrendered. Many, however, refused to do so, and officers needed another ten minutes of hand-to-hand fighting to subdue the rioters. By that point, the guards outnumbered the inmates who still were resisting and they were able to escape relatively unscathed; a number of inmates, however, were wounded. The guards eventually reclaimed control of the yard, strip-searched the inmates, and returned them to their cells. By 3 A.M. Central Prison was quiet.[17]

Although the fighting was over, the consequences were not. Dr. Benjamin Britt, who arrived at the prison at 1:30 A.M., later described seeing "the worst medical disaster in the history of Raleigh." Seventy-six individuals received wounds that required medical treatment. Doctors at Wake Memorial Hospital treated four seriously wounded inmates, while prison doctors treated twenty-nine for injuries that were minor enough for them to return to their cells and another thirty-nine whose injuries required a stay in the prison hospital. Prison doctors also treated and released two state troopers and two prison guards who received minor wounds from ricocheting bullets.[18]

Six inmates died. Doctors pronounced four dead on arrival at the hospital in Central Prison, one died soon after his arrival, and one died at Wake Memorial Hospital on April 17. Andrew Brauch, a forty-year-old white inmate serving fifteen years for assault and intent to commit rape, died in a prison restroom where he and several inmates had holed up during the fighting. When they refused to exit, guards fired a can of tear gas that hit Brauch in the head and killed him. Donald Fox, a twenty-six-year-old white inmate serving two life sentences for burglary and murder, died of a gunshot wound to the chest. Nathaniel Latta, a thirty-three-year-old African American inmate serving fifteen years for assault and intent to commit rape, died of a gunshot wound to the head. William Matthews, a twenty-seven-year-old African American inmate serving eight to ten years for felonious breaking and entering, died of a gunshot wound to the heart. John Scurlock, a twenty-two-year-old African American inmate serving a life sentence for first-degree burglary, died of multiple gunshot wounds to the chest and abdomen. Jerry Walston, a twenty-two-year-old white inmate serving eight to ten years for breaking and entering, larceny, and escape, died from multiple gunshot wounds.[19]

While the living mourned the dead and the injured healed, Bounds confined inmates to their cells, cancelled all visits, shut down all industries, and employed only a skeleton crew of inmates to help staff clean up the mess. Meanwhile, investigators sought out the riot's origins. One inmate interviewed by the *Raleigh News and Observer* explained that the riot's cause was the prison administration's decision to place inmate "leaders" in segregation. Bounds was unhappy that these "leaders" had power over other inmates and seemed to run the prison from the inside. Determined to make clear that he ran the facility, Bounds had segregated the "leaders." The problem, the inmate interviewee explained, was that "punk kids" took control with the leaders locked away. He went on to assert that "the riot would have never come off if the real leaders of Central Prison had not been locked up. It just wouldn't have taken place." Another confirmed that idea, and noted that while inmates had planned a peaceful demonstration to protest the "lock-up of hard-core criminals," it was the restless youth who caused events to spiral out of control. Bounds later seemed to acknowledge this assessment when he told the *Raleigh News and Observer* that the riot's cause was "the administration's determined effort to take over control of our prison system from inmates described as 'bulls' who control other prisoners through extortion, homosexual attacks, and money."[20]

Investigations soon turned from the riot's cause to the violence itself. Not surprisingly, Bounds and the guards blamed the inmates for their refusal to obey rules or to return to their cells as ordered. David Henry later explained, "One thing stands out . . . I recall the tremendous shouting, 'Lie down! Lie down! Lie down!'" He asserted the inmates had the chance to avoid injury, failed to do so, and suffered the consequences. Bounds issued a formal report in which he concurred, justified the order to fire, and claimed all the bullet wounds were consistent with officers following orders and shooting to stop, not to kill.[21]

Inmates, of course, blamed the guards. Several claimed the deaths resulted from "trigger happy" guards who never gave them the opportunity to surrender. One told the *Raleigh News and Observer*, "Not once, not a single time, did the guards come on the loudspeaker and say that we could go back to our cells. Not once." Another claimed, "There was absolutely no warning whatsoever." Another said, "I just can't understand it for the life of me. I can't see all that brutality. Bounds had all the power in North Carolina behind him. All he had to do was talk over the loudspeaker." Prison officials denied the charges, asserted that they did warn the inmates, and noted that many returned to their cells prior to the violence. Despite those arguments, inmates filed forty lawsuits charging officials with everything from murder to making them "unwilling participants" in a riot.[22]

Little came from the lawsuits, as in October 1968 federal judge John Larkins ruled that prison officials used "only such force as was necessary" and acted properly in working to "firmly restore order in the prison." He also dismissed sixteen lawsuits in which inmates claimed prison officials violated their constitutional rights, finding that the prison staff acted in accordance with the Constitution and federal law. Judges disposed of the other suits in similar fashion.[23]

With the lawsuits dismissed, penitentiary administrators worked to recover from the chaos. That recovery took some time, as officials took stock of the situation and oversaw a number of reforms. The stocktaking caused a month-long closing of the printing plant, painting room, and license tag shop—closures that cost the penitentiary $42,000. While the industries eventually reopened, other reforms proved longer lasting. The administration halted the use of maximum security prisoners in prison industries, replacing them with inmates at lower classification levels. When asked if this was a temporary or a permanent change, Commissioner Bounds said, "It is extremely doubtful that we will ever again use maximum custody and dangerous inmates in the prison plants. They have lost their privileges by abusing them." Bounds also instituted a "severe lockup," during which guards moved inmates only in small groups. As he explained to the *Raleigh News and Observer*, "Never again will they be permitted to congregate 200 and 300 at the time like they did before."[24]

Bounds believed even more needed to be done, so he requested $19 million in state funds to hire additional guards, add video surveillance, and remove "visual impediments" from the prison yard. He believed the prison needed significant renovations to prevent a future riot, and as a part of his effort to convince legislators to part with the money, in February 1969 he gave several politicians a tour to show them the issues with which he was dealing.[25]

Bounds was not the only one calling for reform. In 1969, Jesse Steiner and Roy Brown, both professors at the University of North Carolina at Chapel Hill, authored *The North Carolina Chain Gang*. Although focused on the historical use of chain gang labor, the two offered biting commentary on the contemporary state of the penitentiary. They wrote, "In spite of the improvements made in recent years, the management of the state prison has not been removed from political influence; its central building at Raleigh is an out-of-date structure, ill adapted for the proper housing of prisoners; no alienist or psych-pathologist is on the staff of the prison; and little effort is made on the basis of scientific study to classify the prisoners and provide the sort of treatment required by each group."[26]

Despite the violence, the scholarly critique, the General Assembly's previous willingness to fund prison improvement, and the clear need to implement some manner of reform, state legislators refused to act. Although implementing Bounds's suggestion seemingly would have enabled legislators to appear "tough on crime," financial conservatism held sway. Steiner and Brown's suggestions, by contrast, were simply too progressive for the era. Politicians could hardly face the public after the riot and support providing inmates with psychologists, medical staff, and new facilities. Times had changed, and that reality played itself out in the manner in which politicians reacted to the riot.

What they did instead was alter the system's name and organizational structure. In 1967, the General Assembly renamed the Department of Prisons the Department of Correction and reclassified prison guards as "correctional officers." In 1972, the legislature brought together all of the elements of the penal system into one centralized department when it combined the Department of Correction with the Probation Commission and the Department of Youth Development to form the Department of Social Rehabilitation and Control. Two years later, the General Assembly simplified the department's name back to the Department of Correction, but reorganized its structure to create three subgroups: the Division of Prisons, the Division of Adult Probation and Parole, and the Division of Youth Development. In preferring cosmetic name changes to the hard work of addressing the riot's underlying causes, politicians demonstrated the state's changed circumstances. Concern about maintaining its progressive image had waned, the political pendulum had swung to the right, and the public was in no mood for civil unrest. The inmates at Central Prison learned those lessons the hard way.[27]

Bounds also learned the lesson. Stymied by changing public sentiment and legislators who no longer were interested in reforming the penitentiary, he was left to make only minor improvements on his own. He did so by installing new barred doors and erecting several new fences "in order to break up the prison population into smaller units of control." The larger reforms he, Steiner, and Brown suggested would not materialize for another two decades.[28]

In the meantime, inmates and prison administrators once again were left to confront the consequences of a divided state. As a more conservative sensibility developed, inmates rioted, politicians proved intransigent, and finances suddenly tightened. Whereas external social and political forces had once helped prison administrators reform the system, those same forces now undermined the reform effort. At the same time, however, the riot's very methodology—of creating a formal organization, proffering a set of demands, attempting to access journalists, and demonstrating a willingness to risk life and limb—confirmed the inmate's awareness of the manner in which activist groups beyond the prison sought change. They appreciated the mirror and tried to use its reflection to affect change. Additional evidence of that appreciation emerged with yet another round of violence and rioting in the mid-1970s. What made those incidents unique was that they occurred among the women. As the feminist movement made headway among the public, female inmates fought for their rights.[29]

18

THE WOMEN FIGHT BACK

Male prisoners were not the only ones to take matters into their own hands in the 1960s and 1970s; female inmates also challenged the system. That women of the era were fighting for their rights should not be much of surprise given that the feminist movement was in full swing. In North Carolina, Judge Susie Sharp, who in 1962 became the first women to serve on the North Carolina Supreme Court; Margaret Taylor Harper, who in 1968 became the first woman to seek statewide office on a major party ticket when she ran for the Democratic nomination as lieutenant governor; and Crystal Lee Sutton, whose effort to organize workers at the J. P. Stevens Mills in Roanoke Rapids in 1973 later was immortalized in the movie *Norma Rae,* all exemplified the movement. Women in North Carolina's penal system also did their part, as they joined their male colleagues in demanding better treatment and literally fought for their rights.

The fight began in Beaufort County. In August 1974, the county jail housed African American inmate Joan (pronounced Joanne) Little. Born in 1954, she was the eldest of nine children. Wild from a young age, she ran away from home, spent time in a juvenile justice facility, and had frequent run-ins with the law. After years of committing petty crimes and misdemeanors, in January 1974 she graduated to felonies when police arrested her for breaking, entering, and larceny. Convicted, she received a sentence of seven to ten years. By state law, she would be eligible for parole in two years.[1]

Although her crime merited detention in the Women's Prison, Little asked to remain in Beaufort County pending her appeal. The court granted her that right, and she settled into the county jail, where she spent the next eighty-one days. Completed in 1971, the facility, according to Fred Harwell, who wrote about Little's case, was "modern, reasonably comfortable, and well maintained.... It was clean, well-lighted, relatively spacious, and air conditioned."[2]

Not every aspect of the jail was so welcoming. Clarence Alligood was a white correctional officer at the jail. Sixty-two, standing six feet tall, and weighing 185 pounds, he had been working at the facility since 1973, during which time he had earned a reputation for sexually assaulting the female inmates. On the evening of August 26, 1974, he assaulted Joan Little. According to Little, Alligood brought her some sandwiches and a coke, and then demanded sex. She refused, but he entered her cell, touched her breasts, and otherwise fondled her. She tried to fight him off, but Alligood was too big and had an icepick, which he threatened to use unless she complied. When she tried to flee nonetheless, he grabbed her by the neck, threatened her again, and forced her to perform oral sex. Fearing for her life, she submitted. When she finished, Alligood relaxed and dropped the icepick. Seeing her chance, Little grabbed it, attacked him, and fled the jail.[3]

Early the next morning, Officers Johnny Rose and Jerry Helms discovered Alligood's body. As police investigated the murder, Little, with the help of her lawyer, Jerry Paul, fled to Chapel Hill, where they negotiated the terms of her surrender. The basic term was that she not return to the Beaufort County jail. Authorities conceded that point, and she entered the Women's Prison to await the outcome of the police investigation.[4]

What the investigation found was that "Alligood's body was naked from the waist down. Sperm was present on his leg, and an icepick lay loosely cupped in his hand. He had icepick wounds around his temple and his heart." The autopsy determined it was the wound to the heart that killed him. As historians Neal Shirley and Saralee Stafford summarize the coroner's report, "The jailer bled to the death in the cell with his pants around his ankles."[5]

With Little back in custody and the cause of death determined, state prosecutors charged her with first-degree murder. Prosecutors eventually reduced the charge to second-degree murder and manslaughter when they were unable to support the premeditation component of the first-degree charge. That was a notable change, as the reduced charges took the death penalty off the table; however, Little still faced life in prison. The defense team, therefore, prepared a case that charged Alligood with sexual assault and claimed Little acted in self-defense.[6]

After the defense expressed concerns that Little would not get a fair trial in Beaufort, the trial moved to Raleigh and opened on July 14, 1975. The jury was equally divided by race, with seven women and five men. According to Fred Harwell, Little's lawyer, Jerry Paul, portrayed her as the innocent victim of a racist, sexually charged, white, southern cop. He tried to make her stand for "every degraded woman, every persecuted black, every victim of racism and sexual oppression. . . . [He] made it seem that she was a symbol of them all." Not only that, Paul "also brought together civil rights, women's rights, black power, judicial bias, rights of the poor, court reform, prosecutorial reprisals, prison reform, Southern justice, and Southern history" in her defense. The public bought that portrayal, Harwell contends, because it "had a certain historical vitality, and it appeared to confirm a suspicion held in other parts of the country that things had not changed very much in the so-called New South." That public purchase was further evident by the creation of the Joan Little Defense Fund and by the willingness of the Southern Poverty Law Center to raise money for Little's defense. Working together, the two groups raised more than $350,000.[7]

The public was not the only group to buy the defense tactic. So too did the jury. After five weeks of testimony, the jury retired at 11:15 A.M. on August 15. They deliberated for seventy-eight minutes and returned with a verdict of not guilty. The decision made Joan Little "the first American woman to ever be acquitted of murdering her rapist." Not only that, we need to remember that Little was black and her attacker was white. The case thus crossed the racial divide as well, and would seem to demonstrate some manner of racial progress.[8]

Author James Reston sees the case as having additional implications: "in the months that followed her acquittal on the murder charges, she became a symbol of women's groups, civil-rights groups, prisoner-rights groups, and the opponents of capital punishment." In other words, not only did her case reflect larger social conditions, it also caused society to reflect back on the prison. As Reston notes, "the case opened the North Carolina jail system to scrutiny, revealing that there are more prisoners per capita there than anywhere in the nation; that in Jones County in the East, one person in ten is in jail; that the overcrowding in the nineteenth-century Bastille in Raleigh, otherwise known as Central Prison, is a disgrace." Little's trial thus demonstrates the dual nature of the social/penal relationship: society is evident in and has an impact on the prison, but the prison also can be evident in and affect changes on society.[9]

The Little case was not the only example of this relationship, nor was it the only time women fought back. An even more notable example emerged almost simultaneously with the Little case. This one occurred in the Women's Prison.

A 1972 study of the North Carolina Correctional Institution for Women, as the Women's Prison was officially known, found the facility housed 350 women, all of whom worked forty hours a week but were allowed only four hours of schooling. A subsequent study found the "vocational programs offered . . . are very limited and traditional. Secretarial Science, Cosmetology, and Upholstery are the only courses offered." This was so despite the fact that 40 percent of the inmates had less than a ninth-grade education and 83 percent had not completed high school.[10]

The prison itself was "old and drab, surrounded by chain link and barbed wire fences." Nearly 43 percent of the women (150 of 350) stayed in dormitory-style housing, which offered "little living or recreation space," and created a setting in which "privacy [was] virtually non-existent." Similarly lacking were health and recreation services. There were only one full-time and two part-time psychologists, but they spent most of their time dealing with crises rather than managing the women's issues. Problems thus exploded rather than being massaged and dealt with before they reached the point of crisis. Similarly, the five nurses enjoyed no support staff, so they spent their time typing, filing, and doing secretarial work rather than focusing on inmates. Finally, the lack of recreational supplies and a gymnasium floor that was so badly maintained that it was "hardly useable" limited the way women could pass the time.[11]

In preceding years, women in the prison had received literature and support from outside groups like the North Carolina Hard Times Prison Project, the Triangle Area Lesbian Feminist Prison Book Project, and Action for Forgotten Women, all of which encouraged the inmates to fight back against the litany of wrongs. Frustrated with their limited opportunities, encouraged by the aforementioned activist groups, and undoubtedly aware of the Little case and the Central Prison riot, the women finally had enough. On the evening of June 15, 1975, a prisoner at the Women's Prison contacted members of the Triangle Area Lesbian Feminist Prison Book Project and Action for Forgotten Women and informed them of a sit-in planned for later that night.[12]

That sit-in began at 8 P.M. when officers attempted to clear the yard and return inmates to their cells. An interracial mix of 150 refused to leave. Instead they organized benches into a large circle and began to discuss their grievances and what they should do next. Although later studies found the women most outraged by the general inhumanity of their confinement, quoting one participant as saying they wanted "to be recognized as human beings and not as animals in a cage," the protestors had specific demands. Those included better medical treatment and the closing of the laundry, where many inmates worked, often in temperatures reaching 120 degrees, cleaning the clothes of every inmate in the state. That clothing included the untreated garments of tubercular inmates, and workers did not receive any protection while handling their clothing. The protestors also called out nurses for refusing to treat ailing inmates and charged the all-white administration with racism. Finally, thanks to the interaction with the previously mentioned outside groups, they framed their cause as a continuation of the civil rights and feminist movements.[13]

As their complaints rose through the prison's chain of command, the women settled in for an evening in the yard, while their supporters gathered beyond the chain-link fence in solidarity. Those supporters included members of the Triangle Area Lesbian Feminist Prison Book Project and Action for Forgotten Women, but the vast majority were people who had wives, sisters, mothers, or girlfriends in the prison. As authors Neal Shirley and Saralee Stafford note, taken together "the crowd outside became a perfect mirror of the war being fought on the grounds of the prison: small children threw the Black Power salute while riding their bikes, older women with Afros screamed into bullhorns, young white women in combat boots with short cropped hair clenched their fists, and husbands and brothers looked on in anger and concern, all while the guards stood nearby, small in number, cautious but also angry and embarrassed at their humiliating defeat."[14]

Unmoved by the protest, the supporters, or their brief "humiliation," at 5 A.M. on June 16, officers, augmented by forces from Central Prison, set out to reclaim control. They entered the yard with batons and ordered the women into the gymnasium. Unwilling to give in without their demands being met, and fearful of what would happen when they were out of their allies' sight, the women refused. Thirty-five officers responded by coming at the inmates from three different directions, attacking them with batons, and driving them into the gym. According to eyewitnesses, once the inmates were inside, "the sounds of breaking glass, screams, and pounding noises could be heard."[15]

Those sounds came from the inmates' efforts to defend themselves by gathering makeshift weapons in the form of "mop handles, brooms, and concrete blocks." Others used the metal poles from volleyball nets, while some broke windows and gathered shards of glass. Once armed, the inmates, who outnumbered the guards, drove them out and regained "control."[16]

Humiliated once again, administrators allowed several outside supporters to meet with the inmates in the hopes of reaching an accord. They also contacted State Director of Prisons Ralph Edwards, who arrived on the scene to direct the response. Among the first actions Edwards took was to meet with an inmate committee to hear their demands. During the meeting, he promised to close the prison laundry within ninety days and to have an external audit performed of the medical services. When pressed, however, he refused to put the agreement in writing. Despite that, the committee took Edwards at his word, returned to the yard triumphant, and led the inmates back to their cells. It appeared the riot was over.[17]

The subsequent morning, however, the inmates refused to return to work. While the sit-in had ended, the larger conflict had not. Indeed, Director Edwards helped extend the struggle when he told the press that he might reopen the laundry in an emergency, while another paper reported him suggesting it would remain open but would operate at a reduced workload. Already suspicious from his refusal to put his promises in writing, the inmates "sensed betrayal" and employed the strike to demonstrate their unhappiness. That sense of betrayal and unhappiness would only grow in subsequent days.[18]

On June 19, Edwards agreed to another meeting with the inmates, during which he denied ever promising to close the laundry. He then asked the inmates to write out their list of demands. When they did so he rejected them all, left the meeting, and ordered in 125 armed guards, who once again attacked the inmates. To ensure the attack had full force, the administrators locked all the cell doors, trapping the women in the corridors: "apparently the police had driven them there . . . to beat them away from the prying eyes of media and supporters. This is exactly what happened. According to one participant, prisoners were 'beaten and stomped' and teargassed inside the building." Like Little and their male counterparts years earlier, the inmates fought back. By the time the skirmish was over, twenty-eight people were injured: seventeen inmates and eleven officers. While the officers went to the hospital, the prison's nurses, whom the inmates already had complained about, attended the women. Such treatment further enraged the inmates and led them to stand firm and continue their protest.[19]

Determined to prevent more unrest and to end the strike once and for all, on June 20 officers rounded up thirty-four "ringleaders" and shipped them to the prison in Morganton. Officers placed sixty other inmates in isolation, revoked privileges from ninety more, and denied all inmates the right to communicate with members of the Triangle Area Lesbian Feminist Prison Book Project and Action for Forgotten Women. Authorities, however, did not stop there. They also issued "retaliatory threats" should the protests continue. Faced with the loss of their leaders and confronted with the threat of even more punishment, the inmates ended the strike.[20]

As with the riot in Central Prison, however, the end was not actually the end. Whereas Central Prison authorities used the riot to demand increased funding to make prison time even harder, in this case authorities used the riot to demand increased funding to alleviate the hardships. Indeed, in subsequent weeks it appeared the women might actually have "won," as administrators purchased new medical equipment and closed the laundry.[21]

Although the women seemed to get what they wanted, they remained unhappy. One complained that the changes were just "pacifiers," while another said what took place was "just sugar coating to make it look like changes have happened. But that's just on the surface. We still have all the ingredients that brought on the protest."[22]

Evidence of the reform's shortcomings emerged two decades later when a study of the Women's Prison found it housing one thousand inmates and suffering from "long lines, high noise levels, waits to see everyone's case manager, running out of food at meals, inadequate medical care, and the general problems of overcrowding." One former inmate said, "I hated that place. I felt that was the pits of hell. . . . The officers there, they don't have the means or control of that place. It's so overcrowded that someone could get hurt there very easily. That's happened. I was on reception there and a girl got attacked with a straight razor, and by the time . . . they could get any help to that girl, she was cut all to pieces. And I remember laying on my bed crying, thinking 'Dear God, I can't live like this.' It was hell."[23]

When asked what caused the problems, inmates offered three answers. One argued it was the fault of the correctional officers: "They have an ego thing going. . . . They tell you you should act like adults and then talk to you like you're two." Another argued it was the lack of clearly defined regulations: "The rules will change from day to day, like one officer will say do it this way and another will say, 'No, you can't do that.' And write you up. . . . You just go through a lot of mental anguish every day." Another inmate concurred, explaining, "it seems like they got their own rules. . . . Some of the rules here you wouldn't believe. . . . It's just petty."[24]

It was more than just rules and officer behavior that concerned inmates, so too did their care. In June 1997, Prisoner Legal Services filed a class action lawsuit on behalf of nineteen inmates at the Women's Prison claiming "a lack of timely treatment, inadequate emergency services, poor care for inmates with chronic diseases, and a failure to follow the recommendations of outside specialists." The case, *Thebaud v. Jarvis*, resulted in a settlement by which both sides agreed to abide by the findings of an outside investigator. After the investigator presented his findings, prison administrators agreed to implement "virtually all of the recommendations." While it took five years to do so, with an additional year during which the Prisoner Legal Services "monitor[ed] compliance," the result was "substantial improvements in most aspects of the health care delivery system."[25]

Taken together, the Little case, the riot at the Women's Prison, and the subsequent complaints and reforms fit within the state's larger history. During an era of activism and unrest, female inmates joined their male counterparts, organized, and rioted in an effort to affect change. Confronted by forces more powerful than themselves, they put their lives on the line and fought for change when peaceful means proved unavailing. For some, the results seemed to make life a bit healthier. Others, however, charged that the results were inadequate and merely enabled administrators and politicians to pacify the public and burnish their credentials without affecting real reform. Whatever the truth, the events make clear that the era's unrest was not confined to Central Prison, as women too fought for their rights. As the 1970s progressed that fight continued, but with a renewed focus on Central Prison, where inmates employed a new technique that continued to mirror the efforts of those seeking change beyond the prison walls. In this case, they formed a union.

19

A PRISON UNION

Despite the sense some female inmates had that their efforts achieved positive results, the riots at Central Prison and the Women's Prison seemingly changed little, and may have created for inmates an even more hostile environment both within and without the prison. Within, administrators and politicians cracked down on inmate rights and rolled back many of the reforms of the previous generations. Indeed, one inmate who served time in Central Prison in the 1940s and returned in 1969 called it "the worst place," and said, "Do they really call this rehabilitating prisoners? Whatever the N.C. Prison System has anything to do with turns to shit. And that goes for every damn official from Commissioner Lee Bounds right down the list to every dirty bastard who has his stinkin' ass anyplace in the whole fuckin' system." Despite that, the public came to believe inmates still had it too good and demanded they suffer even more severely for their crimes. That belief bred yet more unhappiness for the inmates, but politicians, prison officials, and the public ignored their complaints and refused even the most basic of inmate demands. The consequence was that inmates continued to act out: they formed a union, rioted, and filed countless lawsuits. They thus continued to adopt and adapt external methodologies in an effort to improve their lot.[1]

The first prison unions emerged in Scandinavia in the mid-1960s, and the first American efforts took place in California with the formation of the United Prisoners Union (UPU), which used lawsuits and legislative pressure to address inmate concerns. They did not seek freedom and did not deny society's right to incarcerate them; what they wanted instead was more equitable, fair, and humane treatment. By 1970, however, some inmates wanted to make the UPU more radical, with a focus on direct action. They argued that lawsuits and legislation rarely succeeded, and even when they did, wardens and staff ignored the rulings or laws. In 1971, the divide between those focused on legal action and those focused on activism was such that the union split, with the former organizing the Prisoners Union (PU) and the latter continuing in the UPU. In the end, the UPU remained localized in California, while the PU, through its newsletter *Outlaw,* spread nationwide.[2]

In late 1972, a number of inmates at Central Prison who subscribed to *Outlaw* requested a meeting with PU representatives. Union officials J. D. Richardson and Connor Nixon visited Raleigh on January 15, 1973, and met with African American inmate Wayne Brooks. The meeting led to an agreement, and on March 14, 1973, an interracial group of inmates formed the North Carolina Prisoners' Labor Union (NCPLU) and elected Wayne Brooks president. Brooks soon thereafter gave an interview with the *Winston-Salem Journal* in which he explained, "We're not asking for a release of convicts. We want to only improve conditions, and the right not to be dehumanized." Their specific demands were for "incentive wages," better food, improved healthcare, and additional recreation facilities. The demands, in other words, were remarkably similar to those any union would make.[3]

Hundreds of prisoners statewide soon joined the NCPLU, but leaders realized they needed outside assistance if they wanted any chance of success. Connor Nixon returned from California to offer that assistance and opened an NCPLU office not far from the prison. He solicited funds from sympathetic local businesses and citizens, raising several thousand dollars. Efforts seemed to be going well, but after only a few weeks Nixon fled the state and absconded with union funds.

Fortunately, a woman named Robbie Pruner replaced Nixon and revived the union. Not only that, she brought with her a $14,000 grant from Suburban Partners, a Durham-based nonprofit, as a part of its Prison and Jail Improvement Program. Although initially skeptical, NCPLU members came to appreciate Pruner's work when she helped them complete the paperwork for incorporation. The inmates then elected a board of directors, consisting entirely of inmates, but named Pruner as their external coordinator with the tasks of raising money and finding lawyers and legal aides.[4]

As Pruner addressed her tasks, the union worked to clarify its specific aims. One key issue was a sore spot that remained from the 1968 riot—inmate pay. A 1967 state law required the payment of $1.00 per day to all prisoner workers. Only on July 1, 1975, however, did the prison begin to pay inmates, and then the wages were staggered, beginning at 40 cents per day. The union demanded that penitentiary officials obey the law.[5]

The union further demanded medical coverage for those injured on the job, as well as job placement help for those about to be released. Finally, the union demanded an end to the abuses many inmates faced at the hands of other inmates and staff. Union leaders wrote, "We don't deny that society has a right to punish persons for law violations, but convicts should have the rights of other human beings. Prisoners . . . should be sent to prison *as* punishment, rather than *for* punishment."[6]

Pruner, meanwhile, organized external supporters to speak to legislators and legislative committees, where they described the conditions prisoners faced, called for new laws to protect inmates, and demanded the state pay them for their labor. She also organized similar efforts among the public at large and retained legal representation for the inevitable lawsuits to come. The lawyer Pruner found was Deborah Mailman, and she soon was visiting the penitentiary, work sites, and farms looking for violations. She also wrote articles for *Outlaw* in which she advised inmates on their rights, the law, and how to document violations.[7]

Despite the efforts both inside and outside the prison, the NCPLU faced an uphill battle. Secretary of Correction David Jones refused to recognize the NCPLU, and when asked about it said, "There is no union, there never has been a union, and there will not be so long as I am secretary. The people who are incarcerated have broken the law and they will not dictate to us. There will be no negotiations, no facilities used for meetings, and no solicitations." Jones went on to assert that there was no need for a union because in August 1974 he had created an Inmate Grievance Commission (IGC), which offered "an administrative procedure through which prisoners can file their grievances and get results if so merited." The governor appointed the five-member commission, but inmates hated it because they believed members were partial and acted in the interests of the administration. They also believed the IGC was a ruse designed to keep inmates powerless while providing a public appearance of justice.[8]

Despite that skepticism, inmates abided by the new program and began to submit grievances. In quick order, however, they found themselves harassed by guards, threatened with the loss of honor status, or removed to other facilities. Author Donald Tibbs notes, "This placed North Carolina inmates in a serious bind. On one side, the courts required prisoners to exhaust their administrative remedies through the IGC grievance process before filing civil rights lawsuits. Yet, prison personnel were poisoning the grievance process by arbitrarily punishing prisoners who sought to use it. This meant that prisoners had no safe, unencumbered access to the courts." As a consequence, on December 8, 1974, they filed suit against the IGC claiming its grievance process "denied [inmates] their First Amendment constitutional right to 'petition the government for redress'" and that the prison staff's actions violated their Fourteenth Amendment right to due process. The suit further requested the court close the IGC or stop the administration from intervening in the grievance process.[9]

During the suit, IGC director Fred Morrison offered evidence supporting the inmates' claims. He told of inmates being transferred soon after meeting with him, described others who were threatened for making an IGC appeal, and reported that nearly all inmates found it difficult to get the forms and material needed to make an appeal. Despite such testimony, on December 20, 1975, U.S. District Court Judge Franklin T. Dupree Jr. dismissed the case on the grounds that inmates had failed to exhaust their options through the IGC process. He ignored the inmates' complaints and simply ordered them to follow the law regardless of the implications.[10]

The ruling infuriated inmates and led even more to join the NCPLU, with statewide membership eventually topping five thousand. Prison administrators responded to this growth by attempting to halt the outside aid Mailman and Pruner provided. First, Senior Correction Administrator James Smith informed Mailman that legal aides could no longer visit inmates. When Mailman threatened to sue, Smith backed down, but he then implemented "a blanket censorship of all prisoner union-related mail" despite the fact the Supreme Court had declared such action unconstitutional. He also banned inmates from soliciting new members "whether by newspaper, magazine or personal contact."[11]

The NCPLU responded to those restrictions with yet another lawsuit, charging the state with violating inmates' First Amendment rights by restricting their freedom of speech, association, and assembly. On March 16, 1976, a three-judge panel ruled unanimously in favor of the NCPLU, writing: "1) Inmates . . . shall be permitted to solicit and invite other inmates to join the union by oral or by written or printed communication; 2) the Union shall be afforded the privilege of bulk mailing to the extent it was accorded other organizations; and 3) the Union . . . shall be accorded the privilege of holding meetings also to the extent it was accorded other organizations." The judges acknowledged "that the substantial interest of the DOC was the maintenance of security, but they found not one scintilla of evidence to suggest that the Union was utilized to disrupt the operation of the penal institution."[12]

North Carolina appealed the ruling to the U.S. Supreme Court. On April 19,

1977, the court heard oral arguments and on June 23, 1977, the justices issued their *Jones v. North Carolina Prisoners' Labor Union, Inc.* ruling. In a 7–2 decision, the court found the restrictions "reasonably related to legitimate security concerns," argued that "the fact of confinement . . . imposes limitations on constitutional rights, including those derived from the First Amendment," and chastised the lower court for "not giving appropriate deference to the decisions of prison administrators and appropriate recognition to the peculiar and restrictive circumstances of penal confinement." The ruling thus overturned the lower court's verdict and indicated a move away from its ruling in the *Cooper* case.[13]

The dissenting justices addressed the later point clearly, asserting that the majority argument meant the judiciary was renouncing any power to oversee state prison systems. This meant prison officials alone determined which inmate actions were a threat. That created a situation in which there was no one to whom the prisoners could appeal and no one to whom the officials were accountable. This was a dangerous precedent, the minority justices argued, and threatened the foundations of the entire criminal justice system. In fact, by removing the judiciary from the process, the ruling forced inmates to respond with riots, rebellions, and other outbursts of rage and hopelessness. Despite that reality, the ruling held and the NCPLU lost the case. It also lost its momentum. The union lingered on until 1981, but sputtered to an ignominious end.[14]

The end of the union did not mean the end of inmate activism and unrest; nor did it mean administrators were in complete control. On February 9, 1975, amid the union lawsuits, inmates once again rioted. Outraged when they received only three pieces of bread instead of the traditional four, they refused to go back to their cells. Correctional officers dispersed them with water cannons, but underlying inmate unhappiness lingered. The *Raleigh News and Observer* ran a series of articles about the penitentiary in the aftermath of the tumult in which it asserted, "Central Prison is a time bomb waiting for someone with a match." It even cited an officer who admitted, "We're just keeping a lid on." The paper then quoted Warden Samuel Garrison, who assumed control of the penitentiary in 1973, as saying that the prison had "400 men too many." He went on to tell the paper that overcrowding forced the prison to place inmates and beds in every conceivable place except for those areas "condemned as unfit for human habitation." Garrison also noted that the population excess made addressing life's basic necessities problematic, and explained that staff spent seven hours a day simply feeding the men. He even admitted, "We don't have internal control. We have periphery control in the sense of walls and gun towers. We have internal supervision in the sense of one officer supervising 140 inmates in a dormitory, but that doesn't dictate control."[15]

Proof of this was evident from psychiatric reports. Psychiatrists working in the prison found they had trouble keeping inmates awake during therapy sessions. When they investigated the causes, they learned that the overcrowding and lack of institutional control resulted in increased predation, which left nearly every inmate in constant fear. This fear lingered into the night, causing most to sleep poorly. Once in a secure room with someone who was not a threat, they relaxed and their bodies simply shut down. Scared, exhausted, and stymied by the courts and the administration, it is no wonder inmates rioted.[16]

In February 1976, inmates received some assistance in their struggle when the North Carolina Advisory Committee to the U.S. Commission on Civil Rights authored a study entitled *Prisons in North Carolina*. The report found 905 inmates then incarcerated in a penitentiary designed for 640. In an effort to find bed space for all the inmates, the report noted, Central Prison's administrators had created several dormitory-style housing units. While the dorms provided the needed beds, they did nothing to improve the inmates' lot. The facilities were cramped, fostered the spread of illness, increased stress and mental health problems, and raised concerns about rape and sexual assault. The situation was so bad that Judge Frank Snepp told a report writer, "The dormitories at night are no man's land. A guard would not dare go in there—except in force."[17]

Such conditions, the report found, created the additional problem of low staff retention. The prison's brutality, combined with low pay, caused frequent turnover among correctional officers. The conditions also made it difficult to recruit new employees. The consequence was an inexperienced and often understaffed crew working among an unhappy and violent inmate population. Inmates were aware of that reality, took advantage of it to dominate the weak, and ran the prison from the inside.[18]

The civil rights study next turned to the related issues of race and gender. The committee found that 515 of Central Prison's 905 inmates were African American. Conversely, only 52 of the 262 correctional officers were African American. It found women and minorities especially underemployed in higher-level administrative positions, and documented that of the ten top positions in the Department of Correction in 1974, all of whom the governor appointed, seven were white men, one was an African American man, and one was a white woman. The prison system at large, the report found, was similarly skewed. In 1975, the penal system employed 5,040 people, of whom 3,960 were white, 1,080 were African American, and 1,039 were women. Of the minority employees, the report noted that 449 were hired within the previous year. Additionally, there were no African American or female wardens. The penitentiary also lacked an African American minister, nor did it offer formal services in Islam, Judaism, or any other "minority religions." The racial divide that had long plagued the prison thus continued, exacerbating inmate unrest.[19]

The report concluded with a study of the manner in which prison staff disciplined inmates. After noting that the prison possessed isolation units as places of punishment, it asserted that prison staff often turned instead to water cannons. While the use of the cannons to break up disturbances or protect staff was not a problem in and of itself, the committee discovered that correctional officers often used the cannons as a form of punishment. When asked about the cannons, Warden Garrison seemed to confirm this point when he lamented that "the nozzle pressure was approximately 70 pounds and the pump pressure was about 120 pounds." He explained he would have preferred to increase the pressure to 300 pounds, which "would not only kill a person but destroy a building." Without any seeming bit of irony, he then admitted, "I have been sued in Federal court for having 300-pound water hoses."[20]

Although damning, not everything was dire. The report noted that prisoners enjoyed a number of job opportunities, had access to a gymnasium with a full-time recreation director, and had additional recreation opportunities, including record players, cards, and musical instruments. The penitentiary also had a ninety-eight-bed hospital facility and a seventy-three-bed mental health unit. In the end, the committee found Central Prison better than any of the other penal facilities in the state, but deemed it lacking in staffing, educational opportunities, and oversight.[21]

Based on those findings, the report offered a series of recommendations. It began by demanding that "the Governor and the North Carolina General Assembly immediately restructure the Board of Correction so that more women, blacks, and Native Americans can be appointed to this board." It further called for formal efforts to recruit, hire, and train women and racial minorities as correctional officers, superintendents, and wardens.[22]

After noting that many prisons were located in rural areas that were not easily accessible, lacked adequate rehabilitative quarters, and limited contact with teachers and professors, it urged the erection of new facilities in cities or towns where inmates would have better counseling, educational, and employment opportunities. It then concluded with a demand that prison officials provide better job training programs, liberalize the work release program, pay inmates for their labor, offer more comprehensive recreational opportunities, hire more educational staff, and be more consistent when enforcing rules and implementing punishments. In essence, the report urged administrators to focus more on rehabilitation than punishment and return to the progressivism of old.[23]

In November 1976, administrators from the Department of Correction responded to the commission's report. The reply listed eight positions where women or minorities worked in "upper level management" and noted improved medical efforts and the hiring of one new chaplain. Beyond that, however, officials went no further. Indeed, administrators seemed to grow ever more intractable. Despite numerous efforts by inmates to gain agency and a rather withering analysis of the entire prison system, administrators refused to acknowledge the need to reform. The progressive nature of the past was dead, political intervention, for good or ill seemed to have disappeared, and administrators refused to do anything the public might perceive as being "soft on crime." Criminal justice scholars assert that this was the response nationwide: while inmates enjoyed "better general conditions, better health care, more recreation, education, and religious freedom," overall prisons remained "domains of fear" where the strong brutalized the weak.[24]

That reality, and the state's refusal to acknowledge the report's probity, led Central Prison inmates to make two final efforts to improve their circumstances. In January 1974, they sued North Carolina for denying them access to legal books. Inmates won the suit, but the existence of only one law library for the entire system, in Central Prison, tempered that victory. Not only was there only one facility, inmates complained that administrators kept the library inadequately supplied with outdated codebooks, punished those who used it, and transferred to new institutions those who succeeded in writing appeals. Inmates therefore sued again and took the case to the Supreme Court. In 1977, the court issued its *Bounds v. Smith* case, in which it ruled: "the fundamental constitutional right of access to the courts requires prison authorities to assist inmates in the preparation and filing of meaningful legal papers by providing prisoners with adequate law libraries or adequate assistance from persons trained in the law."[25]

The *Bounds* decision buoyed inmate spirits and encouraged them to initiate one final campaign. A major point of inmate frustration was the belief that administrators maintained an unpublished list of rules and expectations. Prisoners thus found themselves punished for unknown or unwitting violations, and they demanded that prison officials clarify policy. Rather than fight inmates in court for the third time in seven years, in January 1980 administrators revised and published the rule book.

In an effort to convince inmates that it was worth following the rules, the book began with a reminder: "If you will read and follow the rules in this booklet, your time in prison will be shortened and your chances for returning to your home will be greater." It then listed the rules: inmates were to be polite, obey prison staff, do the jobs assigned, and keep their living areas, themselves, and their clothes clean. The rules also forbade possessing weapons, alcohol, drugs, or obscene material, selling or bartering goods or advice, wasting or stealing supplies, fighting, cursing, and having sex. The rule book further broke down violations into major and minor categories, with punishments ranging from a written reprimand or the temporary loss of privileges to time in an isolation cell or a reduction in classification level.[26]

Although the rules did not provide new rights or freedoms, inmates viewed the simple fact that administrators published them as a victory. And that was not their only victory. That same year, and in a clear acknowledgment that the NCPLU was justified in its complaints about the IGC, the prison altered its grievance procedure. Under the new system, prison administrators had to investigate a grievance within twenty-four hours and were required to provide a response within five days. The inmate then had twenty-four hours to appeal the response, and the appeal was to be heard within ten days. If the inmate remained unsatisfied, he could appeal to a newly formed Inmate Grievance Commission, which was "separate from the N.C. Department of Correction with a staff of conscientious investigators drawn from civic-minded and religious groups." The commission acted as an outside sounding board to hear the inmate's concerns, but its ability to affect the inmate's plight was limited. The commission could make recommendations, but it lacked the power "to require implementation of its decisions." Instead, the secretary of correction had that power, and within fifteen days of receiving the commission's report, he was to issue his decision. If the inmate was dissatisfied with the secretary's verdict, his final recourse was to file suit.[27]

The new policy seemed to make the grievance process fairer, but inmates realized that it included a hidden peril: those who appealed spent the process in administrative segregation. Not only could the appeal take weeks, but if the grievance failed the inmate did not receive credit for time served. This meant inmates were punished for making an appeal (since segregation was a form of discipline) and were punished further if they lost the appeal. To many, this seemed like officials were spoiling the process by doubly punishing those who dared challenge the administration. That issue never was resolved to the inmates' satisfaction, and it offers yet another example of state leaders implementing programs that appeared progressive yet provided little real benefit to the inmate.[28]

Clearly, the administrative and public tide had turned against the inmates despite the multiple and varied efforts they made to help themselves. As society at large rejected the 1960s ethos and a more conservative world developed in its stead, inmates found time grow ever harder. They failed to gain a union, lost some of the freedoms they had enjoyed previously, and confronted a legislature, judiciary, and administrative staff that sought to roll back those freedoms even further. While inmates previously had benefitted from the influence of external social forces, with a conservative sensibility dominant those influences turned on the inmates as the public and prison administrators clamped down hard during the 1970s. The sense that administrators were in firm control, however, was deceptive, and during the 1980s the prison population spiraled out of control and created problems that gave lie to administrative dominion. Unfortunately for the inmates, that did not mean a better life; indeed, the loss of administrative control seemed to make things worse.

20

NEW PRISON, OLD PROBLEMS

During the late 1970s, Central Prison administrators struggled with myriad problems, most notably overcrowding, a dilapidated facility, and charges of brutality. All three factors played some role in the riots and the creation of the prison union, but the administration did its best to avoid making any kind of reforms that would appear to have been a consequence of inmate activism. By the turn of the decade, however, legislators and prison officials had to confront the issues. The result was yet more turbulence, as the prison once again became a tool in a political struggle between Democrats and Republicans. Even more problematic was a flare-up of inmate violence and subsequent charges of racism and political deceit. Despite all that, and in a much more positive outcome for the inmates, a new prison arose centered on a new penal philosophy. As with so much of the state's paradoxical past, the new combined with the old and created a mixture of forward-looking reforms and repressive policies.

The overcrowding that affected the prison in the early 1970s only grew worse by the decade's end, with thirteen hundred men crammed into a facility designed for half that number. The situation might well have been worse, except the state converted four minimum security institutions into medium security facilities in order to house some of Central Prison's excess population. Despite that relief, the thirteen hundred inmates still required the prison to double cell inmates in the six-foot by eight-foot cells. This put two men in a confined space of forty-eight square feet and resulted in rising tensions and violence.[1]

What added to the misery was that much of the facility was falling apart. Many of the decorative cupolas and spires were removed for fear they would collapse; on rainy days water leaked through the century-old brickwork; the heating and air conditioning units were inadequate for the task, leaving the prison "cold and dank in winter" and "sweltering" in the summer; the ancient cells proved dangerous for correctional officers to enter; and blind spots offered predators perfect locations to assault other inmates. Such structural failings made it clear to all that Central Prison was in dire straits. Secretary of Correction Amos Reed went so far as to admit the prison was "so old it would have . . . to be renovated even without overcrowding."[2]

Calls to reform or replace Central Prison were nearly as old as the facility itself, and prior to the Depression legislators had made plans to turn the facility into a storage center. The economic catastrophe shelved those plans, and construction of other facilities removed Central Prison from the spotlight in the decades after World War II. By the 1970s, however, overcrowding and the obvious decline of its physical structure led to renewed proposals for renovation. In 1975, Secretary of Correction David Jones made the first such call when he told the *Raleigh News and Observer*, "I think we ought to do society a favor and knock this old thing down and build an entirely new one." When state Attorney General Rufus Edmisten concurred, Jones requested that Governor James Holshouser replace Central Prison with a new $30 million facility.[3]

On October 31, 1975, Governor Holshouser supported just such an action when he proposed a three-phase, $34.5 million construction project for the addition of new housing units, reception and diagnostic areas, medical facilities, and outpatient rooms to the Central Prison complex. In an effort to justify the construction and convince reluctant legislators to foot the bill, Secretary Jones explained to anyone who would listen that in the current institution "many cells [were] packed to double their rated capacity," proved "dehumanizing for the inmates," and frequently "impair[ed] security and rehabilitation services." The state, he argued, desperately needed the new facility.[4]

Although needed, politics got in the way. The previous year Secretary Jones had requested $10 million for renovations. Governor Holshouser, a Republican, had supported the request but the Democrat-controlled General Assembly had refused to comply. Hoping 1975 would be different, the *Raleigh News and Observer* came out in support of the overhaul and pleaded with the General Assembly to tear down the "old, gloomy, obsolete, hard to police" prison where "homosexual rape and other forms of inmate violence flourish." Such was not to be, as the General Assembly again failed to provide funding. As had happened far too often in the state's history, legislators let political opportunism color their votes and used the prison as a political weapon.[5]

Despite that failure, prison officials continued to pressure state politicians, and in 1977 they devised yet another renovation plan. This one was a two-phase, $27 million proposal, which called for the construction of a new 876-bed facility in the place of the current Central Prison. With Democrat James Hunt occupying the governor's mansion, Democrats in the General Assembly suddenly found the construction project worthy and approved funding. By 1980, the contracts were signed and construction was underway, with plans to complete the project by 1982.[6]

While the prospect of a new facility pleased Amos Reed, who succeeded David Jones as secretary of correction in 1977, he soon faced questions from astute critics who pointed out that the plan would not meet current population needs. Reed appreciated that fact and explained that combined with construction were three cost-effective, population-reducing reforms. The first was a restitution program that allowed criminals to repay victims in lieu of prison time. This served two purposes: it compensated the victim and it eased prison crowding. The second was the Local Confinement Act, which required those sentenced to fewer than six months' imprisonment to serve time in local jails rather than state facilities. The Department of Correction subsidized the counties for the added costs at the rate of $10 per day. Despite that expense, keeping inmates in county jails eased the overcrowding in state facilities, and Reed deemed the trade-off a positive. Finally, there was the Pre-Release and After-care Program (PRAC), which offered "assistance to the inmate who would not otherwise receive parole supervision and helps him adopt new attitudes toward society." PRAC sought to reduce the prison population by lowering recidivism rates. Not only did the programs pacify critics, address the crowding issues, and serve the interests of inmates, administrators, and the public, they also suggested a return to the progressive policies of old.[7]

The apparent return to a forward-looking agenda also seemed evident as the new Central Prison took shape. Plans called for gutting the original structure but maintaining more recently erected buildings. Integrated into those existing structures was the new facility, which consisted of a 576-bed unit that included 384 single-bed cells for traditional inmates and another 192 single-bed cells for inmates who had jobs within the prison. The hospital, the mental health unit, and the reception, diagnostic, and processing centers offered an additional 300 beds.[8]

The new facility centered on a "central security corridor" that ran "the entire length of the institution." The corridor connected the new buildings with the existing units, and with the creation of "control stations and sally ports which control access into each building, as well as movement up and down the security corridor," it provided a means of isolating disturbances and maintaining discipline. The corridor also housed the utility connections, which allowed for the safe servicing and maintenance of the facility's electrical, water, heating, and cooling units.[9]

Six four-story housing modules were located at the base of the central security corridor at the facility's front, nearest the entrance. The modules consisted of two units, one atop the other, each a two-story triangle with sixteen cells per story. Each unit thus housed thirty-two inmates. The cells lined two sides of the triangle, while the third consisted of two access ports and the control room. The center of the triangle, meanwhile, included the day room. Each seven-foot by ten-foot 64.04-square-foot trapezoid cell had a five-inch vertical window for natural light, as well as a metal bed, cabinet, toilet, and sink, all affixed to the wall. The cells were so designed and laid out that correctional officers could see each in its entirety from the control room, even with the cell door closed. Although sterile, prison authorities believed the new cells would "contribute to the successful rehabilitation of those who will serve time in Central Prison" since they offered more space and security than the cells in the old structure.[10]

The new facilities also included thirty internal security control stations, an array of two-way intercoms, and a closed-circuit camera system to allow guards to watch inmates as they moved from unit to unit. Each segment of the prison could be isolated from the other units by electronic locks controlled from the control stations, and the control stations also allowed officers to remotely open and close individual cells, limiting the need for face-to-face interaction. Additional updates included new acoustic monitoring devices, electronic flow pattern computers, and automated checkpoints. Further control came from an architectural design that lacked "nooks and crannies out of view of guards, where most prison violence occurs." In all, the interior of the new prison was a world away from the original.[11]

Outside the facility was similarly innovative. In place of the ominous brick wall, the new facility installed a double row of twelve-foot-high fencing topped with razor wire. Along the fence line were seven guard towers. They stood forty feet tall and were located at each corner of the square fence line, with the remainder placed at "strategic points along the perimeter." Armed guards manned each tower and communicated with the other towers and guards within the facility through an intercom system. Beyond the fences was an extended area cleared of trees and brush to hinder escape attempts and create better sightlines for those staffing the towers. Finally, an external visitor's center provided additional security for visitors as well as an opportunity for correctional officers to stymie the ingress of contraband.[12]

While safety and security were the predominating factors in the layout of the new prison, its architects also sought to make it more appealing. The facility included three dining halls, two gymnasiums, four exercise yards, a music room, a ball field, and a four hundred-seat auditorium, available for movies, concerts, and other performances, as well as the requisite support facilities, including a kitchen, bakery, laundry, chapel, library, barber shop, classrooms, counseling space, and canteen. To add some life to the buildings, each cellblock was a different color, and various fixtures throughout were painted bright hues. The new prison thus employed many of the most modern oversight tools, combined with traditional, time-tested methods of inmate control.[13]

Although estimates for the facility's design and construction were set at $27 million, the final cost was $37 million. Despite that overrun, prison officials were pleased with the results, and as the first inmates prepared to enter the facility in early 1983, Warden Samuel Garrison praised the new "state-of-the-art" facility that included "virtually no bars." "No bars," he told the press, "is an indication of security. If you don't have a bar to cut, you have to use a jack hammer to get out." He proudly proclaimed, "it'll be a lot tougher to escape from here," and concluded, "It'll be a hell of an improvement, I can tell you that."[14]

Warden Garrison's bluster, however, hid some trepidation. The electronic features worried him, and he fretted over the ability of the 646 correctional officers to run the new devices. Prior to the formal migration of inmates, therefore, he organized an educational, tutorial, and training program. He also implemented a sixty-day testing period during which the new prison housed minimum custody inmates to give staff practice operating the new system. The testing was important, as not every officer proved competent. As a result, while the first inmates moved into the facility in January 1983, a lack of trained guards prevented full occupation until March. Eventually the full transfer was complete, the old prison was razed, and the second phase began with construction of a $9.8 million, 192-bed unit for inmates working within the prison. That facility was finished in 1985.[15]

When the new facility finally was complete, critics complained that it lacked the formidable presence of its predecessor. Some compared its exterior to a college campus while others saw a luxury hotel. Even Director of Prisons Rae McNamara worried that "some . . . are going to call it a country club; others will say it's too clinical." She rejected those arguments, however, and asserted that the new prison, however it appeared on the outside, was "totally secure, if there is such a thing. Anyway, it's as close as you can get." Warden Garrison affirmed McNamara's claims and assured journalists that while no facility was entirely escape proof, "this is as close as it can be." He also reassured them that despite its facade, "This place is tough."[16]

The new prison may have been "tough," but many came to believe the warden was not. That questioning of Garrison's competence was the result of an incident that erupted amid the hectic final year of construction. It was an incident that shook the prison like nothing since the 1968 riot, and it offered evidence that for all the administrators' efforts, racism and brutality remained a fact of life.

The crisis began at 10:30 A.M. on Tuesday, March 23, 1982, when three African American inmates armed with homemade knives took eight hostages and barricaded themselves in a five-foot by ten-foot office. The three inmates were William Little, a twenty-seven-year-old serving 50–65 years for breaking and entering, larceny, second-degree rape, and robbery by force; twenty-eight-year-old Ezekiel Hall, who was serving life plus 40–70 years for first-degree kidnapping, robbery with a firearm, and assault with a deadly weapon with the intent to kill; and Melvin Surgeon, a thirty-one-year-old who was serving life plus 100 years for four counts of robbery with a firearm. The eight hostages were chaplain Lacy Joyner, correctional officer David Atkins Jr., data compilers Charles Cameron, Hugh Martin Jr., Jimmy Stallings, and William Beckwith, and inmates Bobby Lee Mills and Roger Lee McQueen. The inmates bound each hostage except for Joyner.[17]

Once the three inmates had their hostages under control, they demanded to speak to the press. Warden Garrison acceded, and at 7:30 P.M. WPTF radio news director H. Bart Ritner entered the prison along with North Carolina Parole Commission chairman Walter Johnson. Along with Deputy Warden Nathan Rice, Ritner and Johnson spoke with the inmates. They made no progress in ending the incident but learned the hostages were fine.[18]

After the meeting, Department of Correction spokesman Stuart Shadbolt informed the press that while prison officials were willing to speak to the inmates, they would not negotiate. Indeed, he went so far as to assert, "They could put a knife to their (the hostages') throats and slit them in front of us, and they still wouldn't get out." Although events proved Shadbolt wrong, at the time the administration offered an intransigent front.[19]

On Wednesday, the second day of the standoff, the inmates released Cameron, Beckwith, Mills, and McQueen in exchange for water, bologna sandwiches, and cigarettes. They also issued their demands: to meet with civil rights activists Jesse Jackson, Ben Chavis, and Leon White and to be moved from Central Prison to a federal facility. Administrators rejected the demands but continued the communications.[20]

As the standoff dragged into Wednesday evening, word about what precipitated the hostage taking emerged when journalist Bart Ritner made a second visit to the inmates and reported vaguely that they "were unhappy with conditions at Central Prison." Later accounts indicated that the inmates feared the "racist . . . oppressive . . . predator-type environment" and were dissatisfied with the "poor food, haphazard medical care, inadequate library, roaches, insensitive visiting policy, and the racial segregation of the inmates."[21]

At 10:30 P.M. that second night, civil rights lawyer Irving Joyner entered the prison to negotiate on the inmates' behalf. He met with the three men for half an hour and then met with prison officials for four hours. When that meeting concluded, Joyner met again with the inmates and brought with him a document signed by Department of Correction Secretary James Woodard in which he agreed to remove the men to the federal prison in Petersburg, Virginia. The inmates signed the document and at 4 A.M. released the hostages, put down their weapons, and surrendered. Guards handcuffed and searched the men, and at 5:45 A.M. they loaded them aboard a prison van for the ride to Petersburg.

Before they were even ensconced in their new cells, Secretary Woodard informed the press that he intended to return them to Central Prison as quickly as possible. That admission, along with his original willingness to negotiate and concede to the inmates' demands, met with outrage. Lawyer Irving Joyner assailed Woodard's announcement and asserted that state officials assured the inmates they would remain away from Central Prison "for a reasonable period of time." He argued that "a one-day excursion to Petersburg is not 'a reasonable period of time' under any stretch of the imagination," and reiterated that it was their treatment in prison that caused the hostage taking. Joyner then explained that they needed time away to organize an appeal, worried that they faced possible retribution from correctional officers should they return too soon, and suggested the staff needed time to "cool off."[22]

Woodard dismissed Joyner's claims and told the press that both sides "clearly understood" the transfer was for "a very short time." Warden Garrison supported Woodard and rejected the idea that they had promised an extended stay away from Central Prison. Governor Jim Hunt also approved of the Department of Correction's handling of the incident, although he hedged a little by telling the press he had only received an "outline" of the action.[23]

When authorities released the signed document, it appeared Joyner's complaint had little merit. The full statement read:

The undersigned parties, the state of North Carolina and the United States, hereby agree that prison inmates Ezekiel Hall 20853-OS, Melvin Surgeon 20951-MD, and William D. Little 20954-OS, will be transferred from Central Prison in Raleigh, North Carolina, to the Federal Correctional Institution in Petersburg, Virginia, in accordance with the Interstate Corrections Compact codified at NCGS 148–119 and 148–120 as implemented by previous written agreement. The state of North Carolina will be the state designated "sending" jurisdiction and the United States will be the receiving jurisdiction. This transfer will be contingent upon release of the following individuals now being held hostage at Central Prison:

> 1. David C. Atkins
> 2. Jimmy J. Stallings
> 3. Lacy L. Joyner
> 4. Hugh M. Martin, Jr.

Upon release of these individuals by the prison inmates named above, the transfer will be ordered.

Despite the facts in the agreement, Joyner continued to criticize the Department of Correction and argued that officials acted in bad faith. The *Raleigh News and Observer* editorial board agreed, and asserted that Woodard's actions would cost him authority, respect, and control of the inmates.[24]

Journalists were not the only ones to support Joyner's criticism. Leon White, the director of the United Church of Christ Commission for Racial Justice, held a press conference during which he said he was "shocked and dismayed at the naked deceit used by the state . . . to dishonor the agreement." He concluded by lamenting, "it is now obvious to all of those, both inside and outside of the walls, that the word of the state is meaningless."[25]

Other critics, by contrast, chastised Woodard for giving in to the inmates' demands in the first place. Former Department of Correction Secretary Ralph Edwards worried that removing the three men for even a day gave inmates the idea that they too could get what they wanted through violence. He told the press, "Once you have demonstrated weakness, or the willingness to negotiate under duress, there is a high risk of jeopardizing other staff members in the future." Vernon Bounds, who handled the 1968 riot in a very different manner, also offered critical comments, asserting, "you never reward rebellion" because doing so "invited a repetition."[26]

To counter the critical charges, Woodard tried to make clear that he authorized the inmates' removal solely to win the hostages' freedom. He attempted to thread the needle by asserting that he had not negotiated or conceded anything, and he sought to demonstrate that point by reminding people that the inmates soon would return to the prison. He appreciated the need to make this clear, of course, because he realized that much of the criticism was apt. In fact, Woodard had a very clear message for the inmates who remained: "no inmate incarcerated in our system will be allowed to achieve a desired goal by committing another criminal act."[27]

He further strengthened that message by returning the three inmates to North Carolina on Friday March 26, barely thirty hours after their removal. Rather than place them in Central Prison, however, Woodard sent them to solitary confinement at the Caledonia facility. During the press conference in which he announced their return, Woodard faced a gaggle of reporters who questioned the removal and rapid return. Woodard tried to explain that he had abided by the letter of the agreement, but when journalists accused him of lying, he grew "irate" and "snapped" that he was willing to do "anything to save a life."[28]

As prison officials, the press, and critics argued over Woodard's handling of the incident, the three inmates enjoyed a brief moment of celebrity. They too held a press conference in which they justified their actions. They informed journalists that they had planned the kidnapping for more than a month and saw it as an opportunity to "publicize the 'racist' conditions in the prison and to effectuate a transfer."[29]

They also described how they pulled it off. They explained that they purchased weapons from other inmates, faked illness to avoid their work assignment, used forged passes to make their way through various security checkpoints, and relied on officer apathy to smuggle through the weapons. They further explained that they selected the diagnostic center as their target because "it seemed like an easy area to get into." After describing the rest of the incident, the three men returned to the cause of their actions. They noted that the ease with which they faked illnesses, forged documents, smuggled weapons, and took hostages proved their assertion that the prison was not secure. The need to escape such circumstances, they claimed, was obvious.[30]

While a fascinating tale, the inmates' celebrity soon faded. What did not fade was the state's determination to demonstrate that it had not caved to their demands. As such, in July prosecutors charged the three men with kidnapping, assault, armed robbery, and possession of stolen property. When informed of the charges, the inmates' lawyers proclaimed their defense would be "duress." They claimed "conditions of confinement . . . at Central Prison . . . created an atmosphere of fear and terror, causing the defendants to take steps, which, in their opinion, were absolutely necessary to preserve their lives and sanity."[31]

Superior Court Judge Robert Farmer hindered the duress approach, however, when he refused to provide funds for psychiatric examinations. Unable to prove their clients were under duress, the lawyers sought to demonstrate a systematic pattern of inmate duress. They requested the records "of all inmates who had emotional or physical problems caused by prison conditions," all the "disciplinary reports since January 1978 concerning conflicts involving inmates and guards at Central Prison," and reports on all the "stabbings, assaults and sexual abuse complaints and all the weapons seized at Central since 1978." Their plan was to demonstrate the inherent stress under which every inmate lived, to prove their clients suffered from what we today would call post-traumatic stress disorder, and to justify their actions as a result of psychological strain. That charge would seem to have some merit, if we remember the findings of psychologists from less than a decade earlier who had inmates fall asleep during sessions because the stress of incarceration prevented them from sleeping properly at night.[32]

In October, Judge Maurice Braswell ruled against the defense requests in large part because prosecutors dropped the assault, armed robbery, and possession of stolen property charges. Braswell explained that "the defense would have applied to the case if the charges of assault against the inmates had not been dismissed," but with the charges dropped it no longer was viable. The state thus strengthened its case and weakened the defense by focusing solely on the kidnapping charges, which Braswell ruled were not covered by duress: "there is no law that says deplorable conditions at Central Prison gives a legal right to hold people hostage."[33]

With little left to go on, the defense decided not to offer any witnesses. Despite not taking the stand, the inmates still impacted the proceedings, twice being removed from the courtroom for yelling obscenities. Whether the outbursts affected the jury is unclear, but it deliberated less than three hours before finding the inmates guilty of second-degree kidnapping. The outbursts certainly affected Judge Braswell, who came down hard on the men. He sentenced Ezekiel Hall to 180 years, William Little to 150 years, and Melvin Surgeon to 90 years. To add insult to injury, he decreed the sentences would commence upon completion of their current terms. As all three already had extended terms, the new sentences did little more than demonstrate Judge Braswell's frustration with the men's behavior, which carried into the sentencing phase when Hall called the judge "a vulgar name" and Little "cursed the court" and told Braswell, "You don't give a damn about nobody."[34]

As the inmates vented their frustrations with the judge, the tangential consequences of the incident spiraled in a direction few could have foreseen. A coalition of church groups, along with the Prison and Jail Project of North Carolina, convened the week subsequent to the kidnapping and requested access to the prison so they could see conditions for themselves. The General Baptist State Convention of North Carolina also joined the chorus, demanding that Governor Hunt appoint "a blue ribbon panel to investigate the alleged racism in the total prison system."[35]

Legislators and prison officials rejected all such requests, but Warden Garrison made a fateful error while addressing the issue of racism. During an interview he admitted that elements of Central Prison remained segregated by race. He explained that while the hospital and dormitories were desegregated in 1965, cells housing multiple inmates remained segregated by "race, type of crime and size of the inmate." He claimed, however, that this was done because "the inmates have expressed a desire not to be integrated," although he acknowledged he "deliberately segregated about half the prison population by race 'because it has always been done, and it was traditional.'"[36]

When journalists asked Governor Hunt about Garrison's statement, he offered full support for the warden. Hunt's lawyer, Jack Cozort, also chimed in to argue that the state had attempted integration at the cell level but inmates "made it absolutely clear they do not want it." He further noted that while courts found segregation in prisons unconstitutional, he believed the practices at Central Prison were constitutionally valid due to "concrete security situations." When asked about those situations, he declined to answer, arguing that doing so would "give away our evidentiary position" and might undermine the state's ability to defend itself should "the case come up in litigation."[37]

Cozort had every reason to be concerned about a lawsuit, as just days later the U.S. Justice Department announced it was "monitoring" the segregation charges. Indeed, federal officials had been considering a civil rights suit against the state since 1977 and had drawn up papers citing it for violating the Civil Rights Act of 1964. The department was reluctant to file suit, however, as Central Prison's renovations seemed to render concerns about cell by cell segregation "moot."[38]

Despite that reluctance, in April 1982 Art Peabody and Paul Lawrence, attorneys from the Justice Department, toured the prison and met with officials from the prison and the governor's office. The general consensus was that they were looking to see how close the new prison was to completion in order to determine whether or not to file suit. State officials also came to understand that even should the federal government file suit, it was not seeking "complete integration" of the cells, but rather assurance that race was not the sole factor in determining cell assignment. Considering how far along construction was, and the fact that the state had already claimed the "type of crime and size of the inmate" factored along with race into cell assignment, state attorneys were confident about avoiding a suit.[39]

In December 1982, however, the Justice Department filed the long-held lawsuit. It charged Central Prison administrators with segregating 750 prisoners by race and included an injunction demanding they stop "engaging in any act or practice which has the purpose or effect of discriminating against or segregating any inmate." North Carolina Attorney General Rufus Edmisten called the suit a "publicity stunt" and said he was "flabbergasted" by its timing since the state was only weeks away from moving inmates into the new facility. The Justice Department parried that response by asserting that the suit, despite its stated focus on Central Prison, covered the entire state prison system.[40]

The Justice Department's decision, combined with the criticism of Garrison's handling of the hostage-taking and concerns about his ability to run the modernized facility, ultimately cost Warden Garrison his position. In October 1982, he took "indefinite sick leave" and the governor reassigned him within the prison system. Former Deputy Warden Nathan Rice succeeded Garrison, and he was on hand in May 1983 when the state quietly settled the federal suit by agreeing to desegregate all elements of its prison system. As Rice, Department of Correction leaders, and politicians statewide celebrated the end of the suit and the near simultaneous opening of the new prison, they undoubtedly hoped for a more peaceful future.

It seemed that the future almost had to be more peaceful, as the early 1980s saw politics, finances, race, and progressivism all reflected within the prison. Legislators once again used the prison system as a weapon, leaving inmates and administrators subject to the politics of the moment. Add to that charges of racism from inmates and the federal government, a three-day standoff with unruly prisoners, and the total renovation of Central Prison, and the tumult of the era becomes clear. What also becomes clear is the state's continued para-doxical nature. After a decade of refusing to implement any reform, and indeed making efforts to roll back previous innovations, politicians and prison officials suddenly proved willing to change. That change, however, appeared only super-ficial, as the bright new facility could not hide the system's inherently brutal and violent underpinnings. Once again the state's two minds were apparent, and the external forces that had long affected the institution continued to have their way. Those forces carried through the 1980s and into the early 1990s, as incarceration rates exploded, the inmate population skyrocketed, and prison officials and politicians faced challenges like never before. As the state entered a new decade, the issues of old remained.

21

OVERCROWDING

As Central Prison's inmates settled into their new cells and prison administrators sorted out the aftermath of the hostage taking and segregation cases, the larger prison system confronted its most serious threat since regaining independence in the 1950s. That threat was overcrowding, which was a problem in the 1970s but exploded into an epidemic in the 1980s due to new laws, the continued public demand that inmates serve hard time, and administrative red tape. When inmates responded by flooding the state with lawsuits, federal authorities intervened and threatened to take over the prison system. Fearful that such intervention would embarrass the state, Secretary of Correction Amos Reed begged legislators to act, and publicly "challenged the imagination and creativity of North Carolinians to move out of the counter-productive, fiscally and socially expensive 'folkways' of harsh incarceration" to find new means of handling criminals. Politicians did so by opening the purse strings and building an array of new facilities; they also eased parole rules and created new sentencing guidelines. The early 1980s saw politicians and prison administrators rise to Reed's challenge, but only after stumbling mightily. Both the stumble and the reaction to it further demonstrate the relationship between the state and the prison, as political intervention, financial concerns, progressivism, and new penological policies altered and affected the entire prison system.[1]

Although North Carolina enjoyed a low crime rate, ranking fortieth nationally, during the 1970s its prison population soared. In 1976, North Carolina had "the highest commitment rate of any state," with 240.06 inmates per 100,000 citizens, as compared to the national average of 94.85 per 100,000. It also had the fifth highest total prison population. Based on those facts and the expected continued rise in population, a departmental survey estimated that the inmate population would exceed carrying capacity by seven thousand in 1983.[2]

Theories as to the cause of the predicament were rampant. One popular assertion laid blame on a decline in the number of inmates sentenced to misdemeanors and the concomitant rise in those sentenced to felonies. An article by Secretary Reed in the journal *Popular Government* offered statistical support for that finding. Reed discovered that between 1969 and 1977 the number of felons doubled while the number of misdemeanants fell by one-third. The result was that the average length of an inmate's stay jumped from 2.7 years to 5.3 years. The population increase, in other words, resulted from "an increased average stay in prison rather than from increased admissions." This helped explain why the population rose while the crime rate remained low.[3]

Reed believed an additional cause was the frequent delay in granting parole. The slow process, brought about by a lack of staff, administrators, and infrastructure, hindered the state's ability to clear the prison of inmates otherwise eligible for release.[4]

Historians and penologists have since raised additional reasons for the population problem. Among them were the ongoing "tough on crime" movement, harsh drug laws, and mandatory minimum sentences. Although the crime rate was low, politicians saw the fear of crime as a useful tool. Statewide, therefore, politicians warned about crime as a means of winning office, and once seated they passed stringent criminal measures to appease voters. While the strategy was politically powerful, it caused problems when those same officials failed to fund the Department of Correction to the level required. The ironic result was that one manner of easing overcrowding was to release inmates early, often after serving only a fraction of their sentences. That reality outraged the public, prosecutors, and judges, who responded by demanding and imposing longer sentences, further increasing the prison population.[5]

A final cause was the state's unusual penal organization. North Carolina had more prison units, eighty-six, than any other state in the country. The reason for that was that prison administrators remained determined to control inmate labor. As a result, inmates who in other states would have been under local control found themselves under state administration. The very essence of the state's prison system was the cause of its most pressing problem.[6]

In an effort to address the issue, in 1976 the General Assembly created the Legislative Commission on Correctional Programs and tasked it with affecting sentencing changes to ease prison overcrowding. Headed by former state Senator Eddie Knox of Charlotte, and dubbed the Knox Commission, in 1977 it issued its report.

The commission began by re-examining why the state had so many inmates.

What it found was that North Carolina had some of the harshest punishments in the nation. It noted that a person in North Carolina convicted of breaking into a house and stealing $200 could get twenty years in prison, whereas in California "he would probably be put on probation." It also found armed robbers faced thirty-year terms while other states sentenced them to fifteen years, and those convicted of second-degree murder faced a life sentence while most states punished the crime with a twenty-year term. At the same time, the commission found North Carolina was among the most "conservative" of states in offering parole, creating fewer opportunities to make space for new arrivals. The Knox Commission thus provided concrete evidence to confirm what many already believed to be the causes of overcrowding.[7]

The commission next offered recommendations to relieve the pressure. It first suggested ending disparities in sentence length by creating a presumptive sentencing law. Commission members found sentencing statutes uneven, as some directed judges to impose an allowed punishment range while others left the sentence wholly to the judge's discretion. Judges even had the right to "suspend a sentence and place a defendant on probation for any offense except one punishable by death or life imprisonment." They also had the "inherent discretion to run sentences concurrent with or consecutive to one another." The problem was that this led to "grossly disparate" sentences, with African Americans receiving harsher sentences than whites when they committed the same crime, and the North Carolina Bar Association twice condemned the process. In other words, the Knox Commission found the judicial system lacked coherence, and it called for more equitable, sensible, and rational sentencing.[8]

Second, the commission called for ending parole and replacing it with day for day good time credit. At the time, an inmate was eligible for parole immediately if the judge did not include a minimum sentence; if the judge included a minimum sentence, the prisoner became eligible after reaching the minimum sentence or upon reaching one-fifth of the maximum sentence, whichever came first. For those with life terms, the one-fifth point was twenty years. The commission determined that this system provided the inmate no incentive toward good behavior. Implementing a good time credit system, however, required the inmate to earn time off rather than simply serve his minimum time. Commissioners believed this would result in better-behaved inmates and would reduce the population as inmates had the ability and incentive to shorten their terms.[9]

Third, the commission called for expanding community-based programs, educational opportunities, and vocational training classes. Those programs rehabilitated inmates and reduced recidivism by providing the skills needed to survive beyond the prison walls. This would ease crowding by decreasing the number of reoffenders.

Finally, the commission called for the construction of new facilities. The commission thus confirmed the conclusion Reed reached in his article, and it determined that even were all of its reforms implemented, the state still would lack space. The only way to end overcrowding was to build new jails, prisons, juvenile reformatories, and rehabilitation centers.[10]

The General Assembly took the Knox report seriously and, to the shock of many, voted to fund "the most extensive prison construction program in state history." It did so by apportioning more than $100 million on new construction, with the goal adding 3,604 new beds and renovating old facilities to create an additional 1,280 beds.[11]

The addition of new beds was but part of the solution. In 1980, prison administrators announced a new system of good time credits, which allowed inmates to earn up to 107 days per year off their minimum sentence. They also could earn "gained time," which allowed them to earn additional time off for certain actions. They could earn two days per month for "good performance of short-term work assignments . . . or for attending an on-site academic or vocational training program." They could earn four days per month for "good job performance requiring a minimum of six hours actual work per day or for part-time work release or study release assignments." They could earn six days per month "for the showing of job skills requiring a minimum of six hours actual work per day with requirements for special skills or special responsibilities as well as inmates taking part in full-time study release." Finally, they could earn "emergency gained time" by working more than forty hours a week, working in bad weather, or working in emergency situations. Inmates now had the opportunity to reduce substantially their minimum sentence, and officials hoped the incentive to get out early would inspire good behavior and ease the population pressure on the entire system.[12]

The General Assembly also responded to the Knox report with the 1981 Fair Sentencing Act (FSA), which implemented sentencing and parole reforms in order "to make sentencing more equitable and predictable by setting standard punishment terms—or presumptive sentences that a judge must impose unless there were reasons to lengthen or shorten the sentences." It did so by establishing "presumptive and maximum prison terms for most felonies, which were categorized into offense classes (A through J) based on seriousness." Judges could sentence a prisoner to a "presumptive sentence," a suspended sentence, or to consecutive sentences with no written findings required. If judges wanted to deviate from the presumptive sentence, by either imposing a shorter sentence or a longer one up to a set maximum, they had to provide "a written finding that aggravating factors outweighed mitigating factors or vice versa." However, if judges found even one aggravating factor, they could impose a sentence up to the maximum. The law included a list of mitigating and aggravating factors but allowed judges the discretion to consider additional circumstances that were "reasonably related to the purpose of sentencing," as long as they could demonstrate those factors "by the preponderance of the evidence."[13]

The FSA did not stop there, however, as it also revised the good time credit system. The new law increased the amount of time inmates could cut from their sentences by providing one day of credit for every day served without a major infraction. Whereas inmates previously earned up to 107 days off per year, they now could earn 365 days off per year. The potential result was to cut an inmate's minimum sentence in half. But the FSA did more, adding the opportunity for additional gained time in the form of "meritorious time," which an inmate earned by "heroism or exemplary acts beyond normal expectations." Taken together, the several elements of the FSA seemed to offer a dramatic opportunity to reduce the inmate population.[14]

Studies have found that the FSA succeeded in creating a more logical system that made sentences "less dispersed." Professor Stevens Clarke of the University of North Carolina Institute of Government found the FSA resulted in less variability between those convicted of the same crimes and a reduction in the difference between sentences for white and African American defendants charged with the same crime. Clarke ultimately determined that the FSA eased the system's endemic racism and rationalized prison sentences and the parole process.[15]

While the new law created more uniform sentencing procedures and more rational sentences, it failed to create a more equitable system. Judge Robert Collier argued that the FSA actually proved inequitable because the amount of time a person served was not based on the crime, but on their behavior in prison. A violent felon who did his time quietly, therefore, could win release faster than a nonviolent offender who found trouble in prison.[16]

There was another problem as well: judges and prosecutors hated the good time provisions that allowed inmates to serve only a fraction of their sentence. In the year prior to its imposition, inmates served an average of 42 percent of their terms. Subsequent to the new law that figure fell to 38.5 percent. To combat that reduction, judges worked hard to find aggravating factors in order to sentence inmates beyond the presumptive limits, knowing full well that with good time they would get out much sooner. They indeed became adept at finding those factors, and the percentage of time served quickly returned to near pre-FSA levels.[17]

Despite all of the reforms designed to ease overcrowding, the prison population thus continued to grow: from a daily system-wide average of less than thirteen thousand in 1975 to nineteen thousand in 1990. Subsequent studies determined that "improved rates of apprehension and conviction," an increase in DWI arrests, the increased admittance of "pretrial prisoners," and the increased time "pretrial prisoners" spent in jail conspired to ensure the continued growth. Put simply, new laws and other forms of indirect political intervention filled prison cells faster than the new policies emptied them. The result was that the system remained overburdened.[18]

Actually, it was more than overburdened. In 1987, the prison system had a stated carrying capacity of 16,633, yet it housed 18,022. When journalist Jack Betts interviewed Director of Prisons John Patseavouras about that issue, Patseavouras explained that the situation was even worse than it appeared. The American Correctional Association (ACA) set a standard of fifty square feet of cell space per inmate. North Carolina was nowhere near that standard and, according to Betts, the state "never has conformed to ACA standards, and not one North Carolina state prison unit has *ever* been accredited by the American Correction Association." Employing the ACA's fifty-square-foot guideline would have reduced the system's carrying capacity to 13,200. To make the problem even more obvious, if the state used a forty-square-foot standard, it still had a carrying capacity of only 14,800.[19]

Inmates, obviously, bore the brunt of this problem, often in the form of "triple bunking," by which three inmates were crowded into a cell the size of an average house bathroom. Triple bunking also made life more difficult for correctional officers, as it raised tensions and led to increased violence and sexual assault. Confronted with an untenable situation and a systemic failure by state leaders to solve it, inmates took the offensive. They first appealed to grievance committees. When nothing came from those complaints, they took recourse to the courts. During the 1980s, North Carolina prison administrators faced more than fifty lawsuits brought about by overcrowding.

Those lawsuits did not occur in a void. They actually owe their origins to events in Alabama. In 1971, Alabama inmates claimed at least six deaths resulted from improper treatment in prison hospitals. Federal District Judge Frank Johnson Jr. affirmed the complaint and accused the state of "pervasive and gross neglect" that amounted to the "knowing and intentional" mistreatment of inmates. He ruled that the atmosphere met "any current judicial definition of cruel and unusual punishment" and ordered a federal takeover of the system. That takeover was nearly complete, with federal judges determining the "cell size, urinal space, staff-inmate ratios, the temperature of water in prison showers, and the number of inmates the state could incarcerate." Buoyed by the decision, inmate lawsuits nationwide exploded, and by 1987 ten states found their prison systems wholly under federal control, while another twenty-eight "were operating at least part of their prisons systems under some kind of court order."[20]

North Carolina was not exempt from inmate activism, and in 1980 inmates in the Piedmont Correctional Institute filed suit. Known as the *Hubert v. Ward* case, inmates claimed violations of their Eighth and Fourteenth Amendment rights based on overcrowding, the availability of weapons, the threat of violence, the lack of officer oversight, the fear of "involuntary homosexual activities," the failure to meet state requirements regarding educational, vocational, medical, and mental health services, and the failure to meet state regulations regarding proper classification and housing.[21]

Fearful that a negative ruling would lead to a federal takeover, which would prove expensive and "a critical blow to the confidence of the public in their government's ability to solve its own problems," on September 16, 1985, attorneys reached an out-of-court settlement by which the state agreed to spend $12.5 million to end triple bunking in the facilities that were part of the suit and to reduce the inmate population system-wide by one-third. The agreement also set requirements for any new facilities built: the floor space of each cell had to provide fifty square feet per inmate, the cell ceiling had to be at least eight feet high, there had to be one operable toilet and shower for every eight inmates, and there had to be one operable wash basin with hot and cold running water for every six inmates. The ruling further set requirements for day rooms, temperature, noise, and lighting, and it called for upgraded fireproofing, new educational, vocational, and work programs, proper clothing for each season, improved recreational facilities, improved medical facilities, and the hiring of additional guard staff.[22]

Despite talk of maintaining the public's confidence, the main reason the state conceded the case was that politicians and prison administrators knew the rest of the prison system was similarly overcrowded. Fearful of additional lawsuits and the potential for a federal takeover, they hoped settling the *Hubert* case would give them time to address the other facilities. Such was not to be.[23]

In 1986, the U.S. District Court for the Eastern District of North Carolina certified a lawsuit against "48 other state prison units, essentially all the 'road camp' units outside the south Piedmont area" where the *Hubert* suit was centered. This suit, called *Small v. Martin*, focused on "the constitutionality of the conditions of confinement." U.S. District Court Judge Earl Britt encouraged the two sides to negotiate an agreement. Once again aware they were on thin ice, politicians quickly settled. On December 21, 1988, the parties reached an accord that required the end of triple bunking in all forty-eight units involved in the suit—in this case by December 1989. Legislators also agreed to create "dormitory capacity at each of the affected units based on the standard of fifty square feet of living space per inmate" by July 1, 1994, and to meet the fifty-square-foot requirement in all of the system's facilities, even those not included in the suit, by some unstated future date. In the newly constructed dormitories, as well as those areas renovated to meet the new standards, the agreement further required updated ventilation, heating, and plumbing systems, and the modernization of the lighting, smoke detection units, and fire escapes. The agreement also required a "review and evaluation" procedure for inmate medical care, "set standards" for the day rooms used by inmates, and increased nighttime security in each dormitory. Finally, it created a new "intensive supervision" parole system that freed inmates "who would otherwise enter or remain in prison." The agreement thus created a wide-ranging set of policies designed to solve the immediate problems and to avoid the development of future issues.[24]

Despite the "success" North Carolina had in settling those two suits, dozens of others remained on the docket and journalist Joel Rosch described them as "the most severe threat of federal intervention into the state prison system in the history North Carolina." The prison administration's ability to fulfill the promises made in the two settlements also worried observers, with Department of Correction Executive Administrative Assistant Ben Irons admitting, "the state is in serious danger of losing control of the prison system."[25]

One reason for that fear was that despite the lawsuits, the agreements, and the money spent (some $223 million by 1986), the prison system still had too many inmates. Based on the fifty-square-foot minimum, the system was housing forty-five hundred inmates above capacity.[26]

A second cause of the fear was that Central Prison was especially full. It was not included in any of the lawsuits, and state officials came to believe it was not a "high risk facility for litigation." When correctional officials visited not long after the suits were settled, however, they were discouraged by what they found. "K Dorm," the intake facility where prisoners were processed and housed until assigned to another facility, was triple bunked, its day room was "jammed with bunks," leaving but "a small space for tables and a television," and it had only four toilets for 117 inmates. Correctional officers informed visiting officials that beyond the sanitary issue, the lack of toilets was a problem because it led to fights in the morning when inmates needed to use the facilities prior to breakfast. The lack of toilets was not the only sanitary issue the officials discovered. The 117 prisoners lived in a space designed for thirty-seven; this offered but thirteen square feet per inmate.[27]

Since Central Prison was not included in the lawsuits, the agreed-to fifty-square-foot accommodation would only be implemented at some unstated point in the future. Using that vague framework, prison administrators shuttled inmates to Raleigh from facilities that were part of the suits in order to meet the fifty-square-foot agreement. Inmates stayed at Central Prison until room opened up at other facilities, which typically took four to six months. While this enabled the state to meet its legally binding agreements, it resulted in misery for inmates in the penitentiary. According to one inmate, "There is nothing to do but lay in bed. You get up and walk in a circle and go back to bed. With triple high bunks you can't sit in your bed." Yet another called the prison a "death trap," while one more deemed it a "powder keg waiting to explode."[28]

Determined to prevent that explosion, by the late 1980s officials realized their previous efforts had been only half measures. If they were going to solve the problem, they needed "to fix the entire prison system." That fix would prove hard to come by, however, as the factors that precipitated the problem lingered.[29]

Throughout the 1980s, finances, battles between politicians and judges, and changing social forces conspired to explode the inmate population well beyond the system's carrying capacity. Although lawsuits won some relief, the causes of overcrowding were deep-seated and endemic. The need "to fix the entire prison system" was real but incomplete, and to finish the task required politicians and prison administrators to become more innovative and insightful. As the 1980s waned, however, financial fears combined with yet another round of political battles to stymie any such change. The question was, could anyone or anything overcome those fears, alter the state's psyche, and induce the needed changes? Governor Jim Martin and Secretary of the Department of Correction Aaron Johnson set out to answer that question.

22

THE TEN-YEAR PLAN

Between 1980 and 2000, North Carolina's population grew by 37 percent. Unfortunately, the state failed to respond to that growth with increased infrastructure funding, leaving "schools . . . hospitals, mental institutions, and prisons understaffed and overfilled." By 1989, North Carolina had more than seventeen thousand inmates, a figure that gave it the tenth highest prison population and the fourteenth highest incarceration rate in the nation. While the reforms of the early 1980s slowed prison population growth, and although inmate lawsuits from the middle part of the decade forced the state to accede to yet more improvements, overcrowding remained a problem. More determined than ever to solve the issue rather than simply address its consequences, during the late 1980s and throughout the 1990s politicians and prison officials continued to implement new sentencing guidelines and rehabilitation programs. Those efforts were not without controversy, however, as political infighting once again affected policy. Despite that, the state's paradoxical politics briefly enabled Republicans to overcome Democratic intransigence and enact reforms. They even succeeded in putting a minor dent in the state's racist past with the appointment of the first African American to run the Department of Correction. While many of the traditional problems faced by legislators and prison officials remained, new social and political forces were beginning to emerge.[1]

The first innovation of the era came with the creation of the Special Committee on Prisons. The General Assembly ordered the sixteen-member committee to ensure all facilities met federal guidelines and "to identify problems resulting from overcrowding, pending litigation, and other issues pertaining to the operation of prisons in North Carolina." The committee met, and in May 1988 it proposed three "short-term solutions": "parole release, the housing of inmates out-of-state and the imposition of a population limitation on the system." The housing of inmates in other states never came to be, but the General Assembly did enact the other two suggestions. First, it passed legislation allowing parole "180 days before the final release date," a figure soon raised to 270 days. Second, it passed the Emergency Prison Population Stabilization Act, which created a hard cap on the prison population based on the fifty-square-foot-per-inmate minimum. As it stood, the state could house eighteen thousand inmates, but if the population exceeded 97 percent of that maximum, or 17,460, for fifteen straight days, the legislation required administrators to reduce the population below 17,280 within sixty days.[2]

Although founded on good intentions, neither law worked well. This was not a legislative failure but rather the consequence of a skyrocketing crime rate. Between 1984 and 1989, the crime rate increased 39 percent, as compared to 21 percent nationally. That meant North Carolina's crime rate increased at the seventh highest rate in the nation, dropping the state from fortieth to twenty-eighth in the crime rate index. Prison admissions subsequently rose 62 percent, but due to the population cap the prison population increased only 7 percent. This occurred at a time when many states saw their prison populations increase by 100 percent, while California's and Alaska's prison populations tripled. To achieve the limited growth necessary to remain under the caps despite the spike in crime, the number of inmates paroled increased by 136 percent. The end result was that some felons served as little as 20 percent of their sentences and some misdemeanants served as little as 10 percent. Administrators realized that "offenders, knowing they would serve only a small portion of their sentences, chose prison over probation or refused to comply with probation requirements because revocation would result in serving only a short time." One study concluded that "time served in some instances is so brief . . . that it hardly interferes with their criminal activity."[3]

Appreciating the relative failure of this first reform effort, on March 6, 1986, Governor Jim Martin proposed "the largest prison construction program in the state's history." He first called for a ten-year, $203 million plan to add 9,500 new beds—more than double the cost and number of beds proposed a decade earlier in the aftermath of the Knox Commission report. Next, he proposed the creation of private prison facilities. Martin argued that outsourcing incarceration would benefit the state in a number of manners. First, private prisons would save the state money as the firms bore the construction and operation costs. Second, they would provide a means of comparison to see if there were better ways to house inmates. Finally, allowing private firms to run prisons would "hold North Carolina and the Department of Correction harmless for any and all costs associated with the defense of suits filed against them." Such an idea certainly was appealing, coming as it did after the welter of lawsuits earlier in the decade. While the state did experiment with private prisons in the late 1990s, at the time Martin decided against this approach.[4]

Realizing new construction was only part of the solution, he also proposed alternatives to incarceration, with the goal of diverting five thousand convicts to external programs. The plan thus worked to increase the number of inmates sentenced to probation, parole, or community-based punishments. Martin noted that all three were less expensive than incarceration, allowed individuals to work and pay taxes, thus funding their own punishment, and, in the case of community-based punishments, provided the opportunity for restitution. Martin argued that half of the overcrowding issue could be addressed by better utilization of the alternative programs. He also noted that they provided the added benefit of limiting renovation expenses by reducing the number of required beds.[5]

To meet the increased number of inmates in these programs, Martin called for hiring additional probation and parole officers. The costs of those hires, he assured the public, would be offset by the fact that parole and probation were "the most cost effective means" of addressing the overcrowding problem. As proof, in 1987 "to keep *one* inmate locked up at Central Prison for *one* year cost the taxpayer $24,871." For each inmate on probation, however, the state spent $470.[6]

Related to this suggestion, Martin called for the expansion of the "intensive supervision" parole program. The proposal called for hiring seventy-eight new parole officers, which would give prison administrators the ability to release an additional 1,215 inmates. The plan also urged the expansion of the Pre-Release and Aftercare Program (PRAC) by adding new "pre-release adjustment and training" programs, improving the "community supervision of parolees" to ensure those released obeyed parole regulations, and hiring twenty-eight new PRAC officers. Martin contended that those changes would expand the program by 21 percent.[7]

In one final move, the governor called for the increased use of "house arrest with enhanced surveillance." This included the use of transmitters to detect the location of individuals who were allowed to leave home for work, but otherwise were to remain home as part of their punishment. Summarizing this section,

Martin urged legislators to reexamine the issues every year to "adjust the balance of construction versus probation as needed."[8]

The Ten-Year Plan, as the proposals became known, was a broad and audacious proposition, but one in which Martin truly believed. The man given the task of implementing the plan was Aaron Johnson, who, by his own admission, "knew nothing about corrections." Although a questionable appointment, Johnson made history when he took office on January 7, 1985, as the first African American to head the state's correction system and the first ordained minister in the nation to do so.[9]

His first move to reduce the prison population was to release outright 1,875 inmates, including murderers, rapists, child molesters, and armed robbers, many of whom had served less than half their sentences. Johnson later called the decision a "nightmare." Despite that nightmare, he still needed to reduce overcrowding. The reality of that need, and of overcrowding's consequences, hit home during Johnson's first visit to a field prison in Durham County, where he saw triple-bunked cells in which three inmates were "squeezed into an eight-by-fifteen-foot cell, alongside a sink and a toilet." He recognized that the cramped cells created "space ripe for an epidemic of violence" and realized something had to be done or the entire system would explode. As he left the prison that cold and rainy day, he witnessed another consequence of overcrowding when he came across inmates working outside without long sleeves, jackets, or hats. When he asked why they were inadequately dressed, they informed him the prison did not have the necessary clothes. Incredulous, Johnson demanded to see the "clothes house" where uniforms were stored. Instead of a warehouse packed with the required and "seasonally appropriate" attire, he encountered an empty building.[10]

Not long after his visit to Durham County, Johnson made his first visit to Central Prison. His time in Durham failed to prepare him for what he found in the state penitentiary. The prison hospital, he later described, had "puke green walls" that were so dirty "it seemed like they'd stick to you if you touched them." The linens were soiled and vermin infested, there were maggots on the floors, and the only piece of medical equipment was a thirty-five-year-old X-ray machine. When he asked Parker Eales, the penitentiary's director of nursing, "when was the last time any piece of medical equipment was purchased," Eales replied, "we're still using thermometers from the 1950s . . . and tongue depressors from the twenties." Although Johnson managed to joke that he hated to think "how old the magazines are in your waiting room," he was appalled. He was even further distraught when Eales explained that the prison housed elderly inmates who needed geriatric care that the prison could not provide, inmates with heart conditions the prison could not monitor, and inmates with "cancer, AIDS, kidney disease," and a litany of other diseases for which there was no treatment available. Indeed, Eales lamented that "Central Prison hospital is not equipped to set a broken finger," much less treat these more severe ailments.[11]

Outraged, Johnson became a vocal advocate of Martin's Ten-Year Plan. He first made arrangements with medical companies and philanthropists to provide the penitentiary hospital with supplies and money for a complete overhaul. Less than a year later, Central Prison's hospital was fully equipped and revitalized. When he visited again, Johnson found that "freshly painted white and yellow walls adorned every nook and cranny of the hospital. Cheery, huge murals hung in each infirmary. Clean curtains and bedspreads now covered those bare windows and stark beds. Privacy curtains hung between examination cubicles. Plants were placed throughout the facility." Additionally, the hospital had proper medical machinery and devices, new offices, records rooms, and an emergency room were opened, and twelve new nurses had been hired. As a result, the hospital passed an audit by the National Commission on Correctional Health Care and earned accreditation by the American Medical Association. For his efforts overseeing the reforms, Johnson promoted Parker Eales to director of health operations.[12]

To implement elements of the Ten-Year Plan that focused on overcrowding, Johnson next embarked on an ambitious and multipronged agenda. He took state funds and created a first-in-the-nation program employing electronic ankle surveillance on those sentenced to house arrest. He also created the Building, Rehabilitating, Instructing, Developing, Growing, and Employing program (BRIDGE), which was a "cooperative effort between the North Carolina Division of Prisons and the Division of Forest Resources" to train young, nonviolent offenders to fight forest fires and preserve the state's timberland while teaching them "a strong work ethic and marketable skills." The BRIDGE program remains operative, and according to prison records the recidivism rate among BRIDGE "graduates" is 12 percent—one-third the rate for nonparticipants. Associated with BRIDGE were newly implemented efforts to treat inmates with alcohol and drug issues; the Motheread program, designed to improve inmate literacy so they could read to their children during visits; the Family Service Program Center, which helped inmates' families navigate the prison system; the IMPACT program, a boot camp for inmates aged eighteen to twenty-two, completion of which reduced their sentences; and a first-in-the-nation AIDS screening and treatment plan. Johnson's efforts proved that with a supportive governor, prison administrators could address serious problems with innovative and useful reforms. While problems certainly remained, Johnson seemed to have addressed a number of shortcomings and made a slight dent in the prison population.[13]

But Governor Martin needed more than a slight decline in the inmate population, and the Ten-Year Plan found itself caught up in a round of political infighting. During much of his administration, Martin, a Republican, confronted a Democrat-controlled legislature. Much as it had a decade earlier under James Holshouser, the General Assembly showed little interest in helping Martin implement his proposals no matter how badly needed. Legislators did pass the Emergency Prison Facilities Development Program, but it provided only $30 million in construction funds to create 2,554 new beds. This gave the governor 15 percent of the money and 33 percent of the new beds he had requested. Democrats, it seems, hoped the much-feared federal takeover would occur under the Republican governor, gifting them a political hammer.[14]

Realizing those political machinations doomed his program, despite Secretary Johnson's best efforts, in December 1989 Governor Martin scrapped the Ten-Year Plan and created the Governor's Advisory Board on Prisons and Punishment. The board was evenly divided between Republicans and Democrats, whom Martin tasked with reducing the prison population while ensuring drug kingpins served 100 percent of their sentences, serious offenders served at least 40 percent of their sentences, and all other felons and misdemeanants served at least 25 percent of their sentences.[15]

The board held five public meetings to discuss constructing new prisons, to study data about "crime, incarceration rates, sentences levied and actual sentences served," and to determine how North Carolina could "restore credibility to the criminal justice system." After two and a half months of work, the board concluded that "North Carolina's unique and extraordinarily high increase in crime over the past several years" led to the overcrowding problem. That problem led to the reduction in time served, which eroded "public confidence in the criminal justice system" and destroyed "the effectiveness of the alternative punishment programs." Lamenting that "our prisons have been neglected for too long," the board demanded "a significant expansion of the state's prison system."[16]

To achieve that expansion, the board supported the governor's previous call for prison construction, but raised the ante by demanding the state spend $400 million over the next five years to add 11,280 beds. Additionally, it supported the expansion of alternative programs, but urged that expenditures for those programs occur only after the creation of new bed space. It also suggested cutting construction costs by using inmate labor, duplicating plans for numerous facilities, converting existing units, and implementing other "innovative measures." Finally, it called for the use of public bonds to fund the efforts.[17]

Democrats eventually acceded to the suggestions, although they refused to admit those were the very reforms they had opposed as a part of the Ten-Year Plan, and in 1990 North Carolinians voted on a construction referendum and bond issue. The initiatives succeeded, but only barely. The referendum passed by less than one half of 1 percent and the bond issue was only $200 million— half the amount suggested by the advisory board. Although a narrow victory, it demonstrated what politicians could achieve if they worked together, overcame their financial qualms, and embraced a reformative penal model.[18]

As construction on the new facilities began, including 192 new beds at Central Prison, legislators realized that if they were ever truly to solve the crowding issue they needed to regain the support of the state's judiciary, many of whom remained unhappy with the FSA. As a result, in 1990 the General Assembly created the Sentencing and Policy Advisory Commission and ordered it to replace the FSA with something that reduced the prison population and satisfied the state's judges.[19]

The commissioners studied efforts in Minnesota, Pennsylvania, Washington, and Florida, all of which had introduced "structured sentencing" programs in the early 1980s. Impressed with the programs, the commissioners created a new penal rubric that devised ten criminal offense categories labeled A–J, which focused on the impact the crime had on the victim. Class A crimes, for instance, caused death, Class B crimes caused "serious debilitating long-term injury," and Class C crimes caused "serious long-term personal injury or serious long-term or widespread societal injury." The impact of the crimes diminished as the classification progressed.[20]

The commission next created a "prior criminal record level" for each defendant, which assigned a numerical figure to the seriousness of previous crimes. The commission then devised a grid, with the class level on one axis and the prior criminal record on the other. On the grid itself, the commission placed an assigned punishment range, but with a change from earlier systems. The commission proposed that the inmate serve at least his minimum sentence, and while he could earn time off for good behavior, that time came off the back end. In other words, the inmate could shorten his maximum time in prison, not his minimum. The commission then used computer modeling to examine the results of various sentencing rates and tweaked the sentences accordingly so as to not overburden the system.[21]

The commission's work took three years, but in 1993 the General Assembly passed the Structured Sentencing Act. It went into effect on October 1, 1994, and for more than a decade it stabilized the prison population. It proved so successful that in 1997 North Carolina was among ten winners of the "Innovations in American Government Award," presented by the Ford Foundation and Harvard University. The award committee called the Structured Sentencing Act "an innovative sentencing law that . . . put North Carolina at the forefront of the nascent but increasingly popular concept of criminal justice: balancing prison sentences with available cell capacity."[22]

A rising crime rate in the 2000s, however, caused renewed problems, and in 2009 the state hit its population cap, with projections that it would "exceed the capacity for the next ten years." The legislature responded by tweaking the sentencing grid to reduce the population level by approximately two thousand inmates. Added to that was a decline in the state's crime rate in 2010 that, when combined with the grid reforms, led to a leveling off of the statewide prison population at approximately forty-one thousand. Despite that, politicians continued to address population concerns, and in 2011 Governor Beverly Perdue signed into law the Justice Reinvestment Act, which was "designed to reduce the state's prison population and free up resources for programs aimed at reducing recidivism." The act expanded opportunities for probation and community service sentences; created programs designed to reduce the risk of recidivism that, if completed, made inmates eligible for early release; and increased the "period of post-release supervision" for most felons. Computer models forecasted that the reforms would reduce the prison population by five thousand inmates and save the state $267 million. A 2016 study found that since the act's imposition, the prison population had declined by slightly more than four thousand inmates, saving the state $195 million. Equally notable, the study found a 65 percent decline in "admissions due to probation revocation." The Justice Reinvestment Act thus seems successful: not only has it reduced the inmate population and saved the state money, it has reduced recidivism as well.[23]

Initially, the era's growing crime rate failed to alter the state's traditional political battles as Republicans and Democrats proved unwilling to cooperate, undermining Governor Martin's Ten-Year Plan. Appreciating the circumstances and the true dangers prison overcrowding engendered, however, the two parties eventually worked together, implemented new penal policies, and made a significant effort to address those crowding issues. Although not every program proved a success, the era's many and varied efforts suggested a possible end to the use of the prison as a political weapon, demonstrated a return to the progressivism of yore, and showed a renewed political willingness to spend money on the most advanced penal policies. The system's future seemed bright, but a whole new array of problems soon arose that shocked the public, challenged the state's image, led to yet more social unrest, and toppled Department of Correction Secretary Aaron Johnson.

23

CORRUPTION AND CONTROVERSY

Department of Correction Secretary Aaron Johnson may have been an unorthodox choice for the job, but no one doubted his determination to improve the prison system. His inexperience, however, eventually caught up with him as he faced a massive corruption scandal, ongoing racial dilemmas, continuing financial issues, and a major battle over the death penalty. Those developments once again turned the prison into a political battlefield, demonstrated the paradoxical nature of the public's sensibilities, and called into question the state's progressive image. As public sentiment and the political winds swirled, inmates and prison administrators found themselves caught amid the fury. As the new millennium neared, the ways of old continued apace.

The tumultuous era began when Secretary Johnson set out to address the lack of adequate clothing he witnessed during his visit to the Durham County field prison. In 1985, he ordered controller C. R. Creech, purchasing service officer Rick Hursey, and warehouse manager Jerry Thompson to see that all inmates had at least four sets of clothing at all times, while inmates who worked in the kitchen or on the highways had five sets.[1]

To bring that about, the administrators decided each inmate needed to have "four sets in their lockers, four sets in the Clothes House, four sets in the laundry and four sets at the warehouse." That meant the prison needed sixteen sets of clothing for every inmate in the system. With the amount of clothes determined, the three administrators set about finding a firm to fill the order. Rather than take bids, as was required, Hursey offered no-bid contracts to companies owned by his friends and family. Johnson, his faith in his appointees complete and his attention distracted by so many other issues, was unaware of the impropriety. That unawareness was so complete that for the next five years he did not even read the purchasing contracts Hursey placed before him. This enabled the impropriety to continue and cost the state a small fortune as the firms over-charged and under-delivered.[2]

In October 1991, budget officer Julie Carpenter became aware of the problem and raised her concerns to Creech, the controller. Creech, however, ignored her warning. Undeterred, Carpenter continued to look into the matter, and in November she presented Creech and Assistant Secretary of Management B. J. Mooneyham with a list of thirty-three no-bid contracts that violated the spirit if not the letter of state laws. Once again the two men ignored the report. Unsure how to respond to management disinterested in blatant corruption, Carpenter pondered her next move.[3]

That next move was made for her thanks to the incompetence of those organizing the scam. In December, Hursey placed his order unaware that the firm had altered its packaging to include four uniform sets per box, rather than one. That oversight led Hursey to purchase four times the required number of uniforms. Fearful the mistake would unmask his incompetence and years-long scam, Hursey compounded his error by trying to cover it up. He did this by convincing warehouse manager Jerry Thompson to "hide the overflow" by renting external storage facilities to hold the excess clothing.[4]

The expenses incurred in procuring and hiding the excess clothing finally gave Carpenter the evidence she needed to push through Creech's intransigence and reach the secretary. Johnson was shocked by what he learned upon meeting with Carpenter in January 1992. She demonstrated that over five years Hursey had exceeded costs by $12.3 million and had stockpiled enough clothing to last the system, in some cases, for more than a century. Johnson promptly fired Hursey, Creech, and Thompson, but realized the house cleaning was incomplete as long as he remained. He had appointed the people guilty of the fraud and had failed to oversee their actions. The fault was as much his as theirs. Determined not to cause further harm to the prison system or to Governor Martin, Johnson resigned on February 28, 1992. Seventy-three-year-old Vernon Bounds succeeded him.[5]

Bounds had retired from the prison system in 1973 and spent the next thir-teen years as the William Rand Kenan Jr. Professor of Public Law and Adminis-tration at the University of North Carolina at Chapel Hill. He retired from the university in 1986, but accepted Governor Martin's request that he return to the prison administration. Bounds's first act as secretary was to order an inves-tigation into the corruption scandal. In September 1992 state auditor Edward Renfrow issued his findings.

The "Special Report" offered explicit evidence of how excessive was Hursey's over-purchasing. From June 30, 1990, to May 31, 1991, the number of "green pants" that the Department of Correction owned rose from 3,072 to 51,420 pair, the number of "green shirt jackets" rose from 1,572 to 114,168, and the pairs of socks rose from 2,808 to 825,984. The result, the report explained, was that the per-inmate clothing supply on May 31, 1991, was: 44 pairs of socks, 4 pairs of tennis shoes, 21 pairs of boxer shorts, and 14 tee shirts. The report also found the prison system had 165 years worth of triple-X boxer shorts, 113 years worth of triple-X brown shirts, 27 years worth of green shirts, and 15 years worth of size 13 steel-toed safety boots. What makes the figures even more staggering is that they only include the clothing in the warehouses; when the clothing in use is added in, the numbers grow even higher, with the prison possessing 59 pairs of socks for each inmate. The oversupply was so massive that it cost the state an additional $85,312.46 annually in storage fees. Despite the staggering totals, the report summarized the results in a decidedly understated tone, asserting simply that the "DOC purchased excessive amounts of inmate clothing."[6]

After stating the obvious, the report looked into the means by which this travesty occurred. It discovered that the Department of Correction failed to offer contracts out for bids, and in several cases offered no-bid contracts to companies that charged higher than standard prices. Despite the excessive costs, the report found that on several occasions the Department of Correction "purchased [products] at a price higher than the price stipulated in the contract," with the result being an additional $346,555 in costs. The report also found the Department of Correction performed its own contract negotiations, in "violation of state purchasing regulations," and failed to provide the Department of Purchasing and Contracts with copies of its purchasing orders. The report further noted that several employees traveled, played golf with, and dined at the expense of the companies with whom the Department of Correction did business. In its summary of this section, the report passively concluded: "purchasing policies were violated."[7]

Moving beyond the excessive clothing purchases, investigators found additional violations of state policy. The report noted that the Department of Correction agreed to a deal with CoinTel by which the company collected the coins and maintained the prison's pay phones. The agreement granted the firm 80 percent of the pay phone income and gave the Department of Correction 20 percent. The problem was that the contract included no language allowing the Department of Correction to oversee the amount of money collected. As a result, on several occasions CoinTel failed to pay the Department of Correction any money from the pay phone collections. The report also determined that the

Department of Correction employed CoinTel to maintain the phones without taking competitive bids, and did so despite the fact that AT&T offered a plan of $377 per phone per year while CoinTel charged $643 per phone per year. Worse still, the contract "did not specifically define the details of the maintenance of the pay phones." Not only did the prison pay more for the service, the scope of that service was left undefined. The report noted, "this raises serious questions concerning the integrity of the contract arrangement with CoinTel."[8]

In another case, the report found that the Department of Correction hired CoinTel to operate "privately owned pay phones," with CoinTel retaining 38 percent of the income and the Department of Correction receiving the remaining 62 percent. The problem was that Southern Bell already had a contract to operate the phones, and the report "could not determine that any service had been performed by CoinTel." Despite that, the Department of Correction directed Southern Bell to provide 38 percent of the profits from the phones to CoinTel, giving the company "$59,783 while performing no service other than depositing the Southern Bell check."[9]

The report went on to describe improper contracts for the purchase of lockers, steam cleaners, ammunition, and rifles, and it concluded that the Department of Correction was guilty of the "circumvention of state rules and regulations, wasteful expenditure of funds, less than 'arms length' transactions, and failure on the part of those responsible for insuring that internal management controls [were] in place and working effectively." Those failures cost the state more than $6.5 million in "wasted funds" and another $680,000 in "improperly controlled funds."[10]

In response to the findings, Secretary Bounds hired a collection of new administrators who "engaged as a team in tightening the Department of Correction's financial controls and regularizing . . . purchasing procedures, stressing strict adherence to relevant statues and rules." He also purchased new computer software to better oversee and regulate the purchasing, itemization, and warehousing of goods, instituted a new "purchasing ethics policy" to educate employees on what constituted "a proper relationship" with vendors, opened negotiations with the various companies involved to recover some of the funds, and worked with the state attorney general to determine whether or not prosecutions were in order. Ultimately, the state recovered a few thousand dollars, and none of those involved were indicted.[11]

As Bounds worked to revitalize the Department of Correction and overcome the embarrassing scandal that undermined the secretariat of the first African

American to run the state's prison system, other developments proved decid-
edly sunnier. In 1994, James B. French became the Central Prison warden. A
Vietnam veteran who worked his way through the ranks during twenty-two
years of service, French was the first African American head of the penitentiary.
French's position as warden proved especially notable as the disparity between
the number of white correctional officers and the number of African American inmates appeared emblematic of the state's long-standing racial dilemma.
From 1991 to 2001, the average percentage of white prison officers was 66.2
percent. Although the percentage fell from a high of 70 percent in 1991 to a low
of 61 percent in 2001, it virtually mirrored the percentage of African American
inmates: 63 percent. The presence of an African American warden, especially
one who had earned the position through decades of work in the prison system,
helped offset somewhat this racial imbalance and was a special blessing after
Johnson's corruption fiasco.[12]

More importantly, French proved a good administrator. In 1995, the International Association of Correctional Officers named him Correctional Supervisor of the Year. Among the efforts that earned him the distinction was the
creation of the Palliative Care Unit. This five-person ward offered hospice-type
care and provided "a place for inmates to die with dignity . . . in a supportive
environment." It included "a care team made up of physicians, nurses, chaplains,
social workers and others, [to] provide the physical care as well as a spiritual
environment to meet the concerns of the dying inmates."[13]

French continued to improve the daily lives of inmates when, in March
1998, he invited the University of North Carolina men's basketball team to the
prison. The players and coaches took time off from their preparations for the
NCAA tournament to answer questions, sign autographs, and "show off the
team's talents in the prison gym." More than one hundred inmates attended
the event, and administrators noted the improved morale of those "who often
feel lonely and forgotten."[14]

Understanding that inmates were not the only ones who needed to feel
appreciated, in 1999 Warden French won a 10 percent pay increase for his
correctional officers. While this was a reward for a job well done and for their
role in implementing his agenda, French also realized the raise would affect
retention. Annually, Central Prison lost 45 percent of its new staff within a year
of employment due to the availability of better paying jobs. Understanding that
it was expensive to train new officers and that the constant influx of new blood
undermined security, French pushed hard for the raise.

For those efforts, in April 1999 Warden French won the Lewyn M. Hayes Award during the annual Reunion of the Minority Pioneers, which celebrated minority workers in the Department of Correction. Later that year, French earned promotion to director of the Division of Prisons, and Robey Lee succeeded him as warden. Marvin Polk succeeded Lee in 2003, making him the second African American warden of Central Prison. Polk carried on French's success, and in 2006 he won the Warden of the Year award presented by the North Carolina Division of Prisons.[15]

French's and Polk's achievements were clear bright spots for the Department of Correction and seemed to demonstrate a changing racial perception within the state. Their efforts to ease the inmates' circumstances and to improve the lives of the officers further embodied the continued efforts by prison administrators to implement at least some forward-looking reforms, while making clear the system's fundamental shortcomings and the lengths that remained to make the system humane. Unfortunately, the way the state carried out capital punishment mitigated those steps forward, especially those related to race.

Between 1910 and 1961, North Carolina executed 361 people, an average of seven per year. Of that number, 78 percent were black men, and most had committed crimes against whites. By contrast, only two white men were executed in the entire twentieth century for crimes against African Americans. Like the prison system at large, African Americans were overrepresented on death row.[16]

Despite rising racial tensions and the aforementioned post-civil rights era move to the political right, between 1961 and 1983 North Carolina did not execute anyone. Part of the reason was a national debate about the constitutionality of the death penalty—a debate that culminated in the 1972 U.S. Supreme Court ruling of *Furman v. Georgia* in which the justices ruled that the death penalty was an unconstitutionally cruel and unusual punishment. The basis of that ruling was that juries had no mandate to assign the death sentence nor did they have any criteria with which to justify it.[17]

Determined to maintain the right to execute prisoners, North Carolina legislators revised the death penalty statute to make execution mandatory for murder and rape. In 1976, the Supreme Court's *Woodson v. North Carolina* ruling struck down the law as "unduly harsh and unworkably rigid." Later that year, however, the court offered a pathway to a constitutionally acceptable death penalty in its *Gregg v. Georgia* ruling, and legislators adopted those conditions in 1977. Under this newly revised death penalty law, after convicting a person of murder (rape was no longer a capital offense), a jury was to examine a list of nine mitigating factors and eleven aggravating factors. Based on those factors, the jury would determine whether or not death was the requisite punishment. Although the law passed in 1977, not until 1984 did North Carolina carry out another execution.[18]

Although no executions took place, the number of inmates sentenced to death exploded, and by 1975 North Carolina had 120 inmates on death row, more than any other state. In keeping with much of the state's history, 65 percent of them were African American. What might be even more shocking is that a number of them were women. In fact, in the 1970s North Carolina took the lead in sentencing women to death. In the "modern era," which, penologically speaking, began in 1973, North Carolina was the first state to sentence a woman to death—doing so with Mamie Lee Ward, an African American woman convicted of murdering her boyfriend. She was not alone, as North Carolina sentenced six women to death between 1973 and 1978, fully one-third of all the women sentenced to death nationally. Since 1979, however, North Carolina has sentenced only ten women to death, just 15 percent of sentences nationally. Of those sixteen women sentenced to die since 1973, ten were white, four were African American, and two were Native American. Only one, as we shall see, has been executed. Eleven, including Mamie Lee Ward, had their sentences commuted, while four remain on death row.[19]

As the Supreme Court hashed out the constitutionality of capital punishment and the population on death row swelled, North Carolina's legislators made preparations to recommence executions. As a part of those preparations, in 1983 the General Assembly gave condemned inmates the option to die in the gas chamber or by lethal injection. The gas chamber was the default choice, and inmates who wanted lethal injection had to inform prison authorities at least five days in advance.[20]

The legislature also clarified the procedures for execution. When an inmate exhausted his or her appeals and the time for execution neared, correctional officers removed the individual from the general population and placed them in Central Prison's "death watch area," which sat adjacent to the execution chamber. There were four cells in the area, each with its own bed, lavatory, commode, and table. The inmate enjoyed a fifteen-minute daily shower, but otherwise spent their time in the cell. When execution day arrived, those who selected gas faced the same process as had all capital inmates since Allen Foster's gruesome 1936 execution. Few inmates opted for gas. The last to do so was David Lawson in 1994, and in 1998 the state closed the option, offering only lethal injection.[21]

Those facing injection endured a more clinical process: guards placed the inmate on a gurney, and then nurses attached a cardiac monitor and inserted two saline intravenous lines—one in each arm. The inmate next had a chance to speak and to pray with a chaplain. After the prayer, guards drew a curtain and withdrew. Once the inmate was alone, the warden ended the flow of the saline solution and began injecting thiopental sodium, which put the inmate to sleep. After the drug put the inmate to sleep, the warden injected procuronium bromide, a muscle relaxant, which stopped the inmate's breathing and brought about death. According to experts, this method was more humane than the gas chamber, and the General Assembly adopted it for that very reason.[22]

With a new form of execution and a backlog of death row inmates, North Carolina inaugurated its return to capital punishment precipitously in 1984 by executing James Hutchins and Velma Barfield. Those executions, however, became entangled in politics. It was an election year, and among the contested offices was the U.S. Senate seat occupied by Republican Jesse Helms. Governor James Hunt, a Democrat serving the final year of his second term, set his sights on the seat. The campaign was close and hotly contested, and both sides appreciated that any misstep could cost them the election. Hunt, however, faced the greater challenge as it was he who had to confront Barfield's execution. As governor, he had the authority to intervene in the case and commute her sentence.

Hunt found himself in an unenviable position. If he commuted the sentence of a woman who admitted to killing four people, including her own mother, he opened himself up to charges that he was "soft on crime." At the same time, Barfield was in line to become the first woman executed in North Carolina since 1944, the first person executed in North Carolina since 1961, and the first woman executed in the United States since 1962. Even those who supported capital punishment appreciated the political implications of making a return to the death penalty under such precedents. Unwilling to appear "soft on crime" or to sully the state's progressive reputation, Hunt had to find an acceptable middle ground.

He did this by engineering a delicate swap. Barfield had received her death sentence in May 1978. More than a year later, in October 1979, a judge sentenced James Hutchins to death. North Carolina traditionally executed inmates in the order of conviction, so Barfield's original execution date preceded that of Hutchins. To assuage those concerned about ruining the state's image, Hunt pushed forward Hutchins's death to March 16, 1984. That opened the path to executing Barfield on November 2 without offending the state's progressive traditions or requiring Hunt to endanger his political campaign by commuting her sentence. Despite the dance, the swap failed to secure his election. Hunt lost by eighty-six thousand votes, and both Hutchins and Barfield met their end via lethal injection.[23]

The rapidity with which these two executions were carried out suggested a state anxious to resume capital punishment. And yet, North Carolina performed only three additional executions in the decade subsequent, and from the reimposition of the death penalty through 2006, authorities performed only forty-three executions. None has taken place since 2006. The origins of the current hiatus began in 1997 when the American Bar Association called for a moratorium on death sentences due to inadequate council, improper processes, racial discrimination, and the "execution of the mentally retarded and juveniles." In North Carolina, the numbers seem to support at least the racial element. Although the state resumed capital punishment by executing Barfield and Hutchins, who were white, most of those on death row were African American. In 1998, African Americans made up approximately 22 percent of the state's population but 54.2 percent of the state's death row inmates (96 out of 177). Research on the topic also indicates that minorities, the poor, and those from rural areas are more likely to receive a death sentence than are those who are white, well off, or from urban centers. Any racial progress the state had made seemed challenged by such statistics.[24]

Although the state ignored the ABA call, additional factors soon intruded. In 2007, the North Carolina Medical Board deemed participating in executions a violation of medical ethics. Despite the fact that doctors were mere observers, played no role in the execution, and simply declared the inmate deceased and assigned a time of death, the board voted to punish any doctor who participated in capital punishment. This halted executions, as state law required a doctor's presence at every procedure.[25]

In 2009, the state Supreme Court heard the *North Carolina Department of Correction v. North Carolina Medical Board* case, in which the attorney general claimed the board had no legal right to ban doctors from observing executions. The court affirmed that position in a 4–3 decision and ruled that the board had overstepped its bounds and violated state law. Although a victory for the state, the General Assembly wanted to prevent future conflicts, and in 2015 it revised the capital punishment statute to excise the requirement that doctors attend an execution. It did so by declaring executions "non-medical procedures."[26]

Just months after the court's decision opened the door to a renewal of capital punishment, the General Assembly closed it with passage of the Racial Justice Act. The act allowed inmates to appeal their sentences if they believed racial bias played a role in the decision to pursue or impose death. The General Assembly justified the act by arguing that it wanted to make sure that "when North Carolina hands down our state's harshest punishment . . . the decision is based on the facts and the law, not racial prejudice." By January 2010, 151 of the 158 inmates on death row, including white inmates, had filed suit. As a result, the possibility of executing anyone virtually vanished.[27]

To many citizens, the new law seemed an enlightened achievement. Just as many, however, expressed their frustration. The frustrations, confusions, and mixed messages continued as the courts intervened. In 2012, Superior Court Judge Greg Weeks overturned the death sentence of Marcus Robinson based on statistical evidence that showed state prosecutors discriminated against African Americans when selecting juries in capital cases. This is what the Racial Justice Act required—not that discrimination occurred in the specific case, but that a statistically provable pattern of discrimination existed. As a result of Weeks's decision, the Republican-dominated legislature revised the law, requiring a defendant to prove discrimination in the particular case. Despite that new, higher hurdle, in December 2012 Judge Weeks overturned the death sentences of three additional inmates (Christina Walters, Quintel Augustine, and Tilmon Golphin) after lawyers demonstrated, through both statistical evidence and the prosecutors' handwritten notes, that race played a role in jury selection. In all four cases, Judge Weeks revised the sentences to life in prison without parole, and in so doing pitted the judiciary against the legislature.[28]

This battle between the branches did not end the traditional political struggles. Indeed, the political battles of old carried on in 2011 when the Republican-dominated legislature repealed the Racial Justice Act only to have Governor Beverly Perdue (a Democrat) veto the repeal. In June 2013, however, with Republican Pat McCrory occupying the governor's mansion, legislators successfully repealed the law. Not only did they repeal it, the General Assembly challenged the four cases in which Judge Weeks reduced the inmates' sentences to life in prison. In 2015, the state Supreme Court ruled that Judge Weeks had erred in reducing the sentences and ordered the cases reheard. The decision also placed in limbo the appeals of 150 other inmates, with the result that many, including Democratic state representative Rick Glazier, foresee "intense years of litigation." How that litigation will be resolved remains unclear.[29]

What is clear is that politicians once again intruded in a very intimate manner into the lives of inmates, and they did so for political purposes. As Seth Kotch writes, although the death penalty failed "as a crime-fighting weapon, as a tool of state power, as a way to give closure to victims, and from a technical perspective, it has succeeded in channeling lethal white rage that modern values constrain or should constrain. Support for today's death penalty sends a powerful signal to members of one's political tribe."[30]

What is equally clear is that throughout the 1990s and 2000s legislators, judges, prison administrators, and inmates struggled not only with the death penalty and racism, but with the ongoing battle over public financing, fallout from a corruption scandal, and a series of ever-changing and seemingly contradictory political pronouncements. Prisoners, of course, had it worst, as they found little opportunity to affect the policies that directly impacted them. Greed, corruption, racism, politics, and morality combined in a tempestuous era during which the state took several steps forward, but just as many back. That dance continued in the new millennium, as the treatment of mentally ill inmates and the overuse of solitary confinement caused continued inmate suffering, led to additional political intervention, and resulted in the state's progressive image taking yet another hit.

24

MENTAL HEALTH

While the capital punishment cases made their way through the judicial system, the Department of Correction's focus once again returned to Central Prison, where a new set of dilemmas arose over mental illness and solitary confinement. Although long a national leader in providing facilities and treatment for the mentally ill, there appeared to be something amiss with the prison's mental health unit. Part of that was the result of the legislature's decision to privatize mental health services. According to the American Civil Liberties Union (ACLU), "instead of providing meaningfully integrated services . . . this experiment . . . wreaked havoc on North Carolina's mental health system," creating a situation in which prisons and jails became the state's primary mental health providers. The ACLU further alleged that by 2000 "North Carolina's jails and prisons house[d] more people with mental illness than our state psychiatric hospitals." What made those issues even more significant was the unprecedented use of long-term solitary confinement—a policy psychologists and doctors argued both caused and exacerbated mental health problems. Together, these developments resulted in another disruptive decade as political intervention, a rejection of the progressive tradition, and a reticence to spend money undermined efforts to address either issue and created serious problems for inmates and administrators alike.[1]

The first signs that Central Prison had an unaddressed mental health crisis on its hands arose in 1996. Glen Mabrey, a white, forty-seven-year-old Vietnam War veteran who suffered from post-traumatic stress disorder (PTSD) and had a long history of alcohol abuse, was arrested for drunk driving. It was his fourth charge, and upon conviction a judge sentenced him to two years at the Umstead Correctional Center. While there, his PTSD morphed into full-blown psychosis. He did not know who he was or where he was, and officers at the facility proved unable to attend to his needs. On February 21, 1996, they trans-ferred him to Central Prison's mental health unit. Doctors treated Mabrey with thorazine, but the drug had little effect. As the psychosis worsened so too did his behavior. For a brief time guards placed him in restraints, but upon release he continued to act out, at one point clogging his toilet and flooding his cell. In response, officers turned off his water. For five days he made do without water in his cell, reliant solely on the liquids delivered to him at meal times. Thorazine, however, increases the body's need for water, and Mabrey began to suffer. The staff failed to provide the oversight the National Commission on Correctional Health Care recommends for mentally ill inmates. The reasons for this failure now seem evident: the mental health unit staff was not large enough nor prop-erly trained to meet the needs and demands of its residents. The seventy-six-staff-member unit had not increased in size for five years despite a 50 percent increase in inmate population. Mabrey suffered from this combination of thora-zine treatment, lack of water, and staff inattention, and on February 29 he died of dehydration. Although several nurses received reprimands, no substantive changes took place and press coverage was minimal. As a result, the poor and inadequate treatment of mentally ill inmates continued.[2]

Five years after Mabrey's death, Central Prison administrators performed an internal review during which they "found that prison staff neglected the needs of prisoners suffering from serious mental illness." The cause of this failure was space: the mental health unit did not have enough beds, leaving many inmates untreated amid the general population.[3]

Prison administrators ignored their own damning report. That decision was based on the realization that they could do little in the present circumstances, but also with the knowledge that plans were underway to construct a new mental health facility that would alleviate the problem. Officials simply hoped another Mabrey-type incident would not occur before the new unit opened. Those hopes went unmet.

On August 31, 2010, police arrested Winston-Salem resident Levon Wilson on misdemeanor charges and sent him to Central Prison pending trial. Wilson suffered from bipolar disorder and had a prescription for lithium. High dosages of lithium can be dangerous, and those prescribed the medicine need constant monitoring. Blood tests are especially important to determine if a patient is suffering from kidney problems, an obstructed bowel, or other side effects. Wilson received no such monitoring and fell ill. Guards took him to the Wake

Medical Center on September 30, where doctors discovered "moderately high levels" of lithium in his blood. Despite the doctors' best efforts, he died on October 9 from kidney failure and an obstructed bowel brought about by "complications from lithium therapy." Unlike Mabrey's death more than a decade earlier, officials proved unable to keep Wilson's death quiet, and popular outrage was enough to force the Department of Correction to employ an external audit.[4]

The audit, conducted by the mental health quality assurance coordinator and the central office assistant director of nursing, began in February 2011 and lasted through May. The subsequent report began by noting that since 1999 the Department of Correction had been requesting funds to expand and modernize Central Prison's mental health unit. The General Assembly approved funding in 2009, and construction was nearly complete, with plans to put the new unit on-line later in 2011. That new unit, the report asserted, appeared to be a substantial upgrade and would employ "markedly different" staffing and physical features from the old unit. Since the new unit was not yet operational, however, the remainder of the report focused on the old unit; what it described was a staggering betrayal.[5]

The review found that the original 1970s-era facility was built to handle a state prison population of ten thousand; forty years later the state's prison population was forty-one thousand. That population explosion had not been met with an increase in housing or staffing. The unit offered 144 beds, with separate facilities for safe-keepers (those who needed protection from other inmates) and youthful inmates. On average, the unit housed 125 inmates, and that number included those with long-term mental health issues as well as those suffering from acute crises. The problem, the report found, was that staff maintained those numbers by returning mentally ill inmates to the general population. There were many more ill inmates in the system, but they were not actively treated.[6]

Although the unit was not technically full, the report found it understaffed, noting that staffing had decreased from seventy-four to fifty-nine between 2009 and 2011. That short-staffing prevented the optimal assignment of three nurses in each of the six units. The report noted that although three was optimal, the state-approved minimum was two, one of whom had to be licensed. In reality, the report found that "for the entire month of February 2011 each day on the 11 P.M.–7 A.M. shift, there were some units with no assigned RN" while "58% of the time only one staff member was assigned to a unit." Thus, even minimal requirements were not met.[7]

The results of this short staffing were treatment delays and the frequent failure to provide proper "on-going supervision, care and services." Additionally, the frequent rotation of staff from unit to unit to meet immediate staffing needs meant nurses often were unaware of each inmate's diagnosis and were unable to develop relationships that might have facilitated treatment or prevented crises. Two related points also concerned the auditors: most mental health staff were not trained to deal with inmates who threatened to harm themselves, nor were they trained to attend to the physical needs of ailing inmates. Thus, a mentally ill inmate who also suffered from a health-related malady found little assistance.[8]

Nurses were not the only staff members lacking. The report found the unit did not have an adequate contingent of licensed rehabilitation therapists, psychiatrists, psychologists, social workers, or medical records staff. The psychiatrists were overworked, with the result that gaps often occurred when no doctor was available. The psychologists worked only part time, offering once weekly group therapy sessions and once weekly Alcoholics Anonymous meetings. Worse still, the report found there existed no standard operating procedure to determine how often an inmate should see a psychiatrist or a psychologist.[9]

The unit employed only a single social worker, with the result that several important and legally required tasks often went unfulfilled. For instance, the report discovered that most new inmates did not receive a unit orientation, with one particular survey finding twenty of twenty-one inmates going without. The report also discovered that most inmates did not have a social history record despite the fact that prison policy required one for all inmates receiving mental health care. The report noted that "social history information is an integral component of the treatment planning process" as it provided caregivers information about the inmate's family, doctors, and prior medical treatment. All of this was needed to best treat the patient, but a lack of social workers meant few inmates underwent such a history. Finally, the lack of social workers meant most inmates did not receive a "complete rehabilitation assessment" to chart their development through the treatment process.[10]

The medical records staff also proved understaffed, and those employed lacked "knowledge and understanding of the importance of the medical record." As a result, the unit did not possess complete medical data for most inmates and suffered from a great deal of misfiled material. The incomplete data hindered the ability of doctors and nurses to give proper services and resulted in "fragmented care." The misfiled material, meanwhile, slowed the ability of doctors and nurses to recall important medical histories and provide timely treatment.[11]

This section of the report concluded with a litany of other notable problems. It reported occasions when emergency bags lacked required drugs or equipment, and even noted one instance when "all emergency bags were non-compliant with Health Services Policy." The report cited several cases of improperly administered medicine and a general failure to create a "comprehensive treatment plan" for inmates. The investigation also uncovered a lack of soap in day room restrooms, the smell of urine in stairwells and hallways, roach and ant infestations, one floor that was "caked with dirt and grime," locked doors that were propped open, keys that were left within reach of inmates, broken locks, and broken equipment.[12]

After that damning collection of failures and shortcomings, the report followed with a list of necessary corrections. It first stressed the need to hire additional staff; the demand for licensed nurses, psychiatrists, psychologists, social workers, and medical records staff was acute, and had to be addressed as the most compelling issue confronting the unit. Fully staffing the facility, the report explained, would enable the better monitoring and treatment of inmates, would ensure staff safety, and would make possible the execution of state laws regarding the proper handling of inmates and their files.[13]

The report next stressed the need to create a standard operating procedure regarding the frequency of an inmate's interaction with medical doctors, and an increase in the number of "active treatment programs." The opportunity to meet regularly with doctors and to participate in therapy sessions was a central component of mental health care, and the report all but demanded the unit provide inmates with the requisite services.[14]

The remainder of the recommendation was a straightforward call to address the specific issues noted in the report: the hiring of licensed rehabilitation therapists, improved record keeping, proper treatment of physically ill inmates, the creation of a more hygienic environment with adequate soap and proper clean-up facilities, improved security, and better oversight of staff by administrators.[15]

The report then concluded, "if individuals with mental illness are not engaged and receiving appropriate active treatment, they may continue to exhibit the behaviors that got them there (segregation, seclusion or on an inpatient psychiatric unit) in the first place. If anything, it heightens their behavior, which keeps them in that setting. Instead of getting out, individuals wind up staying longer and longer, and they may deteriorate." Administrators were responsible for making sure that did not happen, and they needed to address the report's issues.[16]

The findings and recommendations were straightforward, and yet Alvin Keller, who in 2009 became just the third African American Department of Correction secretary, only responded to the report in November, six months after it was issued. Keller began by disingenuously suggesting the Department of Correction requested the investigation, and he asserted that "within one business day" the Department of Correction had "assembled a multi-disciplinary subject matter expert team that reviewed the report line by line." He assured the public that "assignments for immediate actions were made to take care of sanitation, cleanliness, supervisory roles, staffing, records management, and other areas," went on to note that "the facility is clean and appropriately staffed," and claimed the department would correct the other issues.[17]

After such assurances, Keller then sought to "clarify some mischaracterizations and exaggerations." He rejected the finding that roaches and ants infested the unit, and noted that an exterminator visited regularly. He admitted that some inmates spread urine or feces in their cells as they acted out, but claimed such incidents were rare, that the messes were cleaned up quickly, and that the charge that the unit smelled of human waste was incorrect. Finally, he reported that he had invited journalists, television crews, and members of the General Assembly to visit the mental health unit, and they found none of the serious issues raised in the report. He thus made clear that while he would address the problems, he found many of the report's claims exaggerated if not false.[18]

Despite that defiance, the public outcry was immediate, loud, and consequential. Just days after issuing his rebuttal, Keller resigned as Department of Correction secretary. Central Prison warden Gerald Branker, the third African American to hold the position, also succumbed to the report and retired, while the entire executive staff of the mental health unit resigned. Public outrage clearly had a direct impact, and it demonstrated that at least some North Carolinians demanded more from their officials. Refusing to allow the state to be embarrassed by seemingly callous administrators, the public all but forced the changes.[19]

Kenneth Lassiter, the warden at the Charlotte Correctional Center, succeeded Branker as warden, making him the fourth African American to hold the position, and he inherited the task of addressing the report's findings. Lassiter's timing was fortunate, as not long after his accession Central Prison opened its new $155 million medical complex and mental health facility, complete with a fully funded staff, adequate meeting rooms, and much needed diagnostics. Dubbed "Unit 6," the facility offered 216 beds and 160 employees, both dramatic improvements from the old facility. It also had three housing levels: Crisis, Intensive, and Long-term/Residential, to better segregate inmates needing different types of treatment.[20]

Those improvements, however, did not solve all the outstanding problems. In 2012, the Department of Correction joined with the Department of Juvenile Justice and Delinquency Prevention and the Crime Control and Public Safety Agency to create the Department of Public Safety. In October 2012, the newly formed agency requested that consultants Dr. Jeffrey Metzner and Dr. Dean Aufderhide perform a follow-up to the 2011 mental health study. Over the course of four days, the two doctors explored the new facility and found that many of the original problems remained. While the 160 employees was an improvement from the fifty-nine employed a year earlier, the doctors still found shortcomings and inadequate staffing, notably a continued lack of doctors and licensed nurses. Similarly, they discovered the additional beds proved insufficient, as 23 percent of the inmates in Central Prison's "Unit 1," an isolation unit, were "on the mental health caseload." A significant portion of those inmates had been admitted to the hospital on more than one occasion, only to be sent back to isolation, where "mental health rounds were not conducted." The doctors determined that the "inadequate treatment" and "harsh conditions of confinement" only exacerbated the mental health issues among those inmates.[21]

Beyond their own observations, the researchers also interviewed inmates, who had two major complaints. The first was that any contact they had with medical staff was done publicly with the doctor yelling through the cell door. The lack of privacy made them less likely to engage.[22]

The more notable complaint was that inmates did not participate in sufficient group therapy sessions. The inmates seemed to benefit from interacting with other sufferers and wanted more contact with their fellows. One inmate explained that initially he went "just to get out of my cell before I went clear nuts," but he soon found the sessions were "a good place to gripe and blow off steam. Cuss out the world and everyone in it! You could come out loud and strong against anything and everything you hated." More importantly, he noted that "the group gradually changed from a bitch session into a sensible talk. . . . We were really hitting out at all those gray walls and a thousand other things we couldn't get away from." Another inmate exclaimed, "I was trying to survive this hell without it changing who I was but the 'system' began to take its toll on me. I fell into a deep depression and was starting to feel righteous anger swell inside of me that would surely take me down the road of physical aggression.

Realizing this would only make matters worse . . . I decided to seek psychiatric counseling." Doing so not only enabled the inmate to reclaim a sense of himself, it led to a job and eventually to a position teaching others. The sessions seemed useful, but they occurred too infrequently.[23]

In a summary of their findings, the doctors praised the new mental health facility, noting that the physical plant was well designed and offered adequate space to meet the needs of the inmates, that the warden was "clearly committed to facilitating implementation of the Central Prison Healthcare Complex's mission," that there was support for that mission from the Department of Public Safety, and that the staffing had improved. On the contrary, they offered sharp criticism, pointing to numerous vacancies in important staffing positions, inadequate treatment programs, the lack of privacy, and the need for new policies with respect to isolation. The doctors suggested offering more group sessions, allowing inmates some say in which group sessions they participated in, offering weekly confidential meetings with doctors, and providing more out of cell recreation.[24]

As had so often happened in the prison's history, the changes administrators made proved insufficient to meet the problems they faced. Whether they did so from a lack of resources, from a lack of appreciation for the depths of the problem they faced, or if they simply hoped public apathy or the mere appearance of reform would suffice is irrelevant. The Metzner and Aufderhide report described major concerns, laid out significant and much needed improvements, and urged administrators to implement a more thorough reform of the mental health system. That follow through, sadly, was not forthcoming.

On March 13, 2013, Warden Lassiter issued a "Mental Health Plan of Improvement" in response to the Metzner and Aufderhide report. In it he explained that inmates had enjoyed expanded group therapy sessions since January, that psychologists were doing weekly rounds, that the Department of Public Safety had created a crisis intervention training program, and that inmates were being allowed more time outside of their cells. As a result, he said, the unit had seen a decline in violence and an overall improvement in inmate behavior. Lassiter seemed content to stop there. While he did not outright reject the Metzner and Aufderhide report, he made clear that he felt administrators had done enough and that further changes were unnecessary.[25]

Metzner returned to Central Prison in October 2014 and determined that administrators had not done enough. He claimed mentally ill inmates in "Unit 6" received "one check-up with psychological services every 45 days," but those check-ups continued to lack privacy. He concluded that "inmates receive no meaningful ongoing therapy or out-of-cell treatment modalities." More disturbingly, Metzner visited "Unit 1" during his return and continued to see a significant number of mentally ill inmates housed in isolation. He was even more outraged when he learned that inmates Guanghui Lei, a Chinese immigrant convicted of murdering his wife and sister, and Edward Campbell, a white inmate who had engaged in a three-state crime and murder spree, had been housed in "Unit 1" despite the fact that they suffered from mental illness. Both committed suicide in the sixteen months prior to his visit, and yet administrators had done nothing to address the causative circumstances. As with each previous mental health crisis, prison authorities seemed to hope minor tweaks to the system and public apathy would protect them from the consequences of their inaction.[26]

They largely got away with such a policy, as politicians generally evinced little interest in the state's mentally ill in the new millennium. Indeed, the disinterest was so extreme that even multiple reports demanding reform failed to elicit a response. Such behavior was in keeping with the all too frequent willingness of state leaders to tinker around the edges and to make minor reforms when fundamental change was required. Rather than address the causes of the problem, causes we should remember that were brought about by the legislature's decision to close down public mental health facilities, legislators and prison officials took the easy way out. The lack of concern and the refusal to intervene in a meaningful manner had serious consequences for the prison system and the inmates involved. The state's progressive facade also once more was exposed. It was exposed again when the excessive use of isolation emerged and confronted legislators and administrators alike with yet another crisis that negatively affected inmates.

25

ISOLATION

The mental health crisis that emerged in the early years of the twenty-first century was but one element of the troubles faced by inmates and prison officials. Related to that crisis, but a substantial problem in its own right, was the frequent, excessive, and seemingly irrational use of isolation. Inmates complained about extended stays in solitary confinement, experts warned about the resultant irreparable harm to inmate sanity, and prison administrators and politicians worried about the consequences of such complaints coming on top of the mental health issues. Once again, politicians had to intervene in the prison system as the state's reputation took another hit.

When the penitentiary model first emerged two centuries ago, both the Pennsylvania and Auburn systems employed isolation as a central component. Both envisioned it as reformative—providing inmates time to reflect on their crimes and change their behavior. That perspective evolved, and until three decades ago prisons employed isolation and solitary confinement sparingly, as punishment for rules violations or when necessitated by safety concerns. Studies, however, have found administrators using the policies with ever greater frequency during the last thirty years. Not only is the use more common, but findings demonstrate that staff now use it as a matter of "administrative strategy." That is, as other forms of punishment were proscribed by law or public sentiment, guards employed solitary confinement as a punishment of first resort.[1]

Three studies find this frequent use problematic. The first is the 2011 study by Juan Mendez, the United Nations Special Rapporteur on Torture, who declared that any sentence of solitary confinement over fifteen days constitutes torture "because it imposes severe mental pain and suffering beyond any reasonable retribution for criminal behavior." The second finding was the result of medical studies that showed the impact of solitary confinement on the brain can be witnessed in as few as six days, while a confinement duration of over six months "is certain to lead to psychological harm." The final study demonstrated that a significant portion of inmates in isolation and solitary confinement are mentally ill. It is worth remembering that during Metzner and Aufderhide's initial investigation they found that 23 percent of inmates in one of Central Prison's isolation units suffered from mental illness. What makes that percentage even more damning is the doctors' assertion that the prison used "solitary confinement as a way of responding to the symptoms of mentally ill prisoners." The doctors found such a response—punishing mental illness rather than treating it—"cruel and irrational." A separate report concurred, and it accused prison officials of failing mentally ill inmates by punishing them for "manifestations of their illnesses"—a punishment that exacerbated their illness and behavior.[2]

Despite those findings, administrators continue to use isolation in part because courts have been reluctant "to accept the mental and emotional pain and suffering caused by extreme isolation." Judges seem unmoved by medical and sociological reports of the damage isolation causes, and "even when faced with . . . overwhelming evidence that solitary confinement is at least inhumane and pushes the boundaries of cruel and barbaric, the judiciary has consistently failed to find that it contravenes the Eighth Amendment."[3]

Those failures have led critics to demand the abolition of solitary confinement, or at the very least a dramatic curtailment in terms of its "prevalence of use, the amount of time prisoners are kept in solitary confinement, and the conditions under which they are held." Others have called for stricter regulations relating to the "minimum standards for conditions of confinement" in an effort to ensure that inmates are secure, humanely treated, and maintained in an environment that is physically and mentally healthy.[4]

North Carolina is among the states facing such demands, in large part because it has a much lower standard than does the American Bar Association for placing inmates in solitary confinement. A 2014 study found that the state shows "almost a complete disregard of prisoners' average mental health needs," with the result that "North Carolina falls extremely short in protecting prisoners' health and well-being in its implementation of solitary confinement."[5]

This is of note because North Carolina isolates inmates at twice the national average: with 3,464 of its 37,465 inmates housed in some form of "control unit" as of March 2014. Central Prison alone maintains two solitary confinement units. The Maximum Control Unit (MCON) is for inmates "who pose an immi-

nent threat to the safety of staff or other inmates or who otherwise pose a serious threat to the security and operational integrity of the prison facility." They
remain in isolation "for the period of time necessary to minimize their threat to
staff and other inmates," but officials must review their status every six months.
The Intensive Control Unit (ICON) is for inmates in long-term isolation. These
are inmates who have "shown disruptive behavior through disciplinary offenses,
assaultive actions or confrontations, or who are so continuously a disruptive
influence on the operation of the facility that they require more structured
management by prison authorities." In both units, inmates live in their solitary
cells twenty-three to twenty-four hours a day, receiving one hour of recreation
in a cage five days a week, and three ten-minute showers each week in a separate shower facility.[6]

Such numbers and conditions appall prisoner rights advocates. For some,
the issue is expense: it costs North Carolina $6,000 per year more to house
inmates in isolation than it does in medium security facilities. For others, it is
the sheer number of inmates affected. For most, however, the real concern is
the impact isolation has on the inmates.[7]

Advocacy groups are not the only ones concerned about this impact—so are
the inmates. On July 16, 2012, an interracial group of prisoners at Central Prison
began a hunger strike to protest the treatment and conditions of those housed
in isolation. They called for an end to locking inmates in their cells for weeks
on end without allowing them access to recreation, an end to the physical and
mental abuse inflicted by officers working the isolation wards, the addition of
educational programs for inmates in isolation, and the release of inmates who
had been in solitary confinement "for years without infractions." The number of
participants fluctuated, as some joined and others left, but about one hundred
inmates participated in the hunger strike during its extent.[8]

The same month that the hunger strike erupted, Central Prison inmate
Chris McBride wrote a letter to *Indy Week*, a Durham-based progressive journal, describing what life was like in solitary confinement. He explained:

> Solitary confinement is hell . . . it is a form of torture. It is a tiny cell about
> 6 feet by 8 feet. . . . We are in this cell 23 hours a day. We are allowed to
> come out for recreation five times a week for one hour. The rec is a cage.
> They just stick us in a little cage and we can walk around. That's it. We
> are only allowed to take three showers a week. Only three! And we can
> only take 5 minutes. If we are lucky, we get 10 minutes. So if you add

up five 1-hour recs, and three 10-minute showers, that's 5½ hours. Let's round that up to 6 hours. There's your answer. Out of the 168 hours in a week, we are out of our cell 6 hours. If that ain't a form of torture, I don't know what is.

McBride, a white inmate, went on to assert that officers punished inmates by spitting in their food. He complained that the cells were filthy, and he called the medical care "ridiculous." McBride asserted that staff ignored inmate requests to see nurses and refused to aid those who suffered seizures, fainting spells, or attempted suicide. He concluded by lamenting, "normal rules don't apply to solitary. They're supposed to, but they don't."[9]

When neither the hunger strike nor press reports improved conditions, in May 2013 nine inmates filed suit. The claim began with two separate instances of alleged officer brutality. African American inmate Jerome Peters claimed that on December 3, 2012, while housed in isolation, he was "handcuffed and escorted by two correctional officers from his cell to an outdoor recreation area" where "one of the guards punched him in the face while the other grabbed a leg and pulled him to the ground." He further asserted that "a third correctional officer then helped the other two kick, stomp and punch" him. As a result of the alleged beating, Peters suffered "a broken right hip and fractured bones in his hand and face," and was confined to a wheelchair.[10]

In early 2013, white inmate John Davis, a diagnosed schizophrenic and diabetic, began to yell and bang on his cell when correctional officers did not deliver his evening meal. According to his lawsuit, officers responded by cuffing him, removing him from his cell, taking him to a place called "the desert," which was a blind spot in the prison's security camera system, and beating him so badly that he suffered broken ribs. After the beating, Davis alleged, the officers returned him to his cell without medical help, which only came after the shift change.[11]

Both men subsequently sued, and soon thereafter seven others living in isolation units joined the suit with their own claims of abuse. Davis settled out of court, but the other eight litigants carried on and cited additional instances of violence and abuse at the hands of twenty-one officers who used similar surveillance blind spots to assault inmates. According to one report, "the abuse claims made by the eight prisoners were substantiated by medical records which documented 'blunt force injuries,' including broken bones and concussions, sustained while they were isolated from other prisoners. One man was unable to walk for months after his hip was fractured." Inmate Will Smith corroborated the claims, allegedly witnessing "repeated beatings by guards" on inmates who failed to obey orders.[12]

Responding with even more intransigence than they had to the mental health cases, prison officials denied the abuse and took the offensive. Spokesmen for the Department of Public Safety informed the press that inmates were in isolation for a reason, and that those involved in the suit had racked up nearly six hundred violations. Prison authorities thus implied the men had "earned" their beatings. Elizabeth Simpson, an attorney for North Carolina Prisoner Legal Services who represented the inmates, responded to that implication by noting that no matter the number of violations, correctional officers had no right to assault them. She concluded, "For years, the inmates of Unit One have pursued every avenue available to them to put an end to the violence that is routinely inflicted upon them. They have filed grievances, engaged in letter writing campaigns to public officials, gone on hunger strikes, and exhausted all of the administrative remedies available to them. The violence has not stopped." Despite her charges, a state court simply ordered administrators to install additional cameras, to remove the blind spots, and to maintain video records "sufficiently long enough to be used by any prisoners who file complaints." Judges seemed uninterested in wading into the legality of isolation or the conduct of the officers who oversaw the isolation complexes.[13]

While prison officials and the state's judiciary proved unwilling to help the inmates, the public came to their rescue. Stirred up in no small measure by Simpson and the North Carolina Prisoner Legal Service team, public pressure forced the prison to concede some reforms. In December 2014, Department of Public Safety head David Guice requested $20 million to expand Central Prison's mental health unit and to hire sixty-four new employees. In making the request, he explained that previous budget cuts had forced the unit to empty one-third of its beds set aside for "severely mentally ill inmates." Without treatment, many of those inmates committed infractions and ended up in isolation, where their illnesses intensified and they acted out, leading to confrontations with correctional officers. The additional funds, Guice argued, would help prison officials solve both the concern over its handling of mentally ill inmates and its overuse of isolation.[14]

Ever fearful of spending more than necessary, and seemingly uninterested in the well-being of the prisoners, in 2015 the Republican-controlled legislature provided Guice with $12 million. Despite the shortfall, prisoners' rights advocates continued to push for reforms, and were rewarded on three fronts. The Vera Institute of Justice chose North Carolina as one of five states to participate in a two-year study designed to reduce the use of solitary confinement. In July 2015, Governor Pat McCrory created the Governor's Task Force on Mental Health and Substance Use, a wide-ranging program that included in its agenda an effort to reduce the use of isolation. Then, in June 2016, Guice announced several major changes in the state's use of solitary confinement and its handling of mentally ill inmates. He first acknowledged the failure of "the state's heavy use of solitary confinement" and promised "to do something different or new." He then announced that the prison system was moving "away from using [isolation] as a tool that is going to keep people locked down for long periods of time," and explained that between June 2015 and June 2016 it had reduced the number of inmates serving time in isolation from 5,330 to 2,530. Guice then described plans to open four new "therapeutic diversion units" designed to "move mentally ill inmates out of solitary confinement and have them participate in programs outside their cells."[15]

Prisoners' rights advocates hope this is just the beginning, and that Guice will continue to implement those and other much needed reforms. That hope may be misplaced, as recent history seems to show the General Assembly and the Department of Public Safety are more interested in the appearance of reform than the reality. Alvin Keller's rather truculent reply to the committee report issued in the aftermath of Levon Wilson's death, the timid response to the Metzner and Aufderhide report, and the willingness to blame the victims during the most recent accusations of officer violence all call into question the legislature's inclination and the prison officials' ability to address the combined issues of mental health and solitary confinement. Indeed, one scholar accused the Department of Public Safety of using committees and public promises of reform as a "way of covering its backside and warding off criticisms." The same critic went further and asserted that the prison system's recent method of operation was to create "task forces to solve problems which should never have existed in the first place," and then to take "a very half-hearted approach to implementing many task force recommendations." Whether or not Guice and his successors will buck that trend and implement lasting reforms is anyone's guess.[16]

However that future may unfold, the isolation debate once again revealed the penitentiary as a social microcosm. Politicians and administrators ignored the system's brutality until inmates took up the traditional mantle of social activism to raise public awareness. Always wary of expenditures, and perceiving a political weapon, the legislature's initial response was half-hearted. Only when public pressure grew and threatened the state's reputation was the response more forthcoming. As they had for more than a century, politics, public sentiment, finances, and a desire to appear forward looking shaped penitentiary policy and directly impacted the lives of inmates. The challenge for North Carolina going forward is to find a balance between these competing forces in order to avoid the sweeping policy swings of the past and to create a healthy relationship that benefits the inmates, the public, the politicians, and the prison's administrators.

CONCLUSION

Since 2015, North Carolina has demonstrated its inability to find the aforementioned balance. Despite promises to the contrary and a brief moment when officials did reduce the use of solitary confinement, prison administrators continue to send inmates with mental illnesses to isolation at a rate far exceeding that of most other states. Indeed, current studies show that about five thousand of the state's thirty-seven thousand inmates are serving time in some form of isolation, and 10.6 percent of them suffer from "serious mental health issues." According to a 2015 Yale Law School study, nationwide about eighty thousand individuals are housed in isolation, and of that number 5 percent suffer from "serious mental health issues." While the number of inmates in isolation places North Carolina on average with other states, the percentage of inmates with "serious mental health issues" housed in isolation puts it in the top ten. Despite promises of reform, it seems little has changed.[1]

Among those affected by the state's continued isolation policy was Devon Davis, who entered Central Prison in 2012 after a conviction on firearms charges. Officers sent him to isolation for various rules violations, and he spent 1,001 consecutive days in solitary confinement. Not surprisingly, he developed mental health issues. As he later explained, "It just did something to me. You stay back there for so long, you start to get comfortable. As you start to get comfortable, it does something to you physically. It does something to you mentally. Now you don't know if you're coming or going. Walls close in on you. You're so anxious to get out of your room, but they [the guards] don't want you to come out." Davis responded by injuring himself and attempting suicide on several occasions. He survived and earned release, but he was a changed man.[2]

In 2017, Davis returned to Central Prison after resisting arrest. Despite having a mental health diagnosis, prison officials reinstalled him in isolation due to a Department of Public Safety policy of placing returning inmates "in the same custody level they left." He remained in isolation for the next 154 days despite the fact that he committed "no infractions—such as fighting, spitting, cursing or disobeying orders" during that period. Not only does that seem excessive, it violated Department of Public Safety policy, which "prohibits housing inmates with mental illness in restrictive housing for more than 30 days." And to make it all the more egregious, Davis twice requested that authorities provide him with prescribed mental health medication. According to Disability Rights North Carolina attorney Susan Pollitt, who had access to Davis's medical records, from October 13, 2017, until February 2, 2018, a total of 113 days, authorities failed to provide him the medicine.[3]

Davis was not the only mentally ill inmate who spent excessive time in isolation. The *Raleigh News and Observer* found at least "half a dozen inmates who have been in solitary confinement for more than a decade." Among them was Jason Swain, a white inmate serving time for aiding and abetting murder. Swain suffered from depression and bipolar disorder, yet spent more than thirteen years in solitary confinement. Swain's response to his illness and isolation was to "repeatedly swallow razor blades, rip open his surgical incisions, and plunge sharp objects into his open wounds." Shawn Minnich, a white inmate serving a thirty-one-year sentence for armed robbery and statutory rape, also spent thirteen years in isolation despite suffering from PTSD, which he contends was exacerbated by the extended stay. Other inmates proved unable to handle the isolation or their illness and took the ultimate step: in the first six months of 2018 alone, five inmates who had served time in isolation committed suicide.[4]

The issue is such that in October 2019 the ACLU and North Carolina Prisoner Legal Services filed suit against the state, charging that isolating inmates puts them at risk of "serious psychological and physiological harm." Indeed, the suit asserted that "the practice is virtually guaranteed to inflict pain." Professors at the University of North Carolina found that inmates who served time in isolation were 78 percent more likely to commit suicide and 54 percent more likely to die from homicide within a year of their release from prison than other inmates. The *Charlotte Observer*, meanwhile, found that despite news of the extended stays in isolation for Swain and Minnich, two other inmates in Central Prison remain in isolation after more than a decade.[5]

The issues surrounding isolation and mentally ill inmates are not the only examples demonstrating the state's continued inability to find a balance between punishment and security. So too is staff safety, as North Carolina's eleven thousand correctional officers confront increased instances of assault and murder, all while enduring short-staffing, low pay, and inadequate training. The assaults occur on a near daily basis, and while some are minor, many more are career or even life threatening.

On August 26, 2015, African American inmate Sammy Whittington, who was serving a sixteen-year sentence for murdering his wife and had twice before assaulted officers, attacked correctional officer Rosie Anderson while she was working in the mental health unit at Central Prison. Surveillance video shows Anderson sitting at her desk completing paperwork as Whittington approached from behind "with his pants lowered and his genitals exposed." Officer Anderson saw him at the last moment, but not in time to defend herself. Whittington grabbed her, threw her to the ground, punched her repeatedly in the face and head, and attempted to sexually assault her. The attack lasted forty-three seconds and ended only when Whittington inexplicably stopped. When he backed away, Anderson scrambled to her feet and doused him with pepper spray. Only then, more than seventy-five seconds after the attack began, did fellow officers arrive on the scene.[6]

Medics transported Anderson to Wake Medical Center, where doctors treated her for a concussion, nerve damage in her back, and broken bones in her hands. Despite treatment, Anderson continued to suffer from "periodic bouts of vertigo so severe that 'it feels like the ground is moving.'" Although she tried to return to work, the injuries, the fear, and the danger that a subsequent assault could lead to another concussion forced her to resign as a correctional officer and accept worker's compensation.[7]

Three years later, on June 19, 2018, African American inmates Jaquan Lane, who was serving four years on weapons charges and had been cited four times for assaulting officers, and Andrew Ellis, who was serving seven years for robbery, attacked unit manager and nineteen-year Central Prison veteran Brent Soucier, leaving him with "traumatic brain trauma, acute respiratory failure, extensive hemorrhages and facial fractures." He spent three weeks in the hospital and was unable to return to work for months. Subsequent investigations suggested that Lane and Ellis targeted Soucier because of allegations that he had abused handcuffed inmates. Indeed, Soucier was one of those implicated in the abuse allegations addressed in the previous chapter.[8]

Regardless of the causes underlying the assault, the fact remains that it was only one of hundreds. Department of Public Safety officials acknowledge that while the number of attacks statewide dropped from 845 in 2015–2016 to 790 in 2016–2017, the latter year was "the deadliest year in the history of the state's prison system." Early data for 2018, meanwhile, showed that violence remained a fact of life, with inmates committing 245 assaults on prison workers during the first six months alone. Thirty-two of those attacks involved weapons. Central Prison was the state's most dangerous facility, with inmate assaults on officers occurring more than one hundred times a year, but officers at every facility were under attack.[9]

Sadly, several of those attacks resulted in officer fatalities. On April 26, 2017, Craig Wissink, a white inmate who was serving a life sentence for murder at the Bertie Correctional Institution, started a fire in a trash can. When officer Meggan Callahan brought a fire extinguisher into the dormitory to put it out, Wissnik grabbed the extinguisher and used it to beat her to death. Six months later, on October 12, 2017, white inmates Mikel Brady, Seth Frazier, and Jonathan Monk and African American inmate Wisezah Buckman used hammers and homemade knives to kill "Officers Wendy Shannon and Justin Smith, sewing plant operator Veronica Darden, and maintenance worker Geoffrey Howe" during an escape attempt from the Pasquotank Correctional Institution in Elizabeth City.[10]

Such violence ultimately led the Department of Public Safety and outside agencies to investigate. The findings suggest the attacks arose from three related causes: understaffing, insufficient funding, and poor officer training.

The understaffing issue is especially acute, with one study finding that North Carolina needs "to hire and train an additional 1,300 correctional officers in addition to filling hundreds of vacant positions." Another finding put the total officer shortfall at two thousand. The studies also found those shortfalls had a direct impact on the violence officers confront. According to a review of the events surrounding Officer Anderson's attack, on the day of the assault Central Prison's mental health unit was supposed to have twenty-one officers overseeing the two hundred inmates, but only sixteen were on duty. Those officers worked twelve-hour shifts as a result of the short staffing, but even then there were not enough officers to fulfill protocol. Indeed, moments before she was attacked, Anderson was left alone when a fellow officer stepped out for a break. Although Department of Public Safety officials claimed officers "responded per policy," when the press followed up administrators refused to reply. Others, however, did. Former Pennsylvania Secretary of Correction Martin Horn called it "unconscionable not to have a second officer there," while the executive director of the American Correctional Officer Intelligence Network, Brian Dawe, rhetorically asked how it was possible to leave "one officer on a mental health ward with murderous inmates." Dawe even went so far as to suggest that "there's a real good chance" the presence of a second officer would have prevented the attack.[11]

Additional studies found similar staffing issues in the other attacks. An investigation by the National Institute of Corrections found Central Prison was suffering a 25 percent understaffing rate and was "unsafe to fully operate" on the day Lane and Ellis attacked Officer Soucier. On the day of her murder, Callahan was one of only four officers guarding 250 inmates at the Bertie Correctional Institution—half the recommended force. Officials speaking anonymously to the *Charlotte Observer* admitted, "Better staffing might have saved the lives of five prison employees who were attacked by inmates last year."[12]

Those two facilities are not alone, and understaffing remains a problem throughout the prison system. In 2018, the Pasquotank prison suffered from a 28 percent understaffing rate, the Alexander Correctional Institution had a 28 percent rate, the Bertie facility had at 31 percent rate, while the Lanesboro Correctional Institution, a maximum security prison, had a 37 percent vacancy rate. The staffing issue there was so bad that Department of Public Safety officials required officers from other facilities to work overtime at Lanesboro. This forced some officers to drive as far as thirty-five miles after normal working hours to complete their compulsory overtime, while others had to work nine straight days or sixteen-hour shifts. Despite that, guards reported on many occasions that the facility remained understaffed, often with two officers overseeing two hundred inmates.[13]

Not surprisingly, security was compromised. Reports found that officers suffered from "burnout," which resulted in "complacency and taking of shortcuts." Among the shortcuts, one study discovered, was that required strip searches occurred only 20 percent of the time, making it easier for inmates to carry and conceal contraband. Officer retention also has suffered. According to state representative Justin Burr, a Republican who represents Stanly and Montgomery Counties, officers "don't want to go. They're retiring. They're quitting. They don't want to put their lives in danger."[14]

Beyond understaffing, studies blamed the attacks on the failure to fully fund the prison system. According to press reports, "prison officials and the state lawmakers who provide their funding have failed to adopt strategies that have proven successful in other states. Prison officials rarely bring in drug-sniffing dogs, for instance." Financial exigencies not only undermined drug prevention programs, they resulted in Prisoner Legal Services, "the state funded agency that once filed lawsuits on behalf of inmates who alleged mistreatment," having its budget "slashed." That left inmates with "no one to go to" for legal advice and forced many to file their own lawsuits. Finally, legislative parsimony has led to poor pay for correctional officers. According to the Bureau of Labor Statistics, the national average salary for correctional officers in 2018 was $47,600, but in North Carolina the average was $35,000. Director of Prisons Kenneth Lassiter admitted, "It's tough to recruit people for such little compensation."[15]

The final causative agent for many of the problems plaguing the prison system is poor officer training. Press reports assert that correctional officers often went to work with "just one week of orientation," after which "new hires [were] routinely put on the job guarding career criminals in situations that can turn violent." That lack of training not only created situations in which inexperienced and undertrained officers found themselves in danger, it left them without the skills required to defuse potentially violent situations, it meant many did not know the rights inmates possessed nor the limits of their own powers, and it created the potential for inmate abuse. Taken together, the lack of funding, understaffing, and limited officer training have put officers and inmates alike at risk, and they make clear that both the poor treatment inmates faced and the concomitant assaults officers endured emerged from the same set of factors.[16]

Director of Prisons Kenneth Lassiter responded to those findings in the spring of 2018 with the announcement of a four-part plan. The plan included efforts to "remove maximum-security inmates from job assignments involving cutting and impact tools," to reduce "the number of untrained prison officers from 700 last summer to about 50," to select a cadre of "field training officers, who will work with new hires to prepare them for work inside the prisons," and to request that local law enforcement "drive by prison perimeters during their regular patrols in hopes of reducing the amount of contraband thrown over the fence to inmates." He also called for increased funding to provide officers additional Tasers and stab-resistant shirts. Finally, he supported a move by Central Prison administrators, who fortified inmate punishments, ironically enough, with "more segregation time" for those who disobeyed an officer's orders, those who possessed drugs, and those caught with weapons.[17]

The aforementioned issues, examples, and responses are by no means complete, but rather represent the ongoing state of affairs. As they have for decades, administrators at Central Prison and the state's other penal facilities struggle to balance punishment and rehabilitation with safety and security for all those involved. Sadly, they seem to be losing that battle.

While the cause of these most recent issues cannot be ascribed directly to contemporary social, political, and economic conditions, the history of such a relationship suggests that conclusion. So too does the fact that when faced with the problems, politicians resorted to form: they lashed out and used them as political weapons. State Representative Bob Steinburg, a Republican from Edenton, for instance, responded to the rash of violence by demanding that Democratic Governor Roy Moore "get off his duff and do something." Such a response seems in keeping with tradition, as is the financial frugality that led the legislature to limit officer pay, underfund officer training programs, and ignore programs such as the drug-sniffing dog force.[18]

Those traditions and the manner in which they reflect society have made Central Prison a useful tool for understanding the larger forces affecting North Carolina. From its earliest incarnation the prison has embodied any number of the state's political, philosophical, social, and economic circumstances, and reflected back on the state its successes and failures. At the individual level, the horrors African Americans faced, the difficulties mentally ill inmates confronted, the determined exploitation inmates suffered at the hands of business leaders, the explosive nature of 1960s civil unrest, and the ever-evolving public attitude toward capital punishment all became manifest in exaggerated form in Central Prison. At one step removed, the state's regional divide, its paradoxical politics, it progressive image, and the manner in which politicians and prison officials both exploited that image and subverted it also are evident. And if we scale back ever further, the entire scope of the state's history is evident in the prison. From the earliest refusals to construct a penitentiary, the omnipresent funding battles, and the frequent bouts of political chicanery, to questions about inmate labor, the incarceration of youthful offenders, and the implementation of modern reforms, the history of North Carolina is writ large in Central Prison. As a social microcosm, the prison offers a unique view of North Carolina's development: to know the prison's history is to know the state's history; their stories are linked intimately.

Central Prison also serves as a prism through which to appreciate evolving penal methodologies. Originally modeled on the Auburn System, which sought redemption through isolation, prison administrators slowly adopted the reformatory model, quickly shifted gears due to the financial lures of convict leasing, grudgingly adopted rehabilitation, succumbed to public pressure and implemented hard time, and currently employ a diversified system that incorporates elements of each system. Put another way, to know the history of the prison's penal policy is to know the history of penal policy.

We must acknowledge, of course, that Central Prison is far from the only public institution in which those developments are manifest. Many of the nation's oldest prisons followed the same trajectory and adopted new penal policies as they evolved. More notably, there are countless other venues in which the various elements of North Carolina's history are evident. From education and industry to culture and the economy, there are myriad windows into the state's essence—and some of them undoubtedly offer clearer insights. This is especially so if we remember Lawrence Friedman's admonition to understand prison as society's equivalent to a "funhouse mirror." Despite that, we should not diminish the utility of studying prisons. As Churchill, Dostoevsky, and countless other scholars have made clear, the penitentiary was and is a social microcosm.[19]

Two hundred years after the public first contemplated it, 140 years after construction first began, 125 years after it finally opened, and thirty years since it was rebuilt, Central Prison remains the centerpiece of North Carolina's penal system and stands as evidence that all elements of a society, even those we tend to ignore, are joined together to create our world. The state and its prison are one.

NOTES

INTRODUCTION

1. Churchill, *House of Commons Debate,* 1354.

2. Barnes, *The Evolution of Penology in Pennsylvania,* 4; McKelvey, *American Prisons: A Study in American Social History Prior to 1915,* 2.

3. Smith, "Reform and Research," 34–35; Sparks, Bottoms, and Hay, *Prisons and the Problem of Order,* 65.

4. Clemmer, *The Prison Community,* xi; Friedman, *Crime and Punishment in American History,* 312, 315.

5. Friedman, *Crime and Punishment in American History,* 125; Friedman, *A History of American Law,* 68; Siegel and Bartollas, *Corrections Today,* 137; New York State Special Commission on Attica, *Attica,* 82.

6. Alexander, *The New Jim Crow,* 4, 237; Gopnik, "The Caging of America."

7. Perkinson, *Texas Tough,* 2, 8, 328, 362–63; Alexander, *The New Jim Crow,* 98–99.

8. Dyer, *Perpetual Prisoner Machine,* 2, 10–11, 204, 208; Gopnik, "The Caging of America."

9. Federal Bureau of Investigation, "Crime in the United States by Volume and Rate, per 100,000 Inhabitants, 1995–2014"; Carson, "Prisoners in 2014," 1.

10. Dyer, *Perpetual Prisoner Machine,* 182, 255, 260; Herivel and Wright, *Prison Nation,* 168–69, 178; U.S. Department of Education, National Center for Education Statistics, *The Condition of Education 2016;* "Annual Determination of Average Cost of Incarceration," *Federal Register: The Daily Journal of the United States Government.*

11. Jacobs, *Stateville,* 6–7, 10.

12. Gopnik, "The Caging of America."

13. Herivel and Wright, *Prison Profiteers,* 103.

14. Christensen, *Paradox of Tar Heel Politics.*

15. Key, *Southern Politics in State and Nation,* 205.

16. Ibid., 211, 214.

17. Ready, *Tar Heel State,* 333.

18. Key, *Southern Politics in State and Nation,* 219.

19. North Carolina Department of Correction, *Research Bulletin,* 1991–2001; 20; Berger, *Captive Nation,* 16.

21. Ibid., 93–94.

1. THE PENITENTIARY ARGUMENT

1. McLennan, *The Crisis of Imprisonment*, 36.

2. Ibid., 38; Friedman, *Crime and Punishment in American History*, 77; Morris and Rothman, *The Oxford History of the Prison*, 100.

3. Christianson, *With Liberty for Some*, 132, 133; "Annual Report of the Inspectors of the Western Penitentiary of Pennsylvania, for the Year 1856," 581; McKelvey, *American Prisons*, 16–17; McLennan, *The Crisis of Imprisonment*, 56.

4. Christianson, *With Liberty for Some*, 115; *Report on Punishments and Prison Discipline*, 72; McKelvey, *American Prisons*, 14–15; Martin, *Break Down the Walls*, 115; Ayers, *Vengeance and Justice*, 39; McLennan, *The Crisis of Imprisonment*, 57, 60–61, 63–64, 67.

5. Powell, *North Carolina Through Four Centuries*, 247–48, 267.

6. Brown, *Growth of a State Program of Public Welfare*, 2–3; Hackney, "Prison Reform in North Carolina," 6; Johnson, *Ante-Bellum North Carolina*, 661–62. For information about the national opposition to the penitentiary model, see McLennan, *The Crisis of Imprisonment*, 39–46.

7. Jones, *Dr. Jones' Speech on the Bill to Amend the Penal Laws by Establishing a Penitentiary House for Criminals*.

8. Ibid.

9. Ibid. For similar arguments at the national level, see McLennan, *The Crisis of Imprisonment*, 49–50.

10. Jones, *Dr. Jones' Speech on the Bill to Amend the Penal Laws by Establishing a Penitentiary House for Criminals*.

11. Hackney, "Prison Reform in North Carolina," 6.

12. Brown, *Growth of a State Program of Public Welfare*, 5; Johnson, *Ante-Bellum North Carolina*, 664–65; Ayers, *Vengeance and Justice*, 50.

13. Mangum, "Oration Delivered at the University of North Carolina Commencement."

14. Ibid.

15. Ibid.

16. Johnson, *Ante-Bellum North Carolina*, 668.

17. Brown, *Growth of a State Program of Public Welfare*, 6.

18. North Carolina General Assembly, *Report of the Committee on the Penitentiary*, 2.

19. Ibid., 2–3.

20. Ibid., 3–4.

21. Ibid., 5–6.

22. Ayers, *Vengeance and Justice*, 50.

23. Powell, *North Carolina Through Four Centuries*, 259–61.

24. U.S. Census Bureau, *Abstract of the Returns of the Fifth Census*, 20; Zimmerman, "Penal Systems and Penal Reforms in the South Since the Civil War," 25.

25. Powell, *North Carolina Through Four Centuries*, 271, 280, 281.

26. *Raleigh Register*, April 7, 1846; Hackney, "Prison Reform in North Carolina," 2.

27. Ayers, *Vengeance and Justice*, 44, 50.

28. *North Carolina Standard*, October 8, 1845; Ayers, *Vengeance and Justice*, 54.

29. Ayers, *Vengeance and Justice*, 44, 50.

30. Ibid., 46, 48; Johnson, *Ante-Bellum North Carolina*, 663; *North Carolina Standard*, April 22, 1846.

31. *North Carolina Standard,* April 22, 1846; Ayers, *Vengeance and Justice*, 48, 57.

2. THE CIVIL WAR ERA AND THE PENITENTIARY

1. Ready, *Tar Heel State*, 235; Mangum, "History of the Salisbury, N.C. Confederate Prison."

2. Ready, *Tar Heel State*, 235–36; Mangum, "History of the Salisbury, N.C. Confederate Prison."

3. Rosenbaum, "Relationship Between War and Crime in the United States," 725–29; Olds, "History of the State's Prison," 4.

4. Ready, *Tar Heel State*, 256, 257.

5. North Carolina Constitutional Convention, "Report of the Committee on Punishments, Penal Institutions, and Public Charities," 292–93; North Carolina Constitution, 1868, Article XI; Thomas, "Chain Gangs, Roads, and Reform in North Carolina," 10–11. By 1837 there were thirty capital crimes. These included the four crimes which remained punishable by death as well as stealing a slave, inciting slaves to rebel, buggery, sodomy, bestiality, dueling, and mayhem, among many others.

6. Zimmerman, "Penal Systems and Penal Reforms in the South Since the Civil War," 57; Powell, *North Carolina Through Four Centuries*, 392.

7. Powell, *North Carolina Through Four Centuries*, 399–403. In 2011, the North Carolina State Senate voted 48–0 to pardon Holden.

8. Olds, "History of the State's Prison," 5; North Carolina General Assembly, "An Act for the Employment of Convicts and the Erection of a Penitentiary," 82–85.

9. Olds, "History of the State's Prison," 5.

10. North Carolina General Assembly, "Report on the Penitentiary and Its Location," *Laws and Resolutions Passed by the General Assembly of the State of North Carolina At the Special Session, Begun and Held in the City of Raleigh on the First of July 1868,* 82; Harris et al., "Report of Committee on Penitentiary and Its Location," *Executive and Legislative Documents Laid Before the General Assembly of North Carolina, Session 1868–69,* 1–10; Olds, "History of the State's Prison."

11. Robbins, "Minority Report From the Committee for the Location of the Penitentiary," *Executive and Legislative Documents Laid Before the General Assembly of North Carolina, Session 1868–69,* 9–13.

12. Olds, "History of the State's Prison," 5.

13. Daniels, *Prince of Carpetbaggers*, 185; Harris et al., "Communication from the Penitentiary Committee, November 17, 1868," *Executive and Legislative Documents Laid Before the General Assembly of North Carolina, Session 1868–69,* 1, 2–3.

14. Welker et al., "Report of the Committee Appointed by the Senate of North Carolina to Inquire into the Facts Attending the Purchase of the Site for the Penitentiary," *Executive and Legislative Documents Laid Before the General Assembly of North Carolina, Session 1868–69,* 1–2; Olds, "History of the State's Prison."

15. Welker et al., "Report of the Committee Appointed by the Senate of North Carolina to Inquire into the Facts Attending the Purchase of the Site for the Penitentiary," *Executive and Legislative Documents Laid Before the General Assembly of North Carolina, Session 1868–69,* 3; Olds, "History of the State's Prison."

16. Welker et al., "Report of the Committee Appointed by the Senate of North Carolina to

Inquire into the Facts Attending the Purchase of the Site for the Penitentiary," *Executive and Legislative Documents Laid Before the General Assembly of North Carolina, Session 1868–69,* 3, 5.

17. Ibid., 5–6.

18. Ibid., 9.

19. Daniels, *Prince of Carpetbaggers,* 175, 176.

20. Zimmerman, "Penal Systems and Penal Reforms in the South Since the Civil War," 80; Brown, *Growth of a State Program of Public Welfare,* 34–35.

3. CONSTRUCTION BEGINS

1. North Carolina General Assembly, "An Act to Provide for the Erection of a Penitentiary," 587–88; Olds, "History of the State's Prison," 5.

2. "Report of the Commission to Erect a Penitentiary," *Executive and Legislative Documents Laid Before the General Assembly of North Carolina, Session 1869–70,* 1; Olds, "History of the State's Prison."

3. "Report of Dr. G.W. Blacknall, Special Agent, Board of Public Charities, November 15, 1868," *First Annual Report of the Board of Public Charities of North Carolina,* 105.

4. North Carolina Penitentiary Commission, *The Rules and By-Laws for the Government and Discipline of the North Carolina Penitentiary During Its Management by the Commission, 1869,* 3–4.

5. Ibid., 5–10.

6. Ibid., 3; Olds, "History of the State's Prison," 5.

7. North Carolina Penitentiary Commission, *The Rules and By-Laws for the Government and Discipline of the North Carolina Penitentiary During Its Management by the Commission, 1869,* 15–18.

8. Ibid., 20–21.

9. "Report of the Commission to Erect a Penitentiary," *Executive and Legislative Documents Laid Before the General Assembly of North Carolina, Session 1869–70,* 4; North Carolina General Assembly, "An Act to Provide for the Erection of a Penitentiary," 588.

10. North Carolina Penitentiary Commission, *Report of the Penitentiary Commission to the General Assembly of North Carolina: Made December 8, 1870,* 4, 5–6; "Report of Assistant Architect of Penitentiary," *Executive and Legislative Documents Laid Before the General Assembly of North Carolina, Session 1871–72,*10; Olds, "History of the State's Prison," 5.

11. "Report of Assistant Architect of Penitentiary," *Executive and Legislative Documents Laid Before the General Assembly of North Carolina, Session 1871–72,* 2, 8, 20; Olds, "History of the State's Prison," 5.

12. North Carolina Penitentiary Commission, *Report of the Penitentiary Commission to the General Assembly of North Carolina: Made December 8, 1870,* 6.

13. Ibid., 7–8, 9.

14. Ibid., 15–18.

15. Ibid., 16–17.

16. Ibid., 18–19.

17. North Carolina Penitentiary Commission, *Report of the Penitentiary Commission to the General Assembly of North Carolina: Made December 8, 1870,* 16–17.

18. "Annual Report of the Board of Directors, Assistant Architect, Deputy Warden, Steward, Physician, of the Penitentiary," *Executive and Legislative Documents Laid Before the General Assembly*

of North Carolina, Session 1871–72, 4; "Report of Assistant Architect of Penitentiary," *Executive and Legislative Documents Laid Before the General Assembly of North Carolina, Session 1871–72,* 11; Olds, "History of the State's Prison," 5.

19. "Report of the Joint Select Committee to Inquire into the Management of the Penitentiary," *Executive and Legislative Documents Laid Before the General Assembly of North Carolina, Session 1871–72,* 5.

20. "Annual Report of the Board of Directors, Assistant Architect, Deputy Warden, Steward, Physician, of the Penitentiary. For the Year Ending October 31, 1872," *Executive and Legislative Documents Laid Before the General Assembly of North Carolina, Session 1872–73,* 3–4.

21. Ibid., 5–6.

4. POLITICIZING THE PENITENTIARY

1. "Annual Report of the Board of Directors, Assistant Architect, Deputy Warden, Steward, Physician, of the Penitentiary. For the Year Ending October 31, 1872," *Executive and Legislative Documents Laid Before the General Assembly of North Carolina, Session 1872–73,* 2–3.

2. "Report of the Joint Select Committee to Investigate Matters Connected with the State Penitentiary," *Executive and Legislative Documents Laid Before the General Assembly of North Carolina, Session 1872–73,* 2.

3. "Report of the Joint Select Committee to Inquire into the Management of the Penitentiary," *Executive and Legislative Documents Laid Before the General Assembly of North Carolina, Session 1871–72,* 6–12.

4. Ibid., 59–62.

5. "Annual Report of the Board of Directors, Assistant Architect, Deputy Warden, Steward, Physician, of the Penitentiary. For the Year Ending October 31, 1871," *Executive and Legislative Documents Laid Before the General Assembly of North Carolina, Session 1871–72,* 27.

6. "Report of the Joint Select Committee to Inquire into the Management of the Penitentiary," *Executive and Legislative Documents Laid Before the General Assembly of North Carolina, Session 1871–72,* 14–15.

7. Ibid., 16–17.

8. Ibid., 18.

9. "Report of the Joint Select Committee to Inquire into the Management of the Penitentiary, January 23 and 24, 1872," *Executive and Legislative Documents Laid Before the General Assembly of North Carolina, Session 1871–72,* 18–19.

10. Ibid., 20–55.

11. Ibid., 56–59.

12. "Report of the Joint Select Committee to Investigate Matters Connected with the State Penitentiary," *Executive and Legislative Documents Laid Before the General Assembly of North Carolina, Session 1872–73,* 3.

13. "Annual Report of the Board of Directors, Assistant Architect, Deputy Warden, Steward, Physician, of the Penitentiary. For the Year Ending October 31, 1872," *Executive and Legislative Documents Laid Before the General Assembly of North Carolina, Session 1872–73,* 1, 7.

14. "Testimony in Regard to the Irregularity in the Report of the Board of Managers, Febru-

ary 6, 1873," *Executive and Legislative Documents Laid Before the General Assembly of North Carolina, Session 1872–73,* 4–14.

15. "Testimony Before Committee Appointed to Investigate Charges Against Board of Directors of Penitentiary," *Executive and Legislative Documents Laid Before the General Assembly of North Carolina, Session 1872–73,* 14–17, 22, 35.

16. Ibid., 17–18.

17. Ibid., 18, 21.

18. Ibid., 24, 33, 40.

19. Ibid., 32–33.

20. "Report of the Joint Select Committee to Investigate Matters Connected with the State Penitentiary," *Executive and Legislative Documents Laid Before the General Assembly of North Carolina, Session 1872–73,* 1.

21. *Welker v. Bledsoe,* 68 N.C. 457, 464 (N.C. 1873); Bounds, *Report on North Carolina's Penal-Correctional System, Prepared for the Commission on the Reorganization of the State Government,* 86; Brown, *Growth of a State Program of Public Welfare,* 38–39; Craven, "North Carolina's Prison System," 33–34.

5. CONVICT LEASING

1. "Annual Report of the Board of Directors, Architect, Deputy Warden, Steward, Physician, and Etcetera of the Penitentiary" and "Communication from the Governor of North Carolina to the Honorable General Assembly of the State of North Carolina, December 12, 1874," *Executive and Legislative Documents Laid Before the General Assembly of North Carolina, Session 1874–75,* 3, 4, 5–6, 8; Cable, *The Silent South,* 126.

2. Powell, *North Carolina Through Four Centuries,* 406–13; Ready, *Tar Heel State,* 267–77.

3. Zimmerman, "Penal Systems and Penal Reforms in the South Since the Civil War," 82–83; "Communication from the Governor of North Carolina to the Honorable General Assembly of the State of North Carolina, December 12, 1874," *Executive and Legislative Documents Laid Before the General Assembly of North Carolina, Session 1874–75,* 1–2; McLennan, *The Crisis of Imprisonment,* 102.

4. McKay, "Convict Leasing in North Carolina," 14–15; Zimmerman, "Penal Systems and Penal Reforms in the South since the Civil War," 83, 84.

5. Zimmerman, "Penal Systems and Penal Reforms in the South since the Civil War," 84; McKay, "Convict Leasing in North Carolina," 14–15, 17, 19–20.

6. Craven, "North Carolina's Prison System," 37.

7. "Report of Directors, November 1, 1878," *Public Documents of the General Assembly of North Carolina, Session 1879,* 1–7; Olds, "History of the State's Prison," 7; McLennan, *The Crisis of Imprisonment,* 110–11, 118.

8. "Report of the Architect and Warden," *Biennial Report of the Board of Directors, Architect and Warden, Steward and Physician. For the Two Years Ending November 30, 1884,* 9–26; McLennan, *The Crisis of Imprisonment,* 105.

9. Blackmon, *Slavery by Another Name,* 66; *Atlanta Constitution,* September 2, 1904; Cohen, "Negro Involuntary Servitude in the South," 50; Roback, "Exploitation in the Jim Crow South," 39.

10. McKay, "Convict Leasing in North Carolina," 9, 60.

11. Carson, "Penal Reform and the Western North Carolina Railroad," 205.

12. Poole, *A History of Railroading in Western North Carolina*, 22–24; Pitzer, *Myths and Mysteries of North Carolina*, 115–18; *Raleigh News and Observer*, January 3, 1883; Carson, "Penal Reform and Construction of the Western North Carolina Railroad," 205–25.

13. Zimmerman, "Penal Systems and Penal Reforms in the South since the Civil War," 129; Olds, "History of the State's Prison," 7; McLennan, *The Crisis of Imprisonment*, 87; Mancini, *One Dies, Get Another*, 3, 30.

14. Logan, *The Negro in North Carolina*, 194; Carson, "Penal Reform and Construction of the Western North Carolina Railroad," 221.

15. Steiner and Brown, *The North Carolina Chain Gang*, 15; Berger, *Captive Nation*, 22, 28; Friedman, *Crime and Punishment in American History*, 94; Blackmon, *Slavery by Another Name*, 99.

16. Cobb, *Industrialization and Southern Society*, 68–69; Lichtenstein, *Twice the Work of Free Labor*, 77, 80–83; Mancini, *One Dies, Get Another*, 20; Blackmon, *Slavery by Another Name*, 56, 57, 96; McLennan, *The Crisis of Imprisonment*, 122.

17. Carson, "Penal Reform and Construction of the Western North Carolina Railroad," 205; "Report of the Architect and Warden," *Executive and Legislative Documents Laid Before the General Assembly of North Carolina, Session 1885*, 10.

18. McKay, "Convict Leasing in North Carolina," 23, 29.

19. Zimmerman, "Penal Systems and Penal Reforms in the South since the Civil War," 127, 129.

20. "Report of the Architect and Warden, November 30, 1890," *Biennial Report of the Board of Directors, Architect and Warden, Steward and Physician. For the Two Years Ending November 30, 1890*, 13–55; "Deputy Warden's Report, November 1, 1876," *The First Biennial Report of the Directors of the N.C. State Penitentiary*, 20.

21. Zimmerman, "Penal Systems and Penal Reforms in the South Since the Civil War," 129.

6. COMPLETING THE PENITENTIARY

1. "Annual Report of the Board of Directors, Assistant Architect, Deputy Warden, Steward, Physician, of the Penitentiary. For the Year Ending October 31, 1872," *Executive and Legislative Documents Laid Before the General Assembly of North Carolina, Session 1872–73*, 28.

2. "Annual Report of the Board of Directors, Assistant Architect, Deputy Warden, Steward, Physician, of the Penitentiary. For the Year Ending October 31, 1874," *Executive and Legislative Documents Laid Before the General Assembly of North Carolina, Session 1874–75*, 19.

3. "Report of the Architect," *The First Biennial Report of the Directors of the N.C. State Penitentiary*, 16.

4. "Report of Directors, November 1, 1878," *Biennial Report of the Board of Directors of the North Carolina State Penitentiary (November 1, 1876 to November 1, 1878)*, 2.

5. "Report of the Board of Directors," *Biennial Report of the Board of Directors of the North Carolina State Penitentiary (November 1, 1876 to November 1, 1878)*, 10; "Report of the Architect," *The First Biennial Report of the Directors of the N.C. State Penitentiary*, 7–8; Olds, "History of the State's Prison," 5–6.

6. "Steward's Report," *The First Biennial Report of the Directors of the N.C. State Penitentiary*, 42.

7. "Annual Report of the Board of Directors, Assistant Architect, Deputy Warden, Steward,

Physician, of the Penitentiary. For the Year Ending October 31, 1874," *Executive and Legislative Documents Laid Before the General Assembly of North Carolina, Session 1874–75*, 14.

8. "Report of the Physician, November 1, 1876," *The First Biennial Report of the Directors of the N.C. State Penitentiary*, 47–56.

9. "Report of Architect and Warden" and "Report of the Steward," *Biennial Report of the Board of Directors of the North Carolina State Penitentiary (November 1, 1876 to November 1, 1878)*, 18, 40; "Biennial Report of the Officers of the North Carolina Penitentiary," *Executive and Legislative Documents of the State of North Carolina, Session 1885*, 21; "Report of the Steward," *Biennial Report of the Board of Directors, Architect and Warden, Steward and Physician. For the Two Years Ending October 31, 1882*, 34; *Reports of the Superintendent, Warden and Other Officials of the State's Prison for the Years 1911–1912*, 8.

10. "Report of Architect and Warden," *Biennial Report of the Board of Directors of the North Carolina State Penitentiary (November 1, 1876 to November 1, 1878)*, 12.

11. Ibid., 9.

12. "Report of the President of the Board of Directors of the North Carolina Penitentiary," *North Carolina Executive and Legislative Documents, Session 1881*, 9–10; "Report of Architect and Warden," *Biennial Report of the Board of Directors of the North Carolina State Penitentiary (November 1, 1876 to November 1, 1878)*, 12.

13. "Report of the Board of Directors," *The First Biennial Report of the Directors of the N.C. State Penitentiary*, 6; "Report of the President of the Board of Directors of the North Carolina Penitentiary," *North Carolina Executive and Legislative Documents, Session 1881*, 2; "Biennial Report of the Officers of the North Carolina Penitentiary," *Executive and Legislative Documents of the State of North Carolina, Session 1883*, 3.

14. "Report of the President of the Board of Directors of the North Carolina Penitentiary," *North Carolina Executive and Legislative Documents, Session 1881*, 19; "Biennial Report of the Officers of the North Carolina Penitentiary," *Biennial Report of the Board of Directors, Architect and Warden, Steward and Physician. For the Two Years Ending October 31, 1882*, 3, 4.

15. "Biennial Report of the Officers of the North Carolina Penitentiary," *Biennial Report of the Board of Directors, Architect and Warden, Steward and Physician. For the Two Years Ending October 31, 1882*, 2–3.

16. "Report of the Superintendent," *Biennial Report of The State Prison Department, July 1, 1930–June 30, 1932*, 10; Department of Correction, *Central Prison: North Carolina's Maximum Security Institution*, 1.

17. "Biennial Report of the Officers of the North Carolina Penitentiary," *Executive and Legislative Documents of the State of North Carolina, Session 1885*, 13.

18. Ibid., 12–13.

7. THE FIRST TWO DECADES

1. Morris and Rothman, *The Oxford History of the Prison*, 151.

2. Ibid., 154; Wines and Dwight, *Report on the Prisons and Reformatories of the United States and Canada*.

3. Hinkle and Whitmarsh, *Elmira Reformatory*, 67, 107; McKelvey, *American Prisons: A History of Good Intentions*, 133–35; Martin, *Break Down the Walls*, 117–18.

4. "Biennial Report of the Officers of the North Carolina Penitentiary," *Biennial Report of the Board of Directors, Architect and Warden, Steward and Physician. For the Two Years Ending October 31, 1882,* 5.

5. Craven, "North Carolina's Prison System," 41.

6. "Report of the Architect and Warden," *Biennial Report of the Board of Directors, Architect and Warden, Steward and Physician. For the Two Years Ending November 30, 1888,* 23.

7. McLennan, *The Crisis of Imprisonment,* 73, 163–64.

8. "Biennial Report of the Officers of the North Carolina Penitentiary" and "Report of the Architect and Warden," *Biennial Report of the Board of Directors, Architect and Warden, Steward and Physician. For the Two Years Ending November 30, 1886,* 2, 7.

9. "Biennial Report of the Officers of the North Carolina Penitentiary," *Biennial Report of the Board of Directors, Architect and Warden, Steward and Physician. For the Two Years Ending November 30, 1886,* 7–8.

10. Ibid., 8.

11. Roberts, *Juvenile Justice Sourcebook,* 131.

12. "Report of the Architect and Warden," *Biennial Report of the Board of Directors, Architect and Warden, Steward and Physician. For the Two Years Ending November 30, 1888,* 23; "Report of the Architect and Warden," *Biennial Report of the Board of Directors, Architect and Warden, Steward and Physician. For the Two Years Ending November 30, 1890,* 23; "Report of the Architect and Warden," *Biennial Report of the Board of Directors, Architect and Warden, Steward and Physician. For the Two Years Ending November 30, 1892,* 37.

13. "Report of Directors," *Biennial Report of the Board of Directors, Architect and Warden, Steward and Physician. For the Two Years Ending November 30, 1888,* 6–7.

14. "Biennial Report of the Board of Directors," *Biennial Report of the Board of Directors, Architect and Warden, Steward and Physician. For the Two Years Ending November 30, 1892,* 5, 36.

15. Zimmerman, "The Penal Reform Movement in the South During the Progressive Era," 463–64; McKay, "Convict Leasing in North Carolina," 82.

16. "Report of the Architect and Warden," *Biennial Report of the Board of Directors, Architect and Warden, Steward and Physician. For the Two Years Ending November 30, 1892,* 19; McKay, "Convict Leasing in North Carolina," 86–87.

17. "Biennial Message of Elias Carr, Governor of North Carolina to the General Assembly, Session 1897," 29, 30–31; "Report Directors," *The Report of the Board of Directors and of the General Manager for the Two Years of 1897 and 1898,* 5–6.

8. THE EXPLOSIVE POWERS OF FUSION

1. Ready, *The Tar Heel State,* 287, 292–99; Powell, *North Carolina Through Four Centuries,* 429–30; Christensen, *The Paradox of Tar Heel Politics,* 7, 10, 11.

2. "Annual Report of the North Carolina Penitentiary," *Public Documents of the General Assembly of North Carolina, Session 1899,* 81.

3. Cooke, *Caledonia,* 33–35, 48; "Annual Report of the North Carolina Penitentiary," *Public Documents of the General Assembly of North Carolina, Session 1899,* 83 (emphasis in the original).

4. "Report of the Superintendent, January 1, 1901," *Biennial Report of the State's Prison for the Years 1899–1900,* 8; Craven, "North Carolina's Prison System," 59, 64.

5. *Raleigh News and Observer,* January 16, 1898.

6. State Democratic Executive Committee of North Carolina, *The Democratic Handbook, 1898,* 71, 73.

7. Ibid., 100, 101.

8. *Raleigh Post,* July 27, 1898.

9. State Democratic Executive Committee of North Carolina, *The Democratic Handbook, 1898,* 102; Powell, *North Carolina Through Four Centuries,* 433–38; Ready, *The Tar Heel State,* 304–5; Christensen, *The Paradox of Tar Heel Politics,* 17–18, 23–27, 43.

10. Craven, "North Carolina's Prison System," 52; Bounds, *Report on North Carolina's Penal-Correctional System, Prepared for the Commission on the Reorganization of the State Government,* 88–89; *State's Prison of North Carolina et al. v. Day* (124 N.C. 362) Supreme Court of North Carolina, April 11, 1899; Craven, "North Carolina's Prison System," 53–54.

11. North Carolina General Assembly, *Report of the Investigating Committee Appointed to Investigate the Affairs of the Department of Agriculture and the State's Prison,* 3, 9, 10–11.

12. Ibid., 10.

13. Ibid., 12–13, 63.

14. McKay, "Convict Leasing in North Carolina," 92, 94; "Report of the Superintendent," *Biennial Report of the State's Prison for the Years 1901–1902,* 12. Such changed policies took place throughout the South. See McLennan, *The Crisis of Imprisonment,* 101–2.

15. "Report of the Warden," *Biennial Report of the State's Prison for the Years 1899–1900,* 106; "Physician's Report," *Biennial Report of the Board of Directors, Architect and Warden, Steward and Physician. For the Two Years Ending November 30, 1890,* 62–63.

16. "Report of the Physician," *Biennial Report of the State's Prison for the Years 1899–1900,* 17, 119.

17. "Report of Superintendent State Hospital for Dangerous Insane," *Biennial Report of the State's Prison for the Years 1901–1902,* 28.

18. "Report of the Superintendent," *Reports of the Superintendent, Warden and Other Officials of the State's Prison, For the Years 1903–1904,* 10, 11; "Report of the Superintendent, January 1, 1911," *Biennial Report of the State's Prison for the Years 1909–1910,* 7.

19. "Report of the Superintendent," *Biennial Report of the State's Prison for the Years 1901–1902,* 8–9.

20. Ibid., 9–11.

21. Ibid., 11.

22. Goodwyn, *The Populist Moment.*

9. THE ERA OF HIGH HOPES

1. McLennan, *The Crisis of Imprisonment,* 240, 242.

2. McKay, "Convict Leasing in North Carolina," 108; Steiner and Brown, *The North Carolina Chain Gang,* 6–7.

3. Terrell, *Prison Bars to Shining Stars,* 46–47, 65–66; Thomas, "Chain Gangs, Roads, and Reform," 60; Knepper and Jones, *North Carolina's Criminal Justice System,* 166.

4. "Report of the General Manager of the State's Prison for the Years 1895 and 1896," *The Report of the Board of Directors and of the General Manager for the Two Years of 1895 and 1896,* 7; Knepper and Jones, *North Carolina's Criminal Justice System,* 166.

5. Zimmerman, "The Penal Reform Movement in the South During the Progressive Era," 469.

6. "Report of the Superintendent," *Reports of the Superintendent, Warden and Other Officials of the State's Prison for the Years 1903–1904*, 8.

7. McKay, "Convict Leasing in North Carolina," 121; Ireland, "Prison Reform, Road Building, and Southern Progressivism," 136.

8. "Report of the Superintendent," *Reports of the Superintendent, Warden and Other Officials of the State's Prison for the Years 1907–1908*, 12.

9. Watson, *Been There and Back*, 41–42; North Carolina State Board of Charities and Public Welfare, "A Study of Prison Conditions in North Carolina," 16–17.

10. Smith, *The Life of George L. Smith*, 12–13.

11. Watson, *Been There and Back*, 41; Terrell, *Prison Bars to Shining Stars*, 47–48; North Carolina State Board of Charities and Public Welfare, "A Study of Prison Conditions in North Carolina," 16–17.

12. "Report of the Superintendent," *Reports of the Superintendent, Warden and Other Officials of the State's Prison for the Years 1907–1908*, 12–15; McKay, "Convict Leasing in North Carolina," 120–21; Ireland, "Prison Reform, Road Building, and Southern Progressivism," 136.

13. McKay, "Convict Leasing in North Carolina," 123.

14. "Report of the Superintendent," *Reports of the Superintendent, Warden and Other Officials of the State's Prison for the Years 1903–1904*, 9.

15. Henderson, *North Carolina, the Old North State and the New*, 505–6; Brown, *Growth of a State Program of Public Welfare*, 82–83.

16. Terrell, *Prison Bars to Shining Stars*, 40–41.

17. Cahn, *Sexual Reckoning*, 46–47; *The Prison News*, May 1, 1927; Zipf, *Bad Girls at Samarcand*, 3.

18. Weare, *Black Businesses in the New South*, 198; Leonard, "The History of the Eastern Carolina Industrial Training School for Boys"; Bounds, *Report on North Carolina's Penal-Correctional System, Prepared for the Commission on the Reorganization of the State Government*, 114; Zipf, *Bad Girls at Samarcand*, 69.

19. "Report of the Superintendent," *Reports of the Superintendent, Warden and Other Officials of the State's Prison for the Years 1909–1910*, 6.

20. Kotch, "Unduly Harsh and Unworkably Rigid," 34, 36, 40–41; Kotch, *Lethal State*, 61–62, 64–66.

21. "Report of the Superintendent," *Reports of the Superintendent, Warden and Other Officials of the State's Prison for the Years 1909–1910*, 7.

22. North Carolina State Board of Charities and Public Welfare, *Capital Punishment in North Carolina*, 15; Seitz, "The Killing Chair," 40; Kotch, *Lethal State*, 67–69.

10. "AN ALMOST PERFECT LAW"

1. "Report of the Warden," *Reports of the Superintendent, Warden and Other Officials of the State's Prison for the Years 1909–1910*, 10–12; "Report of the Warden," *Reports of the Superintendent, Warden and Other Officials of the State's Prison for the Years 1911–1912*, 9–10.

2. Witmer, "The History, Theory and Results of Parole," 28–29, 36, 47, 52, 59; "Report of the Warden," *Reports of the Superintendent, Warden and Other Officials of the State's Prison for the Years 1911–1912*, 4–5, 13.

3. "Report of the Warden," *Reports of the Superintendent, Warden and Other Officials of the State's Prison for the Years 1911–1912*, 13; Terrell, *Prison Bars to Shining Stars*, 90.

4. "Report of the Warden," *Reports of the Superintendent, Warden and Other Officials of the State's Prison for the Years 1911–1912*, 14.

5. Ibid.

6. *Greensboro News*, March 4, 1917.

7. North Carolina General Assembly, *An Act to Regulate the Treatment, Handling, and Work of Prisoners*, 5.

8. Ibid., 3–4.

9. Ibid.

10. Ibid. In 1919, inmates received a raise: "A Grade" inmates earned 15 cents, "B Grade" inmates earned 10 cents, and "C Grade" inmates earned 5 cents.

11. North Carolina General Assembly, *An Act to Regulate the Treatment, Handling, and Work of Prisoners*, 5, 6.

12. Ibid., 6–8; McQuillan, *North Carolina Department of Correction*, 6.

13. "Report of the Superintendent," *Biennial Report of The State's Prison, 1919–1920*, 5; *The Prison News*, June 1, 1927.

14. "Report of the Superintendent," *Biennial Report of The State's Prison, 1919–1920*, 5–6, 10.

15. Ibid., 15–18; Cooke, *Caledonia*, 56–60.

16. "Report of the Superintendent," *Biennial Report of The State's Prison, 1919–1920*, 15–18; Cooke, *Caledonia*, 56–60.

17. "Report of the Superintendent," *Reports of the Superintendent, Warden and Other Officials of the State's Prison for the Years 1915–1916*, 5.

18. "Report of the Superintendent," *Biennial Report of The State's Prison, 1917–1918*, 11–12.

19. Ibid., 13–14.

20. Ibid., 21; "Report of the Physician," *Biennial Report of The State's Prison, 1917–1918*, 27.

11. GEORGE POU

1. "Report of Superintendent Collie," *Biennial Report of The State's Prison, 1919–1920*, 7; "The Employment of Prison Labor," *Biennial Report of The State's Prison, July 1, 1928–June 30, 1930*, 30.

2. Lindsay, *Inside the Prison*, 22, 23, 24–25, 28.

3. Cooke, *Caledonia*, 203–4.

4. "Report of the Superintendent" and "Report of Dr. Norman," *Biennial Report of The State's Prison, 1921–1922*, 8, 15.

5. "Report of Superintendent Pou," *Biennial Report of The State's Prison, 1923–1924*, 6, 13.

6. Powell, "Morrison, Cameron," *Dictionary of North Carolina Biography*.

7. "Report of Superintendent Pou," *Biennial Report of The State's Prison, 1925–1926*, 9.

8. "Report of Superintendent Pou," *Biennial Report of The State's Prison, 1923–1924*, 10.

9. Ibid., 10–12; McLennan, *The Crisis of Imprisonment*, 227.

10. McLennan, *The Crisis of Imprisonment*, 217; "Report of Superintendent Pou," *Biennial Report of The State's Prison, 1923–1924*, 15.

11. McLean, *Special Message of Angus W. McLean, Governor to the General Assembly of North Carolina in Respect to the Conditions and Needs of the State's Prison*, 5.

12. Ibid., 6–7.

13. Bounds, *Report on North Carolina's Penal-Correctional System, Prepared for the Commission on the Reorganization of the State Government*, 92.

14. "Report of the Physician-Warden" and "Report of the Deputy Warden," *Biennial Report of The*

State's Prison, 1925–1926, 17, 23; "Report of the Deputy Warden," *Biennial Report of The State's Prison, 1927–1928,* 21; "Report of the Deputy Warden," *Biennial Report of The State's Prison, July 1, 1928–June 30, 1930,* 37.

15. "Report of the Warden-Physician," *Biennial Report of The State's Prison, 1925–1926,* 20; Craven, "North Carolina's Prison System," 125; Hackney, "Prison Reform in North Carolina," 21.

16. "Report of the Superintendent," *Biennial Report of The State's Prison, 1925–1926,* 15; "Report of the Superintendent," *Biennial Report of The State's Prison, July 1, 1928–June 30, 1930,* 8.

17. Bounds, *Report on North Carolina's Penal-Correctional System, Prepared for the Commission on the Reorganization of the State Government,* 254–55.

18. *The Prison News,* September 1, 1927.

19. McLean, *Special Message of Angus W. McLean, Governor to the General Assembly of North Carolina in Respect to the Conditions and Needs of the State's Prison,* 5.

20. *The Prison News,* June 1, 1927; December 1, 1927; May 1, 1928.

21. Beard, *Carbine,* 66–80, 128.

22. Ibid., 137.

23. "Report of Superintendent Pou," *Biennial Report of The State's Prison, 1927–1928,* 9–10, 16; "Report of Physician," *Biennial Report of The State Prison Department, July 1, 1930–June 30, 1932,* 47.

24. "Report of the Superintendent," *Biennial Report of The State's Prison, 1927–1928,* 10; "Report of the Superintendent," *Biennial Report of The State's Prison, July 1, 1928–June 30, 1930,* 8.

25. *The Prison News,* October 1, 1929; November 15, 1926.

26. Ibid., November 1, 1928.

12. O. MAX GARDNER

1. McKenzie, "Robin Hood of the Blue Ridge," 68; North Carolina State Board of Charities and Public Welfare, *Capital Punishment in North Carolina,* 23–24.

2. Wood, *The Life of Otto Wood,* 35–36, 40–41, 57; McKenzie, "Robin Hood of the Blue Ridge," 36.

3. McKenzie, "Robin Hood of the Blue Ridge," 68–73, 107–8; Wood, *The Life of Otto Wood,* 57–58.

4. Wood, *The Life of Otto Wood,* 61, 63; McKenzie, "Robin Hood of the Blue Ridge," 75, 83–84.

5. Lallier, "'A Place of Beginning Again,'" 4; *Biennial Report of the State's Prison, 1928–1930,* 31.

6. Zipf, *Bad Girls at Samarcand,* 175, 177, 179, 184; Rafter, *Partial Justice,* xxi, xxiv.

7. Zipf, *Bad Girls at Samarcand,* 153–54, 179.

8. Rafter, *Partial Justice,* xxiii; Lallier, "'A Place of Beginning Again,'" 4.

9. Zipf, *Bad Girls at Samarcand,* 1–2.

10. Ibid., 1–2, 177–78, 180.

11. North Carolina Correctional Center for Women, *Inside Outlook,* January 1980; Rafter, *Partial Justice,* 55–56, 65.

12. Rafter, *Partial Justice,* 24, 26.

13. Ibid., 38, 60, 68–69, 97, 100, 128.

14. Ibid., 78, 116, 142, 146–47.

15. *Report of Sub-Committee of State Prison Advisory Commission,* 5.

16. Ibid.; Ready, *The Tar Heel State,* 369; "Report of the Subcommittee on North Carolina's Prison Problem," *Biennial Report of The State's Prison, July 1, 1928–June 30, 1930,* 14.

17. "Report of the Subcommittee on North Carolina's Prison Problem," *Biennial Report of The State's Prison, July 1, 1928–June 30, 1930,* 21.

18. Ibid., 12–13.

19. Ibid.

20. Ibid., 11–12.

21. Ibid.

22. Ibid., 11, 17.

23. Ibid., 12.

24. Ibid., 12, 19; Martin, *Break Down the Walls,* 19.

25. "Report of the Subcommittee on North Carolina's Prison Problem," *Biennial Report of The State's Prison, July 1, 1928–June 30, 1930,* 12.

26. *Report of Sub-Committee of State Prison Advisory Commission,* 16.

13. THE DEPRESSION YEARS

1. Craven, "North Carolina's Prison System," 132; "Biennial Report of the Superintendent of the State Prison Department for the Year Ended June 30, 1932," *Biennial Report of The State Prison Department, July 1, 1930–June 30, 1932,* 26.

2. Martin, *Break Down the Walls,* 120; Bounds, *Report on North Carolina's Penal-Correctional System, Prepared for the Commission on the Reorganization of the State Government,* 101–2.

3. Martin, *Break Down the Walls,* 125–26.

4. Ibid., 21.

5. Ibid., 21–22, 24.

6. Ibid., 26.

7. Bounds, *Report on North Carolina's Penal-Correctional System, Prepared for the Commission on the Reorganization of the State Government,* 103; McKay, "Convict Leasing in North Carolina," 136; Craven, "North Carolina's Prison System," 142.

8. Bounds, *Report on North Carolina's Penal-Correctional System, Prepared for the Commission on the Reorganization of the State Government,* 103.

9. Ibid., 104, 145, 153. New York was the first state to employ state-use on a mass scale. See McLennan, *The Crisis of Imprisonment,* 202.

10. Thomas, "Chain Gangs, Roads, and Reform," 191–92; McKay, "Convict Leasing in North Carolina," 136; "Report of Prison Department Operations," *Biennial Report. State Highway and Public Works Commission, Prison Department. For the Two Years Ended June 30, 1938,* 380–81.

11. Hackney, "Prison Reform in North Carolina," 25.

12. Thomas, "Chain Gangs, Roads, and Reform in North Carolina," 192; *Raleigh News and Observer,* October 21, 1937.

13. *Raleigh News and Observer,* March 17, 1935; Craven, "North Carolina's Prison System," 155, 164, 167–68, 172.

14. *The Prison News,* November 15, 1926; December 15, 1926.

15. Ibid., November 15, 1926.

16. Ibid., March 1, 1927; August 1, 1934.

17. Ibid., June 1, 1927.

18. Ibid., January 1, 1928; February 1, 1931.

19. Kennard, "Confessions of a Boy From Hell's Forty Acres," 65.

20. Ibid.

21. Mebane, "The Torture Chamber in North Carolina," 214, 221.

22. Ibid.

23. Ibid.

24. Ibid.; Watson, *Been There and Back*, 50.

25. Mebane, "The Torture Chamber in North Carolina," 214, 221.

26. *Raleigh News and Observer*, May 10, 1936; November 6, 1936; January 3, 1937.

27. "Biennial Report of the Superintendent of the State Prison Department for the Year Ended June 30, 1932," *Biennial Report of The State Prison Department, July 1, 1930–June 30, 1932*, 37–38.

28. "Report of the Superintendent," *Biennial Report. State Highway and Public Works Commission, Prison Department. For the Two Years Ended June 30, 1934*, 36–37.

29. Bounds, *Report on North Carolina's Penal-Correctional System, Prepared for the Commission on the Reorganization of the State Government*, 41, 43–44.

30. Ibid., 48, 49, 51–52, 54.

14. DEATH PENALTY REFORMS

1. Seitz, "The Killing Chair," 46.

2. North Carolina State Board of Charities and Public Welfare, *Capital Punishment in North Carolina*, 7–8.

3. *Raleigh News and Observer*, March 4, 1984.

4. Kotch, *Lethal State*, 82.

5. *Raleigh News and Observer*, January 25, 1936; Seitz, "The Killing Chair."

6. *Raleigh News and Observer*, January 25, 1936.

7. North Carolina State Board of Charities and Public Welfare, *Capital Punishment in North Carolina*, 18–19, 28–29; Kotch, "Unduly Harsh and Unworkably Rigid," 263; Seitz, "The Killing Chair," 38; Brown, "Crime and Its Treatment," 595.

8. Rapaport and Streib, "Death Penalty for Women in North Carolina," 76–77; *Gaston Gazette*, January 28, 1892.

9. Seitz, "The Wounds of Savagery," 44–46; Baker, "Black Female Executions in Historical Context," 77–78.

10. Seitz, "The Wounds of Savagery," 49.

11. Ibid., 50.

12. Ibid., 44, 51.

13. *Statesville Daily*, January 1, 1943; Seitz, "The Wounds of Savagery," 42–44, 51; Baker, "Black Female Executions in Historical Context," 77–78.

14. Seitz, "The Wounds of Savagery," 30, 55, 56.

15. Gillespie, *Executed Women of the 20th and 21st Centuries*, xxiii–xxv; O'Shea, *Women and the Death Penalty in the United States*, 261.

16. Gillespie, *Executed Women of the 20th and 21st Centuries*, xxiii–xxv.

15. THE MACCORMICK REPORT

1. Rustin, "Report on Twenty-Two Days on the Chain Gang at Roxboro, North Carolina," 8; *The Robesonian*, January 11, 1950.

2. Craven, "North Carolina's Prison System," 193; *Asheville Citizen*, November 29, 1949.

3. Watson, *Been There and Back*, 130; Terrell, *Prison Bars to Shining Stars*, 67, 68, 69.

4. Craven, "North Carolina's Prison System," 210.

5. *Raleigh News and Observer*, June 3, 1952.

6. Ibid.

7. Ibid.

8. Ibid., June 3, 1952; June 5, 1952.

9. Ibid., June 5, 1952.

10. Ibid., June 5, 1952; June 28, 1952.

11. North Carolina Prison Department, *History of Ivy Bluff Prison*, 1–2.

12. *Raleigh News and Observer*, August 25, 1954; Shirley and Stafford, *Dixie Be Damned*, 225.

13. *Raleigh Times*, September 8, 1954; *Durham Sun*, September 8, 1954; Cahn, *Sexual Reckonings*, 176.

14. *Raleigh News and Observer*, September 9, 1954; October 13, 1955; January 12, 1957; *Asheville Citizen*, September 9, 1954; Cahn, *Sexual Reckonings*, 176.

15. As quoted in Christensen, *The Paradox of Tar Heel Politics*, 115–16; North Carolina Conference for Social Service Committee on Adult and Juvenile Delinquency, *Report of the Subcommittee to Summarize the MacCormick Report and Summarize Progress in Implementing It*, 1.

16. *Asheville Citizen*, June 8, 1950; North Carolina Conference for Social Service Committee on Adult and Juvenile Delinquency, *Report of the Subcommittee to Summarize the MacCormick Report and Summarize Progress in Implementing It*, 1–2.

17. North Carolina Conference for Social Service Committee on Adult and Juvenile Delinquency, *Report of the Subcommittee to Summarize the MacCormick Report and Summarize Progress in Implementing It*, 1–2.

18. Ibid.

19. Ibid., 3–5.

20. Ibid., 5–6.

21. Ibid., 6.

22. Ibid., 7–8, 10–12; Hackney, "Prison Reform in North Carolina," 29; "Introduction," *Twentieth Biennial Report of the State Highway and Public Works Commission, For the Biennium of 1952–1954*, vii, xi.

23. "Introduction," *Twenty-First Biennial Report of the State Highway and Public Works Commission, For the Biennium of 1954–1956*, viii.

24. Ibid., ix.

25. Ibid., ix–x.

26. "Summary of Prison Operations, 1956–1958," *Twenty-Second Biennial Report of North Carolina Prison System, For the Biennium 1956–1958*, ix–xi, viii, xiii.

27. North Carolina State Highway and Public Works Commission, *Osborne Association Survey Report on North Carolina Prison System*, chapter 1, 1–2.

28. Ibid.

29. Ibid., chapter 10, 1.

30. Ibid., chapter 1, 1–3; chapter 8, 10–11.

16. FREEDOM

1. North Carolina State Highway and Public Works Commission, *Report on the Feasibility of Separating the State Prison System from the State Highway and Public Works Commission*, 246; McLennan, *The Crisis of Imprisonment*, 271; North Carolina Prison Department, *History of Ivy Bluff Prison*, 2–3.

2. North Carolina Prison Department, *History of Ivy Bluff Prison*, 2–3.

3. Watson, *Been There and Back*, 80–81.

4. North Carolina Prison Department, *History of Ivy Bluff Prison*, 4–5.

5. Ibid., 7–8.

6. O'Neill, *The Professional Convict's Tale*, 91–93; Hackney, "Prison Reform in North Carolina," 35; North Carolina Prison Department, *History of Ivy Bluff Prison*, 8.

7. Hackney, "Prison Reform in North Carolina," 29, 34.

8. North Carolina State Highway and Public Works Commission, *Report on the Feasibility of Separating the State Prison System from the State Highway and Public Works Commission*, 23.

9. Ibid., 48, 58, 62.

10. Ibid., 257–58.

11. Ibid., 333.

12. Ibid., 341.

13. Ibid., 15; *North Carolina Prison Department*, 5–6; North Carolina Prison Department, *Report of Department Operations First Year after Separation, July 1, 1957–June 30, 1958*, 1.

14. "Introduction," *Twenty-First Biennial Report of the State Highway and Public Works Commission, For the Biennium of 1954–1956*, vii; McQuillan, *North Carolina Department of Correction*, 6; *Report of Department Operations First Year after Separation, July 1, 1957–June 30, 1958*, 7; *North Carolina Prison Department*, 14.

15. *North Carolina Prison Department*, 12–15; North Carolina Prison Department, *Report of Department Operations First Year after Separation, July 1, 1957–June 30, 1958*, 8.

16. North Carolina Prison Department, *Report of Department Operations First Year after Separation, July 1, 1957–June 30, 1958*, 4, 14.

17. *North Carolina Prison Department*, 12–13; McQuillan, *North Carolina Department of Correction*, 6; North Carolina Prison Department, *Report of Department Operations First Year after Separation, July 1, 1957–June 30, 1958*, 5, 16.

18. "Summary of Prison Operations, 1958–1960," *Twenty-Third Biennial Report of North Carolina Prison System, For the Biennium 1958–1960*, vi.

19. Knepper and Jones, *North Carolina's Criminal Justice System*, 167; Rucker, "A Study of the North Carolina Work Release Program," 15.

20. Rucker, "A Study of the North Carolina Work Release Program," 16–17.

21. Ibid., 19; Witte, "Work Release in North Carolina—A Program That Works!," 230.

22. "Summary of Prison Operations, 1960–1962," *Twenty-Fourth Biennial Report of North Carolina Prison System, For the Biennium 1960–1962,* 7.

23. Ibid., 5–6.

24. North Carolina Prison Department, *Report of Department Operations First Year after Separation, July 1, 1957–June 30, 1958,* 3; *Raleigh News and Observer,* December 4, 1963.

17. RIGHTS AND REBELLION

1. Christensen, *The Paradox of Tar Heel Politics,* 155, 227.

2. Jacobs, "The Prisoner's Rights Movement and Its Impact," 431; Martin, *Break Down the Walls,* 224; Zinn, *A People's History,* 505; Berger, *Captive Nation,* 2–3, 11.

3. *Monroe v. Pape,* 365 U.S. 167 (1961); Rosch, "Will the Federal Courts Run N.C.'s Prison System?," 31.

4. *Cooper v. Pate,* 378 U.S. 546 (1964); Jacobs, "The Prisoner's Rights Movement and Its Impact," 434.

5. Federal Bureau of Investigation and the Department of Justice, "Crime in the United States," *Uniform Crime Reports for the United States, 1959;* Federal Bureau of Investigation and the Department of Justice, "Crime in the United States," *Uniform Crime Reports for the United States, 1975.*

6. Friedman, *Crime and Punishment in American History,* 305 (emphasis in the original).

7. Bounds, *Riot at Central Prison,* 1.

8. Ibid., 2–6.

9. Ibid., 6.

10. Ibid., 6–7.

11. Ibid., 10.

12. Ibid., 17–18, 20–22.

13. Ibid., 27–28.

14. Ibid., 33–34.

15. Ibid., 35–36.

16. Ibid., 37–38.

17. Ibid., 39–40.

18. Ibid., 45.

19. *Raleigh News and Observer,* April 18, 1968.

20. Ibid., April 18, 1968; April 20, 1968.

21. Bounds, *Riot at Central Prison,* 39, 46.

22. *Raleigh News and Observer,* April 20, 1968.

23. Ibid., October 23, 1968.

24. Ibid., June 15, 1968.

25. Ibid., January 11, 1969; February 14, 1969.

26. Steiner and Brown, *The North Carolina Chain Gang,* 182–83.

27. McQuillan, *North Carolina Department of Correction,* 7; Department of Correction, *A Changing Direction,* 4.

28. *Raleigh News and Observer,* April 23, 1968.

29. McLennan, *The Crisis of Imprisonment,* 314.

18. THE WOMEN FIGHT BACK

1. Reston, *The Innocence of Joan Little*, 284, 285; Harwell, *A True Deliverance*, 33.

2. Harwell, *A True Deliverance*, 40.

3. Ibid., 41, 55, 64, 246–56; Reston, *The Innocence of Joan Little*, 23, 293–306.

4. Harwell, *A True Deliverance*, 101, 103.

5. Ibid., 74–75, 111; Reston, *The Innocence of Joan Little*, xii; Shirley and Stafford, *Dixie Be Damned*, 227.

6. Harwell, *A True Deliverance*, 9–10.

7. Ibid., 12, 14, 135, 138, 156, 281–82; Reston, *The Innocence of Joan Little*, 223, 335.

8. Reston, *The Innocence of Joan Little*, 324–25; Shirley and Stafford, *Dixie Be Damned*, 228; Berger, *Captive Nation*, 212. Little served the remainder of her original term in Women's Prison and moved to New York City upon her release in 1979.

9. Reston, *The Innocence of Joan Little*, xii, 332–333.

10. The Governor's Advisory Council on Children and Youth, *Women, Families, and Prison*, 9; Post, "Women in Prison," 2–3, 10.

11. The Governor's Advisory Council on Children and Youth, *Women, Families, and Prison*, 3, 11.

12. Shirley and Stafford, *Dixie Be Damned*, 233.

13. Ibid., 233–36.

14. Ibid., 239.

15. Ibid., 236–37.

16. Ibid., 237.

17. Ibid., 238.

18. Ibid., 238–39.

19. Ibid., 240–41.

20. Ibid., 240–42.

21. Ibid., 244.

22. Ibid.

23. Girshick, *No Safe Haven*, 76

24. Ibid., 78–80.

25. Ibid., 154; *Thebaud v. Jarvis*, No. 5: 97-CT-463-BO(3) (EDNC 1997); Hamden, "North Carolina Prisoner Legal Services: A Model for Other States?," 157–58.

19. A PRISON UNION

1. Watson, *Been There and Back*, 141.

2. Tibbs, *From Black Power to Prison Power*, 118, 121–24; Berger, *Captive Nation*, 186–87.

3. Tibbs, *From Black Power to Prison Power*, 136; Berger, *Captive Nation*, 187.

4. Tibbs, *From Black Power to Prison Power*, 137–38.

5. Chin, *Prisons in North Carolina*, 64.

6. Tibbs, *From Black Power to Prison Power*, 139–40 (emphasis in the original).

7. Ibid., 142.

8. McQuillan, *North Carolina Department of Correction*, 12; Tibbs, *From Black Power to Prison Power*, 144.

9. Tibbs, *From Black Power to Prison Power*, 148.

10. Ibid., 149.

11. Ibid., 153, 154.

12. Ibid., 165, 166.

13. Ibid., 178–79, 192–94; *Jones v. North Carolina Prisoners' Labor Union, Inc.*, 433 U.S. 119 (1977).

14. Tibbs, *From Black Power to Prison Power*, 178–79, 192–94; Herivel and Wright, *Prison Nation*, 293.

15. *Raleigh News and Observer*, March 30, 1975; June 9, 1976.

16. Ibid., March 30, 1975.

17. Chin, *Prisons in North Carolina*, 7, 19.

18. Ibid., 10, 33, 34, 42.

19. Ibid., iii, iv, 3, 4–5, 10–11, 34.

20. Ibid., 49.

21. Ibid., 20, 31, 36, 44.

22. Ibid., 56–59.

23. Ibid.

24. Ibid., 63–65; Friedman, *Crime and Punishment in American History*, 314.

25. *Bounds v. Smith*, 430 U.S. 817 (1977).

26. North Carolina Department of Correction, *Rules and Policies: Governing the Management and Conduct of Inmates*, 1, 7, 9, 21–28.

27. Ibid., 35–36; Quin, *The Tree of Thorns*, 13.

28. Chin, *Prisons in North Carolina*, 44–45, 52.

20. NEW PRISON, OLD PROBLEMS

1. Reed, "The North Carolina Department of Correction: Problems, Progress, and Plans," 1.

2. Ibid., 2; *Raleigh News and Observer*, March 30, 1975.

3. *Raleigh News and Observer*, October 1, 1975.

4. Ibid., October 31, 1975.

5. Ibid., November 2, 1987; Finger and Betts, "Prisons Policy: Who's in Charge?," 20–22, 28.

6. *Raleigh News and Observer*, September 8, 1978; November 17, 1977.

7. Reed, "The North Carolina Department of Correction: Problems, Progress, and Plans," 2, 7.

8. North Carolina Department of Correction, *Maximum Custody Design*, 1.

9. Ibid., 3.

10. Ibid., 4; *Raleigh News and Observer*, April 19, 1982.

11. *Raleigh News and Observer*, September 3, 1982; September 5, 1982.

12. North Carolina Department of Correction, *Maximum Custody Design*, 4; *Raleigh News and Observer*, April 19, 1982.

13. North Carolina Department of Correction, *Maximum Custody Design*, 6.

14. Ibid., *Raleigh News and Observer*, April 19, 1982; September 3, 1982.

15. *Raleigh News and Observer*, April 19, 1982; September 3, 1982; December 29, 1982.

16. Ibid., September 5, 1982.

17. Ibid., March 24, 1982.

18. Ibid.

19. Ibid.

20. Ibid., March 25, 1982.

21. Ibid., March 25, 1982; March 26, 1982; March 30, 1982.

22. Ibid., March 26, 1982.

23. Ibid.

24. Ibid.

25. Ibid., March 27, 1982.

26. Ibid., March 26, 1982.

27. Ibid.

28. Ibid., March 27, 1982.

29. Ibid., March 30, 1982.

30. Ibid.

31. Ibid., July 28, 1982.

32. Ibid., August 1, 1982; October 9, 1982.

33. Ibid., October 12, 1982; October 15, 1982.

34. Ibid., October 15, 1982; October 20, 1982.

35. Ibid., March 30, 1982; March 31, 1982.

36. Ibid., March 31, 1982; December 30, 1982.

37. Ibid., April 2, 1982.

38. *The Civil Rights Act of 1964*, Public Law 88–352, July 2, 1964; *Raleigh News and Observer*, April 6, 1982.

39. *Raleigh News and Observer*, April 15, 1982.

40. Ibid., December 30, 1982.

21. OVERCROWDING

1. Quin, *The Tree of Thorns*, 17.

2. Reed, "The North Carolina Department of Correction: Problems, Progress, and Plans," 1; Department of Correction, *Long Range Construction and Conversion Plan*, 1.

3. Reed, "The North Carolina Department of Correction: Problems, Progress, and Plans," 1.

4. Ibid.

5. North Carolina Department of Correction, *Research Bulletin*, February 26, 1991; Freeman, "The North Carolina Sentencing and Policy Advisory Commission," 1.

6. Betts, "Behind Bars," 6.

7. *Raleigh News and Observer*, April 13, 1975.

8. Quin, *The Tree of Thorns*, 16; Markham and Welty, "Sexual Assault Cases," 3–5; Freeman, "The North Carolina Sentencing and Policy Advisory Commission," 1.

9. Markham and Welty, "Sexual Assault Cases," 10–11.

10. Quin, *The Tree of Thorns*, 16.

11. Christensen, *The Paradox of Tar Heel Politics*, 244; North Carolina General Assembly Special Committee on Prisons, *Report of the Special Committee on Prisons: Final Report to the 1989 General Assembly*, 3

12. North Carolina Department of Correction, *Rules and Policies: Governing the Management and Conduct of Inmates*, 11–12.

13. Reid, "The Fair Sentencing Act," 42; Finger and Betts, "Prisons Policy: Who's in Charge?," 19; Freeman, "The North Carolina Sentencing and Policy Advisory Commission," 2; Markham and Welty, "Sexual Assault Cases," 5–6.

14. Markham and Welty, "Sexual Assault Cases," 10–11.

15. Reid, "The Fair Sentencing Act," 45.

16. Ibid., 43.

17. Ibid., 42; Freeman, "The North Carolina Sentencing and Policy Advisory Commission," 2; North Carolina Department of Correction, *Research Bulletin*, February 26, 1991.

18. Reid, "The Fair Sentencing Act," 43; North Carolina Department of Administration, Office of Policy and Planning, *Decade in Review*, 89, 90.

19. Betts, "Behind Bars," 10 (emphasis in the original).

20. *New York Times*, January 15, 1989; Rosch, "Will the Federal Courts Run N.C.'s Prison System?," 31.

21. *Hubert v. Ward*, No. C-E-80-414-M (W.D. N.C. 1985); Rosch, "Will the Federal Courts Run N.C.'s Prison System?," 32.

22. Rosch, "Will the Federal Courts Run N.C.'s Prison System?," 33; North Carolina Department of Correction, *A Master Plan for the Allocation of $87,500,000*, 24–25; North Carolina Department of Correction, *Corrections at the Crossroads*, 21–22.

23. Rosch, "Will the Federal Courts Run N.C.'s Prison System?," 32; Hood, *Catalyst*, 187.

24. *Small v. Martin*, 5:85-cv-00987 (E.D. N.C.); Rosch, "Will the Federal Courts Run N.C.'s Prison System?," 29; North Carolina Department of Correction, *Report to the Governor: Annual Report of the North Carolina Department of Corrections*, 5 6, 8; Finger and Betts, "Prisons Policy: Who's in Charge?," 19; North Carolina Department of Correction, *A Master Plan for the Allocation of $87,500,000*, 25.

25. Rosch, "Will the Federal Courts Run N.C.'s Prison System?," 29.

26. Finger and Betts, "Prisons Policy: Who's in Charge?," 18.

27. North Carolina Department of Correction, *A Master Plan for the Allocation of $87,500,000*, 5A-8; McLaughlin, "North Carolina's Prison System," 29.

28. McLaughlin, "North Carolina's Prison System," 29, 30.

29. North Carolina Department of Correction, *A Master Plan for the Allocation of $87,500,000*, 25.

22. THE TEN-YEAR PLAN

1. Ready, *The Tar Heel State*, 376, 385, 389; North Carolina Department of Correction, *Research Bulletin*, April 15, 1988; February 28, 1989.

2. Freeman, "The North Carolina Sentencing and Policy Advisory Commission," 3–4; Johnson, *Man From Macedonia*, 198; North Carolina Department of Correction, *Report to the Governor: Annual Report of the North Carolina Department of Corrections*, 5.

3. The Governor's Advisory Board on Prisons and Punishment, *A Report to the Governor: North Carolina's Prison Crisis*, 3, 9–11; Freeman, "The North Carolina Sentencing and Policy Advisory Commission," 4; Mark Jones, "Voluntary Revocations and the 'Elect-to-Serve' Option in North Carolina Probation," 36–49.

4. North Carolina Department of Correction, *Report to the Governor: Annual Report of the North Carolina Department of Corrections*, 4, 15; North Carolina Department of Correction, *Corrections at the Crossroads*, 3–6, 39–40.

5. North Carolina Department of Correction, *Corrections at the Crossroads*, 4–6; Powell, *North Carolina Through Four Centuries*, 542–43.

6. North Carolina Department of Correction, *Corrections at the Crossroads*, 35; Betts, "Behind Bars," 15 (emphasis in the original); McLaughlin, "North Carolina's Prison System," 23.

7. North Carolina Department of Correction, *Corrections at the Crossroads*, 28, 30–31.

8. Ibid., 33; North Carolina Department of Administration, Office of Policy and Planning, *Decade in Review*, 90.

9. Johnson, *Man From Macedonia*, 7, 70, 75, 89, 173, 181, 187, 189, 190.

10. Ibid., 194–95, 198.

11. Ibid., 206–7; Department of Correction, *What's Up, D.O.C.?* (fall 1989), 1.

12. Johnson, *Man From Macedonia*, 208–9.

13. Ibid., 211–13; North Carolina Division of Forest Resources, *Young Offenders Forest Conservation Program: BRIDGE*.

14. Finger and Betts, "Prisons Policy: Who's in Charge?," 20–22, 28.

15. The Governor's Advisory Board on Prisons and Punishment, *A Report to the Governor: North Carolina's Prison Crisis*, 1.

16. Ibid., 1, 14, 20.

17. Ibid., 14–19.

18. Freeman, "The North Carolina Sentencing and Policy Advisory Commission," 5; North Carolina Department of Correction, *A Master Plan for the Allocation of $87,500,000*, 26, 44.

19. Freeman, "The North Carolina Sentencing and Policy Advisory Commission," 7.

20. Ibid., 27.

21. Ibid., 11, 15–18.

22. Ibid., 20; Markham and Welty, "Sexual Assault Cases," 4; Duncan et al., "The Effects of Adopting North Carolina's Sentencing Guidelines in Georgia," 2; Freeman, "The North Carolina Sentencing and Policy Advisory Commission," 20–21.

23. Freeman, "The North Carolina Sentencing and Policy Advisory Commission," 23–25; Department of Public Safety, Division of Adult Correction and Juvenile Justice, "Justice Reinvestment Performance Measures, Fiscal Year 2014–2015," 3–4, 16; North Carolina Sentencing and Policy Advisory Commission, "Justice Reinvestment Act Implementation Evaluation Report," 45; Department of Public Safety, Division of Adult Correction and Juvenile Justice, "Justice Reinvestment Performance Measures, Fiscal Year 2014–2015," 5.

23. CORRUPTION AND CONTROVERSY

1. Johnson, *Man From Macedonia*, 231–32.

2. Ibid.

3. Ibid., 232.

4. Ibid., 233.

5. Ibid., 237.

6. Bounds, *Special Report*, 6–9.

7. Ibid., 10–11.

8. Ibid., 16.

9. Ibid., 18.

10. Ibid., 36–37.

11. Ibid., 50–54.

12. Department of Correction, *North Carolina Department of Correction News*, 1, 5; North Carolina Department of Correction, *Research Bulletin*, March 8, 1991, and May 10, 2001.

13. Department of Correction, *Correction News*, June 1997, 7.

14. Ibid., April 1998, 1, 3.

15. Ibid., July 5, 1999; May 1999; July 1999, 5; February 2006.

16. Kotch, *Lethal State*, 30, 117.

17. *Furman v. Georgia*, 408 U.S. 238 (1972); Department of Correction, *The Death Penalty and North Carolina Department of Correction*, 1; Mandery, *A Wild Justice*, 117–18, 236–37.

18. *Woodson v. North Carolina*, 428 U.S. 280 (1976); *Gregg v. Georgia*, 428 U.S. 153 (1976); Mandery, *A Wild Justice*, 258–59, 277, 411, 419–20; Friedman, *Crime and Punishment in American History*, 317; Kotch, "The Death Penalty in North Carolina," 252–56; Kotch, *Lethal State*, 170–71, 177.

19. Department of Correction, *The Death Penalty and North Carolina Department of Correction*, 1; Rapaport and Streib "Death Penalty for Women in North Carolina," 75.

20. Department of Correction, *The Death Penalty and North Carolina Department of Correction*, 1.

21. Ibid., 3.

22. Ibid., 4–5.

23. Ibid., 281, 349; *New York Times*, November 2, 1984.

24. McQuillan, *North Carolina Department of Correction*, 7–8; Department of Correction, *The Death Penalty and North Carolina Department of Correction*, 6; Kotch, "Unduly Harsh and Unworkably Rigid," appendix B, 263; Kytle and Pollitt, *Unjust in the Much*, 1–2, 8.

25. Kotch, "Unduly Harsh and Unworkably Rigid," 256.

26. *North Carolina Department of Correction v. North Carolina Medical Board*, 363 N.C. 189 (May 1, 2009); *Raleigh News and Observer*, May 2, 2009.

27. Bowers, *Solitary Confinement as Torture*, 195; Kotch, *Lethal State*, 181.

28. *Raleigh News and Observer*, December 18, 2015; *New York Times*, December 13, 2012.

29. *New York Times*, June 5, 2013.

30. Kotch, *Lethal State*, 185.

24. MENTAL HEALTH

1. Letter from Amy Fettig to Vanita Gupta, August 10, 2015, 11–12.

2. *Raleigh News and Observer*, November 2, 1997; *Wilmington Morning Star*, November 3, 1997; Dawson, "Under Fire for Negligence, North Carolina Prison's Chief Seeks New Mental Health Funding."

3. Dawson, "Under Fire for Negligence, North Carolina Prison's Chief Seeks New Mental Health Funding."

4. *Winston-Salem Journal*, November 19, 2011.

5. *Interim Summary "Old" Central Prison Inpatient Mental Health Review*, 1.

6. Letter from Robert Lewis to James French, August 23, 2011, "Interim Report Reference Central Prison Inpatient Mental Health Program," 1, 2.

7. Ibid., 2, 3–4, 6.

8. Ibid., 6, 14–15, 16, 17, 19.

9. Ibid., 8–9.

10. Ibid., 10, 11, 14.

11. Ibid., 13.

12. Ibid., 20, 21–24, 30–31, 35–40.

13. Ibid., 7–8.

14. Ibid., 9–10.

15. *Interim Summary "Old" Central Prison Inpatient Mental Health Review*, 1–5.

16. Letter from Robert Lewis to James French, August 23, 2011, "Interim Report Reference Central Prison Inpatient Mental Health Program," 41.

17. Keller, "Statement from Secretary Alvin Keller regarding Central Prison Mental Health Report."

18. Ibid.

19. Ibid.

20. *Winston-Salem Journal*, November 19, 2011; Bowers, *Solitary Confinement as Torture*, 48.

21. Metzner and Aufderhide, "2012 Report on Central Prison," 6, 9, 10; Bowers, *Solitary Confinement as Torture*, 9, 47.

22. Metzner and Aufderhide, "2012 Report on Central Prison," 18; Bowers, *Solitary Confinement as Torture*, 49.

23. Watson, *Been There and Back*, 144–45; Smith, *Squawk 7500*, 91–92.

24. Metzner and Aufderhide, "2012 Report on Central Prison," 21–22; Bowers, *Solitary Confinement as Torture*, 49, 51–52.

25. Bowers, *Solitary Confinement as Torture*, 53–54; *Raleigh News and Observer*, May 5, 2013.

26. Letter from Amy Fettig to Vanita Gupta, August 10, 2015, 7–8.

25. ISOLATION

1. Bowers, *Solitary Confinement as Torture*, 113, 130.

2. Ibid., 45, 78, 79, 160; letter from Amy Fettig to Vanita Gupta, August 10, 2015, 12.

3. Bowers, *Solitary Confinement as Torture*, 117, 121.

4. Ibid., 155, 172.

5. Ibid., 185.

6. Ibid., 173, 176–77.

7. Ibid.; Ball, "What Life Is Like in Solitary Confinement in North Carolina's Central Prison."

8. Rodriguez, "North Carolina Prisoners Launch Hunger Strike."

9. Ball, "What Life Is Like in Solitary Confinement in North Carolina's Central Prison."

10. Dawson, "Under Fire for Negligence, North Carolina Prison's Chief Seeks New Mental Health Funding."

11. Ibid.; letter from Amy Fettig to Vanita Gupta, August 10, 2015, 8.

12. Dawson, "Under Fire for Negligence, North Carolina Prison's Chief Seeks New Mental Health Funding"; letter from Amy Fettig to Vanita Gupta, August 10, 2015, 8; Smith, *Squawk 7500*, 90–91.

13. Reutter, "Federal Court Orders Cameras to Cover Blind Spots at North Carolina Prison," 35; Dawson, "Under Fire for Negligence, North Carolina Prison's Chief Seeks New Mental Health Funding."

14. Dawson, "Under Fire for Negligence, North Carolina Prison's Chief Seeks New Mental Health Funding."

15. *Raleigh News and Observer*, May 27, 2016.

16. Quotation from Mark Jones, January 2017. Transcript in possession of author.

CONCLUSION

1. Travis, "Problems at North Carolina Prisons Have Festered for Years"; Association of State Correctional Administrators, "Aiming to Reduce Time-in-Cell," 5, 50.

2. Knopf, "NC Prison Breaks Its Own Rules for Suicide Prevention."

3. Ibid.

4. Ibid.; *Raleigh News and Observer*, November 12, 2016; November 23, 2016.

5. *Charlotte Observer*, October 16, 2019.

6. Ibid., October 28, 2017.

7. Ibid.

8. *Raleigh News and Observer*, June 19, 2018; Travis, "Problems at North Carolina Prisons Have Festered for Years."

9. WITN.com, May 29, 2018; *Star-Telegram*, October 29, 2017; *Charlotte Observer*, August 17, 2018.

10. WITN.com, May 29, 2018; *Star-Telegram*, October 29, 2017; *The Citizen Times*, January 26, 2018.

11. *Charlotte Observer*, October 28, 2017.

12. *Star-Telegram*, October 29, 2017; WRAL.com, June 21, 2018; *Charlotte Observer*, March 20, 2018; WITN.com, May 29, 2018.

13. *Charlotte Observer*, March 20, 2018; WITN.com, May 29, 2018.

14. WITN.com, May 29, 2018.

15. Ibid.

16. *Charlotte Observer*, May 31, 2017.

17. Ibid., March 20, 2018; WITN.com, May 29, 2018.

18. *Raleigh News and Observer*, June 19, 2018.

19. Friedman, *Crime and Punishment in American History*, 125; Friedman, *A History of American Law*, 68; Churchill, *House of Commons Debate*, 1354.

BIBLIOGRAPHY

PRIMARY SOURCES

North Carolina Collection at the University of North Carolina at Chapel Hill

Bureau of Sanitary Engineering and Inspection, North Carolina State Board of Health. *Convict Prison Camps: Rules and Regulations Governing Sanitary Management.* 1925.

Bounds, Vernon Leland. *Changes Made in Prison Law and Administration, 1953–1960.* Chapel Hill: University of North Carolina Institute of Government, 1960.

———. *Report on North Carolina's Penal-Correctional System, Prepared for the Commission on the Reorganization of the State Government.* Chapel Hill: University of North Carolina Institute of Government, 1954.

———. *Riot at Central Prison, April, 1968; Report of V.L. Bounds.* Raleigh, N.C.: N.p., 1968.

Brown, Roy M. *Growth of a State Program of Public Welfare*, vol. 2. N.p.: N.p., 1950.

Chavis, Benjamin. *An American Political Prisoner Appeals for Human Rights in the United States of America.* Cleveland: United Church of Christ, Commission for Racial Justice, 1978.

———. *Psalms from Prison.* Cleveland: Pilgrim Press, 1994.

Clarke, Stevens, Susan Kurtz, Elizabeth Rubinsky, and Donna Schliecher. *Felony Prosecution and Sentencing in North Carolina: A Report to the Governor's Crime Commission and the National Institute of Justice.* Chapel Hill: Institute of Government, the University of North Carolina, May 1982.

Cooke, Alfred. *Caledonia: From Antebellum Plantation, 1713–1892, to State Prison and Farm, 1892–1988.* Tillery, N.C.: W. A. Cooke, 1988.

The Governor's Advisory Board on Prisons and Punishment. *A Report to the Governor: North Carolina's Prison Crisis.* 1990.

The Governor's Advisory Council on Children and Youth. *Women, Families, and Prison.* 1981.

Jones, Calvin. *Dr. Jones' Speech on the Bill to Amend the Penal Laws by Establishing a Penitentiary House for Criminals, Delivered in the House of Commons of North Carolina, November 20, 1802.*

Kennard, John. "Confessions of a Boy from Hell's Forty Acres." *Success Magazine*, May 1924.

Mangum, Adolphus Williamson. *History of the Salisbury, N.C., Confederate Prison.* N.p., N.d.

Mangum, Priestly. "Oration Delivered at the University of North Carolina Commencement." June 1815.

McLean, Angus. *Special Message of Angus McLean, Governor to the General Assembly of North Carolina in Respect to the Conditions and Needs of the State's Prison.* Raleigh: Edwards, Broughton, Printers and Binders, 1925.

North Carolina Conference for Social Service Committee on Adult and Juvenile Delinquency. *Report of the Subcommittee to Summarize the MacCormick Report and Summarize Progress in Implementing It.* April 12, 1954.

North Carolina Correctional Center for Women. *Inside Outlook.* 1979–1985.

North Carolina Department of Administration, Office of Policy and Planning. *Decade in Review: Issues North Carolina Faced in the 1980s.* 1990.

North Carolina Department of Correction. *Central Prison: North Carolina's Maximum Security Institution.* Raleigh: Department of Correction, 1974.

———. *A Changing Direction.* Raleigh: Department of Correction, 1976.

———. *Correction News.* Raleigh: Department of Correction, 1996–2008.

———. *The Death Penalty and North Carolina Department of Correction.* Raleigh: Department of Correction, 1994.

———. *Long Range Construction and Conversion Plan, 1974–1983, Division of Prisons, Department of Correction.* Raleigh: Department of Correction, 1974.

———. *A Master Plan for the Allocation of $87,500,000: A Report to the 1993 Session of the General Assembly of North Carolina,* 1993.

———. *North Carolina Department of Correction News.* Raleigh: Department of Correction, 1993–1996.

———. *Report to the Governor: Annual Report of the North Carolina Department of Corrections,* 1987.

———. *Research Bulletin.* Raleigh: Office of Research and Planning, 1980–2001.

———. *Rules and Policies: Governing the Management and Conduct of Inmates under the Control of the Division of Prisons.* Raleigh: Department of Correction, January 1980.

———. *What's Up, D.O.C.?: A Newsletter for Department of Correction Employees.* Raleigh: Department of Correction, 1988–1992.

North Carolina Division of Forest Resources. *Young Offenders Forest Conservation Program: BRIDGE: Building, Rehabilitating, Instructing, Developing, Growing, Employing.* Raleigh: North Carolina Division of Forest Resources, 2008.

North Carolina General Assembly. *An Act to Regulate the Treatment, Handling, and Work of Prisoners.* Raleigh: Edwards, Broughton, Printers and Binders, 1917.

———. *Report of the Investigating Committee Appointed to Investigate the Affairs of the Department of Agriculture and the State's Prison.* Raleigh: Edwards, Broughton, Printers and Binders, 1900.

———. *Report of the Joint Select Committee to Inquire into the Management of the Penitentiary.* 1872.

———. *Report of the Joint Select Committee on the Subject of a Penitentiary and Lunatic Asylum.* December 30, 1826.

North Carolina General Assembly Special Committee on Prisons. *Report of the Special Committee on Prisons: Final Report to the 1989 General Assembly of North Carolina, 1990 Session.* 1990.

North Carolina Penitentiary. *Special Report of Architect of the State Penitentiary.* 1876.

North Carolina Penitentiary Commission. *Report of the Penitentiary Commission to the General Assembly of North Carolina: Made December 8, 1870.*

———. *The Rules and By-Laws for the Government and Discipline of the North Carolina Penitentiary During Its Management by the Commission.* Raleigh: M.S. Littlefield, 1869.

North Carolina Prison Department. *History of Ivy Bluff Prison.* 1959.

———. *Report of Department Operations First Year after Separation, July 1, 1957–June 30, 1958.* Raleigh: North Carolina Prison Department, 1958.

North Carolina Prison Department. Raleigh: Prison Enterprises, 1958.

North Carolina State Board of Charities and Public Welfare. *Capital Punishment in North Carolina, Special Bulletin Number 10.* 1929.

North Carolina State Highway and Public Works Commission. *Osborne Association Survey Report on North Carolina Prison System.* 1950.

———. *Report on the Feasibility of Separating the State Prison System from the State Highway and Public Works Commission.* Chapel Hill: University of North Carolina Institute of Government, 1956.

North Carolina State Prison. *Rules and Regulations Governing the North Carolina Prison: Adopted May 17, 1899, by the Executive Committee.* 1899.

Olds, Fred. "History of the State's Prison," *The Prison News* 1, no. 11 (November 15, 1926): 5.

Report of Sub-Committee of State Prison Advisory Commission: Submitted to Governor O. Max Gardner. Raleigh: Edwards, Broughton, Printers and Binders, 1930.

Rustin, Bayard. "Report on Twenty-Two Days on the Chain Gang at Roxboro, North Carolina." 1949.

Smith, George L. *The Life of George L. Smith, North Carolina's Ex-Convict: Boldest and Bravest Blind Tiger Man.* N.p., n.d.

State Democratic Executive Committee of North Carolina. *The Democratic Handbook, 1898.* Raleigh: Edwards, Broughton, Printers and Binders, 1898.

The Prison News.

Wood, Otto. *Life History of Otto Wood: Inmate North Carolina State Prison.* Raleigh: Commercial Printing Company, 1926.

———. *The Life of Otto Wood.* Wadesboro, N.C. Pee Dee Publishing Company, 1931.

Federal Government

"Annual Determination of Average Cost of Incarceration." *Federal Register: The Daily Journal of the United States Government.*

Carson, E. Ann. "Prisoners in 2014." Bureau of Justice Statistics, September 2015.

Federal Bureau of Investigation. "Crime in the United States by Volume and Rate, Per 100,000 Inhabitants, 1995–2014." *2014 Crime in the United States.*

Federal Bureau of Investigation and the Department of Justice. "Crime in the United States." *Uniform Crime Reports for the United States, 1959.* Washington, D.C.: United States Government Printing Office, 1960.

———. "Crime in the United States." *Uniform Crime Reports for the United States, 1975.* Washington, D.C.: United States Government Printing Office, 1976.

U.S. Census Bureau. *Abstract of the Returns of the Fifth Census, Showing the Number of Free People, the Number of Slaves, the Federal or Representative Number and the Aggregate of Each County of Each State of the United States.* Washington, D.C.: Duff Green, 1832.

U.S. Department of Education, National Center for Education Statistics. *The Condition of Education 2016* (NCES 2016–144). Public School Expenditures.

Prison Reports

The First Biennial Report of the Directors of the N.C. State Penitentiary. Raleigh: Josiah Turner, November 13, 1876.

Biennial Report of the Board of Directors of the North Carolina State Penitentiary (November 1, 1876 to November 1, 1878).

Biennial Report of the Board of Directors, Architect and Warden, Steward and Physician. For the Two Years Ending October 31, 1880.

Biennial Report of the Board of Directors, Architect and Warden, Steward and Physician. For the Two Years Ending October 31, 1882.

Biennial Report of the Board of Directors, Architect and Warden, Steward and Physician. For the Two Years Ending November 30, 1884.

Biennial Report of the Board of Directors, Architect and Warden, Steward and Physician. For the Two Years Ending November 30, 1886.

Biennial Report of the Board of Directors, Architect and Warden, Steward and Physician. For the Two Years Ending November 30, 1888.

Biennial Report of the Board of Directors, Architect and Warden, Steward and Physician. For the Two Years Ending November 30, 1890.

Biennial Report of the Board of Directors, Architect and Warden, Steward and Physician. For the Two Years Ending November 30, 1892.

Annual Report of the Board of Directors and of the Superintendent of the State's Prison, for the Year Ending December 31, 1893.

Annual Report of the Board of Directors and of the Superintendent of the State's Prison, for the Year Ending December 31, 1894.

The Report of the Board of Directors and of the General Manager for the Two Years of 1895 and 1896.

The Report of the Board of Directors and of the General Manager for the Two Years of 1897 and 1898.

The State's Prison: Reports of the Superintendent, Executive Board, and Other Officers, 1899/1900. Raleigh: Edwards and Broughton Printing, 1901.

Reports of the Superintendent, Warden and Other Officials of the State's Prison for the Years 1901–1902. Raleigh: Edwards and Broughton Printing, 1903.

Reports of the Superintendent, Warden and Other Officials of the State's Prison for the Years 1903–1904. Raleigh: E. M. Uzzell, 1905.

Reports of the Superintendent, Warden and Other Officials of the State's Prison for the Years 1905–1906. Raleigh: E. M. Uzzell, 1907.

Reports of the Superintendent, Warden and Other Officials of the State's Prison for the Years 1907–1908. Raleigh: E. M. Uzzell, 1909

Reports of the Superintendent, Warden and Other Officials of the State's Prison for the Years 1909–1910. Raleigh: Edwards and Broughton Printing, 1911.

Reports of the Superintendent, Warden and Other Officials of the State's Prison for the Years 1911–1912. Raleigh: Edwards and Broughton Printing, 1913.

Reports of the Superintendent, Warden and Other Officials of the State's Prison for the Years 1913–1914. Raleigh: Edwards and Broughton Printing, 1915.

Reports of the Superintendent, Warden and Other Officials of the State's Prison for the Years 1915–1916. Raleigh: E. M. Uzzell, 1917.

Biennial Report of The State's Prison, 1917–1918. Raleigh: Commercial Printing, 1919.

Biennial Report of The State's Prison, 1919–1920. Raleigh: Commercial Printing, 1921.

Biennial Report of The State's Prison, 1921–1922. Raleigh: Edwards and Broughton Printing, 1923.

Biennial Report of The State's Prison, 1923–1924. Raleigh: Edwards and Broughton Printing, 1925.

Biennial Report of The State's Prison, 1925–1926. Raleigh: State Prison Printery, 1926.

Biennial Report of The State's Prison, 1927–1928. Raleigh: State Prison Printery, 1928.

Biennial Report of The State's Prison, July 1, 1928–June 30, 1930. Raleigh: State Prison Printery, 1930.

Biennial Report of The State Prison Department, July 1, 1930–June 30, 1932.

Biennial Report. State Highway and Public Works Commission, Prison Department. For the Two Years Ended June 30, 1934.

Biennial Report. State Highway and Public Works Commission, Prison Department. For the Two Years Ended June 30, 1936.

Biennial Report. State Highway and Public Works Commission, Prison Department. For the Two Years Ended June 30, 1938.

Biennial Report. State Highway and Public Works Commission, Prison Department. For the Two Years Ended June 30, 1940.

Biennial Report. State Highway and Public Works Commission, Prison Department. For the Two Years Ended June 30, 1942.

Biennial Report. State Highway and Public Works Commission, Prison Department. For the Two Years Ended June 30, 1944.

Biennial Report. State Highway and Public Works Commission, Prison Department. For the Two Years Ended June 30, 1946.

Biennial Report. State Highway and Public Works Commission, Prison Department. For the Two Years Ended June 30, 1948.

Biennial Report. State Highway and Public Works Commission, Prison Department. For the Two Years Ended June 30, 1950. Winston-Salem: Winston Printing, 1951.

Nineteenth Biennial Report of the State Highway and Public Works Commission, For the Biennium of 1950–1952. Raleigh: State Prison Printery, 1953.

Twentieth Biennial Report of the State Highway and Public Works Commission, For the Biennium of 1952–1954. Raleigh: State Prison Printery, 1955.

Twenty-First Biennial Report of the State Highway and Public Works Commission, For the Biennium of 1954–1956. Raleigh: State Prison Printery, 1957.

Twenty-Second Biennial Report of North Carolina Prison System, For the Biennium 1956–1958. Raleigh: Prison Enterprises, 1959.

Twenty-Third Biennial Report of North Carolina Prison System, For the Biennium 1958–1960. Raleigh: Prison Enterprises, 1961.

Twenty-Fourth Biennial Report of North Carolina Prison System, For the Biennium 1960–1962. Raleigh: Prison Enterprises, 1963.

Twenty-Fifth Biennial Report of North Carolina Prison System, For the Biennium 1962–1964. Raleigh: Prison Enterprises, 1965.

State Library of North Carolina

North Carolina Department of Correction. *Maximum Custody Design, Central Prison, 1982.*
———. *Corrections at the Crossroads: Plan for the Future.* March 6, 1986.

North Carolina Department of Correction

Bounds, V. Lee. *Special Report, North Carolina Department of Corrections.* September 1992.

Department of Public Safety, Division of Adult Correction and Juvenile Justice. "Justice Reinvestment Performance Measures, Fiscal Year 2014–2015." March 1, 2016.

Interim Summary "Old" Central Prison Inpatient Mental Health Review.

Keller, Alvin. "Statement from Secretary Alvin Keller Regarding Central Prison Mental Health Report." November 17, 2011.

Letter from Robert Lewis to James French, August 23, 2011. "Interim Report Reference Central Prison Inpatient Mental Health Review."

McQuillan, Patty. *North Carolina Department of Correction.* Raleigh: Department of Correction, 1987.

Metzner, Jeffery, and Dean Aufderhide. "2012 Report on Central Prison."

North Carolina Sentencing and Policy Advisory Commission. "Justice Reinvestment Act Implementation Evaluation Report." April 15, 2017.

State of North Carolina Department of Public Safety, Prisons: Policies and Procedures. Chapter C, Section. 1600, Safekeepers. November 1, 2011. 1–8

North Carolina State Government

Biennial Message of Elias Carr, Governor of North Carolina to the General Assembly, Session 1897. Raleigh: E.M. Uzzell, 1897.

Executive and Legislative Documents Laid Before the General Assembly of North Carolina, Session 1868–69.

Executive and Legislative Documents Laid Before the General Assembly of North Carolina, Session 1869–70. Raleigh: Jo. W. Holden, 1870.

Executive and Legislative Documents Laid Before the General Assembly of North Carolina, Session 1870–71.

Executive and Legislative Documents Laid Before the General Assembly of North Carolina, Session 1871–72. Raleigh: Theodore N. Ramsey, 1872.

Executive and Legislative Documents Laid Before the General Assembly of North Carolina, Session 1872–73. Raleigh: Stone and Uzzell, 1873.

Executive and Legislative Documents Laid Before the General Assembly of North Carolina, Session 1873–74. Raleigh: Stone and Uzzell, 1873.

Executive and Legislative Documents Laid Before the General Assembly of North Carolina, Session 1874–75. Raleigh: Josiah Turner, 1875.

Executive and Legislative Documents Laid Before the General Assembly of North Carolina, Session 1875–76. Raleigh: Stone and Uzzell, 1873.

Executive and Legislative Documents Laid Before the General Assembly of North Carolina, Session 1885. Raleigh: P. M. Hale, 1885.

First Annual Report of the Board of Public Charities of North Carolina. February 1870.

Freeman, Lorrin. "The North Carolina Sentencing and Policy Advisory Commission: A History of its Creation and its Development of Structured Sentencing." November 2000.

Laws and Resolutions Passed by the General Assembly of the State of North Carolina at the Special Session, Begun and Held in the City of Raleigh on the First of July 1868. Raleigh: N. Paige, 1868.

Legislative Research Commission. *Report to the 1977 General Assembly of North Carolina: "Females in the Department of Correction."* 1977.

Mitchell, Memory F., ed. *Addresses and Papers of James Baxter Hunt, Jr., Governor of North Carolina.* Raleigh: Division of Archives and History, Department of Cultural Resources, 1982.

North Carolina Board of Charities. *First Annual Report of the Board of Charities, February 10, 1870.*

North Carolina Constitutional Convention. "Report of the Committee on Punishments, Penal Institutions, and Public Charities." *Journal of the Constitutional Convention of the State of North Carolina at its Session 1868.* Raleigh: J. W. Holden, 1868.

North Carolina Criminal Justice Analysis Center. *A Discussion of Incarceration and Its Alternatives in North Carolina: Crime and Justice Perspective from the N.C. Governor's Crime Commission.* Raleigh, N.C., July 2007.

North Carolina Executive and Legislative Documents, Session 1881. Raleigh, N.C., 1881.

North Carolina State Constitution. 1868.

North Carolina General Assembly. "An Act for the Employment of Convicts and the Erection of a Penitentiary, August 24, 1868." *Laws and Regulations Passed by the General Assembly of the State of North Carolina.* Raleigh: N. Paige, 1868.

———. "An Act to Provide for the Erection of a Penitentiary, April 12, 1869." *Public Laws of the State of North Carolina Passed by the General Assembly at Its Session 1868–69.* Raleigh: M. S. Littlefield, 1869.

North Carolina State Board of Charities and Public Welfare. "A Study of Prison Conditions in North Carolina." *The Bulletin of the North Carolina State Board of Charities and Public Welfare* 6, no. 1 (first quarter, January—March 1923): 2–25.

Public Documents of the General Assembly of North Carolina, Session 1879. Raleigh: The Observer, 1879.

Public Documents of the General Assembly of North Carolina, Session 1899. Raleigh: The Observer, 1899.

Public Laws of the State of North Carolina Passed by the General Assembly, 1868–1869. Raleigh: Holden and Wilson, 1872.

Robert W. Woodruff Library, Atlanta University Center

Rucker, Sheridine. "A Study of the North Carolina Work Release Program" (1968). ETD Collection for AUC Robert W. Woodruff Library. Paper 2230.

American Correctional Association

Declaration of Principles Adopted and Promulgated by the 1870 Congress of the National Prison Association.
"Annual Report of the Inspectors of the Western Penitentiary of Pennsylvania, for the Year 1856." *Miscellaneous Documents Read in the Legislature of the Commonwealth of Pennsylvania During the Session Which Commenced at Harrisburg on the Sixth Day of January 1856, 581–83.*

Pennsylvania State Government

"Annual Report of the Inspectors of the Western Penitentiary of Pennsylvania, for the Year 1856." *Miscellaneous Documents Read in the Legislature of the Commonwealth of Pennsylvania During the Session Which Commenced at Harrisburg on the Sixth Day of January 1856.* 581–83.
Report on Punishments and Prison Discipline: By the Commissioners Appointed to Revise the Penal Code of Pennsylvania. Philadelphia: John Clarke, 1828.

Internet Sources

Churchill, Winston. *Class III. House of Commons Debate,* 20 July 1910, vol. 19, cc1326–57, https://api.parliament.uk/historic-hansard/commons/1910/jul/20/class-iii.
Letter from Amy Fettig et al. to Vanita Gupta. August 10, 2015. https://www.acluofnorth carolina.org/sites/default/files/SolitarylettertoUSDOJ.pdf.
New York State Special Commission on Attica. *Attica: The Official Report of the New York State Special Commission on Attica.* New York: Bantam Books, 1972. https://nysl.ptfs .com/data/Library1/Library1/pdf/14815273.pdf

SECONDARY SOURCES

Adamson, Christopher R. "Punishment and Slavery: Southern State Penal Systems, 1865–1890." *Social Problems* 30, no. 5 (June 1983): 555–69.
Alexander, Michelle. *The New Jim Crow: Mass Incarceration in the Age of Colorblindness.* New York: New Press, 2012.
Anderson, Barbara Shaw. "Struggling with the Burden of Feminine Virtue: The Case of Ida Ball Warren in North Carolina, 1914–1916." Master's thesis, University of North Carolina at Chapel Hill, 1988.

Anderson, Lloyd C. *Voices from a Southern Prison*. Athens: Univ. of Georgia Press, 2000.

Ashman, Allan. *Jails and Prisons in North Carolina: A Brief History*. Chapel Hill: University of North Carolina at Chapel Hill Institute of Government, 1963.

Association of State Correctional Administrators, The Arthur Liman Public Interest Program, Yale Law School. "Aiming to Reduce Time-In-Cell: Reports from Correctional Systems on the Numbers of Prisoners in Restricted Housing and on the Potential of Policy Changes to Bring About Reforms." November 2016. https://law.yale.edu/sites/default/files/area/center/liman/document/aimingtoreducetic.pdf.

Ayers, Edward L. *Vengeance and Justice: Crime and Punishment in the 19th-Century American South*. New York: Oxford Univ. Press, 1984.

Baker, David V. "Black Female Executions in Historical Context." *Criminal Justice Review* 33, no. 1 (March 2008): 77–78.

Ball, Billy. "What Life Is Like in Solitary Confinement in North Carolina's Central Prison." *Indy Week*, July 4, 2012. https://indyweek.com/news/life-like-solitary-confinement-north-carolina-s-central-prison/.

Barfield, Velma. *Woman on Death Row*. Minneapolis, Minn.: Worldwide Publications, 1985.

Barnes, Harry Elmer. *The Evolution of Penology in Pennsylvania: A Study in American Social History*. Montclair, N.J.: Patterson Smith, 1968.

Battle, Kemp Plummer. *Memories of an Old-Time Tar Heel*. Chapel Hill: Univ. of North Carolina Press, 1945.

Beard, Ross E. *Carbine: The Story of David Marshall Williams*. Lexington, S.C.: Sandpaper Store, 1977.

Berger, Dan. *Captive Nation: Black Prison Organizing in the Civil Rights Era*. Chapel Hill: Univ of North Carolina Press, 2016.

Betts, Jack. "Behind Bars: North Carolina's Growing Prison Population." *North Carolina Insight Magazine* 9, no. 3 (March 1987): 4–16.

———. "The Correction Conundrum—What Punishment Is Appropriate?" *North Carolina Insight Magazine* 9, no. 3 (March 1987): 2–3.

———."An Interview with Aaron Johnson, North Carolina Secretary of Correction." *North Carolina Insight Magazine* 9, no. 3 (March 1987): 38–41.

Blackmon, Douglas A. *Slavery by Another Name: The Re-Enslavement of Black Americans from the Civil War to World War II*. New York: Doubleday, 2008.

Bledsoe, Jerry. *Death Sentence: The True Story of Velma Barfield's Life, Crimes, and Execution*. New York: Dutton Adult, 1998.

Blumstein, Alfred. "American Prisons in a Time of Crisis." In *The American Prison: Issues in Research and Policy, Law, Society, and Policy*, edited by Lynn Goodstein and Doris Layton Mackenzie, 13–22. New York: Plenum Press, 1988.

Bowers, Mark, et al. *Solitary Confinement as Torture*. Chapel Hill: University of North

Carolina School of Law Immigration/Human Rights Clinic, in association with the American Civil Liberties Union of North Carolina and North Carolina Stop Torture Now, 2014.

Brown, Roy. "Crime and Its Treatment." *Social Forces* 8, no. 4 (June 1930): 591–95.

Cable, George W. *The Silent South Together with the Freedman's Case: Inequality and the Convict Lease System.* New York: Charles Scribner's Sons, 1889.

Cahn, Susan K. *Sexual Reckonings: Southern Girls in a Troubling Age.* Cambridge, Mass.: Harvard Univ. Press, 2007.

Carlson, Peter M., and Judith Simon Garrett. *Prison and Jail Administration: Practice and Theory,* 3rd ed. Burlington, Mass.: Jones and Bartlett Learning, 2013.

Carson, Homer S., III. "Penal Reform and Construction of the Western North Carolina Railroad 1875–1892." *Journal of Appalachian Studies* 11, no. 1/2 (spring/fall 2005): 205–25.

Carter, Dan T. "Prisons, Politics, and Business: The Convict Lease System in the Post-Civil War South." Master's thesis, University of Wisconsin, 1964.

Cash, W. J. *The Mind of the South.* New York: Vintage, 1991.

Chin, Laura, ed. *Prisons in North Carolina: Report of the North Carolina Advisory Committee to the United States Commission on Civil Rights.* Washington, D.C., 1976.

Christianson, Scott. *With Liberty for Some: 500 Years of Imprisonment in America.* Boston: Northeastern Univ. Press, 1998.

Christensen, Rob. *The Paradox of Tar Heel Politics: The Personalities, Elections, and Events That Shaped Modern North Carolina.* Chapel Hill: Univ. of North Carolina Press, 2008.

Clear, Todd R., and George F. Cole. *American Corrections,* 3rd ed. Belmont, Calif.: Wadsworth, 1994.

Clemmer, Donald. *The Prison Community.* New York: Rinehart, 1958.

Coates, Albert. "Punishment for Crime in North Carolina." *North Carolina Law Review* 17, no. 2 (April 1939): 205–32.

Cobb, James C. *Industrialization and Southern Society, 1887–1984.* Lexington: Univ. Press of Kentucky, 2004.

Cohen, William. "Negro Involuntary Servitude in the South, 1865–1940: A Preliminary Analysis." *Journal of Southern History* 42, no. 1 (February 1976): 31–60.

Connor, R.D.W. *History of North Carolina.* Vol. 1, *The Colonial and Revolutionary Periods, 1584–1783.* New York: Lewis, 1919.

Contardo, Jeanne Bayer. "Against the Grain: A Study of North Carolina's Plan to Provide College to Its Prison Inmates." Ph.D. diss., University of Maryland, College Park. 2008.

Craddock, Amy. "The Imprisonment of Women as Formal Social Control: A Constructive Critique of Theoretical Perspectives and Empirical Research." Master's thesis, University of North Carolina at Chapel Hill, 1985.

Craven, Charles Kinsman. "North Carolina's Prison System: A Chronological History Through 1950." Master's thesis, University of North Carolina at Charlotte, 1987.

Daniels, Jonathan. *Prince of Carpetbaggers.* New York: Lippincott, 1958.

Dawson, Lisa. "Under Fire for Negligence, North Carolina Prison's Chief Seeks New Mental Health Funding." *Solitary Watch,* December 15, 2014.

———. "Federal Lawsuit Challenges Brutality in Solitary Confinement Unit at North Carolina Prison." *Solitary Watch,* May 18, 2013.

Davis, Earl Warren. *From Carolina Chain Gang to Earl of Alaska: An Autobiography.* Bloomington, Ind.: Author House, 2006.

Duncan, Randall W, John C. Speir, and Tammy S. Meredith. "The Effects of Adopting North Carolina's Sentencing Guidelines in Georgia." Atlanta: Georgia Public Policy Foundation, February 2, 1999.

Dyer, Joel. *The Perpetual Prisoner Machine: How America Profits from Crime.* Boulder, Colo.: Westview, 2000.

Ekirch, A. Roger. *"Poor Carolina": Politics and Society in Colonial North Carolina, 1729–1776.* Chapel Hill: Univ. of North Carolina Press, 1981.

Finger, Bill, and Jack Betts. "Prisons Policy: Who's in Charge?" *North Carolina Insight Magazine* 9, no. 3 (March 1987): 17–28.

Foucault, Michel. *Discipline and Punish: The Birth of the Prison.* New York: Vintage, 1995.

Friedman, Lawrence M. *Crime and Punishment in American History.* New York: Basic Books, 1993.

———. *A History of American Law.* New York: Simon and Schuster, 1973.

Gillespie, L. Kay. *Executed Women of the 20th and 21st Centuries.* Lanham, Md.: Univ. Press of America, 2009.

Girshick, Lori B. *No Safe Haven: Stories of Women in Prison.* Boston: Northeastern Univ. Press, 1999.

Goodwyn, Lawrence. *The Populist Moment: A Short History of the Agrarian Revolt in America.* New York: Oxford Univ. Press, 1978.

Gopnik, Adam. "The Caging of America." *New Yorker,* January 30, 2012. https://www.newyorker.com/magazine/2012/01/30/the-caging-of-america.

Greenberg, Janelle R., and Martin S. Greenberg. "Crime and Punishment in Tudor-Stuart England and the Modern United States." *Law and Human Behavior* 6, no. 3–4 (1982): 261–72.

Hackney, John Joseph. "Prison Reform in North Carolina." Honors thesis, University of North Carolina at Chapel Hill, 1967.

Hamden, Michael S. "North Carolina Prisoner Legal Services: A Model for Other States?" *Criminal Law Bulletin* 40, no. 2 (2004): 157–62.

Hartnett, Stephen John. *Executing Democracy.* Vol. 1, *Capital Punishment and the Making of America, 1683–1807.* East Lansing: Michigan State Univ. Press, 2010.

Harwell, Fred. *A True Deliverance.* New York: Knopf, 1979.

Hearn, Daniel Allen. *Legal Executions in North Carolina and South Carolina: A Comprehensive Registry, 1866–1962.* Jefferson, N.C.: McFarland, 2015.

Henderson, Archibald. *North Carolina, the Old North State and the New.* Chicago: Lewis, 1941.

Herivel, Tara, and Paul Wright, eds. *Prison Nation: The Warehousing of America's Poor.* New York: Routledge, 2003.

———. *Prison Profiteers: Who Makes Money From Mass Incarceration.* New York: New Press, 2007.

Hinkle, William, and Bruce Whitmarsh. *Elmira Reformatory.* Charleston, S.C.: Arcadia Publishers, 2014.

Hood, John M. *Catalyst: Jim Martin and the Rise of North Carolina Republicans.* Winston-Salem, N.C.: Blair, 2015.

Ingle, Joseph B. "Final Hours: The Execution of Velma Barfield." *Loyola of Los Angeles Law Review* 23, no. 1 (1989): 221–36.

Ireland, Robert E. "Prison Reform, Road Building, and Southern Progressivism: Joseph Hyde Pratt and the Campaign for 'Good Roads and Good Men.'" *North Carolina Historical Review* 68, no. 2 (April 1991): 125–57.

Jacobs, James B. "The Prisoner's Rights Movement and Its Impact, 1960–1980." *Crime and Justice* 2 (1980): 429–70.

———. *Stateville: The Penitentiary in Mass Society.* Chicago: Univ. of Chicago Press, 1977.

Johnson, Aaron. *Man From Macedonia: My Life of Service, Struggle, Faith, and Hope.* Bloomington, Ind.: West Bow Press, 2010.

Johnson, Guion Griffis. *Ante-Bellum North Carolina: A Social History.* Chapel Hill: Univ. of North Carolina Press, 1937.

Jones, Clifford A. "A Study of the Inequities of Justice as Reflected in the Prison System of North Carolina." Master's thesis, Southeastern Baptist Theological Seminary, 1977.

Jones, Mark. "Voluntary Revocations and the 'Elect-to-Serve' Option in North Carolina Probation." *Crime and Delinquency* 42, no. 1 (January 1996): 36–49.

Key, Valdimir Orlando. *Southern Politics in State and Nation.* Knoxville: Univ. of Tennessee Press, 2006.

Knepper, Paul, and Mark Jones. *North Carolina's Criminal Justice System,* 2nd ed. Durham, N.C.: Carolina Academic Press, 2011.

Knopf, Taylor. "NC Prison Breaks Its Own Rules for Suicide Prevention." *North Carolina Health News,* May 22, 2018.

Kolchin, Peter. *American Slavery: 1619–1877.* New York: Hill and Wang, 2003.

Kotch, Seth. *Lethal State: A History of the Death Penalty in North Carolina.* Chapel Hill: Univ. of North Carolina Press, 2019.

———. "Unduly Harsh and Unworkably Rigid: The Death Penalty in North Carolina, 1910–1961." Ph.D. diss., University of North Carolina at Chapel Hill, 2008.

Kytle, Calvin, and Daniel H. Pollitt, eds. *Unjust in the Much: The Death Penalty in North Carolina*. Chapel Hill, N.C.: Chestnutt Tree Press, 1999.

Lallier, Rebecca Ragsdale. "'A Place of Beginning Again': The North Carolina Industrial Farm Colony for Women, 1929–1947." Master's thesis, University of North Carolina at Chapel Hill, 1990.

Law, Victoria. *Resistance Behind Bars: The Struggles of Incarcerated Women*. Oakland, Calif.: PM Press, 2009.

Lefler, Hugh Talmage, ed. *North Carolina History Told by Contemporaries*. Chapel Hill: Univ. of North Carolina Press, 1956.

Leonard, Samuel Erwin. "The History of the Eastern Carolina Industrial Training School for Boys, Rocky Mount, North Carolina." *North Carolina Historical Review* 22, no. 3 (July 1945): 276–92.

Lichtenstein, Alex. *Twice the Work of Free Labor: The Political Economy of Convict Labor in the New South*. New York: Verso, 1996.

Lindsay, J. J. *Inside the Prison, or, In Chains and Stripes*. Weldon, N.C.: Harrell's Printing House, 1913.

Logan, Frenise A. *The Negro in North Carolina, 1876–1894*. Chapel Hill: Univ. of North Carolina Press, 1964.

Mandery, Evan J. *A Wild Justice: The Death Penalty and Resurrection of Capital Punishment in America*. New York: Norton, 2013.

Mancini, Matthew J. *One Dies, Get Another: Convict Leasing in the American South, 1866–1928*. Columbia: Univ. of South Carolina Press, 1996.

Markham, James M., and Jeffery B. Welty. "Sexual Assault Cases Based on Conduct Before 2001." *UNC School of Government Administration of Justice Bulletin* (July 2009): 1–29.

Martin, John Bartlow. *Break Down the Walls: American Prisons, Past, Present, and Future*. New York: Ballantine, 1954.

McCleery, Richard. "Communication Systems as Bases of Systems of Authority and Power." In *Theoretical Studies in Social Organization of the Prison*, edited by Richard A. Cloward et al. New York: Social Science Research Council, 1960.

McKay, Herbert Stacy. "Convict Leasing in North Carolina, 1870–1934." Master's thesis, University of North Carolina at Chapel Hill, 1942.

McKelvey, Blake. *American Prisons: A History of Good Intentions*. Montclair, N.J.: Patterson Smith, 1977.

———. *American Prisons: A Study in American Social History Prior to 1915*. Chicago: Univ. of Chicago Press, 1936.

McKenzie, Trevor Jackson. "'Robin Hood of the Blue Ridge': The Life, Legend, and Songs of Otto Wood, the Bandit." Master's thesis, Appalachian State University, 2012.

McLaughlin, Mike. "North Carolina's Prison System: Is the Crisis Corrected?" *North Carolina Insight Magazine* 11, no. 4 (August 1989): 21–32.

McLennan, Rebecca M. *The Crisis of Imprisonment: Protest, Politics, and the Making of the American Penal State, 1776–1941.* New York: Cambridge Univ. Press, 2008.

Mebane, John. "The Torture Chamber in North Carolina." *Modern Monthly* 9, no. 4 (June 1935): 214, 221.

Morris, Norval, and David J. Rothman, eds. *The Oxford History of the Prison: The Practice of Punishment in Western Society.* New York: Oxford Univ. Press, 1998.

O'Neill, John. *The Professional Convict's Tale: The Survival of John O'Neill In and Out of Prison,* edited by Elmer H. Johnson. Carbondale: Southern Illinois Univ. Press, 2007.

O'Shea, Kathleen. *Women and the Death Penalty in the United States, 1900–1998.* Westport, Conn.: Praeger, 1999.

Pearce, Gary. *Jim Hunt: A Biography.* Winston-Salem, N.C.: Blair, 2010.

Perkinson, Robert. *Texas Tough: The Rise of America's Prison Empire.* New York: Picador, 2010.

Pitzer, Sara. *Myths and Mysteries of North Carolina: True Stories of the Unsolved and Unexplained.* Guilford, Conn.: Morris Book Publishing, 2010.

Poole, Cary Franklin. *A History of Railroading in Western North Carolina.* Johnson City, Tenn.: Overmountain Press, 1995.

Post, Phyllis. "Women in Prison: A Study of Their Prospects and Problems." Honors essay, University of North Carolina at Chapel Hill, 1972.

Poster, Mark. *Foucault, Marxism and History.* Cambridge: Polity Press, 1984.

Powell, William S. *Dictionary of North Carolina Biography.* Chapel Hill: Univ. of North Carolina Press, 1979–1996.

———. *North Carolina Through Four Centuries.* Chapel Hill: Univ. of North Carolina Press, 1989.

Quin, Harroitt Johnson. *The Tree of Thorns: A Brief History of the Interaction of Values and Practices in Criminal Justice in North Carolina.* Raleigh: North Carolina Council of Churches, 1980.

Rafter, Nicole Hahn. *Partial Justice: Women in State Prisons, 1800–1935.* Boston: Northeastern Univ. Press, 1985.

Rapaport, Elizabeth, and Victor Streib. "Death Penalty for Women in North Carolina." *Elon Law Review* 01.1, no. 65 (2009): 65–94.

Ready, Milton. *The Tar Heel State: A History of North Carolina.* Columbia: Univ. of South Carolina Press, 2005.

Reed, Amos. "The North Carolina Department of Correction: Problems, Progress, and Plans." *Popular Government* 44, no. 4 (spring 1979): 1–7.

Reid, Dee. "The Fair Sentencing Act: Setting the Record Straight." *North Carolina Insight Magazine* 9, no. 3 (March 1987): 42–49.

Reston, James. *The Innocence of Joan Little: A Southern Mystery.* New York: Times Books, 1977.

Reutter, David. "Federal Court Orders Cameras to Cover Blind Spots at North Carolina Prison." *Prison Legal News*, September 2015.

Roback, Jennifer. "Exploitation in the Jim Crow South: The Market of the Law?" *Regulation* (September/December 1984): 37–43.

Roberts, Albert R. *Juvenile Justice Sourcebook: Past, Present, and Future*. New York: Oxford Univ. Press, 2004.

Rodriguez, Sal. "North Carolina Prisoners Launch Hunger Strike." *Solitary Watch*, August 1, 2012.

Rosch, Joel. "Will the Federal Courts Run N.C.'s Prison System?" *North Carolina Insight Magazine* 9, no. 3 (March 1987): 29–37.

Rosenbaum, Betty B. "Relationship Between War and Crime in the United States." *Journal of Criminal Law and Criminology* 30, no. 5 (January–February 1940): 725–29.

Seitz, Trina N. "The Killing Chair: North Carolina's Experiment in Civility and the Execution of Allen Foster." *North Carolina Historical Review* 81, no. 1 (January 2004): 38–72.

———. "The Wounds of Savagery: Negro Primitivism, Gender Parity, and the Execution of Rosanna Lightner Phillips." *Women and Criminal Justice* 16, no. 1–2 (2005): 29–64.

Shirley, Neal, and Saralee Stafford. *Dixie Be Damned: 300 Years of Insurrection in the American South*. Oakland, Calif.: AK Press, 2015.

Siegel, Larry J., and Clemens Bartollas. *Corrections Today*, 2nd ed. Belmont, Calif.: Wadsworth, 2014.

Smith, Peter Scharff. "Reform and Research: Re-Connecting Prison and Society in the 21st Century." *International Journal for Crime, Justice and Social Democracy* 4, no. 1 (2015): 33–49.

Smith, Will. *Squawk 7500: The True Story of a Pilot Hijacked by the North Carolina Justice System*. Lutz, Fla.: Down and Out Books, 2015.

Sparks, Richard, Anthony Bottoms, and Will Hay. *Prisons and the Problem of Order*. Oxford, UK: Clarendon Press, 1996.

Spindel, Donna J. *Crime and Society in North Carolina, 1663–1776*. Baton Rouge: Louisiana State Univ. Press, 1989.

Steiner, Jesse Frederick, and Roy Brown. *The North Carolina Chain Gang: A Study of County Convict Road Work*. Santa Barbara, Calif.: Greenwood, 1970.

Sykes, Gresham M. *The Society of Captives*. New York: Atteneur, 1966.

Terrell, Bob. *Prison Bars to Shining Stars*. Alexander, N.C.: WorldComm, 1997.

Thomas, Susan W. "Chain Gangs, Roads, and Reform in North Carolina, 1900–1935." Ph.D. diss., University of North Carolina at Greensboro, 2011.

Thompson, Heather Ann. *Blood in the Water: The Attica Prison Uprising of 1971 and Its Legacy*. New York: Pantheon, 2016.

Tibbs, Donald F. *From Black Power to Prison Power: The Making of Jones v. North Carolina Prisoners' Labor Union*. New York: Palgrave Macmillan, 2012.

Tonry, Michael, and Kathleen Sonosky, eds. *Sentencing Reform in Overcrowded Times: A Comparative Perspective*. New York: Oxford Univ. Press, 1997.

Travis, Kari. "Problems at North Carolina Prisons Have Festered for Years." Carolinajournal.com, February 12, 2018.

Watson, Frank. *Been There and Back*. Winston-Salem, N.C.: Blair, 1976.

Weare, Walter B. *Black Businesses in the New South: Social History of the North Carolina Mutual Life Insurance Co*. Urbana: Univ. of Illinois Press, 1973.

Wellman, Manly Wade. *Dead and Gone: Classic Crimes of North Carolina*. Chapel Hill: Univ. of North Carolina Press, 1980.

Welty, Jeff. "The Death Penalty in North Carolina: History and Overview." Chapel Hill: University of North Carolina School of Government, April 2012.

Wines, Enoch C., and Theodore W. Dwight. *Report on the Prisons and Reformatories of the United States and Canada*. Albany, N.Y.: Van Benthuysen and Sons, Steam Printing House, 1867.

Witmer, Helen Leland. "The History, Theory and Results of Parole." *Journal of Criminal Law and Criminology* 18, no. 1 (spring 1927): 24–64.

Witte, Ann D. "Work Release in North Carolina—A Program That Works!" *Law and Contemporary Problems* 41, no. 1 (winter 1977): 230–51.

Zimmerman, Hilda Jane. "The Penal Reform Movement in the South During the Progressive Era, 1890–1917." *Journal of Southern History* 17, no. 4 (1951): 462–92.

———. "Penal Systems and Penal Reforms in the South Since the Civil War." Ph.D. diss., University of North Carolina at Chapel Hill, 1947.

Zinn, Howard. *A People's History of the United States, 1492–Present*. New York: Harper Perennial, 1995.

Zipf, Karin L. *Bad Girls at Samarcand: Sexuality and Sterilization in a Southern Juvenile Reformatory*. Baton Rouge: Louisiana State Univ. Press, 2016.

INDEX

Electric chair: construction and first usage of, 88–89; debates about, 128–31

Ellis, Andrew, 252, 254

Elmira Reformatory, 9, 63–64, 95

Emergency Prison Facilities Development Program, 219

Emergency Prison Population Stabilization Act, 215

Fair Sentencing Act (FSA), 208–10, 220

Family Service Program Center, 218

Faribault, George, 31

Farm Colony for Women, 111–12

Farmer, Robert, 201

Federal Bureau of Investigation (FBI), 3, 165

Ferrell, Granville, 43

First Amendment, 185–86

Fleming, John, 69

Foster, Jimmie Lee "Allen," 130–31, 229

Foster, William, 50

Foucault, Michele, 1–2, 4

Fourteenth Amendment, 22, 185, 211

Fowler, Columbus, 43

Fox, Donald, 169

Frazier, Seth, 253

Friedman, Lawrence M., 2, 51, 165

French, James, 227–28

Furman v. Georgia, 228

Fusion, 71–74, 79

Gardner, O. Max, and Otto Wood, 108–9; and female inmates, 109–112; and prison reform, 112–13, 116

Garrett, Judith Simon, 164

Garrison, Samuel: on prison overcrowding, 186–87; on inmate control, 188; and the new Central Prison, 196–97; and 1982 hostage taking, 197–98, 202–3

Gas chamber: debates about, 128–29; construction of, 130; first use of, 130–31; victims of, 134–35; closure of, 229–30

Glazier, Rick, 232

Goldsboro Youth Center, 159

Golphin, Tilmon, 232

Good Roads Movement, 82, 96

Good time credits, 207–10

Goodwin, Miles, 41, 43

Gopnik, Adam, 3, 4

Governor's Advisory Board on Prisons and Punishment, 219–20

Governor's Task Force on Mental Health and Substance Use, 248

Green Mile, The, 5

Gregg v. Georgia, 228–29

Guice, David, 247–48

Hall, Ezekiel: and kidnapping, 197–99; trial of, 202

Hanging: debates about, 87–88, 130; of Caroline Shipp, 132

Hardaway Company, 96

Harper, J. C., 22

Harper, Margaret Taylor, 174

Harris, Cebern, 25, 27, 29–30

Harris, J. H., 25

Harrison, John, 30, 45

Harwell, Fred, 174–76

Heck, John, 26

Helms, Jerry, 175

Helms, Jesse, 230

Henry, David, 166–68, 170

Hicks, William: appointment of, 30–31; and prison construction, 57–58; as prison administrator, 58, 65–69, 72

Hill, William, testimony of, 39–40, 43; medical reports by, 40, 54–55, 57

Hinton, Ivan, 140

Holden, William Woods, 24, 38–39, 71

Holshouser, James, 193, 219

Homosexuality, 170, 193, 211

Honeycutt, H. H., 103, 121, 130

Horn, Martin, 253

Hospital for the Insane, 48

Howe, Alfred, 29, 45

Howe, Geoffrey, 253

Hubert v. Ward, 211–12